DATE DUE

THE INDEPENDENCE MOVEMENTS IN ARAB NORTH AFRICA

American Council of Learned Societies
Near Eastern Translation Program
Number Eight

THE INDEPENDENCE MOVEMENTS IN ARAB NORTH AFRICA

'Alāl al-Fāsi

Translated from the Arabic by
Hazem Zaki Nuseibeh

1970
OCTAGON BOOKS
New York

This work is a complete translation of *al-Harakāt al-Istiqlāli yah fi al-Maghrib al-'Arabi* by 'Alāl al-Fāsi, published by Matba'ah al-Risālah, Cạiro, 1948.

Reprinted 1970

by special arrangement with the American Council of Learned Societies

OCTAGON BOOKS
A DIVISION OF FARRAR, STRAUS & GIROUX, INC.
19 Union Square West
New York, N. Y. 10003

LIBRARY OF CONGRESS CATALOG CARD NUMBER: 70-96201

Printed in U.S.A. by
NOBLE OFFSET PRINTERS, INC.
NEW YORK 3, N. Y.

FOREWORD

The Near Eastern Translation Program as an operation of the American Council of Learned Societies effected through its Committee on Near Eastern Studies, was initiated in 1950 with the aid of a subsidy from The Rockefeller Foundation. The aim of the program is the translation into English of significant works in all the important Near Eastern languages, in the fields of the humanities and of the social sciences, to provide an insight into local life and thought.

In the difficult problem of choosing books for translation, the Committee has had the counsel and cooperation of scholars throughout the United States and Canada, as well as in Europe and the Near East generally. It is thought that the selections will be of increasing use to readers interested in world affairs, and will also serve as collateral reading material for courses in our colleges and universities.

The volumes translated are of various recent dates and have been restricted by the fundamental aim of the program--the discovery and selection of the best in contemporary thought written by the various peoples of this region for themselves. Only in this way, it is believed, can American readers be made aware of the concepts and ideologies by which the thinking and attitudes of the various peoples of the Near East are being molded. The translations are unabridged English versions of the original text, made to represent the closest approximation in the English language of what the author said to his own readers.

It should, of course, be clearly understood that the views expressed in the works translated are the opinions of the writers and not of the American Council of Learned Societies or the Committee on Near Eastern Studies. Both the Council and the Committee, however, wish to express their appreciation for the generous service of the various authors who have willingly facilitated translation and publication of their work in this way.

The American Council of Learned Societies
acknowledges with special gratitude
the cooperation of the author
Mr. 'Alāl al-Fāsi
in this translation of his work
as an element in creating a better understanding
among American readers of the thinking and problems
of the Near Eastern peoples

CONTENTS

PREFACE

The genesis of this book was a program sponsored by the Cultural Bureau of the League of Arab States for a study and depiction of contemporary problems in the Arab world. The chairman of the Bureau, Dr. Aḥmad Amīn, asked me to contribute a section on "the independence movements in Arab North Africa".

It was my view that a topic of such considerable importance could not be adequately covered in a limited report for publication in a current magazine. I therefore decided to write a comprehensive treatise on the resistance movement of the North Africans in its manifold diplomatic, military, and political aspects. Thus the present work has come to be written and I now dedicate it to the Arab League and its supporters.

In preparing this work I have been prompted by laudable national motivations. In the first place, it has been my aim to familiarize the new generation of Arab youths, and particularly those of North Africa, with the phases through which our movement has passed, and to acquaint them with the efforts which the founders of the movement and their followers have expended in successive generations. The history of the movement should serve as a worthy model; it should also facilitate a comprehension of the present-day struggle for liberation and rejuvenation as an unfolding of a well-integrated panorama, in which the past and the present achieve that unity which gives to music its lofty and magnificent harmony.

In the second place, my purpose has been to acquaint the Arabs, and particularly those in responsible office, with the aspirations of the Arabs of North Africa and their strivings for the achievement of their aims. Such a knowledge would drive home conclusively to them the unity of purpose that underlies our mutual struggle and would convince them of the necessity for coordination in the Arab conflict, notwithstanding its seemingly varying aspects and manifestations. This will induce a wider perspective in Arab outlook, which would supersede the present parochialism so that no Arab province would continue to look after its own narrow interests to the exclusion of the more general Arab interest. Then, and only then, would the Arab League be capable of leading the seventy million Arabs in a determined struggle for the attainment of complete liberation and a great rejuvenation.

Thirdly, my aim has been to establish before the world forum the fact that the peoples of Arab North Africa have never accepted foreign occupation, and that neither the military might of the conqueror nor his political machinations could make them acquiesce in the bitter reality of French and Spanish domination over their lands. The struggle I shall depict in this book will serve as evidence that the problems of North Africa have but one solution. It is the solution that is consonant with reason and justice: the eclipse of colonialism and the dawn of complete and unequivocal independence.

I have exerted my utmost to be free from partiality and dogmatism in the preparation of this work. I consider the facts embodied in this book to be self-evident and to need no artificial support based on falsehoods.

The reader will observe that the section on Morocco is larger in space and richer in material than the other two sections. There are several reasons for this, the foremost being that I have more documents and papers on Morocco than on the two sister countries, Tunisia and Algeria. Moreover, I have thought it proper and legitimate, in the course of expounding our independence movements, to speak in the name of the "Istiqlāl Party" which I represent. Such a presumption of authority would not be justifiable in the case of the other friendly parties, although I have no doubt that their leaders are in agreement with the views I have expressed. Another consideration has been the avoidance of cumbersome repetition, as in narrating the history of the fundamentalist movement "al-Salafīyah" and its political orientation. This lofty movement went through a parallel growth in the three countries and I shall therefore confine my discussion to its development in Morocco. The reality is, that the movements in North Africa, although under different names and labels, are but one movement seeking liberty, unity, and rejuvenation.

If I can plead good intention and well-meaningness as an

excuse, then I seek forgiveness for any mistakes that may have occurred inadvertently in the writing of this book. Error is after all a human virtue which stems from the exercise of reason and its critical faculties.

In conclusion, I wish to thank my friend Aḥmad al-Malīḥ for his assistance in proof-reading and in seeing this manuscript through the press. I also wish to thank al-Risālah press for its meticulous care in the printing of the book.

'Alāl al-Fāsi

Cairo
October 1948

INTRODUCTION

If we study the history of Arab North Africa we find that nationalism, in the sense of self-defense and love of freedom for both the individual and the social group, is one of the strongest and most prevalent attributes of the peoples of North Africa. It is a characteristic that has permeated their manifold activities and historical experiences.

No nation has defied a conquering power or a surging alien immigration so steadfastly as the people of North Africa have done throughout their history. If on occasion the conquerors succeeded in establishing footholds, without, however, ever taking hold of the impregnable heights of Morocco, their presence, no matter how long-lived, has been but a passing phase that left no lasting marks or impact.

A number of Western writers, blinded by their colonial orientation and prejudices, have misinterpreted the perpertual struggle for self-defense and freedom as a manifestation of extreme individualism, love of anarchy, and internecine warfare. This led them to conclude that North Africa was incapable of forming a national unity in the true sense of the term; they further contended that the countries of this region had never known complete independence in their history. Finally, they surmised that the peoples of North Africa were more closely akin to the conquering European nations of today than to the Eastern Arab nations.

The learned French author Gautier was in the forefront among those diehards who subordinated the tools and the techniques of research to the service of their colonial aims. Their purpose was to undermine the faith of the North African youths in themselves and to reorient them with a view to their eventual integration into alien units, so that their striving would be for a unity other than their own and an independence other than their national independence.

We the people of al-Maghrib (North Africa), nevertheless, derive from our present unflinching resistance to colonial domination a sense of communion with the spirit that permeated our forefathers from time immemorial. Gautier went so far as to deny the Arab Maghrib its historic name. This is the worst error possible, however, because the Maghrib was known as the country of Amāzīgh (the land of the free) before the Franks were even heard of. Her people, the ancestors of the Berbers, were known as Imāzīghen, meaning "the free men". This name alone is sufficient proof that freedom in a land of freedom was the spirit that permeated our forefathers. The ancient Egyptians called these countries Amanti (the bride of Maghrib). The Greeks called the land Hesperia (al-Maghrib), and it was from the Greeks that the Arabs and the Semites derived the name al-Maghrib to designate the entire area.

The Amāzīgh were later known as Berbers. Ibn Khaldūn advanced the thesis that it was the Canaanites who brought about the change of name. Other writers attribute it to the Romans. Whether this is true or not, it indicates at any rate that the word Berber was used by the Canaanites and the Romans to denote an unfamiliar language.

It is our view that the name Berber antedates the Canaanite and the Roman associations. What then is the origin of the word Berber?

An ancient Roman song in honor of Mars, the god of war, included the following verse: Satur tu Fere Mars, Limen Sali! Sta! Berber. [Sic, Latin alphabet in Arabic text.] Thus the word Berber stood for speed and mobility. The ancient historians used it to describe the Berbers inhabiting the banks of the Nile. Renan, the French historian, writes: "A family of Berber-speaking nations inhabited an area that extended from Egypt and the Red Sea to Senegal and from the Mediterranean to Nigeria. It appears that the word Berber stood for the Libyans and the ancient Numidians." It is known, further, that the Nile valley included what was called the Berber valley.

Thus, the name had been used to designate this Berber-speaking people on account of their mobility and nomadism or because of their habitation along the fast-moving water of the Nile. It was from this source that it found its way into the Roman and Canaanite languages. Whatever may have been the genesis of the term, it is evident that it antedated the Greeks, the Romans, and the Arabs, who were familiar with it before the Islamic conquests.

The linguistic genealogy of the term has a deeper significance in that it illustrates the unity of the peoples who inhabit the area between the Mediterranean and the Red Sea and as far as Senegal and Nigeria. This African family has exhibited an unfailing attachment to freedom in its struggle to defend its honor and dignity.

The countries of this region had been subjected to similar foreign conquests and to identical waves of immigration from both East and West. They were successful at all times, however, in preserving their regional integrity and in absorbing both conqueror and immigrant.

It is superfluous to recount here the contributions of Egyptian civilization because they are universally acknowledged. What the imperialists do not recognize, however, is the North African civilization, although it was parallel to the Egyptian and contributed to it. Historians have proved that the city of Carthage was known in the Maghrib before the advent of the Phoenicians. It was built by our ancestors the Berbers, who also built other towns which were similar in their architectural design to the Mediterranean style. The city of Carthage was the capital of the Berber king Irbas. The Phoenician immigrants maintained an extensive commercial intercourse with its inhabitants. They established thriving commercial communities in Carthage and its environs, until by 810 [B.C.?] they had impressed their stamp upon it. This community of merchants and immigrants had been integrated into the life of the country, and it was the admixture of the two elements which established the state of Carthage. Carthage, therefore, did not constitute an alien dominion but merely represented the hegemony of a foreign family over the country, by virtue of a dynamism greater than that of the indigenous population. The resistance of the people of North Africa to the Carthaginians was not a resistance to a foreign conqueror or to an imperialist power seeking to dominate them. It was rather in the nature of a resistance to a government that had imposed itself upon them against their will. Thus, Carthage was able to survive in Africa for a long span of time. She succeeded in effecting a fusion of Semitic and Berber civilizations which gave to North Africa a unified national existence embracing language, religion, and aspirations. There were no serious internal upheavals to disrupt or undermine this basic unity.

If evidence is needed to prove that the peoples of North Africa did not look upon the Phoenicians as an imperialist power, such evidence may be deduced from the united rally of the citizens of North Africa to the support of Hannibal in response to his call for the defense of the fatherland against Roman imperialism. The Second Punic War exemplified this inherent unity, when the entire citizenry rallied behind one banner for the defense of a well-defined geographic unity, hedged in on all sides by the sea and unconquerable except from across the desert. And it was, in fact, from across the desert that North Africa resumed intercourse with the countries from which the brothers of the Phoenicians came, heralding the enlightenment of Islam and the unity of the Arabic tongue.

When news of Hannibal's victory was received and the Maghrib armies crossed the seas in hot pursuit of the invader, celebrations were held in every corner of the land from Tangier to Carthage. Thus, the people of al-Maghrib looked upon Carthage as a symbol of their nationhood and upon the Phoenicians as their brethren. Their resistance to the tyrannical rule of Carthage was no different from the resistance they displayed later under the Fatimid state, in protest against tyrannical government. But they always submerged parochial and regional loyalties whenever the integrity or the freedom of the greater homeland was in peril.

The state of Carthage endured for nine centuries prior to the Roman onslaught and six more centuries after it [sic]. The Roman destruction of Carthage and of the five cities affiliated to it, including the city of Thunes (Tunis), did not succeed in erasing the Semitism of North Africa which had been implanted by the Phoenician state, nor did it destroy the unity of these territories in respect to language and national orientation. Currency remained Phoenician, that is, Maghrib, currency. The vernacular throughout the land was also Phoenician and it remained the official medium in contracts, wills, and other transactions until the third century A.D. Pline [sic] spoke most highly of the twenty-eight books, which the Roman Senate had entrusted D. Silanus [?] with translating from Phoenician to Latin. There are records of many prominent Latin, Greek, and Carthaginian writers who expressed their thoughts in the Phoenician language. St. Augustine, the Maghrib saint, asserted that the Phoenician language was in his lifetime the dominant language throughout North Africa.

The Romans themselves were compelled to use the Phoenician language in their administration of the Maghrib, in the same way as France and Spain have to use Arabic at the present time. Translators were assigned to all offices of state, because the inhabitants refused to use the language of the imperial power even though they had been well-versed in it.

Gautier writes, "If the Berbers had been Arabicized with such ease, it is because they had not forgotten Phoenician."

The preceding discussion is significant because it proves one thing: the preponderance of the Semitic or Eastern over the European or Latin influence in North Africa. (I should not say Western influence because I consider all Semites Western). This is undoubtedly due to the fact that the Semites were not conquerors but had merely forced their way into the Maghrib family, which soon after forgot their style of entry and fraternised with them. The great similarities in outlook and temperament between the indigenous people and the newcomers replaced the initial enmity.

The Latin conquest, on the other hand, though it lasted five centuries, left no trace of influence on the land and its people. The cause of this failure is not inherent in the nature of East or West but must be sought in the policies of ruthless exploitation and domination which the Romans had pursued in the conquered territories. The Romans catered to nothing but their own selfish interests; no wonder they failed, because power no matter how great cannot break the moral fibre of a people who believe in themselves and who are willing to sacrifice all they have in the cause of freedom.

A number of imperialist historians have attempted to demonstrate the success of Roman rule in North Africa. All historical evidence, however, disproves this claim and underlines Rome's political failure in North Africa. Boisset writes: "Rome made no attempt whatever to become the fatherland; she merely exploited the conquered peoples of Europe and Africa. She also failed as a carrier of civilization. In fact, the Romanized Berber kings ruled Rome better than she ruled herself."

It was the Carthaginians who built the road system in al-Maghrib, as Isidore asserts, while the Romans demolished what the Carthaginians had built.

It was the Carthaginians who established unity and peace throughout the country, whereas the Roman emperor himself could not move about in North Africa without an escorting army ten thousand strong.

D.H. Muller expresses the view that Rome came to know the Twelve Tables through the Phoenician Carthaginian community in the Roman domains. That there are similarities between this law and the code of Hammurabi is well established.

Rome did not have in North Africa a large community which could have influenced the inhabitants, as the imperialists claim. Even M. Louis Bertrand, well-known for his antipathy to Islam and his fidelity to Latin civilization, asserts this fact.

The peoples of North Africa have consistently rejected any link with the Romans. They were Judaic or Christian when Rome was still pagan. They supported the Carthaginian bishop of al-Maghrib, Donatus, when he broke away from the Roman Papacy to form a Maghrib church. They refused, however, to support St. Augustine, who remained loyal to Rome and the Papacy, and accused him of seeking to subjugate his countrymen to the spiritual domination of the imperialist power. Their aversion on similar grounds to Eastern Roman Christianity and Byzantium was no less pronounced.

The peoples of al-Maghrib, however, enthusiastically embraced Islam because they found in it the avenue to national liberation and independence, in addition to intellectual and spiritual enhancement. The Islamic movement was to them an extension of the monotheistic principles which were compatible with their general outlook on life.

Thus, the ancient history of North Africa discloses a perpetual struggle for dominance between the Latin family on the one hand, and on the other, the family that is known in the contemporary period as Arab, whose intellectual heritage comprises Greek, Semitic, and Maghrib civilizations. But we also find that victory has always been on the side of this Arab civilization which forms the real cornerstone of

Mediterranean civilization. It is a foundation in which the material did not contribute so much as the spiritual elements. It is upon this basis that the people of al-Maghrib feel their profound affinity to the rest of the Arab world.

The Maghrib, however, despite its acceptance of Islam as its religion and Arabic as its language has always felt pride in its own entity, seeking a proper place within the Arab world and refusing to be relegated to a position in the rear of the Arab convoy or far away from the center of leadership. The unswerving loyalty of al-Maghrib to Arabism was exemplified beyond doubt in the careers of the first Muslim monarchs of purely Berber extraction. Their record is one of wholehearted devotion to the cause of Islam and the expansion of Arab rule beyond the seas. Internally, their attention was concentrated on the Arabicizing of local culture. A Maghribi national consciousness became so articulate and widespread that when al-Mahdi ibn Tūmert of southern Morocco and founder of the Muwaḥḥidīn dynasty died, he named 'Abd al-Mu'min al-Jūmi of Algeria to succeed him as caliph.

National consciousness existed in al-Maghrib before and after the advent of Islam. Evidences of deep-rooted nationalism may be discerned in the books of Ibn Jubayr, Ibn Khaldūn, in the poems of Ibn Hāni, and others. It was this strong nationalism which enabled our nation to beat back European aggression, particularly that of Spain and Portugal, throughout the Middle Ages. Modern times find the imperialist states of Europe embarked upon a concerted attack against the Arab and Muslim world in its entirety. The Arab lands of North Africa were early victims of this onslaught, but their record of resistance, in spite of great odds, has been no less heroic than that of their forefathers.

Roman, Byzantine, and Vandal imperialisms failed to destroy the national entity of al-Maghrib despite their long-lived sway over the land. In the present day, French and Spanish rule is becoming more and more onerous. The two states entertain the hope that by terror and oppression they can destroy our existence as an independent Arab nation, but history will repeat itself and this imperialism will wither away as did the earlier ones.

The tyranny of Rome and its record of exploitation have been resuscitated by those who proudly claim to have inherited the Roman Empire in the twentieth century. The heroism of the people of al-Maghrib, which they have inherited from their Berber and Arab ancestors, is also being renewed in them and mobilized within their independence movements for the struggle to lift the shame of occupation and to wrest from the usurpers their freedom and independence.

The following pages are a record of al-Maghrib's extended struggle. It is a struggle between the Arab East and the Latin West. The Maghrib has pledged itself to struggle until victory is achieved. The glory of tomorrow will be built by the sweat and blood which our fighters for independence will expend today.

Chapter I

IN CENTRAL MAGHRIB OR ALGERIA

In 1947 a delegation representing the "Movement for the Victory of Democratic Freedoms", which represents the Sha'b (people's) Party in Algeria, approached the authorities with a request for the transfer of the remains of Amīr 'Abd al-Qādir, the first hero of Algerian independence, from its resting abode on the outskirts of Damascus to his birthplace in Central Maghrib. The aim of those freedom-loving delegates was to reiterate to the French Governor a statement by Maṣāli al-Ḥaj, their leader, in which he said, "Our movement is but the hoisting anew of the banner of Amīr 'Abd al-Qādir, who struggled throughout his life for the freedom and independence of the Algerian people."

Thus the contemporary independence movement in Algeria is an extension of the first resistance movement, put up by the Amīr 'Abd al-Qādir and his successors, since Marshal Bourmont attacked Sīdi Faraj on June 13, 1830.

France committed her aggression against Algeria at a time when sovereignty was vested in the Ottoman Empire.

Turkey offered no serious resistance; but no sooner had the Turkish vālis (governors) in Algeria surrendered than Arab resistance was launched. This was made possible by the arrival of the Moroccan army, under Abu al-Ḥassan, at the city of Tlemcen in October 1830. This Moroccan commander succeeded in mobilizing the tribes of the area under his banner for resistance to the French and rejection of the Turkish surrender. When Muḥyi al-Dīn joined the movement it was decided to rally to the support of the Sultan of al-Maghrib in the jihād (holy war) for the protection of the area against foreign aggression. In spite of the intrigues of the French and their appointment of a Tunisian bey over Oran, with a view to playing off one Arab faction against another, Maghrib solidarity continued unimpaired. It gained added strength by the refusal of the Amīr 'Abd al-Qādir to cooperate in any form of government except with the full concurrence of the government of Morocco. Following numerous incidents and vicissitudes into which we shall not delve here, the Amīr 'Abd al-Qādir instituted an Algerian government independently of both the French and the Turks. He also formed a united national front in the face of the enemy which aroused an Algerian national consciousness, hitherto dormant under the yoke of Turkish oppression and tribal turmoils. 'Abd al-Qādir's genius is exemplified in his early alertness to the necessity of uniting the entire Maghrib for common self-defense. The failure of Morocco to continue to lend support to Algeria, though for reasons beyond her control, and Tunisia's failure to apprehend the magnitude of the French danger, must, together with Ottoman neglect, share the blame for the Western onslaught on the Arab world and the resulting spoliation of all the Arab nations by the Anglo-Saxons and the Latins.

One of the heroes of Algerian resistance was Abu Ma'zi, a Moroccan, who came to Algeria in 1835 in order to mobilize popular support against the French in the districts of Southern Oran. Later, he moved his headquarters to Zawāwah, where he gathered considerable support. The fact that his movement had been organized independently of the Amīr 'Abd al-Qādir enticed the French into the belief that he could be counted upon to undermine the authority of the latter. They were forced to retract their plan, however, following costly campaigns against his forces which lasted two years. Abu Ma'zi crowned his achievements by joining the camp of 'Abd al-Qādir, who subsequently appointed him governor of the mountainous region of Zawāwah. Abu Ma'zi continued to fight in the ranks of 'Abd al-Qādir until the latter was forced to take refuge in Morocco in 1845. When he returned to Algeria in the same year, Abu Ma'zi joined his ranks. They succeeded in mobilizing all the tribes of Oran and Algeria and in scoring a decisive victory over the French in the battle of Sīdi Ibrāhīm, to the west of Jāmi' al-Ghazawāt. The position of French forces became so precarious that General Bugeaud was compelled to ask for substantial reinforcements. With a reinforced army of ten thousand men, General Bugeaud mounted a successful offensive against 'Abd al-Qādir. Abu Ma'zi fought with utmost heroism until his line was pierced and overwhelmed by French troops and he was taken prisoner. Upon his release he went to Turkey where he was accorded a warm welcome by the authorities and took up residence as guest of the government.

During the Crimean war he enlisted in the Ottoman army and was taken prisoner by the Russians in the Caucasus where he remained until his death in the city of Batum.

After his death six Algerian individuals claimed to be Abu Ma'zi; one of them asserted that he was his brother and assumed the name of Mawlāyi Aḥmad abu Ma'zi. He was wounded in one of the battles, captured, and turned over to the court-martial. In spite of his terrifying position, the following debate took place between him and the head of the court:

The head of the court asked him who he was and he answered, "I am Abu Ma'zi."

"Why did you fight against France?"

"Because it is an unjust and tyrannical government which is attacking us."

"Don't you see that the Arabs are joining us?"

"Those Arabs are of two kinds. The majority of them are innocent people who fear for their lives. The minority are the low and treacherous, who are only interested in satisfying the ruler, whoever he may be, and who wish to wear red braid on their chests."

"What do you expect from us?"

"Whatever I expect from you does not worry me at all."

"If we were to set you free, what would you do?"

"I should return to fight for God's cause."

"And if we killed you?"

"I should proceed to God saying two shahādas [that is, confessions of faith]."

"And if we imprisoned you?"

"I should spend my time worshipping and asking God to grant victory to justice over injustice."

"Why do you detest us?"

"Because you are tyrannical oppressors."

After being condemned to prison for some time he was set free.

In 1849 the governor of the Za'āṭashah (a tribe in the south of Constantine near the city of Biskra) made an attempt on the life of their previous chief Abu Zayyān, who had been appointed by Amīr 'Abd al-Qādir. Abu Zayyān then began to incite the people who had submitted to France in 1847 to resume the war. He actually gathered around him a group that was able to destroy a large French army on maneuvers near Biskra. The French sent a strong punitive force to besiege this oasis, which supported no more than 3,000 inhabitants, all of whom raised date palms. In spite of their limited numbers they were able to hold out for six full months, and Abu Zayyān was able to gain victories over three French commanders who were sent successively to destroy this simple oasis. Finally the Governor-General was compelled to equip an army of 10,000 men with forty-five cannon and a large number of military engineers who specialized in mine-laying. Even then they were able to overcome it only after a severe fight, which took place among the date trees and along the sides of the houses. The people of the oasis suffered the loss of more than a thousand dead. After the French had occupied the oasis, the Commander in Chief General Herbieu ordered Colonel Cribère, who later became A French marshal, to direct the army to collect all the population that remained, including the women who had fought and suffered side by side with the men throughout the battle. The army crowded the remainder of the population together and dispatched them, after taking Abu Zayyān, who had been wounded. They cut off his head and the heads of his three sons, the oldest of whom was not over sixteen years old; these heads and others were sent to Biskra where they were hung over the gates of the city. None of the inhabitants of the oasis escaped; some died durin the battle and the others, including 117 women, were bayonetted after they capitulated.

The war of national independence lasted for eighteen years and ended with a victory of brute force over right and justice. All the while the French authorities continued their frantic efforts toward the consolidation of their influence in the face of native hostility. We shall see how all their repressive acts failed to divert the Algerian people from their cherished aim--freedom and independence.

The French, in astute tactical maneuvers, offered the Algerians equality and freedom within the French orbit whenever national sentiment became threateningly pronounce Their objective was to deflect the liberation movement from its original course and circumscribe its scope. We shall see the vacillation of French policy in this regard and its impact upon the Algerian national movement.

On July 22, 1834 a royal decree was issued by Louis Philippe, King of the French, as a result of which Algeria became a French possession. The annexation remained ineffective, however, because the Franco-Algerian war was still raging unabated. In 1846 France abolished the idea of a "special regime" for Algeria and decided on an outright assimilation of the country. This step, embodied in the French Constitution of 1848, was a decisive milestone in the struggle between an independent Algerian entity and outright French rule. It ended the period of tact and diplomacy in the relations of the two countries. That is why the people of Algeria refer to the date of its inception as the commencement of the rule of the sword. The ensuing reign of terror lasted until the Emperor Napoleon III acceded to the throne. The Emperor promulgated in 1865 his famous Senatus Consultum which conferred upon the Algerians equal rights with the French. Henceforth the Algerians could hold civil offices, serve in the French army and assume French citizenship at will, without prejudice to their personal status under the jurisdiction of the Islamic Sharī'ah. The Emperor visited Algeria and delivered a historic speech in which he declared: "Algeria is not a colony but an Arab kingdom. I am as much Emperor of the Arabs as of the French. Both are equal in my eyes."

Napoleon's far-sighted policy was wholly unpalatable to the French colonists in Algeria. They reacted vigorously to his placating the Muslims, thus proving, as they did on many later occasions, that they placed their own selfish and immediate interests above those of the mother country.

Although Napoleon's attempt failed to surmount the colonists' opposition, it served nevertheless as a model which the French utilized to divert Arab resistance from a forthright struggle for independence to a mere quest for equality.

Following the downfall of the Empire in 1871 [sic] and the establishment of the Third Republic, Gambetta, the idol of the Republicans, initiated two iniquitous enactments reimposing a regime of slavery upon the Algerian people. The first was the Crémieux Decree. (Crémieux, a Jew, was Minister of Justice in the Gambetta government.)

The decree accorded French citizenship to the Jews of Àlgeria, en masse, with a view to increasing the proportion of French colonists vis-à-vis the indigenous population. The second consisted in a series of measures highly inimical to the Algerian people, including a complete denial of civil rights. This placed them under the absolute rule of the governor-general and his administration. The administration was empowered to imprison every Algerian without due process of law, if there was the slightest doubt concerning his loyalty to French sovereignty. The administration was also empowered to exile any recalcitrant Algerian and to impound or confiscate his property. Gambetta went so far as to deny the government of Paris or Parliament the right to review the administrative acts of the governorship in its persecution of the Algerian people.

The people of Algeria did not take these arbitrary measures lying down. Outbursts of popular indignation against the French meddling in the religious affairs of the Muslims, and their policies of racial discrimination and religious persecution, culminated in a full-fledged rebellion which encompassed the whole Zawāwah area, the districts of Constantine and of Algiers. The rebellion was led by the distinguished pasha of a district in Constantine, Agha al-Ḥaj Muḥammad al-Muqrāni, and also by Sheikh Muḥammad al-Ḥaddād, Sheikh of the al-Raḥmānīyah al-Darqāwīyah religious order.

This serious rebellion lasted six whole months. It cost the Muslims no less than sixty thousand martyrs, while French losses amounted to twenty thousand killed. The rebellion was only quelled when Bismarck released the French army which had been taken prisoner during the Franco-Prussian war of 1870. This army was dispatched to Algeria to quell the rebellion. In the course of the campaign Ḥaj Muḥammad al-Muqrāni, the commander, was killed in action on May 5, 1871 and was succeeded by his uncle Sheikh Abu Muzrāq.

The atrocities committed by the French army in vengeance are beyond description; I only refer the reader to a book entitled "al-Ikhwānīyah" in which the author details the unspeakable acts of savagery inflicted upon the rebels.

When fighting ended, six thousand rebels were sentenced

to death. Abu Muzrāq, Sheikh al-Ḥaddād and his two sons, Muḥammad and 'Azīz, together with five hundred rebel leaders, were exiled to the island of New Caledonia in the Pacific. They remained in this remote exile until their death. A levy of thirty-six million francs was imposed on Algeria. When the inhabitants found themselves unable to pay this sum they were deported en masse and their land sequestered. Immigrants from Alsace-Lorraine were settled in their place.

The rebellion, though successfully put down by the French, had far-reaching effects upon the entire Algerian nation. It was followed by another large-scale rebellion in Oran under the leadership of al-Pasha Āgha Sulaymān ibn Ḥamzah, which lasted without interruption for five years. The leader al-Pasha Āgha was killed in action in the course of this campaign.

In 1882 the Muḥrānīyah tribes rose in rebellion against the French under the leadership of Sheikh Abi 'Umāmah, the Moroccan. The rebellion lasted until 1885.

In addition to these armed insurrections, peaceful agitation was carried on at various intervals in response to changing political circumstances. The first of these peaceful movements was organized in 1871 by Sayyid Muḥammad al-Badawi, an Algerian intellectual, who seized upon the opportunity presented by the Paris Commune to press for Algerian self-rule. He set up an organization which demanded full rights for the Algerian people. Its activities, however, ceased with the collapse of the Paris Commune.

In 1892 the French, alarmed by the widespread dissatisfaction that had permeated all sections of the Algerian people, put in motion a number of farcical reform measures to placate the unrest. These included the creation of a new elective assembly called the "Délégations Financières Algériennes" consisting of two-thirds French delegates and one-third Algerian.

In 1904 the people of Morocco were lining up to meet the challenge created by the Anglo-French conspiracy. Developments in Morocco had their repercussions in the contiguous region of the Oran. Formations known as the "honorable thieves" came into being with the avowed purpose of killing every French governor or any Algerian guilty of collaboration with the French. The most famous of these heroes was Abu Zayyān al-Qal'i.

This movement subsided only to take a different manifestation in the "protest emigration" to the lands of the Ottoman Empire in the years 1898-1899. During this period a large number of leading families emigrated to the East and to Turkey in order to escape French rule and await a favorable opportunity to seek the support of the Ottoman state in which Algeria continued to place high hopes.

In 1910 Algerian writers took upon themselves the cause of equality for the people of their country. They comprised the first group of educated Algerians who had studied in France, and who upon their return home addressed themselves to exploring ways and means of ameliorating the lot of their people, and of resisting the iron hand that had clamped down upon them. The group was led by Aḥmad abu Darbah, the first Algerian to obtain a barrister-at-law degree from Paris (after seventy-five years of French rule in Algeria). The group also included Sādiq Dandān, a pressman, and Ḥaj 'Ammār, a financial delegate.

The program of the movement aimed at reforms on the basis of the Senatus Consultum of 1865. Its objective was the achievement of Islamic unity. In addition to propagating their cause at home its leaders hoped to enlist the assistance of the Ottoman Empire in whose leaders they had placed great hopes. We must not forget the violent attacks which pressman Sādiq Dandān launched in support of Moroccan independence and in condemnation of the French conquest of Morocco.

When World War I broke out the French started a forcible enlistment of North Africans and particularly Algerians. The people's resistance to enlistment caused serious troubles and bloodshed, and several French officials and colonists were killed. Desertions from the army amounted to 120,000 persons, many of whom took to the mountains. Simultaneously, there was organized agitation in towns and cities in support of freedom and evacuation. A number of Algerian military units, notably the one commanded by Ḥaj Muḥammad Bukabūyah, deserted to the Ottoman army. The Paris government, sensing the dangers to its position in Algeria, resorted to its traditional tactics of false and moonshine promises. M. Briand, the then Prime Minister, sent a message to M. Clemenceau, chairman of the Senate Foreign Relations Committee, and another to the chairman of the House Foreign Relations Committee, conceding that the time had come to accord the Algerian people all their civil rights.

At the termination of hostilities in 1918 a delegation of Algerian officers was formed under the leadership of the Amīr Khālid. The delegation made representations to President Woodrow Wilson in Paris, demanding that Wilson's Fourteen Points be applied to the Algerian people.

The formation of this delegation was only a prelude to the organization of a large-scale political movement. Following the enactment by the French authorities of the laws of February 4, 1919, which abrogated the discriminatory "Code of the Indigénat" and extended the electoral rights of Algerians to municipal and financial office, the Amir Khālid, who was an officer in the French army, was retired on pension. He returned to Algeria and formed an organization known as the "Bloc of Elected Algerian Muslims". The bloc, led by the Amir Khālid, carried on widespread agitation with a view to achieving two principal aims: complete rights for the Algerians, and the amelioration of their social conditions.

In the forefront of the demands advocated by the Bloc was the cessation of foreign immigration to Algeria, on the grounds that Algeria belongs to the Algerians. To propagate the program of the movement the Amir Khālid started a newspaper "al-Iqdām", with Arabic and French editions.

The movement was in essence a reaction to the French reign of terror, and therefore it was violent in its tone and orientation. It lacked precision and clarity in its principles and program of action, but it did succeed in undermining French influence in the fear-ridden hearts of the Algerian people and gave vent to their long-suppressed animosity towards the oppressive colonial rule.

The colonial power, in league with a considerable number of stooges and traitors, conspired against the Amir, demanding his expulsion from his country. The administration, however, was not able to effect this without due process of law. To surmount the difficulty, the colonial power re-enacted the Code of the Indigénat, which gave the administration arbitrary and sweeping powers. As a matter of fact, the Governor-General, M. Steeg, did not await the re-enactments of the Code, but applied it retroactively in the case of the Amir. He was expelled and forced to take refuge in Alexandria.

When the government of M. Poincaré fell in 1924, to be succeeded by a left bloc under the leadership of M. Léon Blum and M. Herriot, the Amir Khālid was permitted to return to France where he formed a committee of North African nationalist leaders. The committee included Maṣāli al-Ḥaj (present leader of the Algerian People's Party), 'Abd al-Qādir ibn al-Ḥaj 'Ali, Abd al-'Azīz al-Munawwar, and 'Ali al-Ḥamāmi from Morocco. The Amir Khālid returned to Alexandria during the intensified phase of the fighting between French forces and the forces of the hero of the Riff, the Amir 'Abd al-Karīm. In 1925 the French accused the Amir Khālid of conspiring against France and British police in Alexandria broke into his residence. The Amir considered this act an insult and challenged the French consul in Alexandria to a duel, whereupon the French Ambassador made representations to the Egyptian Government demanding his extradition. The Amir was chained and expelled to Syria where he remained until his death in 1936.

The movement which the Amir Khālid had set in motion among the Algerian and Moroccan communities during his sojourn in France did not die out with his own death. On the contrary, it grew in intensity, and no historian of North Africa could gloss over or minimize it. One of its main outgrowths and manifestations was a conference, convoked in Paris in 1924, to tackle the political, economic, and labor problems of North Africa. The resolutions of the conference included a demand for freedom of the press and speech, organization of a publicity campaign on behalf of the North African cause, and abrogation of the Code of the Indigénat. The conference concluded its work with a dispatch of cables to the people of Morocco and their leader the Amir 'Abd al-Karīm, and also to the peoples of Egypt and Tunisia. It is pertinent to cite the text of the first cable. It reads: "The North African workers of the Paris area factories, assembled in their first conference on this historic day, December 7, 1924, congratulate their Moroccan brethren and their leader, the hero 'Abd al-Karīm, on the occasion of their victory over Spanish colonialism, and declare their solidarity with them in all steps that might contribute to the liberation of their country. They join with them in hailing the independence of oppressed people and the downfall of world imperialism and French imperialism.

This message alone is evidence of the spirit which has permeated the North African citizens since those days. Colonial rule had suppressed its overt expression at home, but it found within the democratic framework in France a vehicle for self-expression. Is not this lofty message of greeting an embodiment of the entire nationalist program for the attainment of which we are struggling today; complete independence, solidarity with all the Arab peoples, and striving for the liberation of oppressed peoples everywhere?

The movement of our brethren in Paris continued, with varying manifestations. What interests us most at this point is the transformation of the Algerian resistance movement from its futility and indecision to a new phase of unflinching determination.

The new phase found its expression in the formation of "Najm Shamāl Ifrīqia" (Etoile Nord Africaine). The movement was initially an organization for the relief of needy North Africans; it evolved, however, in March 1926, into a political association for the defense of the Arab Maghrib and the realization of its rights. It founded a French-language newspaper known as "al-Ummah" (the Nation).

The movement expended considerable efforts towards organizing North African workers in France and in effecting their political and social indoctrination according to methods of political party organization in France. The work of its leader, Maṣāli al-Ḥaj, and his colleagues is a shining example of selfless devotion and sacrifice, deserving the highest tribute. The intensification of its activities, coupled with its uncompromising demand for all-out liberation of the whole of North Africa, was too much for French imperialism. The French Government found in its continuation a serious threat which could not be allowed to continue unchecked. It worked out a twofold program for dealing with this dissident movement. In the first place, it subjected it to a heavy propaganda barrage in Algeria and Tunisia, alleging that it was an affiliate of the Communist Party, that it was extreme in its demands and served only the interests of Moscow and the Communist International. The propaganda campaign deceived the Algerian deputies and their supporters. Secondly, the Etoile Nord Africaine was sued before a court of the Seine and an order for its dissolution was issued on November 20, 1929, without any specific charges being levelled against it. The court decision, however, was never officially carried out, with the result that members of the organization were able to resume their activities six months after the decision had been handed down, in accordance with article 150 of the French civil code.

Admittedly, the Etoile Nord Africaine moved with great reticence thereafter, in deference to circumstances and on account of the pressure to which it had been subjected. Furthermore, many leaders of public opinion in Algeria misunderstood the aims and motivations of the movement. In 1933 I was exiled to France, where direct contact was established between myself and the leader of the Etoile, Maṣāli. This led to substantial understanding between the Algerian movement and the "Moroccan League for National Action" (Kutlat al-'Amal al-Waṭani) of which I was a member. We participated in several conferences which aimed at enlightening French public opinion concerning our cause. The conference of North African Muslim students in France afforded us an opportunity to defend the principle of Algerian independence against the protagonists of assimilation and integration with France. During one of the sessions of the conference an acrimonious debate occurred over this issue. Two Tunisians, 'Abd al-Raḥmān Yāssīn and Sayīd al-Ya'lāwi, had argued in favor of admitting Algerians who had accepted French naturalization to our North African organizations in France.

I put up a determined stand against this proposal. Sayīd Maṣāli and his Algerian colleague rallied to my view which was eventually adopted by the conference. Thus Algerians, Tunisians, and Moroccans carried at the conference a decisive resolution, underlining the principle of preserving for the countries of North Africa their pure Arab character.

On May 22, 1933 the Etoile Nord Africaine met in plenary session and adopted the following program:

1. Urgent reforms:

a. Freedom of the press, of meetings, and of association.

b. Replacement of the Délégations Financières by an Algerian national parliament elected by universal suffrage.

c. Admission of Algerians to all public offices.

d. Obligatory education in Arabic.

e. Extension of social and syndical rights to North African workers.

2. Evacuation of occupation troops and the formation of a strong army.

3. Complete independence for Algeria and the nationalization of the means of production; the great estates seized by the colonists or their descendents to be returned to their lawful owners.

In March 1934 the court of the Seine resumed trial of Maṣāli al-Ḥaj, Imāsh 'Amār, and al-Ridha abu al-Qāsim, on charges of having resuscitated an organization that had been disbanded by judicial decision. The three accused emerged victorious, however, because the former court decision had not been carried out during the period stipulated by law. Thus the Etoile Nord Africaine continued officially in existence, thanks to the tenacity and untiring activity of its members. In 1936, however, the Etoile engaged in a violent struggle with the French Communist Party which led to a headlong clash with the combined forces of the French Popular Front. Subsequently, M. Léon Blum issued a decree, dated March 26, 1937, dissolving the Etoile Nord Africaine.

In Algeria herself, a great religious leader and reformer achieved renown. He is Sheikh 'Abd al-Ḥamīd ibn Bādīs, a descendant of the old and noble family of al-Zīrīyīn which had founded the two Amirates of Bijāyah and Qal'at Banī Ḥammād. It was at the behest of this family that relations were severed between North Africa and the Fatimid dynasty in Egypt many centuries before.

This learned leader graduated from Jāmi' al-Zaytūnah in Tunis, and upon completion of his studies returned to Algeria, where he initiated a great religious revival, the "Salafīyah" (Fundamentalist). The Sheikh started a weekly publication, "al-Shihāb", which throughout the Riffian war served as a rostrum for all the religious reformers in North Africa and particularly for those in Morocco. In the latter country, we in our turn were engaged in a great reform movement to combat some of the religious orders which the French had exploited in opposition to the Riff war of liberation. In 1928 Sheikh Ibn Bādīs established the "Society of Muslim 'Ulemas" in Algeria. A short while later many men of learning from the sister country Morocco joined hands. The Society performed a most effective task in enlightening Muslim public opinion in Algeria and in spreading Arab culture throughout the land. It also awakened Arab national consciousness among its numerous supporters.

Officially, the aims of this society were non-political. They were concerned with the purification of the Islamic faith in Algeria from the superstitions that had engulfed it. The program also included a revival of the Arabic language and the strengthening of Arab consciousness in Algeria. Nevertheless, in a country suffering under the yoke of French imperialism, which aims officially at the liquidation of Islam, the Arabic language, and Algerian national consciousness, the very principles of the society embroiled it in bitter and sustained conflict with the French rulers on the one hand, and on the other, with members of some of the religious orders, whom the French authorities would not hesitate to exploit for their own ulterior purposes.

The purely religious orientation which the Society had assumed, however, caused its policies to be ambiguous. Its men would not join any political movement except as private individuals, not as members of the Society. Moreover, the Society as a whole did not restrict its cooperation to any one party. It made use of all existing movements for the propagation of its principles and beliefs. We can assert, however, that the true belief of Sheikh Ibn Bādīs was in the independence of Algeria from French rule. No better proof can be cited in support of our contention than the following excerpts from an article that appeared in Sheikh Ibn Bādīs' weekly, "al-Shihāb", in April 1936. It reads in part: "It is our view that the Algerian nation is in being and has developed like the other nations of the earth. It was, and still is, a living reality. It has its glorious history as well as its religious and linguistic unity. It has its culture and its traditions--the good and the bad ones--like the other nations of the world. This Algerian nation is not France; it does not wish to become France; it is impossible that it should ever become France, even if forcible assimilation were attempted

It is impossible for a historian to underrate the role which this Society has played and is still playing in the national life of Algeria. Its program of action included the opening of branches and schools in various parts of the land. It published many newspapers in both Arabic and French, while its active members roamed the country propagating the revivalist (salafīyah) and the nationalist cause. Suffice it here to mention amongst its prominent members Ibn Bādīs, Sheikh al-Ibrāhīmi, Sheikh al-'Amūdi, al-Maylī, and the poet Muḥammad al-'Īd. This religious society in Algeria, and the Etoile Nord Africaine in France, though different in their orientation and programs, continued as the two active organizations striving for the well-being of the Algerian people from 1928 to 1934. In this year an incident occurred in the city of Constantine which had a profound effect upon the development of the Algerian national movement, as we shall see.

On the evening of August 3, 1934, a Jew named Khalīfah Elyālo, a soldier and a native of Constantine, desecrated a Muslim mosque and made insulting references to Muslims. The led to a clash between Muslims and Jews, in the course of which the latter resorted to the use of firearms. The Muslims were compelled to defend themselves by hurling stones. The day ended with several dead and scores wounded from both sides. Next day two Arabs were shot dead by two Jews and were quietly buried. The Muslims held a mass meeting to protest the partiality of the authorities towards the Jews during the clashes. The incident could have ended there, but the military authorities dispatched troops ostensibly to restore order. They included in their ranks many Jews who allied themselves with Jewish civilians in a concerted assault upon the Muslims. This provoked fierce fighting between the people and troops on the one hand and between Muslims and Jews on the other. Several hundred Algerians and others lost their lives.

It is natural that we should attribute such incidents to the policy of social discrimination which the French Government had pursued in Algeria since the Crémieux Decree to which we have already alluded. It is evident that if the Jews had not been accorded the rights of French citizens they would not have dared molest the Muslims, who had become in their eyes an unworthy populace, a sort of second class citizenry undeserving of respect. The incidents thus had profound effects in awakening and sharpening the feelings of self-respect amongst Muslims. They closed their ranks and intensified their agitation for the attainment of their natural rights, while condemning the French policy of racial discrimination and the playing off of one section of the people against another.

The French Government and colonists were alarmed at the turn of events in Algeria. A French financial delegate, who was also mayor of Constantine, requested the Paris government to send five hundred combat planes to restore order in Algeria. In a statement he declared: "We must carry out a military occupation of the country by an adequate and reliable army. As a precaution against the recrudescence of such serious incidents we must have a strong defense setup and a well-organized police force. The governor-general should be empowered to call up all French citizens in cases of emergency."

Thus, Algeria found herself in a state of war with France. The trial of Dr. Ben Jalūl gave the authorities an opportunity to display their military might and the people an occasion to express their longing for freedom and equality. Later M. Régnier, Minister of the Interior, made a circuit of Algeria to study the situation on the spot. His study tour familiarized him with the people's aspirations for liberation; his response was the enactment of the notorious Régnier Decree, which provided that severe penalties be meted out to all recalcitrant elements. The decree was subsequently enfored in Tunisia and Morocco as well.

The Constantine disturbances revealed the stark fact that the people's elected representatives to local councils had no mass support whatever. There also appeared on the political scene, in addition to the Muslim religious leaders, two new faces: Dr. Ben Jalūl and 'Abbas Farḥāt. We have already pointed out the official as well as the unofficial orientation of the Society of Muslim 'Ulemas. Dr. Ben Jalūl has been very erratic and changeable in his views. As for 'Abbas Farḥāt, he is indeed an outstanding personality, both intelligent and cultured. His goal, however, was limited to a demand for equality with the French. In 1933 I had an occasion in Paris to discuss with him his views on this question I was made to understand that the demand for equal rights with the French was only a phase through which Algeria must pass and that the eventual goal should be the independence of the Algerian people.

This particular phase of the movement, aiming at equality with the French, is intended, therefore, to prepare the ground not for integration with France but for separation from her. It is akin to the case of Ireland, which though a British territory at the outset, succeeded eventually in gaining her independent government.

Regardless of what our views might be on this strategy, there is no doubt that the leaders of this period gave to Algeria her best organized and best publicized movement. They succeeded in mobilizing the Algerian people behind them. They also cooperated effectively with the Society of Muslim 'Ulemas as well as with the Etoile Nord Africaine in spite of the differences in their respective orientations. The objective was after all identical, namely, resistance to the policy of racial discrimination and the undermining of colonial hegemony on the one hand and opposition to French assimilation on the other. Thus there came to the fore anew the question of Muslim representation in the French Parliament. An intensive publicity campaign was launched in support of the Viollette scheme which advocated a gradual grant of this right to the Algerians.

'Abbas Farḥāt wrote his book, "al-Shābb al-Jazā'iri" (the Algerian youth), expounding his views and principles, while M. Viollette wrote his book on Algeria defending his scheme. He told his fellow Frenchmen that failure to implement the program with expedition would throw its Algerian supporters into the arms of the protagonists of Arab unity, particularly in the light of the intensified independence movement in Morocco and the active constitutional movement in Tunisia. The publicity campaign for the program continued unabated and was able to win over the support of all the left-wing parties in France. The events of November 6, which witnessed the participation of North African workers in support of democracy against French Fascists, solidified French leftist support of the program.

After the Victory of the French Popular Front

The formation of the Popular Front in France, and its victory in the elections, was widely acclaimed by the people of North Africa, particularly in Algeria. Our countrymen believed that these leftist parties, which had unreservedly dissociated themselves from all the oppressive acts of the reactionary imperialists, would not hesitate to meet the wishes of the people, at least within the scope of their self-proclaimed principles which had installed them in power.

"Bread, peace, freedom"--these expressed the basic principles upon which the government of the Popular Front staked the elections. They were the essentials to the realization of justice for every nation and for every individual. No wonder a substantial number of Algerians placed their hopes and trust in this new government which was itself a manifestation of the will of the underprivileged classes in France. Another section of opinion adopted a wait-and-see policy towards the new government. Its leaders continued to press for the rights of the Algerian people, without changing their attitude to the colonial power as a result of the change in its government. No sooner had the new government taken office than an Algerian Muslim conference was convened on June 7, 1937. The conference, under the chairmanship of Dr. Ben Jalūl, represented all shades of opinion in Algeria, including that of the Society of Muslim 'Ulemas. Only members of the Etoile Nord Africaine did not take part.

The conference adopted the following resolutions:

1. The election of the Algerian Muslims to Parliament in a united electoral bloc and without prejudice to the voters' civil status.
2. Abrogation of the Code of the Indigénat; reform of the Forestry Act; revocation of the Act of August 4, 1926 as amended on April 4, 1928, concerning the movement of Algerians in France; and cancellation of the Régnier Law, intended against those who are opposed to French sovereignty over Algeria.
3. Abolition of the separate administration in charge of native affairs and the "Territories of the South".
4. Recognition of Arabic as a national language in Algeria.
5. A thorough overhaul in the Algerian administrative apparatus.

These were the modest demands adopted by the conference. They were of small significance as compared to the general atmosphere it succeeded in creating throughout Algeria. The leaders of the conference wanted to organize it along the lines of the Indian Congress Party. In the outcome, however, they restricted themselves to various minor points which did not in any way reflect the aspirations of the Algerian people for genuine freedom and rejuvenation.

The conference appointed a delegation to submit its resolutions to the French Government. The delegation left for Paris amidst tumultuous popular demonstrations clamoring for freedom, independence, and the downfall of oppression. On July 23, 1937 the delegation was received by Prime Minister Léon Blum. The Premier told the delegation that as a Frenchman he was happy to welcome Frenchmen, and as a democrat to welcome democrats, and as a Jew to welcome Muslims. He then informed them that the government was preparing to implement a number of reforms in Algeria and that it would study the demands of the Algerians in a spirit of justice and fraternity.

The cordial reception granted to the delegation by the Premier was most favorably received by the people of Algeria. A working alliance was formed between the supporters of the conference and the Popular Front in France for promoting the demands of the underprivileged and resisting the die-hard colonists in Algeria, who think only in terms of their own selfish interests. In the meantime, demonstrations of people shouting the slogan "bread, peace, freedom" continued throughout the land. These were highlighted by an impressive mass parade on June 14, in which Algerian Muslim women formed a phalanx, joining in the democratic slogans and salutations. The phase of peaceful demonstrations lasted, however, for only a few days and was followed by popular agitation for the fulfilment of the promised reforms. The strikes of Muslim workers in plants owned by French colonial companies increased. The call to strike spread even among agricultural laborers, who protested the tyranny of the French colonists and demanded equality and land. The strikers occupied the roads and evacuated the farm estates. Frequent clashes flared up between the strikers and the colonists in which scores of people from both sides were killed or wounded. On February 26, 1937 a serious clash occurred in Sidi 'Abbās. On the first day of the following month hundreds of agricultural workers assembled in a village in the district of Oran and decided to strike and demonstrate. Next day they marched on the great marketplace to bring its operations to a standstill (this is known in tribal customs as "breaking the market" and is usually the symbol of rebellion). The workers blocked all roads leading to the market. The authorities summoned armed forces to meet the challenge of the striking workers, who in the meantime had been joined by close to ten thousand persons from nearby villages. A violent clash occurred between the assembled crowd and forces of the Foreign Legion which had been summoned to deal with the situation.

On March 9 copperminers in the Constantine area struck work. When the European workers refused to side with them a clash occurred, in which several persons lost their lives.

We have deliberately cited a sample of the incidents that occurred following the Muslim Algerian conference. Did the excited masses support the conference in its proclaimed principles, which did not explicitly include a demand for independence? The truth is that the slogans and the demands of the demonstrators went far beyond those of Dr. Ben Jalūl and his supporters. What the conference had done was merely to remove the barrier that had prevented the people from giving vent to their views and aspirations. If the coincidental presence of a leftist government in France had directed the movement into channels of class warfare, we should not be misled into assuming far-fetched implications. Classes in Algeria are a mere reflection of the inequalities that had been implanted by the colonial power. The Algerian proletariat is none other than the entire nation--whether rich or poor, capitalist or worker--in revolt against the imperialists.

An old proverb states that truth is served by its friends and enemies alike. Likewise, the cause of Algerian independence was served by its friends, who came out openly in its support, and by its enemies, the colonials and the defeatists within the ranks of the people. No sooner had the conference met and its aims been presented to national and French circles than the colonists began their widespread agitation to sabotage it. What is interesting for our purpose is the fact that the colonials and the local French administration in Algeria supported the correct view: that it was the duty of France to preserve for the Algerians their national character; that she should not integrate them into France or attempt their assimilation; that any such attempts would be a violation of pledges given to the people of Algeria.

The local administration mobilized for its purpose a number of religious personages, who were known for their pro-French leanings and their antipathy to the Society of Muslim 'Ulemas and its revivalist movement. In the forefront of opposition to the Algerian Muslim conference was the Mufti of Algeria, Ibn Dāli Kaḥḥūl, a staunch supporter of French policies. A number of extremists took advantage of popular excitement on the occasion of the delegation's return from Paris and stabbed the Mufti fatally. His murder had wide repercussions in French circles and was followed by a second conference sponsored by members of religious orders. The conference, meeting under the auspices of the French director of native affairs, adopted a decision claiming that the first conference was not representative of the Algerian people.

Although the conference of those traitors did not have a popular impact comparable to that of the first conference, it did, at any rate, awaken in a section of the people a realization of the peril into which they were being led. The current which Dr. Ben Jalūl had induced began to ebb. A schism occurred in the ranks of the first conference which culminated in the removal of Dr. Ben Jalūl from the chairmanship of the conference. His views, orientation, and statements were unpalatable to the executive committee. On January 22, 1937 the Blum-Viollette plan was submitted to the French Chamber of Deputies. The plan accorded to sections of Algerians the right to elect and be elected to the French Parliament without loss of their Islamic personal status. The French colonists in Algeria fought the plan tooth and nail. A conference of all French mayors in Algeria was convened and declared its opposition to the plan on the ground that it would undermine French supremacy over Algeria.

The Algerian People's Party

The Amir Shakīb Arslān sent me a message from Geneva, early in 1936, in which he informed me that the Algerian leader Maṣāli al-Ḥaj had taken refuge in Geneva. The Amir spoke very highly of him. The Algerian leader remained in Geneva until the government of the Popular Front took over, whereupon he returned to his country, then in the throes of disturbances to which we have already referred. The Etoile Nord Africaine had by then passed out of existence altogether. Maṣāli and his colleagues had fortunately not taken part in either of the two conferences. They were thus free and were able to make use of the circumstances and to carry on the movement in a spirit of genuine nationalism. They urged a rejection of the Viollette plan, insisting instead on Algerian nationalism. In March 1937 they established a new organization, the Algerian People's Party.

The Party saw the dawn of life in a situation of turbulence and tension. Its organizational setup followed the pattern of the Tunisian Constitutional Party and the Moroccan Nationalist Party. It was residuary legatee to the cells and the adherents of the Etoile Nord Africaine. Its leaders had intimate connections with nationalist leaders in both Tunisia and Morocco and also with the Amir Shakīb Arslān. This background explains the French all-out hostility to the newborn party. On August 17 Maṣāli and his colleagues, including the renowned poet, Mufadda Zakarīya, were interned for two years, on charges of having resuscitated the disbanded Etoile Nord Africaine under guise of the People's Party, of resisting French sovereignty over Algeria, and of working for Arab unity.

In 1938 a majority of French deputies turned down the Blum-Viollette plan. This convinced even those who had been in doubt that the policy of integration was no more than a tool employed by the French administration to gain much-needed time until they could strike their next blow. Thus 'Abbas Farḥāt withdrew from the conference, declaring that his experience had convinced him of the necessity for an independent and self-governing Algerian entity, since the rulers would not accord it even the most meager manifestations of equality with other human groups. Maṣāli was released in August 1939 to find all the Algerian leaders united in their condemnation of French intrigues and machinations and anxious to work for the liberation of the Algerian nation from these futile colonial tactics. But the Munich agreement had just taken place; war was knocking at the doors and the French were not ready for anything save violence and the application of force everywhere. Thus, when Maṣāli al-Ḥaj resumed his political activity he was imprisoned along with his main supporters on October 4, 1939, that is, only two months after he had been released. After spending seventeen months in custody he was sentenced on March 28, 1941 to sixteen years in prison at hard labor, and to twenty years exile, and was fined thirty million francs.

The Party of Aṣdiqa' al-Bayān

On February 3, 1943 something entirely unexpected by the French took place. The occupation power had taken all possible precautions; all the leaders, major and minor, of the Algerian People's Party had been interned; the Vichy Government had reverted to the old tactic of offering assimilation. To this end they summoned a number of Muslim deputies for consultations. All these steps, however, did not deflect the Algerian people from their search for the freedom they wanted. The blow this time came from a quarter which in French opinion could not conceivably play other than the French tune. All sections of the Algerian people, including former supporters of assimilation, the many supporters of the People's Party, and members of the Society of 'Ulemas, banded together in a new organization known as Aṣdiqā' al-Bayān under the leadership of 'Abbās Farḥāt. The new bloc decided to disavow all past movements for assimilation. Instead, they decided to press for a purely Algerian entity and the establishment of an Algerian republic, with an Algerian parliament elected freely by the people.

Although this movement was moderate in its demands, as compared with the People's Party, it constituted nevertheless a victory of Algerians over themselves. It represented a departure from the idea of assimilation and perpetual dependence on France, and an unequivocal choice of Algerian independence. The emergence of the movement at a critical moment was the salvation of the entire nationalist movement in Algeria.

To counteract these unadulterated nationalist demands, the Ministry for Islamic Affairs, affiliated to the French Liberation Committee, advised General De Gaulle to declare acceptance of sections of educated Algerians into the French family orbit. The move came too late, however; the Algerian people had found their road to salvation; the old tactics would no longer deceive or convert. Thus General De Gaulle's speech in Constantine embodying the new policy merely aggravated the situation. Maṣāli al-Ḥaj was flown back to Algeria for negotiations. The Algerian leader, however, refused to budge from the principles that had led to his imprisonment. He was exiled for the third time to southern Algeria. 'Abbas Farḥāt and 'Abd al-Qādir al-Sāyeḥ were summoned to a meeting with the authorities; when they declined to attend they were sent to prison also.

Upon his release in 1945, following the surrender of the Axis, Farḥāt resumed political activity within the ranks of the Bayān party. He led the demonstrations in Algiers, Constantine, Oran, and Setif that had been organized by the People's Party. Maṣāli cabled his support from his exile in Shallalah (Oran district). The French called out their armed forces, including tanks and aircraft, to quell the demonstrations. 'Abbās was interned, Maṣāli was transferred to the Congo, and on his way passed through the village of Mayama to which I had been exiled. I made efforts to meet him but the guards accompanying him prevented me from doing so. The authorities even threatened my black cook because he had informed Maṣāli of my presence in the village.

The Tragedy of May 8, 1945

The Algerian Muslims participated in the defense of democracy during World War II. Tens of thousands lost their lives fighting on the side of the Allies; considerable numbers of their Tunisian, Moroccan, and other Arab brethren fought valiantly and died in order to stem Nazi and Fascist aggression. It did not occur to them that their efforts and sacrifices would be made in vain or that humanity would sink to the level to which colonialism in the twentieth century had sunk. It did not occur to them that the French would forget what the enemy had done to them, and would instead turn their wrath and vengeance upon the helpless people of Algeria.

Those who suffer calamities and emerge from them react in two ways. One way is that of people who remember their past sufferings and sorrows and become sensitive to similar sufferings in others. Their conscience is stirred and they are moved to help others relieve their plight. Any help they might extend is its own reward. These are the honorable people; there is no doubt that the Arabs of Algeria, who had transcended and projected their own sufferings in order to share and alleviate the sufferings of their foes and assist them in resisting foreign occupation, belong to this honorable group.

The second group of people react to their emergence from calamity with an obdurate desire to forget all its circumstances and associations. This urge becomes so impelling that its victims attempt to manifest in themselves the spirit, the conscience, and the mentality of their former oppressors and tyrants. Thus they commit against others the same heinous atrocities that had been committed against them. They even exceed their former oppressors in the bestiality of their crimes against their victims. To this second group belong the French colonials in Algeria.

There is no other psychological explanation which enables us to understand the reasons that motivated the French colonials to stage the vile massacre of May 8 and its aftermath.

May 8 is the day on which all the democratic nations celebrated victory, after five years of war, unprecedented in the annals of history for the scale of its human and material losses. Our Algerian brethren thought that their full share in the human and the material sacrifices of the war entitled them to a share in the celebration of victory, like all the other Allies. On that day of celebration they paraded in the streets with other demonstrators, carrying the flag of Algeria which represents the emblem of Amir ʻAbd al-Qādir, founder of Algerian independence. The French colonial oppressors found it too much to allow those people to breathe for a while on that day or to express their hope for the resuscitation of Algerian independence. French troops attacked the unarmed Algerians and pulled down the flag. Fierce fighting ensued between the Muslims and the French, in which the former used stones and sticks while the latter opened up with their firearms and other lethal weapons. In other words, the French used the arms that had been given to them under the American lend-lease. The engagements resulted in the death of one hundred Frenchmen while Muslim dead and wounded ran into tens of thousands.

The clashes were not confined to one place or locality. A most serious clash took place in Setif, while the most atrocious occurred in Qalmah, where thousands of Muslim youths were rounded up and slaughtered en masse.

It is inconceivable that the vicious French attacks could have occurred accidentally. They were rather part of a premeditated plan, in the preparation of which French civilians had been armed for a concerted assault upon the totally unarmed people of Algeria. For what reason? Because the Algerians wanted to reap their share in victory as they had contributed their share to the war; because the Algerians wanted to gain a measure of their national freedom, as they had participated in the liberation of other peoples.

The colonialists attempted to justify the attacks on the ground that Maṣāli, leader of the Algerian People's Party, had made inciting speeches in the course of a political tour of the country. Now is it right that a speech delivered somewhere else, no matter how strong-worded and hostile, should be answered by attacking the unarmed people by the most deadly and concentrated fire?

The truth is that the French became panicky at the sight of Algerian manifestations of national consciousness and their striving for freedom and rejection of assimilation. French citizenship had hitherto been the song by which the French calmed the nerves of the inhabitants. This time, however, they found themselves face to face with the Algerian reality: that the people of Algeria would accept nothing short of complete freedom and independence; that the 120 years under the heels of the colonial oppressor had not eradicated in the people of Algeria their national consciousness, their religious affiliation, and their "Arabism". The occupation had merely accentuated their hatred of colonialism and had strengthened their fidelity to rights that had been usurped. The colonials were unable to swallow this stark reality. They played for time, however, and when the war was over they bristled in the manner of a cat, sprang at the peaceful inhabitants, and inflicted indescribable atrocities upon them. Perhaps they wanted to show the people that French forces were still invincible and that eternal France would as always remain in wait for those who demand freedom or acclaim independence.

At any rate, the incidents revealed to the world the horrors of French imperialism. It also proved to those who did not know it that the people of Algeria had never acquiesced in French rule. This reality was highlighted by the courageous manner in which internees of all Algerian parties conducted themselves. They all reiterated clearly and steadfastly their unequivocal loyalty to their principles and their readiness to sacrifice everything in defense of them. The civilized world protested against these atrocities. The British and the American Governments notified the French Government of their condemnation of those heinous acts, but they did nothing beyond protest. Meanwhile, the Algerians are still being subjected to a reign of terror in the sight and the hearing of the United Nations and its civilized members.

Solutions Offered

In spite of all French acts and claims, the conclusion of the war witnessed a clear retrogression of France's position in Algeria. The French attempted in vain to arrest the nationalist avalanche which had permeated every part of the country and had become the staunch faith of every Algerian regardless of party. The extension to sections of the people of the suffrage for elections to the French Parliament merely complicated the issue. The man in the street became aware of the worthlessness of elections to a foreign assembly, seated in the capital of the occupation power, and drawing its authority from the sovereignty and the ambitions of the conquering nation.

Faced with this fact, the French Government and political parties began to explore solutions that would at one and the same time ensure the preservation of Algeria as part of France and satisfy the aspirations of the Algerian people for independence. But it is beyond human ingenuity to accommodate two diametrically opposed and contradictory postulates. Independence means separation, or at least association by a contract of alliance between two equals. The "prolongation" of France on the other hand requires absorption or at least full-fledged dependence. All solutions submitted by the French were thus a mere restatement of the Blum-Viollette plan to which we have already referred.

One of the solutions was offered by the Communists and the Socialists. It envisioned an independent Algeria, with its own government and parliament, but in which France retained complete sovereignty in the capacity of a "fatherland", as they call it. The parties of the right, however, still clung to the theme of an indivisible and united France. They could not, therefore, but approve of the government plan submitted to the French National Assembly following a visit to Algeria by the Minister of the Interior early in 1947.

The plan gives to Algeria the following governmental framework:

1. That Algeria be organized into a French département with its own civil setup and relative financial independence.

2. Executive power to remain in the hands of the governor-general.

3. That Algeria shall have its own legislature, to function through a governmental council, consisting of six members, three of whom shall be appointed by the governor-general. The other three comprise a chairman, a vice-chairman, and the director of finances. The duties of this council, as provided for in the plan, are control of the Algerian house of representatives, the creation of which was projected in the plan.

4. The Algerian house of representatives shall consist of 120 members, half Algerian, half French. The electoral law provides for a general election to be held every six years, in two degrees and by secret ballot. The jurisdiction of this house is restricted to a discussion and adoption of the Algerian budget, as presented by the various departments of the governorate. The house is also empowered to submit proposals in regard to taxes and dues. Every discussion beyond this circumscribed circle would be null and void. The house has no right in the course of debates, even on strictly financia issues, to vote against government proposals. Any resolutions that it might adopt would not have the force of law unless approved and promulgated in a government decree.

The French National Assembly adopted this plan on August 27, 1947 by 322 votes. All the Muslim and Communis deputies and some of the other leftist members were absent from the session. Representatives of the French community in Algeria voted against it.

The adoption of the plan was of no significance because the Muslims who are most concerned rejected it. Their representatives even refused to be present during its discussion. The Muslim members of the State Council resigned in protest against the submission of such a plan to the National Assembly. The plan, they declared, did not realize the legitimate aspirations or wishes of the Algerian people.

The Bayān Party, presently known as "al-Ittiḥād al-Demoqrāṭi li Muslimi al-Jazā'ir" (the democratic union for Algerian Muslims), offered a counter-proposal, in the belief that it would harmonize the French and the nationalist views on Algeria. The counter-plan provided for the establishment of a somewhat independent Algerian republic, with its own government and parliament, attached to the French Union and in accord with France on foreign, military, and financial affairs. The authors of the plan made it clear, however, that the proposed link with France would be temporary, until Algeria was capable of achieving complete independence.

Naturally, this Algerian home-spun plan received no enthusiastic support either from French or Algerian nationalist circles. To the French, it was incompatible with the policy of assimilation, which dominates the whole field of French-Algerian relationship. The nationalists, on the other hand, found it in conflict with Algerian nationalism which aims at complete and unequivocal liberation. The plan, therefore, did not receive the endorsement of the Algerian People's Party. The platform of the party remained as hitherto in favor of the establishment of an independent Algerian republic with its own constitution to be drawn up by a national assembly freely elected by universal suffrage and without discrimination on account of race or creed. The platform proposed the conclusion of a treaty of alliance between France and Algeria on a basis of equality and mutual interests, without however recognizing any form of subjection, as implied by the proposed membership in the French Union.

The Present Situation

The forthright and unequivocal program adopted by the Algerian People's Party through its leaders in East and West, the continued exile of Maṣāli al-Ḥaj in Abi Zarī'ah in Algeria (after his release from the Congo), the farcical nature of the government-reform program for Algeria, and the Bayān Party's declaration in favor of temporary membership in the French Union--all these factors provided the people of Algeria with an opportunity to decide on alternative courses of action. The results of the recent municipal elections throughout Algeria have shown conclusively that the people's choice was for complete independence. Thus, nominees of the Party for Victory of Democratic Freedoms (this is the subterfuge for the disbanded and outlawed People's Party) obtained more than sixty per cent of the votes, notwithstanding the abstention of one-third of the eligible voters, in protest against high-handed and continual pressure of the authorities. At the same time, the party of Democratic Union (the new name for the Bayān Party) failed in the elections because of its acceptance of the policy of French Union and on account of its alliance with a number of French organizations in Algeria.

Thus, the present situation underlines the unanimity of the Algerian nation in its striving for independence and its willingness to work for it to the utmost of its capabilities.

The two Algerian parties seem to be drawing closer together. The leaders of the Bayān Party have already withdrawn their support from the policy of union with France. The leader of the party, 'Abbās Farḥāt, has given statements that call for optimism. He followed them up by changing the name of the party's newspaper from "Mussāwāh" (Equality) to "al-Jumhurīyah al-Jazā'irīyah" (the Algerian republic). The change of name reflects the party's change of orientation from a mere demand for equality with the French to outright independence.

The leader of the People's Party, Maṣāli al-Ḥaj, has addressed from his exile a fervent appeal to the leaders of the Bayān Party, reminding them of the dire need for united action and stressing the fact that differences had been a mere outgrowth of foreign colonialism.

It is evident that the Society of Muslim 'Ulemas is fully convinced of the need for the strengthening of the independence movement and has exerted its good offices towards reconciling the two main parties on the basis of the people's choice, as was shown by the recent elections. The People's Party has approved of the establishment of the Liberation

Committee in Cairo and has appointed permanent representatives to it. Let us hope that it will not be long before the Bayān Party also joins this Committee, which is working for the liberation of all Arab North Africa.

Chapter II

IN TUNISIA OR THE NEAR MAGHRIB

The occupation of Tunisia and Morocco was the expected outgrowth of the occupation of Algeria. No sooner had the Franco-Algerian war ended than France began to prepare the ground for the occupation of Tunisia and then of Morocco, as we shall see. The excuses proffered by France for its aggression ranged from defense of vested economic interests to the prevention of a strong state bordering on eastern and western Algeria.

Unlike French designs on Algeria, which evoked no serious reaction on the part of the big powers, French designs on Tunisia and Morocco stirred several of these powers to opposition. They had their own designs on the two territories and were averse to letting France grab them for herself. Thus, a diplomatic scramble developed among the big powers which, by creating within them financial complications and internal upheavals, complicated and undermined the ability of Tunisia and Morocco to defend themselves.

We are not concerned here with the various phases of the diplomatic struggle over Tunisia. That is a different topic which needs special study and investigation. What is pertinent to our study is the fact that the signing of the protectorate agreement took place only after Tunisia had put up a continuous struggle,lasting fifty years, against France and other powers. This underlines the fact that Tunisia, like Morocco, had never accepted the protectorate, and that she had exerted her utmost in defense of her independence and the consolidation of friendly relationships with the neighboring territories. We are not implying that the efforts of Tunisia had always been carried out in the right direction. Nations in their periods of sickness are inevitably exposed to varying pressures from without and internal tensions from within. It is unavoidable that we should admit the weaknesses of governmental policies, particularly in their financial manifestations, which greatly facilitated the machinations of France and enabled her to fish in the waters troubled by Tunisian mismanagement. At the same time we must emphasize that the people of Tunisia were at no time unaware or unappreciative of the true situation. They resisted corruption and mismanagement at home with no less vigor than they showed in repelling foreign encroachments.

One of the most significant aspects in the history of that epoch was the awareness of the Tunisian government, under the guidance of the Maghrib thinker-statesman Khayr al-Dīn, that the best way to resist European designs would be through a renascent Tunisia, a thorough overhaul of the anachronistic state machinery, and an enlightened leadership of the nation towards real progress, which had given the West its ascendency.

Khayr al-Dīn was a reformer who had been deeply affected by the principles and the thought of the French Revolution. He was convinced that the East must abandon its tyrannical forms of government. A contemporary of the last phase of the Napoleonic era, he had seen for himself the plight of Algeria and the collapse of the resistance offered by the Amir ʻAbd al-Qādir. Khayr al-Dīn was firmly convinced that the great danger was not posed by European attack against the country; it was rather to be found in the social and moral diseases that had plagued the country and sapped its vitality. Khayr al-Dīn studied the new laws and organizational setup introduced by Turkey in the reign of the Caliph ʻAbd al-Majīd I. He had also listened to the views of such great Ottoman reformers as Fuʼad Muḥammad Pasha and Rashīd ʻAli Pasha. The reformers had been endeavoring to relax the absolutist regime in the Empire and to replace it by a new Ottoman constitution, based upon the Italian Constitution of Cavour. Those were the enlightened and progressive views which had found their highest embodiment in the great Ottoman constitutional reformer, Midḥat Pasha. Khayr al-Dīn wrote a book embodying his views on constitutional and other reforms.

The Tunisian reformer attempted to implement his progressive views in Tunisia. His attempts, however, were foiled by two major obstacles. The first was the authoritarian regime of Prime Minister Mustapha Khazindār, who had ruled Tunisia for 34 years. His was a rule of despotism and terror; the public was bled white by his exploitation and the public treasury ruthlessly squandered. The second obstacle to reform was posed by the religious sheikhs who enjoyed absolute sway over the mentality of the people. A corollary to this was the fear of the people of Tunisia lest reforms derived from the West should imperil their existence as a nation. Khayr al-Dīn did all he could to weaken the power of Khazindār, but to no avail. He became convinced that the only way to do so was to win the sympathy of the Bey. With this end in view he introduced to the court of the Bey a youth named Mustapha ibn Ismā'īl. The youth succeeded in winning favor with the Bey and in influencing his actions. Eventually, Khayr al-Dīn was able to exert influence in the court and he converted the King to the plan for a constitutional government. In 1867 the new Constitution of the Kingdom of Tunisia was proclaimed.

This bold act was the most effective step towards rejuvenating the Tunisian state and ensuring its protection. The powers with designs on Tunisia were not too pleased over such a constructive endeavor. They resorted to various means of sabotage, including incitement of the religious leaders against its adoption. The representatives of France and Italy, who had hitherto been advocating the establishment of a dynamic system in Tunisia, now openly voiced their governments' opposition to the reform. They were supported by the other signatories of the Paris Treaty of 1856, which had concluded the Crimean War and established the status quo in the East. The colonial powers through incitements and interferences succeeded in arousing the people themselves against the new constitution. They found Mustapha ibn Ismā'īl an effective tool of opposition to Khayr al-Dīn, to whom he owed his career and his influence at the court. Thus the Tunisian Constitution remained ink on paper.

Khayr al-Dīn Pasha did not belong to the masses of the people. He was a great landowner with considerable financial connections and interests. The management and development of his properties and assets naturally claimed part of his time and attention. His financial transactions brought him into league with M. Theodore Roustan, French consul-general, who was himself an aggressive financial and bourse manipulator. Thus, he aroused both public opinion and the Bey against him and he was removed from the Cabinet on July 21, 1877.

It must be noted that the Bey had meanwhile renewed Turkey's suzerainty over Tunisia and had conceded to her the right to conduct Tunisia's foreign affairs. This was animated by the Bey's desire to keep out French encroachments and designs on the territory.

Khayr al-Dīn left Tunis to take refuge with the Porte in Turkey. When 'Abd al-Ḥamīd succeeded to the throne, following the assassination of Sultan 'Abd al-'Azīz and the death of Sultan Murad V in internment, he brought Khayr al-Dīn to his inner circle, in appreciation of his high talents. 'Abd al-Ḥamīd in the early part of his reign had been enthusiastic about introducing constitutional reforms. His personal aversion to Midḥat Pasha, father of the Ottoman Constitution, prompted him to appoint Khayr al-Dīn to the post of prime minister in order to carry through the program of reform. The great Tunisian reformer assumed the premiership and attempted with fidelity and painstaking efforts to implement the Constitution of Midḥat Pasha. After one year of effort, however, he found himself in headlong collision with two obstacles: the first was the inflexibility of the Ottomans in their approach to and understanding of Islamic jurisprudence; the second was the vacillation of 'Abd al-Ḥamid who chose to retreat to the traditional ways of government, as they had existed in the reign of his predecessors. Khayr al-Dīn was forced to withdraw but remained in Constantinople until his death.

Khayr al-Dīn's departure from Tunisia, however, the sale of his great estate at "Enfida" to a Marseilles company in 1880, and the refusal of the Bey to sanction the deal on the ground that he had given the land to Khayr al-Dīn for his own use but not for transfer to foreigners, brought the internal situation in Tunisia to a climax. An insignificant raid by the Karmīyīn tribesmen [the Khroumirs] into Algeria in pursuit of tribal enemies gave the French an excuse to intervene. The Bey of Tunis had refused to punish the tribe for its minor incursion across the Algerian frontier and had equally refused the request of M. Roustan, the French consul, for a French protectorate over Tunisia. The French thereupon sent an army of thirty thousand men to Tunis. General Breart and Roustan read an ultimatum to Muḥammad al-Sadūk, the Bey of Tunisia. Under duress, the Bey was forced to sign on May 12, 1881 the Treaty of Bardo, accepting a French military occupation and protectorate.

The people of Tunisia did not acknowledge the protectorate, however; the inhabitants of the south highlighted the many uprisings against the protectorate. They launched a holy war in which they quickly occupied Sfax, Kairouan, and the Oasis of Gabes. The Bey openly declared that the French had forced him to sign the Treaty, which he did not therefore recognize. The French sent another expedition. Sfax was subjected to naval bombardment and after a bitter campaign the French armies succeeded in occupying Jāra, al-Manzel, al-Jabra, and Zāzāy. French troops failed, however, to subdue resistance in the hinterland. Two leaders of the Tunisian resistance, 'Ali ibn Khalīfah and 'Ali ibn Ghaddān, particularly distinguished themselves.

In the fall of the same year [1881] General Saussier led three columns in a concerted attack against Kairouan and occupied it after a fierce battle with the Tunisian defenders. In the spring of 1882, during April and May, the offensive was resumed against the rest of the south. National resistance to the French, however, continued well into the winter months of 1882-1883.

Notwithstanding France's occupation of the whole of Tunisia, resistance groups operating from neighboring Tripolitania continued to wage guerrilla warfare in southern Tunisia until the year 1888, when Turkey formally relinquished her rights over Tunisia.

The Nationalist Movement after the Occupation

The French consolidated their hold upon Tunisia and their armies were stationed at all strategic points. Armed resistance became no longer feasible. This, however, did not break the people's national will particularly after it had become manifest that France was violating all her pledges and was acting as a conqueror, contrary to her allegedly limited objective of helping the national government straighten out its difficulties and of maintaining law and order. A national movement was organized under the leadership of Sheikh Muḥammad al-Senūsi. A deputation was selected to convey to the Bey a petition, signed by people from the various strata of society, protesting the imposition of direct French rule upon the land. The leader of the delegation, Sheikh Senūsi, delivered before the King a speech depicting the people's strong resentment. The King was moved by the address and assured the delegation of his solidarity with them and his determination to strive for Tunisia's legitimate rights.

The following day the occupation authorities deported Sheikh Senūsi and interned Sayyid Hassūna ibn Mustapha and other partisans of the movement.

Sheikh Senūsi, the first leader of the nationalist movement in Tunisia after the occupation, was one of the most accomplished 'ulemas of the Zaytūnah mosque. He was the instructor of Muḥammad Nasir Bey, whose participation in the nationalist movement we shall discuss later on. Sheikh Senūsi was, prior to the occupation, editor of the official gazette, "al-Rā'id".

Two years later a new religious leader, Sheikh al-Makki ibn 'Azūz of the Zaytūnah Salafīyah 'ulemas, launched a campaign against the stagnant attitudes and policies of those theologians who had effectively resisted the reforms of Khayr al-Dīn and his successors. To Sheikh 'Azūz belongs the credit for having formed a circle of enlightened 'ulemas which included the renowned Sheikh 'Abd al-'Azīz al-Tha'ālibi.

Sheikh Makki emigrated to the East where he remained till his death. But the enlightened views which he had implanted in his pupils continued to flourish. A group of them met together and started a newspaper in the French language called "al-Mustaqbal al-Tunisi" (the Tunisian future) for the avowed purpose of defending Tunisian rights and interests. They also published two other newspapers in Arabic, one called "Ḥabīb al-Ummah" (the nation's beloved) and the other, "Sabīl al-Rashad" (the road to truth), which Sheikh Tha'ālibi himself edited. Among the distinguished leaders of this transitional phase in the nationalist movement were 'Ali Kāhiya, Sheikh Zarrūq, and al-Hādi al-Sab'i.

Al-Ḥadhirah group

This was formed by a group of students from al-Sādiki institute, who prior to the occupation had been sent abroad by the government to carry on advanced studies. The French authorities, having consolidated their hold, permitted them to return home. They were animated by the liberating and enlightened views which they had acquired in the course of their studies and were highly qualified to lead and instruct Tunisian public opinion. The most distinguished of these young men was Sayīd 'Ali abu Shūshah, proprietor of the newspaper "al Ḥādhirah". He was able to gather together a strong bloc of friends and supporters, mainly from the ranks of the Zaytūnah University. The group launched a national and religious movement having a dual purpose: one was to strengthen the ties between Tunisia and the Pan-Islamic movement; the other was to seek implementation of the Tunisian Constitution which had not been abrogated by the two occupation statutes, the Treaty of Marsa of June 8, 1883 and the Treaty of Bardo, May 12, 1881.

Spiritually, the movement was a response to the modernist reform movements of Jamāl al-Dīn al-Afghāni and Sheikh Muḥammad 'Abduh in Egypt, and also of the Egyptian nationalist movement under the leadership of Mustapha Kāmil.

The movement was guided and strengthened in its orientation by direct contacts which its leaders had established with Sheikh Muḥammad 'Abduh and Muḥammad Farīd upon the latter's visits to Tunisia. The discussions led to a clarification of and agreement upon the common aims of Islamic movements. The movement also deserves credit for the establishment of the Ibn Khaldūn Institute, designed to provide an Arab modern institution of learning. Of its many members the name of Bashīr Ṣafr, father of the Tunisian cultural rejuvenation, deserves particular mention. His numerous articles published in "al-Ḥādhirah" in defense of the cause of independence and unity of North Africa are unforgettable. 'Umar abu Ḥājib and 'Ali al-Baglāti also deserve special mention.

The group maintained close contacts with the Moroccan constitutional movement, which contributed articles to "al-Ḥādhirah", criticizing the policies of the then Moroccan administration and demanding the initiation of more vigorous policies to safeguard the country from French intrigues, following the Entente Cordiale of 1904.

In 1907 a peasant uprising occurred in Qaşarin (southwest of Tunis), led by the tribal leader 'Ali ibn 'Uthmān, in protest against the sequestration and exploitation of their lands by French colonists. The French dispatched a militar expedition which succeeded in quelling the uprising. The leader was arrested and shot dead.

The Young Tunisia Party

Algeria served the French as a training center for experimentation with ideas which could be carried out in all parts of North Africa. We have see how the Third Republic strove to strengthen the colonists in Algeria through the Crémieux Decree, which provided for the enfranchisement of all Jews en masse. The French attempted an identical policy in Tunisia; in 1907 they incited the Jews of Tunisia to launch an all-out attack upon the Tunisian judiciary and to demand French citizenship. The entire colonial press sided with them, in the hope of increasing the numerical strength of the French community which was weak, not only relative to the Tunisians, but also to the Italian settlers as well. A group of educated Tunisians organized themselves to resist the enfranchisement of the Jews, on the ground that such a step constituted a flagrant violation of the country's sovereignty and the jurisdiction of the king. The movement was led by the late 'Ali Bāsh Ḥambah and it developed into an anti-Jewish movement which successfully advocated the boycott of Jews both materially and socially. Eventually the occupation authority refrained from implementing the Algerian experiment.

Tunisia benefited immensely from her boycott of the Jews. The Muslims experienced an upsurge of economic activity and commercial enterprise which has continued until the present day despite the many obstacles with which it had to contend.

The battle over the Jewish question ended with considerable success. This encouraged the youths, who had rallied to the support of the great leader 'Ali Bāsh Ḥambah, to form a resistance party which in 1908 became known as the Young Tunisia Party. The party issued a newspaper in French with an Arabic edition edited by Sheikh Tha'ālibi.

The early orientation of the movement was nationalist and secular, along lines of the Young Turks, but when the Ḥādhirah group joined in the party veered towards support of Pan-Islamism.

The activity of this group of patriotic young men has not been surpassed in Tunisia, nor has the country in her modern history produced the equal of this highly endowed and amiable leader, 'Ali Bāsh Ḥambah. It is therefore fitting to depict at some length his personality and achievement.

'Ali belongs to one of Tunisia's most renowned families. He was an infant when the occupation statutes were imposed and he grew up at a period when France was anxious to disseminate her culture in the towns and cities of Tunisia. After studying Arabic at the Zaytūnah mosque he enrolled in a number of French schools. Upon completion of his schooling he went to Paris where he joined the law faculty. He returned to his country where he practiced law for a short while. But his undaunted spirit and patriotism compelled him to abandon his personal strivings and dedicate himself instead to the service of his country and the mobilization of the people's energy towards liberation from French rule. His views were similar to those of the Egyptian nationalist leader Mustapha Kāmil and were more extreme than those of the Ḥādhirah group. He was the first leader to conceive of the need for uniting the Arab Maghrib in the common struggle. He cooperated with the Algerian resistance movement. His brother formed a committee in Berlin known as the Tunisian-Algerian committee. At the same time he established contacts with the resistance in Morocco when the latter country was fighting for her existence. In Constantinople he cooperated with the North African leader al-Sayīd al-'Atābi, as we shall show later on.

In Tunisia herself, his movement succeeded in stirring public feeling against the French and in affirming the demand for recognition of the sovereignty of the Ottoman Caliphate over Tunisia. His active campaigning lasted until 1911.

In 1911 Italy occupied Tripolitania, an event that caused a stir in the Islamic world. 'Ali Bāsh and his supporters played an important role as a liaison between the Ottoman Embassy in Paris and the Ottoman Command in Tripolitania Thus, thanks to his efforts, Tunisia served as a secret passage for Ottoman officers on their way from Europe to Tripolitania.

In the same year the "Jallāz" incident took place. The incident was caused by tramway workers who went on a prolonged strike at the behest of 'Ali Bāsh and his group. Ther was a considerable number of Italian immigrants in Tunisia and much antipathy towards them had existed. This now exploded, under the momentum of the strike, into violent clashes between Tunisians and Italians. Both parties suffered numerous casualties in dead and wounded. The astute French Resident-General Alapetite utilized the disturbances to round up the nationalists and disband the Young Tunisia Party. Many were deported to the south. Al-Tha'ālibi, 'Ali Bāsh, and his brother were deported outside the country. Al-Tha'ālibi went to France and thence to Constantinople. Later he visited India and Java until his return to Tunisia just before the outbreak of World War I. 'Ali Bāsh settled in Constantinople until his death.

'Ali Bāsh Ḥambah in Constantinople

During this period Constantinople was the refuge for all the persecuted leaders from the Islamic world. When 'Ali Bāsh arrived in Constantinople he joined the ranks of such exiled leaders as Muḥammad Farīd, 'Abd al-'Azīz Jāwīsh, al-Bārūni, 'Abd al-Ḥamīd, Aḥmad Fu'ad, 'Ali al-Shamsi, Abi Sa'īd Hindi, Sheikh 'Ali Kaspirinki, and Aḥmad Aghayf, the Russian Muslim leader. The group represented the new awakening in the Islamic world--the spiritual revival, modernism, and the growing nationalist consciousness.

The Sultan 'Abd al-Ḥamīd extended a helping hand to many of these leaders while the Party of Unity and Progress sympathized with a particular wing in the group. The Tunisian leader thus found a fertile ground for continuing his activities on behalf of the cause of North Africa in general and that of Tunisia in particular. He contributed numerous articles to pro-Caliphate Turkish newspapers including the "al-Shabāb al-Turki", "Taṣwīr al-Afkār", and "Tanīn", the official Ottoman publication. His press campaign was designed to mobilize Ottoman opinion for the liberation of North Africa. The campaign was instrumental in sensitizing Muslim leadership to the situation in North Africa; it also won for him considerable influence and prestige. He established close friendships with Shakīb Arslān, al-Bārūni, Jāwīsh, and Muḥammad Farīd. He also drew closer to the leading Ottoman statesmen and was appointed legal adviser to the Ministry of Justice and later a member of the State Council. When war broke out he was appointed Director of Publicity. In that capacity he was able to launch a strong anti-French publicity campaign and expose their brutalities in North

Africa. In 1916 he was appointed adviser to the Ministry for Foreign Affairs and thence adviser to the Prime Minister.

During this same year the Ottoman Government decided to establish in Constantinople an organization to make preparations for an invasion of North Africa in cooperation with refugee leaders. As a result of this an uprising took place in Tripolitania and Cyrenaica which drove out the Italians from all save the main towns. Anwar Pasha, at the request of the organization, appointed al-Bārūni governor of all the liberated territories in Libya. He was landed in Tripolitania from a German submarine and from the impregnable mountain area of Gharyan he organized and carried out a powerful resistance movement against the Italians. He also sent emissaries to Algeria and Tunisia and was able to establish contact between Anwar Pasha in Constantinople and Ḥassan Qalāti, one of 'Ali Bāsh's party who remained in the country.

In 1917 the Touareg tribes, led by Mūsa Wa'q al-Muṣṭāti, staged a vigorous rebellion in the Sahara area extending from the upper Nile to Adrar on the Atlantic coast. The French were forced to withdraw all their desert garrisons to the oases. Father Charles de Foucauld, French espionage agent, was assassinated at Tamanrasset. The situation became so critical that the French had to summon from the European front their expert in desert warfare, General Laperrine, to take charge of the situation. He was given command of southern Algeria and remained in that post until he was killed in 1918. The rebels also invaded southern Tunisia, where fierce encounters took place between 1916 and 1921.

Thus, the sons of North Africa succeeded, thanks to the efforts of Bārūni, Bāsh Ḥambah, and their colleagues, in opening a new front against the French, which bogged down a considerable number of their troops in prolonged warfare.

During 1917-1918 a new agency was established at Constantinople for the purpose of organizing North African prisoners of war--both in Germany and Turkey--in a unified military force, which would be provided with arms and equipment and landed in Tripolitania by submarines. It was decided that 'Ali Bāsh Ḥambah should lead the expedition as representative of the Ottoman Caliph for the liberation of North Africa from Western colonialism. Staff officers of the expedition, both Ottoman and North African, were actually landed in Tunisia; these included Prince 'Uthmān Fu'ad, grandson of the Sultan Murad, who served as military attaché to the Governor-General, al-Bārūni.

This expedition was linked to the campaign of 1915-1916 at Sallum along the borders of Egypt, where Anwar Pasha had sent a military force to assist Sheikh Senussi under the command of his brother Nuri Bey and the Iraqi officer Ja'far al-'Askari, who later became prime minister of Iraq. The expedition continued to harass the British until it was defeated. Sheikh Senussi took refuge in Turkey where he was received with great deference in recognition of his exploits. He was even appointed to preside over the coronation of Ottoman sultans, a privilege which since the days of Sultan 'Uthman I had been the prerogative of one of the descendants of the Seljuk kings.

Just before the date set for the launching of the expedition 'Ali Bāsh was afflicted with a serious illness, believed to be cancer, which disabled him from carrying on any further duties. In the meantime the military position of the Central Powers had been seriously deteriorating and the proposed expedition lapsed with the catastrophe of Ottoman surrender. 'Ali Bāsh died a week before the Armistice of Madras. He was given a state funeral in which a representative of Sultan Muḥammad Waḥīd al-Dīn, ministers, and army commanders took part. His remains were interred at the Bashiktash cemetery.

The career of this outstanding Tunisian leader should be emulated by the North African youths and contemporary leaders of the movement. He personifies the untiring and selfless struggle on behalf of a sacred cause. It is our view that the movement of Young Tunisia represents the most impressive phase in the struggle of that country and its lesson should not be lost upon posterity.

Muḥammad, the brother of 'Ali Bāsh, who was also a lawyer, at the behest of his brother had proceeded to Geneva in 1916, where he started a weekly publication in French by the name of "Majallat al-Maghrib" (the magazine of al-Maghrib). The periodical persisted for two years in presenting the North African viewpoint and had finally to suspend publication when financial assistance from Constantinople was no longer forthcoming.

It is just and proper to acknowledge with gratitude the assistance rendered to the publication by the late Fu'ad Salīm al-Ḥijāzi al-Miṣri, friend of the Egyptian nationalist leader Mustapha Kāmil and Ottoman Ambassador at Berne.

When the war ended Muḥammad returned to Berlin where he continued his political activity along with the other Eastern émigrés in Germany until his death in 1920. He was laid to rest in the Islamic cemetery. The Ottoman Prime Minister Tal'at Pasha and the renowned Egyptian nationalist Ismā'īl Labīb contributed towards the construction of his tomb.

Inside Tunisia members of the Young Tunisia Party continued their clandestine resistance under the leadership of Sheikh Tha'ālibi, despite the fact that the French authorities had disbanded the party. Their activities consisted mainly in the distribution of pamphlets and the dissemination of anti-French propaganda. The authorities kept a vigilant watch which compelled them to meet secretly in the home of the Amir Muḥammad al-Ḥabib, who after the death of Muḥammad al-Nāsir became the Bey of Tunis and whose home was inviolable. In spite of their caution, the authorities detained a number of young Tunisia supporters, including Tawfiq al-Madani on the charge of posting pamphlets at the walls of the grand mosque inciting the army to mutiny. When his home was searched, the authorities laid their hands on correspondence which had been going on between him and Ḥussein al-Jazīri, proprietor of the newspaper "al-Nadīm". The latter was also detained and his house searched. Documents were seized which revealed that he had been, together with al-Madani, in contact with Sheikh Omar ibn Qaddūr, one of the Salafīyah religious reformers in Algeria and proprietor of the newspapers "al-Fārūq" and "al-Siddīq". The entire group implicated in the correspondence were detained for the duration of the war.

The National Delegation to the Peace Conference

World War I ended with the defeat of the Ottomans upon whom the Young Tunisia movement had placed great hopes. The close of the war also saw the awakening of the Eastern world in its entirety from the far end of India and China to North Africa. Two powerful currents appeared in the post-war world, both preaching the rights of man and the freedom of peoples. On the one hand there was the Soviet revolution which occurred in Russia in the name of liberation and which filled the world with propaganda against French and other Western imperialism. The other was President Wilson's program for the rehabilitation of the world--embodied in his Fourteen Points.

The Tunisian nationalists were thus able to breathe after the suppressions of the war. It was natural that they did not seek help from the revolutionary Russians. Russian propaganda had been ambiguous from its inception; moreover, accepting the Russian viewpoints would have entailed the sacrifice of many nationalist doctrines in which Tha'ālibi and his compatriots fervently believed. Their orientation, therefore, was towards the Peace Conference which purported to work for the rehabilitation of the world on the basis of justice and freedom.

Tha'ālibi and his colleague Aḥmad al-Saqqa submitted a memorandum to President Wilson demanding the independence of Tunisia, while the Amir Khālid, leading a delegation of Algerian officers, made a similar demand for Algeria. The demands of both Tunisia and Algeria, however, like those of Morocco, Egypt, and Syria, did not meet with any response from the prophets of peace and liberty at the Conference. They were either neglected altogether or distorted to suit rapacious colonialism. Tha'ālibi, therefore, strove to enlighten French public opinion and placed some hopes in the leftist elements which had been strongly opposed to the government of the rightist coalition formed after the war. In 1920 he issued in French a valuable booklet entitled "La Tunisie martyre ses revendications" in which he exposed the misdeeds of colonial rule. He explained how the colonial administration had flouted the national, political, and individual rights of the Tunisian people, with particular emphasis upon the sequestration of land, opposition to education, suppression of public and civil liberties, the influx of Italian and French immigrants, and finally, the French policy of assimilation which had been applied in Algeria. The author included excerpts from the two books, "Le Panama Tunisien" and "La Sueur du Burnous", by French deputy Paul Benedicto, which had caused a big stir both in France and the colonies at the time of their publication. The author had been sent in 1906 on a mission to Tunisia in connection with the budget. His inquiries disclosed the most brazen acts of sequestration of land, perpetrated by and for noted French personages and military commanders, to the extent of twenty-two thousand hectars. He implicated in this racketeering business important sections of the press as well as business establishments. He depicted the abject poverty and misery of the Tunisian masses as a result of these spoliations and concluded by demanding the establishment of a Tunisian government responsible and accountable to a popularly elected assembly, so that it might be able to safeguard and control the destinies of the Tunisian people.

While the delegation led by Tha'ālibi were continuing their efforts in Paris, their colleagues in Tunisia made representations to the Bey and to the French Resident-General. But the structure of the situation in which they found themselves compelled them to tone down their criticisms and demands. Their talks with the Resident-General, Flandin, during a meeting held in May 1919, did not go beyond a demand for granting Tunisia a constitutional system. In June of the same year they submitted to the Bey, on the occasion of 'Id al-Fiṭr (the Bairam feast), a petition demanding in the name of the people the granting of a constituion. The Bey was sympathetic and promised to satisfy their demand.

On the basis of this categorical promise members of the movement decided to form a new party (the Dustūr party) based upon the demand for a constitutional system of government. They stated the objectives of the new party in a manifesto which said, among other things: "The purpose underlying the formation of the party is to help the nation achieve its maturity and to strive for its liberation from bondage so that the people of Tunisia may become free in the enjoyment of all the rights which other free nations enjoy. The party believes that this objective could be attained by a speedy implementation of a constitutional system which enables the people to govern themselves, as is the case throughout the civilized world."

It is clear that the new party had been formed on the basis of a platform differing from that of "Young Tunisia", with the latter's insistence upon unequivocal independence above all. It also differed from the policies pursued by Tha'ālibi and his group in Paris. This does not mean that the founders of the party did not contemplate independence as their objective, but it is evident that they were less doctrinaire than their predecessors. Perhaps through the adoption of their ambiguous program they hoped to gain a breathing spell for reorganizing their ranks. Whatever may have been the motivation, the program remained the official platform of the party until 1925. Was the other wing of the Young Tunisia group satisfied with this new orientation? Was the new program compatible with the views of Tha'ālibi and Aḥmad Saqqa? All we know is that founders of the new movement were all graduated from French universities and that the "Zaytūnah mosque" nationalists had held aloof until the return of Tha'ālibi and his election to leadership of the party.

As for Sheikh Tha'ālibi himself, it is clear that he was not satisfied with the new program but was compelled to swim the general tide until he left Tunisia for other parts of the Arab world where he was able to come out openly and forcefully with his views.

Sayīd Muḥyi al-Dīn al-Qalībi told me of an interview which he had had in his younger days with Tha'ālibi and which throws light on the latter's true convictions. Qalībi had shown Tha'ālibi an article he had written for one of the newspapers. The Sheikh was pleased with the article and asked Qalībi to join the Dustūr Party, whereupon Qalībi said: "I am prepared to work with you, but you are demanding mere constitutional reforms while I stand for the independence of Tunisia; I cannot therefore give my oath of loyalty to the party unless its aim is also for independence." Sheikh Tha'ālibi smiled and replied: "My son, this is a policy which my colleagues had accepted as a tactical move. For my part, I would have preferred the forthright and unequivocal attitude you have mentioned. However, do not give your oath except for independence because it is the aim of all of us."

The new party, in pursuance of its policy, endeavored to utilize every opportunity for the realization of its constitutional reforms. There was considerable public clamor, particularly among those who would have been dispossessed, when Flandin, the Resident-General, attempted to seize private waqf property held in perpetuity according to Sharī'ah law. The agitation was intensified when Flandin attempted to involve Tunisia in a loan to the amount of two hundred and fifty million francs in order to meet a budget deficit. A delegation was formed at the behest of the Dustūr movement, consisting of Sheikh Mustapha al-Bāhi, Sheikh Bashīr al-Bakri, Sheikh Ḥammūdah al-Mastīri, Bashīr 'Akkāshah, and Ṣāliḥ ibn 'Ajūzah. The delegation went to France to protest the decrees of Flandin. It also seized the opportunity to present to the government the following nine demands of the Dustūr Party:

1. The establishment of a legislative assembly, consisting of Tunisian and French delegates to be elected by universal suffrage, with powers to prepare its own agenda and also with extensive powers of supervision over fiscal matters.
2. The establishment of a government responsible to this assembly.
3. Separation of the legislative, judicial, and executive branches of government.
4. The appointment of Tunisians to all government posts if they possess qualifications equal to French candidates.
5. Equal salaries for French and Tunisian employees.
6. The establishment of elected municipal councils.
7. Compulsory education.
8. Eligibility of Tunisians to purchase of lands administered as state domains.
9. Freedom of the press, of meetings, and of association.

The nine-point program reveals a retrogression, even from the standpoint of the initial demands of the Dustūr Party. It appears, however, that the delegation had submitted this watered-down program as a mere supplement to its main mission, namely to defend waqf properties jeopardized by Flandin's proposed decree. The delegation, in fact, returned from Paris without having achieved anything save the repudiation by the French of Flandin's schemes relating to waqf properties and the proposed loan. Another delegation proceeded to Paris in December 1920, but it too obtained no substantial gains.

The failure of the Dustūr experiment for constitutional reforms did not dissuade Tha'ālibi from his publicity campaig in Paris. The authorities arrested him on charges of conspiring against the security of the state and ferried him to Tunisia where he was placed in a military prison. His two colleagues, Sheikh Muḥammad Riyāḥi and Sheikh Ṣāliḥ ibn Yaḥya, were also arrested. Nine months later they were released and immediately resumed their activities within the new party, forming its left wing. They organized it efficiently and extended the party apparatus and publicity organs to the most important districts in Tunisia. Tha'ālibi was elected chairman, while Aḥmad al-Ṣāfi took over as secretary general. The French Government found it prudent to make a temporary shift in its policy. Flandin was replaced by Saint as Resident-General.

The Forty-Man Delegation and the Steadfastness of the Bey

No sooner had the new Resident-General arrived on June 6, 1921 than the Dustūr Party formed a new delegation consisting of forty members representing the various strata of Tunisian society. The delegation submitted anew the demands for constitutional reforms which had previously been presented to Paris. The Resident-General informed the delegates that he was prepared to come to an understanding with them concerning certain reforms that did not conflict with the statutes of occupation. The latter, he declared, was within the jurisdiction of the Ministry of Foreign Affairs. The Resident was referring to a number of partial and inconsequential reforms which had excluded the granting of a constitutional system and governmental responsibility before a popularly elected chamber. At the same time the delegation had an audience with the Bey. They were well received at the court and the Bey expressed his solidarity with them and his readiness to approve the principle of forming a constitutional government.

M. Millerand, President of the French Republic, had been visiting Morocco and it was decided that he should visit Tunisia also. The Ministry of Foreign Affairs was anxious that an atmosphere of quiet prevail during the visit. The Bey was informed that the proposed reforms would be implemented upon the completion of M. Millerand's tour and was requested to exert his influence with the Dustūr

Party with a view to according a cordial welcome to the President during his visit to Tunisia. The Bey sent two of his chief aids to the headquarters of the party to inform Tha'ālibi and Aḥmad al-Ṣāfi of M. Poincaré's categorical promise to implement the requested reforms at the conclusion of the President's visit.

Millerand visited Tunisia and was given a cordial welcome. In the course of the visit, however, he gave a speech in which he said that Tunisia would forever remain linked to France. The speech made a most unfavorable impression upon the people who contrasted it with Poincaré's promise to the Bey and the party. The Resident-General submitted to Bey Muḥammad al-Nāṣir his so-called reforms. The Bey refused to sign them because he thought they were inadequate and distorted.

While the political atmosphere was charged and the relations between the Palace and the Residency had reached the crisis situation, a French journalist published an alleged interview which he claimed he had had with the Bey. The journalist quoted the Bey as condemning the nationalist leaders and accusing them of communism.

When the alleged interview was brought to the notice of the Bey he became furious and instructed the government to issue an official denial. Both the Prime Minister and the Chief of the Royal Cabinet refused to issue the denial, whereupon the Bey summoned the pressmen himself and gave them a denial of the alleged interview. The Bey also decided to fire the Prime Minister and the Chief of his Royal Cabinet for their insubordination. The French Residency, however, was adamant on the subject, fearing that it might set a precedent as regards the prerogatives of the Bey. The courage and integrity of Bey Muḥammad al-Nāṣir was amply demonstrated when he met the challenge and decided to abdicate.

The people, admiring the courage and steadfastness of their King, rallied to his support at this critical moment. A huge demonstration was staged on April 5, 1922 which led to the arrest of a considerable number of prominent persons. When the demonstration ended, Resident-General Saint accompanied by a detachment of Senegal troops surrounded the royal palace and presented to the King a list of thirty-six nationalist leaders with the request that he approve their deportation from the country. The Bey replied: "Your list is incomplete; you should have added to it my name and members of my family." The Resident replied in a discourteous manner and was castigated for doing so by the Crown Prince al-Munṣif, who later became Bey and ended his reign as an exile in the south of France.

The President returned to Paris, and while the people were waiting for the implementation of the promised reforms the Bey died suddenly in mysterious circumstances which have been the subject of much conjecture in Tunisia until the present day. He was succeeded by the Amir, Muḥammad al-Ḥabīb, who approved the reform measures rejected by his predecessor. The policy of repression was launched anew.

Tha'ālibi's Journey to the East

It was stated earlier that the home of Amir Muḥammad al-Ḥabīb had served during the war as the clandestine meeting place for the leaders of the nationalist movement. Their documents and papers had been deposited in that inviolable home to prevent them from falling into the hands of the authorities. The policy of Ḥabīb after his accession to the throne underwent a radical change from that which he had pursued before assumption of office. He signed the decrees providing for the establishment of the mixed "Grand Council" and the two chambers for agriculture and commerce, in spite of his earlier promise to Tha'ālibi and his colleague not to do so. This gave rise to a serious dispute between the Dustūr Party and the Bey. The former feared that the Bey might use his office to take vengeance upon the friends of yesterday and the enemies of today, particularly after the Bey had threatened Tha'ālibi with exposure of the secret documents in his possession. The party decided that Tha'ālibi should journey to the East in the hope of ending an acrimonious dispute which could assume serious proportions to the detriment of the nationalist cause.

Tha'ālibi travelled to the East in 1923 and did not return to Tunisia until 1937. During this period he visited Egypt, Syria, Iraq, Hejaz, India, and other Eastern countries. He conducted a vigorous publicity campaign in Arab and Islamic circles for the Tunisian cause. He participated in the

Palestine conference of 1930 and was elected member of its executive committee. Earlier, he had devoted his attention to the cause of the outcasts in India. Wherever he went, he was received with the greatest deference and appreciation for his learning and accomplishments. One of the best testimonies I have heard was uttered by Sheikh al-Fārūqi, chairman of the eastern section of the Congress Party and one of the distinguished Muslim leaders in India. He said to me, "We have not welcomed to India anyone of greater learning and amiability than Tha'ālibi." This is a testimony which honors the Tunisian Dustūr movement and its great leader.

Meanwhile, the party continued its activities under the direction of its secretary-general, Aḥmad al-Ṣāfi. Muḥyi al-Dīn al-Qalībī took charge of organization, in which capacity he continued to receive directions from Tha'ālibi. In spite of the defection of Qalāti, one of the prominent leaders who advised greater moderation, the party continued its activities without let or hindrance. Nor did this defection weaken the Tunisian people's attachment to the party and its leadership. As a result of this minor defection, however, the party leadership undertook a thorough overhaul and extension of its organizational setup. Seven major branches were opened in the capital alone, while the number of branche elsewhere reached the figure of eighty-three. The organization included several women's formations and youth movements which enabled the party to make considerable headway. One of the important achievements of the Dustūr Party in this period was the establishment of several sport activities and scout movements.

In 1925 the occupation authorities in Tunis erected a statue of the French Cardinal Lavigerie. This caused a furor and the Dustūr Party organized a massive demonstration which came to blows with the French in the vicinity of Bab al-Baḥr. Several leaders and 'Ulemas were either detained or deported.

The Riff war of liberation in Morocco had been raging in its full fury. Its repercussions were strongly felt in Tunisia as in all parts of the Arab world. It was an uplifting experience reminiscent of al-Maghrib's heroic past. The Dustūr Party in Tunisia arranged several plays for the stage, including Fatḥ al-Andalus (the conquest of Spain) by Mustapha Kāmil. The authorities, however, prevented the show.

They also confiscated the sum of money that had been collected for relief of the Riff soldiers wounded in battle. The French did likewise later on when we collected money in Morocco for aid to Palestine. Omar ibn Miqrāsh was sentenced to five years at hard labor, while Tawfīq al-Madani was deported to Algeria, where he still remains, for depicting the heroism of the Riff and the magnanimity of its leader the Amir 'Abd al-Karīm.

In 1926 the authorities designed a new attack on Tunisian sovereignty by appointing French judges to Tunisian courts of law. A general strike was called in which even government employees took part. Large throngs demonstrated in various parts of the kingdom and a delegation was formed under the leadership of Aḥmad al-Ṣāfi, secretary-general of the party, to protest the French move to the Bey. The Bey assured the delegation of his solidarity with the people in their protest. The French were forced to withdraw their plan, but in view of the solidarity of national courts with the people political offenses were henceforth submitted to French courts. The nationalists were subjected to renewed restrictions and repressions.

The Dustūr Party published more than twenty newspapers in Arabic, and one newspaper, "al-Ḥurr" (the free), in French. The apparatus of repression was directed towards these organs of national expression. The press, associations, and public gatherings bore the brunt of the authorities' wrath.

In 1924 the trade union movement had reached the peak of its activities and strength, thanks to its great leader Muḥammad 'Ali, who succeeded in breaking away from French unions and converting it to a purely Tunisian Muslim establishment. A country seeking independence cannot but strive for the independence of its various organs and their liberation from any material or moral dependence upon the occupation power. The Resident-General resisted this new manifestation of national independence. Muḥammad 'Ali and a number of his labor colleagues were deported outside their country where they all died, away from their homes and families. Dr. Ibn Mīlād was also deported on this occasion but he returned five years later.

The Role of the Dustūr Youth

It was stated earlier that the most significant step following the departure of the leader of the party to the East was the reorganization of its apparatus and particularly the enrollment of the youth. The party gave every encouragement to youth participation. Al-Shāthili Khayrallah was appointed secretary to the executive committee in charge of foreign correspondence. When the government suspended the party organ in 1927 he started a newspaper in French by the name of "al-'Alam al-Tūnisi" (the Tunisian flag). The paper succeeded--although it was not the official party organ--in rallying the support of the educated Tunisian youths. The government could not put up with it for long and in 1929 it was suspended also. The Dustūr group immediately put out another newspaper by the name of "Ṣawt al-Tūnisi" (the Tunisian voice). A committee of young Dustūr members was set up to direct its policies. The committee included Ḥabīb abu Raqībah, Sāliḥ Farḥāt, Ṭāhir Ṣafr, Dr. Māṭiri, and others. The paper was successful in giving expression to the discontent of the Tunisian people. Later, the Dustūr youths started another paper independently of Shāthili, by the name of "al-'Amal al-Tunisi" (the Tunisian action). Abu Raqībah was editor of this publication. The Dustūr Party itself issued its own official organ in French by the name of "Ṣawt al-Sha'b" (the voice of the people).

A Dangerous Trend in French Colonialism

While the Tunisian people, like their other North African brethren were striving for the attainment of their usurped rights, the French in their colonial policy resorted to a new tactic more vicious and unscrupulous than any they had had recourse to before. They directed their campaign this time, not against national sovereignty or the national wealth, but against Islamic doctrines and beliefs which had been the mainstay and the sole spiritual armor of the oppressed people of this land. Thus, the French decided to convene the Afkhārasti conference, on the occasion of the fiftieth anniversary since the occupation of Tunisia. The conference coincided with the French Berber policy initiated in Morocco.

The new move did not emanate from the reactionary policies of French administrators abroad; it represented a new policy of the French Government itself. The French Foreign Minister, in the course of a debate on proposed budgetary allocations for missionary societies, replied to left-wing opposition to the bill as follows, "If France is secular at home, she is religious abroad." The issue, therefore, was not extraneous to the official responsibility of the Third Republic, which boasts of its secular, non-sectarian character.

The new orientation encouraged Christian missionaries in North Africa to exploit the authority of the occupation in their endeavors to convert Muslims, to the disregard of the sensitivities of North Africans and their religious beliefs and emotions. In pursuance of this objective the Residency submitted to the newly established Grand Council a bill providing for the allotment of two million francs to subsidize the proposed Afkhārasti conference. When the Muslim deputies objected to the allocation, the authorities closed the discussion and acted upon the bill in toto. The Bishop of Tunis described the proposed conference as a crusade, though characterized by love and peace.

In the face of this onslaught upon the feelings of the Muslims the people resorted to widespread demonstrations and protests. Their gathering places were the clubs and centers of the Dustūr Party. Dock workers in Bizerta and Tunis struck work on the day scheduled for the arrival of the conferees. Cotton merchants and their employees also struck work throughout the country, while youth formations did an outstanding job in aiding the victims of the demonstrations. At the same time the national press launched a vigorous and successful campaign against the proposed conference. The conference failed and the French authorities gave up their proposed semicentennial celebrations.

A non-Muslim reader might find in these demonstrations an indication of Tunisian religious fanaticism. He might conjecture that the conference was nothing more than a meeting of Christian representatives to deliberate on religious affairs, not unlike similar conferences which adherents of different beliefs hold in both Christian as well as Muslim lands. The truth is that the Tunisians were not motivated in their opposition to the conference by religious intolerance. Theirs was a protest against the French policy of Francization of the people through Christianity. The utilization of religion and its men and the exploitation of the spiritual force represented by Christianity, with a view to enabling the colonialists to destroy the Tunisian edifice, were the motivational factors in Tunisian resistance. Furthermore, the occupation forces would never allow the Muslims to call an all-Islamic conference on the lines of the Afkhārasti conference in Tunisia, even though it was purely religious and devoid of politics. The resistance, therefore, was also a protest against the spirit of detested discrimination and partiality. Moreover, the authorities were intent upon reminding the people of the fifty-year occupation of their country and the proposed conference was but a part of these celebrations designed to sensitize the Tunisians to the "blessings" of their own enslavement. Thus, national preservation was what prompted our Tunisian brethren to resist French policies and designs disguised in the name of religion.

The Issue of Assimilation

When the French sensed the failure of their attempt at Francization of the Tunisians through Christianity they initiated a policy of assimilating the Muslims en masse, whereas hitherto only individual naturalization had been attempted. The national spirit could not permit this new onslaught to destroy the nation in the essence of its existence. No sooner had the French Government announced its plans of assimilation than the people launched the most vigorous protest. The press took a leading part in the campaign. The people decided to ostracise anyone who availed himself of assimilation. He would not be allowed to marry a Muslim woman or to enter a mosque. On his death he would not be buried in a Muslim cemetery. This stern policy of boycott achieved considerable success in reducing the number of those who availed themselves of assimilation at the inception of the policy, and it eventually put an end to it altogether. This was a great victory for the nationalist movement over the French policy of integration. The agitation did not pass without its victims. A special booklet, issued by the information bureau of the Dustūr Party, details the events and the casualties that had occurred in the cause of the disturbances; this is available for reference.

The Qism al-Jabal Conference

Encouraged by the support it had received, particularly from the youths, the Dustūr Party convened a conference to formulate a policy consonant with developments in the country. The conference met on May 12 and 13, 1933 at the party club in Qism al-Jabal. Members of the party's executive committee and representatives of the various branches attended. They were joined by Jamā'at al-'Amal al-Tūnisi (the group for Tunisian action) which represents the leftist wing of the Dustūr youth movement. After reviewing developments since the departure of Tha'ālibi, leader of the party to the East, and taking a serious view of the French campaigns of assimilation and its missionary counterpart, the conferees decided to abandon the policy of cooperation with the existing regime and to withhold recognition of the Grand Council. Instead, it was resolved to revert to the firm policy pursued by the party's first delegation to Paris after the war. The following manifesto was issued at the conclusion of the conference: "The objective of the party's political activity is the liberation of the Tunisian people and the attainment of a sound and stable system of government through a constitution that preserves the Tunisian entity and realizes the sovereignty of the people. The objectives stated above are to be secured through:

1. A Tunisian parliament elected by universal suffrage, competent to draw up its own agenda and in possession of full legislative powers.
2. A government responsible before parliament.
3. Separation of legislative, judicial, and executive branches of government.
4. The extension of the jurisdiction of the Tunisian judiciary over all residents of Tunisia.
5. Civil rights and freedoms for all citizens without exception.
6. Compulsory education for all.
7. Safeguarding the economic life of the country.
8. The initiation of all necessary measures for uplifting the country from the moral and material degeneration into which it had relapsed so that it may occupy a worthy place among the self-governing civilized nations.

The Resident-General reacted to these resolutions as would have been expected. He outlawed the liberal Dustūr Party and suspended all its press organs. At the same time, however, he ordered the construction of a special cemetery for those accepting assimilation. Soon after, M. Manceron was relieved of his duties as Resident-General and replaced by M. Peyrouton. The civil administrators attempted to make use of the occasion for compelling the Muslims to acquiesce in the burial of assimilated Tunisians in their cemeteries. This led to an incident on August 8, when the French administrators attempted the forcible burial of one assimilate Tunisian in a Muslim cemetery. A detachment of troops clashed with protesting demonstrators; in the course of this conflict a civilian was killed and numerous others sustained injuries.

Dissension in the Ranks of the Dustūr Party

The new orientation, represented by the "Tunisian Youth Action Bloc", differed regarding intensity of effort and momentum from the old guard represented by members of the party's executive. The latter, however, attempted to avoid an open split. The participation of the Action group at the Qism al-Jabal conference and their inclusion in the executive was intended for this purpose. Unfortunately, the attempt at reconciliation of the old and the new failed. As soon as Peyrouton assumed office as Resident-General, he showed every inclination to cooperate with the Dustūr Party. After meeting with their leaders he announced that he was agreeable to some of their demands, including a reduction in the number of French officials and their replacement by Tunisians, as a step towards the eventual goal of Tunisian self-government. He made a condition, however, that his plan should not be made public for fear of French opposition. Though the promise, trivial as it was, was never implemented, it hastened the much-feared split between the new and the old guard. One of the youth leaders, Sayīd Qīqa, did not hesitate to reveal M. Peyrouton's secret promise concerning the reduction in the number of French officials. His friends blamed him for violating his promise. His bloc retorted, however, that there could be no secret between the nationalists and the Residency of which the public was not made aware. The opponents claimed that prudence shoul have impelled a postponement of the announcement until a more opportune moment and that the interval could have beer used to test the sincerity of the promise. Trivial as this dispute had been, it was directly responsible for the split which gave rise to two combinations, the old and the Neo-Dustūr groups.

Although the old Dustūr Party had been officially disbande

by Manceron's order previously referred to, M. Peyrouton made no attempt to interfere with the Neo-Dustūr party or its official Arabic organ "al-'Amal" (work). This enabled the dissidents to propagate their program and to enlist widespread popular support.

The Neo-Dustūr Party was born on March 2, 1934 during a conference held at Hilāl palace. Dr. Māṭiri was elected president, while Ḥabīb abu Raqībah became secretary general. To distinguish the new from the old setup, its administrative committee was named "al-Dīwān al-Siyāsi" (the political bureau). The old guard retained the name of executive comittee.

The new party did not differ ideologically from its progenitor, but it did criticize bitterly the lack of dynamism in the old group. It therefore set out to create public agitation as a means of pressure on the administration to force it to concede Tunisian rights.

Though Peyrouton had tolerated the newly-established party and though he had attempted to exploit the split by summoning both groups to consultations with him, he soon found himself compelled to face the realities of the situation. He was up against widespread demonstrations and mounting public clamor, induced by violent press campaigns and the entry into the field of a vigorous new generation. On September 2, 1934 he ordered suspension of "al-'Amal" newspaper and deported a number of leaders to desert exiles.

Demonstrations of solidarity with the exiled leaders and their program continued in Tunis as well as in other Tunisian towns. A clash occurred between army troops and the populace, following which the Resident-General appealed to those nationalist leaders who had not been exiled for their cooperation in quieting the situation. Public tension, however, had risen so high that the remaining leaders of the party could no longer control the situation or dissuade the public from its course. The Resident-General thereupon imprisoned the rest of the leaders including members of the political bureau and the old Dustūr executive.

M. Peyrouton had found out that political differences in al-Maghrib did not undermine common action against the occupation. The disturbances continued unabated until the government finally decided to relieve M. Peyrouton of his duties. He was transferred to al-Maghrib where he met his final demise by the solidarity of Moroccan authorities.

Tunisia and the French Popular Front

Tunisia was no less deceived than Algeria by the advent of the French Popular Front, particularly since the French Socialists under Léon Blum had actively opposed Peyrouton and had striven for his removal. The new Resident-General, M. Armand Guillon, adopted a policy of conciliation and showed a desire to improve the lot of the Tunisians with a view to their eventual liberation. His first public utterance upon his arrival at Tunis was that he wished to govern by his heart. He inaugurated his term of office with the release of all political internees and permitted Ḥabīb abu Raqībah, Ṣāliḥ ibn Yūsuf, Ṭāhir Ṣifr, Qīqa, Qulaybi, and other Dustūr leaders to resume their activities.

This liberal policy left a most favorable impression in the minds of the people and gave rise to considerable hope respecting the attitude of the Popular Front. The people participated in the celebrations on the occasion of its accession to power, and their leaders expressed confidence in its men. The spirit of optimism was reinforced by the Resident's decision to permit the reopening of the Dustūr clubs, the freeing of the press, and the removal of the ban on associations and public meetings. The Neo-Dustūr leaders made full use of the opportunity to reorganize their ranks. New formations and party cells were organized throughout the land and particular attention was devoted to the strengthening of sport and scout units. Tunisian union leaders also made use of the new favorable situation to resume their activities. They formed the Federation of Tunisian Trade Unions--independent of French unions--under the leadership of al-Qannāwi. This appeared to the Popular Front as being incompatible with the policy of fraternization and cooperation.

Sheikh Tha'ālibi, who had been in exile since 1923, was permitted to return to his country. He was given a tumultuous welcome by the people of Tunisia for his services to the cause.

In this atmosphere of freedom the Dustūr leaders stepped up their political activities. Public gatherings were organize to discuss the manifold public issues and aspirations. A number of party and non-partisan newspapers made their appearance. Contacts with French circles in Tunisia and in France were sustained and developed.

The Neo-Dustūr Party announced that the platform adopted at the Qism al-Jabal conference of 1933, that is, the achievement of an independent and sovereign Tunisia, remained the basic policy of the party. At the same time, the party decided to proceed to its realization in stages. As an initial step it pressed for a return to the spirit and the letter of the occupation statutes, which either had not been respected or had been mutilated in a manner contrary to its original purport(and this with the understanding that French trusteeship was not intended to be permanent). In pursuance of its aim the party urged the speedy implementation of the following reforms:

1. Abolition of the "colonial allowance". (This is an allowance amounting to one-third of the basic salary paid to French employees in Algeria, Tunisia, and Morocco).
2. Cessation of official colonization of the land.
3. Compulsory education for all.
4. The setting up of elected municipal councils.
5. Appointment of Tunisians to various government jobs, including a greater share in pivotal posts.
6. A more effective relief program.
7. Anti-usury legislation.
8. Abolition of the Grand Council and its replacement by a duly-elected Tunisian parliament and a government responsible to it.

As a matter of fact, this policy of gradualism had deceived many nationalists, not only in Tunisia but throughout al-Maghrib. We had--all of us, to be fair--regarded it as a means for achieving our ultimate objectives. The experiment, we are now convinced, had been a mistake. Granted that the policy of gradualism had been a feasible one in the initial formative phases of the party, it could no longer remain so, even as a means, after its repudiation at the national Dustūr conference of 1933. It lingered on as a result of the successful propaganda carried on by the Popular Front in North Africa and the conciliatory policies of the Resident-General.

The Neo-Dustūr Party should not alone carry the blame

for this gradualist orientation. The old guard of the Dustūr was no less its victim. By recording it here, it is not our intention to criticize our colleagues for a mistake from which we ourselves were not immune. Our aim is merely to expose the futility of those who today still cherish hopes in a policy of gradualism and the attainment of independence by stages. Since we have won victory over ourselves and have succeeded in rallying public support behind a policy of unequivocal independence, it is no longer an error but a crime to retreat to a policy whose unsoundness and futility we have experienced ourselves.

Abu Raqībah visited Paris in 1936 where he carried on a successful publicity campaign and made useful contacts with Popular Front circles. He had discussions with M. Vienot, Under-Secretary at the Foreign Ministry for North African Affairs, who was an advocate of an Islamic-oriented French policy. He was a proponent of a more cordial policy, though devoid of liberality or any spirit of concessions. He made a visit to Tunisia in the course of which he gave a speech in the presence of Dustūr leaders who had gathered to greet him. He attributed the causes of the Tunisian crisis to the selfishness of certain French colonists who could not distinguish between their own narrow interests and those of France. The Under-Secretary urged improvements in the lot of farmers and workers and the reorganization of the country on modern basis. At the same time he reiterated M. Millerand's earlier statement that Tunisia would forever remain linked with France.

The conciliatory tone of M. Vienot's speech and approach impelled the Dustūr leaders to gloss over his disturbing references to an eternal link between the two countries. The public, however, was unimpressed by sweet words and verbal promises. No sooner had M. Vienot departed than Tunisian workers began to press for their legitimate demands. Phosphate-miners of Metlaoui and Mdila in the Sfax region struck work and clashed with security forces; the clash resulted in the death of twenty-five and injuries to thirty others. A wave of labor strikes spread to other areas throughout Tunisia. The situation became so critical that M. Vénéque, President of the French Colonists Association, sent a message to the Residency in January 1937, warning that if the authorities failed to take stringent measures against strikes blood would flow.

Meanwhile, both the people and the Dustūr leaders awaited the fulfillment of the promises made by the representative of the Popular Front. The promises, however, proved illusory. Tensions mounted and the tone of the Dustūr press changed from cordiality and reticence to open threats that Tunisian independence must and would be achieved with or without French help.

The Party Congress, 1937

During this period Morocco was smarting under the repressive colonial policy which continued unaltered during the Popular Front regime. In 1937 widespread arrests of the nationalist party supporters had been in full swing. This led to the convening of al-Ḥizb al-Waṭani (the nationalist party) conference at Rabāt in October of the same year. The party decided to sever all connections with the Residency in Morocco. I was deported on October 20 to Jābūn and several of my colleagues were also deported to various places. Serious disturbances occurred, as we shall explain in a later section. The situation in Algeria was no more auspicious; the policy of repression and persecution had spread there as well.

All these developments, in addition to the Popular Front's failure to effectuate its promises, led the Neo-Dustūr Party to convene a national congress in November 1937 to protest the policies of repression in Algeria and Morocco. It was decided to withdraw confidence from the government and a twenty-four hour general strike was called in sympathy with Morocco and Algeria. The strike was a complete success.

The Occupation Authorities Counteract

The French administration had been planning to extend its repressive measures to Tunisia. An order was issued forbidding all public gatherings. This, however, did not prevent the Dustūr Party from organizing clandestine meetings and gatherings. The authorities thereupon clamped down. They arrested the leader Abu Raqībah, Dr. Ibn Sulayman, Ṣāliḥ ibn Yūsuf, al-Hādi Nuwayrah, and others.

On April 9, 1938 the authorities arrested ʻAlāl al-Bahlawān. The arrest led to serious disturbances in the capital in the course of which one hundred lost their lives and several hundred others sustained injuries. Demonstrations spread to other parts of the country.

The leaders of the Dustūr Party were brought before a military tribunal on charges of conspiring against the state. Several thousand supporters were also detained.

The Committee for Defense of Freedoms in Tunisia

As a result of the policy of repression and the detention of all the leadership in Tunisia, the nationalist struggle could no longer be continued as hitherto. The Tunisian youths who had been studying in Paris, however, decided to carry on the nationalist struggle until the detained leaders had been released. With this end in view they set up a committee for the defense of public freedoms in Tunisia under the leadership of Dr. Sulaymān ibn Sulaymān who is regarded today as one of the most prominent members of the Neo-Dustūr Party's political bureau. The committee organized meetings and press campaigns. A short while later it established what amounted to a continuous clandestine resistance movement. Dr. al-Ḥabīb Thāmir was in charge of these operations which included the secret distribution of pamphlets, sabotage of communications and telephone lines, demonstrations, and other seditious acts.

World War II

It was natural that the advent of World War II should have intensified the activities of the resistance. One of its principal aims was to dissuade the people from joining the army. In this it was successful, for only those who had been forcibly enlisted or were in dire need joined the ranks. Sabotage increased manifold in spite of French warnings and threats. When these were not heeded, the authorities resorted to the most stringent measures including the imposition of death sentences and collective responsibility for sabotage to communications. The Residency became so fearful that Tunisian troops guarding fortifications in the country were disarmed. In spite of this, sabotage did not diminish, and a mutiny threatened in the ranks of Tunisian troops. The authorities had to use force in compelling the troops to board transport ships for the battlefields in Belgium and Italy. Military courts were set up everywhere while prisons and detention camps overflowed with inmates.

When Vichy signed the Armistice Agreement, the Dustūr Party took occasion to press for independence since the protecting country could no longer defend its own territory. On July 5, 1940 a Neo-Dustūr delegation submitted a memorandum to the Bey, requesting release of Abu Raqībah and his colleagues detained in Marseilles as well as the termination of the occupation. At the same time the party branches distributed a manifesto embodying the same demands. The Resident-General, Admiral Stephan, promptly arrested all members of the delegation. Their detention lasted for only a few weeks, thanks to the intervention of the Bey.

Finally, Dr. Thāmir and members of the Dustūr's political bureau, who had not been detained in the earlier wave of arrests, were imprisoned. This, however, did not diminish the resistance movement, which continued until December 1942.

On June 19, 1942 His Highness al-Munṣif succeeded to the throne. He was known for his nationalist sentiments which he had acquired through his father Muḥammad al-Nāṣir. His accession was the occasion for tumultuous public celebrations in which all strata of society participated. The monarch declared his solidarity with the Tunisian nationalists.

On August 2, 1942 the Bey submitted to Admiral Stephan a list of demands which in many respects conformed to the reforms requested by the Dustūr Party in 1936. The French Government promised to implement them but the promise was never fulfilled. On November 9, 1942 German troops occupied Tunisia and the Bey intervened for the release of all political internees. Dr. Thāmir resumed leadership of the Dustūr movement in the open. He reorganized its ranks, increased its cells and branches, started a newspaper in Arabic, and undertook a campaign tour throughout Tunisia. Thus the party was able to regain its position and the people rallied around it. Abu Raqībah and his colleagues were removed to Rome and were not able to return to Tunisia until April 1943.

On May 8, 1943 Tunisia was liberated by the Allies. The French administration took advantage of the state of turmoil to destroy Tunisian nationalists on charges of collaboration with the Axis.

On May 14, 1943 General Giraud announced the ousting of Bey Munṣif from the throne, notwithstanding the fact that he had at the most critical moments declared his neutrality and had turned down all German offers for collaboration. He was exiled to the Algerian Sahara and thence to Po in 1945 where he remained in detention, a martyr of patriotism and fortitude until his death on September 1, 1948. Several hundred persons were executed, while thousands were given prison sentences at hard labor. On intervention of certain foreign circles, Abu Raqībah and a number of his colleagues were spared imprisonment. The people, however, continue their clandestine struggle in the face of the most repressive measures on the part of the authorities.

At this juncture, the Dustūr Party issued a manifesto demanding that Tunisia be given self-government. The party was thus able to focus the minds of the people upon one common platform.

On March 26, 1943, Abu Raqībah and a number of his close associates departed in secret from Tunisia. After an arduous journey they arrived in Cairo to continue their struggle for the liberation of their country.

The leaders who remained in Tunisia set about reorganizing the political bureau under the leadership of Ṣāliḥ ibn Yūsuf. They successfully built upon the basis which had been laid down by their predecessors.

In view of changed circumstances in the post-war period the Neo-Dustūr's political bureau and the old Dustūr executive committee agreed to hold a united conference with a view to devising a common plan of action. The conference met on August 23, 1946 under the chairmanship of al-'Arūsi al-Ḥaddad. In addition to the two Dustūr parties, the Tunisian Trade Union Federation, the Union of Tunisian Government Employees, and the staff of the Zaytūnah University attended. The conferees adopted a national manifesto to which reference will be made later on.

While the conferees were in session, the police forced their way in and occupied the building on the authority of a warrant signed by the Resident-General. The conferees were individually and meticulously searched. Sixty participants were arrested, including the chairman Ḥaddad and Dustūr leaders, on charges of conspiring against the state and of reconstituting a disbanded party. The detainees remained in prison for one month.

Manifesto of the National Tunisian Conference

Following is the text of the manifesto adopted by the conference:

Whereas Tunisia had been, prior to 1881, an independent state linked to the Islamic Caliphate primarily by spiritual rather than by political bonds;

Whereas Tunisian sovereignty had been internationally recognized as evidenced by the treaties into which it had entered with the various powers;

Whereas France, after defending the independence of Tunisia from the Ottoman state, had forced the acceptance of her occupation by a treaty imposed by brazen force upon King Muḥammad al-Ṣādiq, in which treaty the people of Tunisia had never acquiesced;

Whereas the Treaty of Bardo did not exclude the Tunisian state from the international community and did not divest it of its internal or external authority;

Whereas the occupation--after sixty-five years--had turned into a system of colonial exploitation, in which Tunisia has been divested of her sovereignty and her wealth systematically plundered, while both the spirit and the letter of the Treaties of Bardo and of Marsa did not contemplate more than a temporary trusteeship;

Whereas the protecting authority had not confined itself to the duties of supervision but had replaced the protected state in the direct management of government and public affairs;

Whereas the French authority had seized legislative functions belonging to His Majesty the Bey with the result that the latter had become a mere honorary official whose private liberty is curtailed, while Tunisian ministers of state had been reduced to mere dignitaries for ceremonial purposes; whereas governors had been reduced to mere tools for implementing the orders of French civil controllers, while all jurisdiction had been transferred from Tunisian to French officials whose experience or integrity have not in most cases been free of aspersions;

Whereas France, which had been officially obligated to protect the person and the family of the Bey, had violated her pledge once more by forcibly ejecting the legitimate sovereign of the land, His Majesty the Bey al-Munṣif, thereby committing a breach of one of the basic tenets of the Islamic religion;

Whereas these aggressions had given rise to an unstable administrative system which is neither fully taken over nor autonomous, and in which location of authority and responsibility is non-existent;

Whereas France since the imposition of the occupation had pursued a policy of impoverishing the people and plundering their best lands and of allocating more than two-thirds of the budget for the administrative apparatus (almost wholly French), a budget over which the people have no control and which is based on per capita levies rather than on wealth; whereas Tunisia has been subjected to currency, customs, and commercial policies that are detrimental to her economic well-being and place the country in an unfavorable position in its dealing with foreign countries;

Whereas the policy of impoverishment is the consequence of the colonization of the country by colonists and officials, of enticing the people to assimilation, of granting naturalization to Maltese, English, White Russians, Spanish Republicans, and even in the latter phase to Italians, with a view to increasing the number of French citizens in proportion to the indigenous population and of destroying the Tunisian character of the country.

Whereas the financial extravagance indulged in in pursuance of this policy has led to the failure of the protecting power to meet its social obligations towards the Arab population--such as adequate nutrition, housing, medical care, and education.

Whereas the protecting authority had neglected its humanitarian obligations for the benefit of the capitalist exploiters who dominate the country and had failed in its alleged civilizing mission by virtue of which it sought to justify the imposition of its protectorate;

Whereas the representation of the French Tunisian community in the French Parliament constitutes a further aggression against Tunisian sovereignty and a serious breach of the international obligations underlying the occupation;

Whereas the people of Tunisia have been denied in their own country the most fundamental freedoms, that is, the freedom of thought, speech, publication, association, and movement, and have lived for twenty years under military law.

Whereas the protecting state had failed in its obligation to safeguard the security of the country and had delivered it over to the Axis Powers, while the Tunisians had expended their blood on every occasion in defense of France and her allies.

Whereas the Treaty of Bardo had specifically stipulated that the protectorate was essentially an ad hoc arrangement and that French interests arising therefrom could not under any circumstances assume the character of permanence;

Whereas on the other hand, the interests of a protecting power should not stand in the way of the people's inalienable rights to determine freely their own fate;

Whereas colonialism is rightly regarded as a cause of international animosities and conflicts, and considering that the United Nations had explicitly and unequivocally condemned it, and had announced as one of its war-aims the right of all peoples to choose the form of government acceptable to them together with the restoration of independence and sovereignty to the peoples from whom they had been forcibly alienated;

Whereas this new principle has been reiterated and recognized at the various world conferences, and France had been one of the colonial powers which had assented to the principle that no nation has the right to rule over peoples under its authority indefinitely;

For all these reasons, the Tunisian National Conference declares that the protectorate regime is a political and economic system totally incompatible with the sovereignty of the Tunisian nation and its vital interests, and that this colonial regime has shown its bankruptcy before the world after an experiment lasting sixty-five years. The conference also declares the unflinching determination of the people to restore their complete independence and to join as a sovereign state the League of Arab States and the United Nations, and to demand participation in the peace conference.

The Present Situation

The Tunisian Dustūr conference terminated the ambiguities and ambivalence that had clouded the orientation of the nationalist movement. Complete and unconditional independence has become the focal point for the nationalist movement. Both the executive committee of the old Dustūr and the political bureau of the Neo-Dustūr have agreed upon this objective and have pledged to strive for its achievement, with the full backing of the entire people.

The attainment of independence naturally requires a different form of struggle. It requires the closing of ranks and the coordination of activities. The two Tunisian parties therefore agreed to form a coordinating committee to study the existing problems and to direct the movement along a sound course of action.

It is only just to recognize that the majority of the Tunisia people today are on the side of the Neo-Dustūr Party. But the minority is also strong in its fidelity to this common objective and its willingness to cooperate with the Neo-Dustūr. The nationalist movement today is pursuing the right course of action. Its leaders are doing their utmost both inside as well as outside Tunisia for the liberation of their homeland and the realization of their countrymen's aspirations.

Both parties took part in the establishment of the "Committee for the Liberation of the Arab Maghrib" under the leadership of Amir 'Abd al-Karīm. The political bureau of the Neo-Dustūr is represented by Abu Raqībah and Dr. Thāmir, while the executive committee of the old Dustūr is represented by its chairman, Muḥyi al-Dīn al-Qalībi.

Abu Raqībah does not restrict his activities to Cairo but is travelling constantly to the East, to Europe, and to America. In his trips he speaks for the Dustūr movement in its entirety.

Chapter III

MOROCCO OR THE FAR MAGHRIB

Morocco has always regarded Algeria as her first line of defense. For this reason her traditional policy had been oriented towards extending Morocco's moral influence in Algeria, or at least preventing her occupation by a foreign power lest the country should serve as a springboard for expansion to neighboring territories. When Algeria fell under Turkish rule, the Moroccans became apprehensive of Turkish expansion and their successive governments pursued policies of support for all anti-Turkish nationalist movements aiming at the establishment of an independent Algerian kingdom. This was the overriding consideration in Sultan 'Abd al-Raḥmān's support of the Tījānīyah resistance to the Turks, despite the fact that the religious beliefs of his predecessor Sultan Sulaymān had been derived from the Wahhābi movement and was in contradiction to the precepts of the Tījānīyah sect.

If this had been the policy of Morocco towards an Islamic imperialist power, it is natural that her attitude towards a non-Muslim occupying power would be no less pronounced. No sooner had France attempted the occupation of Algeria than Morocco launched a vigorous protest and an intensified resistance to the invader. When the Moroccan Government witnessed the inability of the Turks to defend Algeria, the reigning sovereign initiated Arab resistance in Tlemcen. He also aided in the establishment of Amir 'Abd al-Qādir's sultanate. Abu Ma'zi, the Moroccan, also organized resistance to the French in the region of Zawāwa, at first independently and later in conjunction with 'Abd al-Qādir. The Moroccan Government's assistance to the Algerian resistance movement lasted until the disastrous battle of Isly on August 4, 1844, when North African forces were badly shattered and France was about to occupy the eastern part of Morocco after threatening to bombard the ports of Tangier and Ṣuweirah.

The defeat of the Moroccan army in the battle of Isly, despite its able commander, Crown Prince Muḥammad ibn 'Abd al-Raḥmān, who later became Sultan Muḥammad IV, prompted the Moroccans to engage in a good deal of self-searching with a view to ascertaining the causes of the defeat. The Moroccans recognized from the beginning that the antiquated methods in the army and in the administrative machinery of the state were no longer effective or capable of withstanding modern European tools and techniques. Modernization and regeneration became uppermost in the minds of their leaders. The defeat of Isly, therefore, may be regarded as the first dawn of modern Moroccan awakening. There followed an outpour of literature reflecting on the tragic consequences of defeat and warning of even greater disasters. Al-Kardūdi, an accomplished author, composed a treatise urging the complete reorganization of the army along modern lines. Others emphasized the need for economic regeneration and development, with a view to decreasing the country's dependence upon foreign imports. When Sidi Muḥammad IV succeeded to the throne, he set himself the task of implementing the requested reforms. An artillery school was established; the sugar plantations in the south were revived, and a sugar refinery begun. He was also founder of the Muḥammadīyah printing press, credited with the publication of numerous books.

King Muḥammad IV was succeeded by Mawlay al-Ḥassan (1873-1894) who is justly regarded as one of the great reformers and rulers of al-Maghrib. He devoted his energies to enhancing the moral prestige of the state both at home and abroad and succeeded in safeguarding the independence of Morocco by a wise and farsighted statesmanship. His foremost accomplishment was the reorganization of the Moroccan army according to the most up-to-date standards. He sent student missions to Europe for advanced training and enlisted the services of foreign experts drawn on a non-preferential basis from the various foreign countries. During his reign the Moroccan cabinet discarded its antiquated form and assumed the structure and function of a modern government. Separate ministries for foreign affairs, justice, war, navy, and finance were instituted. Hitherto, all these functions had been concentrated in the hands of al-Ṣadr al-A'zam (equivalent of chief minister) who was himse no more than an adjutant of the king.

He modernized the Moroccan navy and founded an armament industry in the city of Fez.

He encouraged local industry and the investment of local capital in competition with foreign investments. Moroccan manufacturers were urged to display their goods at the various international exhibitions.

He strove to counteract the consequences of the foreign concessions which had been established by the convention of Madrid (1880) and which were threatening to bring about political and social chaos. At the same time he attempted to remove the causes that had prompted the foreign powers to set up their consular courts, by the gradual formation of civil courts. All cases had been within the jurisdiction of Sharī'ah courts. Foreign residents, rightly or wrongly, regarded Sharī'ah courts as clerical councils to which they as non-Muslims could not be subject. The King recognized that the institution of civil courts would remove the causes upon which the foreigners had based their claims to independent consular jurisdiction. He decreed that civil and criminal cases should be referred to pashas and caids who had no connection with Sharī'ah courts. He also abolished slavery and granted Moroccan Jews full citizenship.

The European scramble for control of the Muslim countries was now in full swing. To meet this challenge Sultan al-Ḥassan decided to establish the closest ties of cooperation between these countries within the framework of Pan-Islamism; this cause had been effectively and increasingly propagated in those days. In pursuance of this objective he decided to renew diplomatic relations with the Sublime Porte and to enlist the services of Ottoman experts. Following the Convention of Madrid he sent a delegation to Constantinople led by his minister Barīshah. Sultan 'Abd al-Ḥamīd accorded the delegation a warm welcome. He was profoundly interested in the fate of North Africa because his policy was oriented towards the cause of Pan-Islamism. An agreement was signed for the exchange of diplomatic representatives, and the Ottoman Government appointed Amir Muḥyi al-Dīn, son of Amir 'Abd al-Qādir, its first ambassador to Morocco. When France became acquainted with the successful outcome of the negotiations between the two Islamic states, she made representations to the signatories of the Madrid Convention, urging them to oppose the new trend. France succeeded in convincing the diplomatic representatives at Tangier to resist the spread of the Pan-Islamic movement to Morocco. The ambassadors informed His Majesty Mawlay al-Ḥassan that they viewed unfavorably his policy of rapproachement with the Sublime Porte and that they regarded it as an act hostile to the allies of Morocco. England was the only power that refused to associate herself with this policy, and this was for two main reasons:

1. British policy was anxious to keep Morocco as an instrument with which to threaten France, whenever the latter bickered over the Nile valley.

2. Britain was anxious not to harass Sultan 'Abd al-Ḥamīd in his policy of resistance to Russian expansion which had reached to the south of the Caspian Sea and was threatening the borders of India.

Mawlay al-Ḥassan was compelled to postpone his policy of close collaboration with the Sublime Porte, but such a policy remained uppermost in his mind until his death. His successor, 'Abd al-Ḥamīd al-Malik, made another attempt at carrying out the policy. He sent a delegation led by Sayīd Shams to Sultan Rashād V. The delegation was cordially received and obtained a promise from the Sublime Porte to refuse recognition of a French protectorate should France succeed in occupying Morocco.

Thus, the Pan-Islamic movement on the one hand, and the series of aggressions against neighboring countries on the other, combined to resuscitate Moroccan national consciousness and to mobilize the nation in opposition to foreign designs.

The Salafīyah (fundamentalist) religious reform movement and Arab awakening in the East left their impress upon Morocco. The religious reformer, Sayīd 'Abdullah al-Senūsi had returned from the East carrying the principles and ideas of the religious reformers. He castigated his fellow country men for obedience to the sheikhs of the Sūfi sects and urged them to revert to the puritanism of their great forefathers at the dawn of Islam. He met with such obdurate opposition from the reactionary sheikhs that he almost gave up his mission and would have done so but for the patronage of King Ḥassan and his adoption of the reform movement. We shall see later on how the movement gained in strength and momentum to become today the backbone and the principal driving force behind the independence movement.

Simultaneously there occurred a cultural and a literary revival. There was a prodigious output of literary and historical works which have inspired and guided our contemporary cultural revival.

All these activities were in fact a spontaneous response to the challenge presented by foreign danger and should not therefore be overlooked in a history of the independence movement in Morocco.

The movement was not restricted to defense against the foreign intruder. It became a national faith striving for the removal of all impediments to freedom so that through the instrumentality of freedom the program of reconstruction, interrupted by the occupation, could be carried forward.

The independence movement in Morocco has a dual purpose: resistance to foreign occupation, and progress. Both are inseparable one from the other. The movement will be described under three main topics: (1) diplomatic resistance, (2) political and military resistance, (3) political resistance. Reforms are intended to effectuate a reorganization of the state apparatus, the organization of the people,and the creation of an atmosphere of mutual confidence between government and the people, on the basis of solidarity among the individuals of a nation and with a view to their protection and happiness.

Diplomatic Resistance

The previous section contained a brief description of the diplomatic resistance put up by Mawlay al Ḥassan through out his life. It is not intended here to narrate the diplomatic history of al-Maghrib over a period of fifty years. The aim is merely to deduce the general features of Maghrib policy, as laid down by Mawlay al-Ḥassan and pursued by his successors. There are three basic orientations in Morocco's policy: (1) refusal to accord any single foreign power a privileged position in Morocco; (2) the creation of a modern progressive state in which all citizens enjoy equal rights and obligations, without discrimination on account of creed or race; (3) the preservation of the independence of Morocco. As a result of King Ḥassan's resolute policies, Morocco was spared foreign encroachments and internal upheavals in spite of French and Spanish efforts to establish footholds in his kingdom.

This sound policy placed the foreign powers in feverish competition with one another to secure the favor of the King. It also embroiled France, who had the greatest designs and ambitions, in a tremendous effort to remove the obstacles placed in her way by the other competing powers. Thus in 1902 France had to make a deal with Italy under which she renounced all claims to Libya and Tripolitania in exchange for a free hand in Morocco. In 1904 France concluded the Entente Cordiale with Britain, wherein she renounced all claims on the Nile valley in exchange for a privileged position in Morocco. France's conspiracy was completed by partitioning the country with Spain, who obtained a zone in the north.

Mawlay al-Ḥassan was succeeded to the throne by Mawlay 'Abd al-'Azīz, who was a minor. His chief minister Aḥmad continued the late King's policies of thwarting foreign aggression. He died five years later and the Sheriffian Kingdom was placed in the hands of a well-meaning and intelligent but young and inexperienced monarch. He did not possess the will to resist the machinations of self-seeking politicians in the court, who conspired against the state and were agents of foreigners. The policy of a balance of power remained to the end, however, the foreign policy of the Moroccan state.

French pretensions were naturally accentuated following the conclusion of agreements with three of her major competitors. A fourth power, however, was still waiting for her share. France had ignored the claims of Germany in the belief that she had already secured her assent at the Convention of Madrid. The Government of Morocco preferred to cooperate with Germany, who also had the Sublime Porte on her side. German policy, however, was ambiguous and aimed at little more than a share in political or economic influence somewhere. This was granted when she renounced her claims in exchange for colonial territory in the Congo and Togoland.

The Moroccan people did not remain at a standstill while awaiting assistance from the foes of France. A nationalist movement was organized under the leadership of Sheikh Ma'al-'Aynayn for resistance to the French in the area of Shanqīṭ, at the far end of southern Morocco. All the tribes of the area rallied to its support. The movement was expecting Mawlay 'Abd al-'Azîz to perform superhuman efforts in thwarting foreign aggressions. It also looked forward to obtaining a constitutional system of government which would aid in resistance to foreign invasion.

The King, in response to his people's demands, established a Senate to serve as a nucleus for the constitutional setup visualized by the reformers. The French were loud in complaining about the Senate's opposition to their pretensions. They complained of 'Abd al-'Azîz's refusal to comply with the demands made upon him by French diplomacy on grounds that the representatives of the people had turned them down or that the 'ulemas had found them unacceptable. The King and his advisers were anxious to lift the question of Morocco from the narrow range of a Franco-Moroccan concern to the wider dimensions of the international arena. The cause of Morocco, they felt, would be considerably enhanced if it were thrown into the limelight of international discussion. Thus, the King invited the signatory powers of the Madrid Convention to the Conference of Algeciras on January 15, 1906.

The Conference, in which representatives of fifteen nations participated, nullified the privileges accorded to France by the Convention of Madrid. It also nullified the advantages accruing to her as a result of the secret agreements contracted with other interested powers, and it recognized, further, the territorial integrity and independence of Morocco. The French, however, were entrusted with the implementation of a number of reforms including an international police force. Against her strong wishes, those functions were to be carried out in the name of the international community to which France had been made accountable. The question of Morocco was made an international issue and not a purely Franco-Moroccan affair. The British Foreign Secretary, addressing himself to France, declared that the Conference of Algeciras had nullified entirely all the secret agreements contracted hitherto, but, he went on, if France could establish a privileged position in Morocco and if she handled the issue with Germany discreetly and firmly, his country would eventually have no alternative but to recognize a French protectorate over Morocco.

The people of Morocco were dissatisfied with the outcome

of Algeciras Conference. Though it had averted greater dangers, nevertheless it had accorded France a privileged position. The Moroccans were averse to granting a privileged position to any foreign country. Mawlay 'Abd al-'Azīz, who endorsed his representatives at the Conference, fell into public disfavor. Since he could no longer check French penetration in the remote south, the people decided that revolt was the only efficacious means for annulling his obligations old and new. Nationalist leaders called upon the people to raise the banner of holy war, while religious leaders urged a boycott of French goods. King 'Abd al-'Azīz was deposed and his brother Mawlay 'Abd al-Ḥāfiẓ proclaimed sovereign.

'Abd al-Ḥāfiẓ was provisionally proclaimed sovereign by Sheikh Ma' al-'Aynayn. The official proclamation, however, took place at the Grand Mosque of the city of Fez.

The Ḥāfiẓīyah proclamation, drawn up by the leading personages of Fez and written in final text by Aḥmad ibn al-Mawāz, one of the leading intellectuals, is a national and constitutional charter of the first order. It imposes the following conditions upon the new king:

1. To do his utmost for the restoration of Morocco's territorial integrity.

2. To make every effort for the abrogation of the Treaty of Algeciras, in which the people had not been consulted.

3. To undertake the expulsion of the invader from the Moroccan territories under occupation.

4. To strive for the cancellation of foreign privileges.

5. To refrain from consulting foreigners in the government of the state.

6. To refrain from entering into contractual agreements with foreign powers on commercial or civil matters without prior consultations with the people.

The proclamation is tantamount to a contract between the king and the people transforming the system of government from an absolute to a limited constitutional monarchy. By virtue of it a sultan is no longer entitled to conclude any treaty with foreign powers--commercial or civil--without consultation of and ratification by the people. It significantly precludes both the king and the people from assuming power to conclude treaties touching upon the integrity of the country It is conformable to the spirit of the French declaration on human rights, which places sovereignty in the people and renders it inalienable.

The Ḥāfiẓīyah revolt thus had a dual purpose:

1. Elimination of foreign conspiracies by safeguarding the complete independence of Morocco.

2. Implementation of political reforms with a view to the establishment of a sound and stable constitutional government.

The two objectives have remained until the present day the cornerstone of all our independence movements. Shortly after the enthronment of the new king, the constitutionalists, who had formed the backbone of the revolt and whose earlier efforts had secured the establishment of the Senate, drew up a comprehensive draft constitution which was published in their newspaper "Lisān al-Maghrib" (the mouthpiece of Maghrib) in Tangier. We cannot gloss over this noble movement which is rightly considered as the forerunner of our independence movement.

The Group of "Lisān al-Maghrib"

No other country has suffered so much loss of historical records as Morocco has experienced throughout the ages. Our knowledge of this early nationalist movement, therefore, is meager in the extreme. All we know is that group of youths including al-Mahdi ibn Ṭālib al-Fāsi, Sa'īd al-Fāsi, 'Abd al-Ḥafīẓ al-Fāsi, Aḥmad ibn al-Mawāz, and Aḥmad al-Zabdi had organized a secret society with the avowed purpose of alerting the Moroccan people to the dangers presented by foreign occupation. Members of this group contributed articles to the free press in Tangier as well as to "al-Ḥāḍirah" newspaper, mouthpiece of the Tunisian nationalists. At the same time, a group of sheikhs masquerading as members of Sufi [mystical] orders had been actively engaged in political activities on behalf of one cause or another. Some of them derived their support from the Ottoman Empire while others were backed by certain colonial powers. The latter group met with strong resistance from the nationalists as well as from the Salafīyah reform movement. Sheikh Ma' al-'Aynayn, to whom reference has been made earlier, launched a movement similar to that of Sheikh Senūsi for the unification of Sufi orders and their adherents. The movement was a success and an important group of public figures and nationalists rallied to its support. A spirit of mysticism permeated both the religious and the national life of the country. Sufi beliefs and rituals intermingled with the desire for political reforms. The mystification of the political movement to which the reformer, the superstitious man, the traitor, and the patriot had contributed, had one fundamental aim: liberation and independence as well as political and social reforms.

The inner core of the movement comprised men of the highest intellectual stature who had been in touch with progressive ideas and developments in the Arab and Muslim worlds. They used every available weapon--including superstitions--for the achievement of freedom and reforms. It is not possible to identify the men who had drafted the Maghrib constitutional document; they preferred to remain incognito to ensure the success of their program.

Nevertheless, the nationalist weekly publication "Lisān al-Maghrib" has preserved the text of the draft constitution as well as a number of valuable articles which shed light on the motivations of the nationalist leaders in that period.

"Al-Maghrib al-Jadīd" (the new Maghrib) magazine has reproduced the following excerpt from its progenitor "Lisān al-Maghrib", which shows the vitality and progressive orientation of the movement. It reads in part: "Since the time has come for effectuation of reforms to which the youths of the country ardently look forward, and since His Majesty the new Sultan 'Abd al-Ḥafīẓ recognizes their dire necessity, we shall vigorously and continually demand of the King the expeditious implementation of these reforms. The King knows that we have voluntarily proclaimed him our sovereign and leader, in the hope that he would save us from the brink of disaster to which ignorance and tyranny have brought us. It is the duty of His Majesty to respond to our aspirations and to prove to all his ability and willingness to improve the lot of his people in fulfillment of the trust placed in him by them.

"Our first demand is for the opening of schools and the dissemination of learning. Elementary education should be made compulsory; public offices should be held by men of ability and progressive outlook. The King should beware of spies and mischievous advisers who distort to him the views of his subjects and try to draw a wedge between sovereign and people. The Sheriffian court is plagued with a large army of these deadly microbes. If the King does not beware and resist them they will communicate their infectious germs."

The author then makes a plea for a constitutional form of government. He writes: "Since one hand is incapable of uplifting the nation from the abyss to which it has sunk or of reforming the variegated functions of our government, it is essential that the contributions of all men of ability should be solicited and mobilized for the task of reconstruction. It is therefore imperative that His Majesty should grant his people the blessings of a constitutional government, including a chamber of deputies, and the freedom to work and think for the good of the country, such as are enjoyed in the Muslim and the Christian states of the modern world. When these modern states were under the yoke of tyrannical rule, their voice was not heard nor were they high in the scale of capabilities. Only when liberated from the chains of absolutism and slavery did these states rise from their lethargy to attain their exalted position of today. Suffice it here to cite the example of Japan, this shining sun in the horizon of Asia, which only forty years ago was one of the most backward states and has now risen to the rank of a great power, having scored that miraculous victory over one of the world's greatest powers, Russia. Not far away from us is the impressive transformation that has occurred in Turkey since His Majesty the Commander of the Faithful granted a constitution to his people and ordered the election of al Mab'uthan assembly [parliament]. It is to be hoped that our country will follow suit in the task of reform and reconstruction."

Do not these quotations show that our people were treading the right path to salvation, but for the dislocation caused by the foreign invasion which diverted all our energies to the task of self-defense for a long period of time?

The Maghrib draft constitution consists of four sections: the first embodies the basic law of the land; the second comprises the procedural law of the proposed elective assembly; the third lays down the electoral provisions; the fourth embodies what the drafters called the Maghrib law of torts.

The draft constitution calls for the establishment of

Muntada al-Shūra (the consultative assembly) to consist of two houses--the people's assembly and the assembly of the nobility. The new body, meeting in concert, shall be regarded as the supreme organ in the land. Its decisions are incontrovertible and its jurisdiction includes powers of supervision over the various governmental agencies and functions. The lower house is empowered to propose additions or omissions regarding the provisions of the constitution, subject to royal endorsement.

The first section of the constitution devotes attention to issues arising from special protections and privileges adopted at the Convention of Madrid. Article 75 of the draft constitution declares: No citizen of the Moroccan state is permitted to avail himself of the protection of a foreign state, save in exceptional circumstances provided for in article 79. Article 76 states: Any person who, in secret and without the knowledge of the government, accepts the protection of a foreign state shall forfeit all rights and shall be subject to the penalties provided for in the law of torts. Article 77 states: No citizen who has acquired the protection of a foreign power shall be eligible for employment in government services. Article 78 declares: Any government employee who has secretly acquired foreign protection shall upon disclosure be removed from his job regardless of his protection and shall be liable to all the penalties provided for in the law. Article 81 provides: Any person who had acquired foreign protection prior to the adoption of this constitution shall be treated as a subject of his protecting power without any distinction or discrimination. Article 82 declares: Any person who renounces his foreign affiliation shall be readmitted to citizenship of the state of Morocco and shall be granted complete equality with other citizens.

The draft constitution, in a section on education, provides for the establishment of primary and secondary schools for boys and girls and the reorganization of the Qarawiyīn University on modern lines. Article 88 declares that schooling shall be free for all and that the people's assembly shall vote allocations to meet the government share of the expenses; the remaining expenses of the program shall be drawn from revenues of waqf endowments and state domains as well as from public subscriptions, particularly from well-to-do citizens.

Primary education is compulsory for all boys in the schooling age.

Article 90 permits the establishment of private schools by Moroccans as well as by foreigners who wish to found them. Article 92 lays upon the assembly, in the first year of its existence, the duty of enacting laws and regulations for every government department and agency.

The draft constitution mirrors the thoughts and aspirations of the cultural élite of the country in those days. Although it is not the ideal constitution to which we should aspire today, it nevertheless contains the seeds that have oriented Morocco towards popular democracy. The publication of this draft constitution was enthusiastically acclaimed in Tunisia as well as in other Arab countries.

It is pertinent to emphasize that the popular movement in Morocco looked to Mawlay 'Abd al-Ḥafīẓ as a symbol of resistance to foreign encroachments. It was hoped that he would succeed in terminating foreign privileges. As regards political reforms, it was hoped that he would transform the system of government from an autocracy to a democracy in which the nation would be able to control and reform its affairs. International pressure together with France's refusal to recognize His Majesty led the King to pursue policies which his people regarded as an unexpected sell-out. The situation was brought to a climax by the advance of the French army on Fez and the imposition of the protectorate on March 30, 1912.

Military Resistance

No sooner had the protectorate been announced than the royal army mutinied against its supreme commander. The troops killed their French officers and rebellion became widespread throughout the land. Heavy encounters occurred which are still referred to as the "bloody days". Twenty thousand armed men from the tribal localities around Fez closed in on the city under the command of al-Za'īm al-Ḥijāmi. The rebellion extended to the south and north and to the Middle Atlas. General Gourand, in the course of operations at Hajrah al-Kaḥla, fifteen kilometers from Fez, seized a map of operations skillfully prepared by the command of the rebellion, together with a call for a holy war as the imperative duty of every Muslim without exception.

The French unified their command under Marshal Lyautey. He became Resident-General and supreme commander of French invasion forces for the whole of Morocco. His operations to secure the lines of communications for his dispersed troops cost him heavily in blood and money. His forces suffered 56,000 casualties in 1912, 70,000 in 1913, and 63,000 in 1914. This costly campaigning involved Lyautey in a number of loan-projects which were bitterly contested in the French Parliament.

When World War I broke out, the entire Maghrib, except the largest towns and ports, was in full-fledged rebellion against foreign occupation. The rebellion areas were divided into four main parts: (1) Jabālah and the Riff in north Maghrib; (2) the Middle Atlas area; (3) the High Atlas in south Maghrib; (4) Tafilelt and Ayāt 'Aṭa, in south Maghrib also.

1. Jabālah and the Riff

The Spaniards had settled in the Maghrib towns of Melilla and Ceuta during the fifteenth century when Banu al-Aḥmar were still the ruling dynarty in Granada.

In 1903 an agreement was reached between France and Spain, at the behest of French Colonial Secretary Delcassé, wherein the northern portions of Morocco were to be ceded to Spain in the event of a French conquest of Morocco.

In 1909 the Spaniards amassed an army of three divisions in the environs of Melilla for conquest of the Riff. They were resisted by the first hero of the Riff, Muḥammad Amazyān. There were heavy encounters over a period of two years in the course of which the invaders suffered considerable losses, estimated by Spanish historians at ten thousand killed, including two generals, Benito and Vicario. Al-Qal'īyah tribe fought the war with particular distinction.

In 1913 the Spanish attempted the conquest of al-Sheshuan region. In heavy encounters with the Jabāla tribes Spanish troops were forced to retreat to the city of Tetuan where they were besieged until an armistice was concluded, through the influential tribal leader Raisuli; this armistice lasted until 1918. Thus, Spain had been forced to maintain peace with the Riff tribes throughout World War I in order to safeguard her lines of communications. The area remained quiet until the battles of the Riff hero, 'Abd al-Karīm.

2. The Middle Atlas

Numerous encounters took place in this region between 1911 and 1933. It is possible to distinguish four important phases in these prolonged campaigns:

1. The attempts of the advancing foreign army to establish links with the mountain redoubts. The attempts precipitated four campaigns:

a. The Battle of Bany Maṭīr in 1913.

b. The resistance of Tadla until its occupation in 1913.

c. The battles of Khunayfirah in 1914.

d. Operations in the Tadla area from 1915 to 1917.

2. Attacks against the hard core of the tribal constellation in the Middle Atlas. These included:

a. Battle of Azur-Midlet in 1917.

b. Battles of Zāyān and Banī Maqīlid (1920-1923).

3. Invasion of the northern coast of Wādi al-'Abīd. This precipitated the following engagements:

a. Resistance at 'Arbālah in 1926.

b. Attempts at conquest of Wādi al-'Abīd in 1929, 1930, 1931.

4. Enemy invasion of the Middle Atlas. This includes:

a. Resistance put up by Āyat Yeḥya (1931-1932).

b. Heroic stand of Āyat Yeḥya in 1932.

c. Attack on Bisāṭ al-Buḥayrah in 1932.

d. The Battles of Mulūl, High Atlas, Kardūs, Bado, and al-Kussa in 1933.

3. The High Atlas in South Maghrib

The policy of Marshal Lyautey in this region had been designed to win over the various caids who enjoyed influence and prestige among their respective tribes. National consciousness, however, had reduced considerably the influence of these individual caids. Lyautey's strategy was vitiated here no less effectively than in the Middle Atlas, in view of the inhabitants' democratic way of life which left little scope for individual predominance. Sheikh Mā' al-'Aynayn and his son al-Hibah deserve credit for the unification of the southern tribes and their mobilization in resistance to the French and their local henchmen. His forces occupied the city of Marrakech, but were eventually defeated at the battle of Sidi abī-'Uthmān. Nevertheless, he continued the fight in the area of al-Sāqiyah al-Ḥamrā' throughout

World War I. The resistance movement of the High Atlas and Sūs came to an end only in 1935.

4. Tafilelt and Āyat 'Aṭa in South Maghrib

This region continued in its resistance to the French for twenty-three years. Its commander, Sheriff al-Samlāli, was the hero of Tafilelt, who placed the considerably augmented French forces under General Poeymirau in great jeopardy in 1917. He was assassinated, and Abu al-Qāsim al-Naqqādi took over command of the resistance, which lasted until 1935 when he was forced to surrender. He is still detained in the city of 'Uyūn Sidi Mulūk.

The preceding section highlights the main phases in Morocco's struggle for independence. It would require volumes to record a complete history of this heroic struggle and its leading personages. We shall, therefore, recount only one phase of that struggle--the Riff war--in view of its profound impact upon the contemporary nationalist movement and because its great hero has resumed the struggle as head of the Committee for the Liberation of Arab Maghrib since his arrival in Egypt.

The Riff War

In dealing with the battles of the High Atlas reference was made to the spirit of national consciousness engendered by Sheikh Mā' al-'Aynayn and his son al-Hibah in order to counteract Lyautey's policy of resuscitating inter-tribal conflicts through the various local caids. The parochial nature of the Moroccan resistance movement led the foreign powers, and particularly the French, to believe that inter-tribal animosities and divisions could be exploited to considerable advantage, not only in whittling down armed resistance but also in consolidating France's political hold on the country at the termination of active warfare. The French authorities discerned in al-Hibah's nationalist movement the most potent manifestation of nationalist consolidation in Morocco. The numerous tribes that inhabit an area extending from the city of Marrakech to Senegal were seen pooling their resources under one unified command for defense of Morocco's independence and unity.

General Guillaume, in his book on the Berbers of Morocco and the military operations for pacification of the Central

Atlas, contests Marshall Lyautey's often-repeated dictum that a show of force makes recourse to it unnecessary.

The tenacious resistance put up by the people of Morocco renders Lyautey's favorite dictum wholly inapplicable, Guillaume asserts. He expresses astonishment at the fact that the tribes most loyal to the Sultan were the first to rise against him when he authorized the protectorate. They were more fierce and fanatical in their fight against us, he adds, than some of the other traditionally more turbulent tribes. The General expressed the view that if the French administration on the spot had been unsuccessful, it was because the opponents would never relinquish a position or retreat except after putting up the maximum resistance possible. Earlier in the book the author quotes with approval a statement made by Marshal Bugeaud in which he said: "Indeed it is both amusing and painful to hear and to read what our writers and speakers advise us to do in order to win over our opponents. They suggest that we pursue fair policies in order that the Arabs may feel the sweetness of our traditions and the benefits of our civilization. Undoubtedly this is beautiful and sublime. No one appreciates it more than I do. But how can we follow such a policy towards a people who confront us only with fierce fighters and who reply to sentimental words with bullets?"

This is indeed the spirit of al-Maghrib. The people have never consented to a rapprochement with either France or Spain. They were never taken in by their claims that they had come to al-Maghrib not as conquerors but as civilizers and helpers. The rally of the entire people behind the defense effort is a proof of al-Maghrib's deep-rooted national consciousness, derived from and based upon the right of self-defense which is the natural attribute of the human race in its entirety.

The spirit of resistance, however, shows its greatest manifestation in the Riff war under the brilliant generalship of its hero, 'Abd al-Karīm.

It was the father of 'Abd al-Karīm who resumed organized resistance to the Spanish after the repeated failures of the latter to secure his acquiescence in their rule. He laid siege to Tafersit for more than twenty days but contracted illness in the course of this operation, leaving to his sons the legacy of the struggle for the liberation of al-Maghrib from foreign rule. One of 'Abd al-Karīm's first exploits was the liberation of Dār Abāra from Spanish troops. He accomplished this feat with a force of three hundred fighters after a fierce encounter in which the Spaniards lost four hundred dead (including six officers). The Riff force captured a substantial amount of arms and ammunition from the retreating Spaniards.

'Abd al-Karīm's victory had a profound impact in that it rallied the people of the Riff behind the banner of the Amir and put an end to tendencious rumors circulated by traitors and foreign hirelings against 'Abd al-Karīm and his family. General Silvestre then attacked in the area of Sidi Beisān to the northwest of Anual. The forces of the Riff repulsed the attack, inflicting considerable losses, estimated at 314 killed, upon the Spanish. The Riff losses amounted to 17.

The next major encounter was the battle of Anual which lasted for six days. General Silvestre, the Spanish commander, made desperate efforts to dislodge the Riffian forces from the surrounding area, but was beaten back and forced to abandon Anual and all the positions in its vicinity. The retreat of the Spaniards from Anual deteriorated into a panicky flight. The Riffians, in pursuit of their defeated opponents, found it unnecessary to use firearms. The Spaniards abandoned more than one hundred military posts. The roads were strewn with thousands of their dead while seven hundred were taken prisoners. The military booty seized by the Riffians was prodigious and enabled 'Abd al-Karīm to arm and equip his forces. The booty included two hundred artillery guns, twenty thousand rifles, a considerable number of transport vehicles, stores of ammunition, and other war equipment. The victory of 'Abd al-Karīm considerably bolstered the morale of the Riff population and enhanced their confidence in final victory.

The battle of Anual was followed by another decisive battle at "Monte Arruit" in which the Spaniards suffered a disastrous defeat and were thrown back into the city of Melilla which stood defenseless before the advancing Riff army.

During 1922 and 1923 the Spanish organized and equipped several new armies under the command of General Berenguer. Heavy but indecisive encounters took place all along the Melilla-Cuba-Alhucemas line. Finally, 'Abd al-Karīm launched a counteroffensive which again drove back the Spanish into Melilla after inflicting heavy losses and depriving them of all their arms and equipments.

The Spanish Government, shaken by the revelations of this disaster, decided to end its military operations and to sue for a settlement. General Berenguer, Supreme Commander and Resident-General in Spanish Morocco, was recalled for consultations. He voiced strong disapproval of the government plan. In March 1922 General Berenguer launched a new major offensive in which he deployed fifty thousand soldiers at Alhucemas area and other large contingents around Melilla, in a concerted attack upon Bani ʻArūs and ʻAbd al-Karīm's stronghold of Ajdir.

On March 25 the Riffians began a general counteroffensive all along the front, using artillery, which they had captured from the Spanish, for the first time. The battle, which lasted for a whole week, ended in a complete victory for the Riff forces. Five thousand of General Berenguer's troops were killed and three thousand were taken prisoner. The General himself sustained two serious wounds in the chest. He returned to Madrid where after consultations with the general staff it was decided to call off the offensive and to withdraw to a small enclave around the Bay of Melilla.

In the meantime, the Riff forces continued their operations, capturing and destroying military posts and installations still in Spanish hands. A number of Spanish war vessels were sunk and the Riff's only war vessel participated in the operations. There was a great public furor when news of the Spanish military disasters became known in Spain.

Following the defeat of Alhucemas, the Madrid Government sent feelers to ʻAbd al-Karīm for the conclusion of an armistice as a first step towards a peace settlement. The Spanish envoy, Echevarrita, held several meetings with ʻAbd al-Karīm at Ajdir, which resulted in an provisional agreement for a cease-fire, release of Spanish prisoners of war against payment of ransom to the Riff government, and release of all Riff prisoners in the hands of the Spanish authorities. Negotiations for the conclusion of a peace settlement, however, broke down. The Riff representative insisted on independence of Northern Maghrib from Spain, while Spain was not willing to go beyond the grant of internal self-government.

In 1923 a Riff force of seven thousand men attacked from the mountain plateau of Darsah-Sheshuan and succeeded in overrunning forward enemy positions. Its next objective was the town of Daghīt, where very fierce encounters took place. The Spanish army was placed in serious jeopardy, and responsible Spanish sources conceded that the situation had become very precarious.

The Spanish Government, following an extraordinary meeting in connection with the latest development on the Morocco front, formed a delegation for conducting peace talks with 'Abd al-Karīm. Several meetings between the two delegations were held in Tetuan but to no avail. The Riff delegates adhered meticulously to the nationalist platform, while the Spaniards did not go beyond a number of minor concessions. The secretary of the Spanish delegation addressed a message to the foreign secretary of the Riff in which he maintained that negotiations should be confined to bringing about administrative and economic changes in the Riff area and determining the status of the Amir 'Abd al-Karīm in his capacity as envoy of the Sultan's Khalīfah in Northern Morocco. The Spanish secretary declared that negotiations concerning independence or the abrogation of the protectorate were out of the question.

The foreign minister of the Riff government replied at length to this offer. The reply stated, in part: "The Riff government established on modern ideas, laws, and civilization considers itself independent both politically and economically, and we are priviliged to enjoy our freedom, as we have enjoyed it for centuries, and to live freely as other peoples live. We consider that we have the right to enjoy the possession of our territory in preference to any other nation, and we believe that the Spanish colonial party have transgressed and violated our rights and that they have no justification for their pretense of a claim to make a protectorate of ourRiffian state. We have never recognized this protectorate and we never shall recognize it. We desire to be our own rulers and to maintain and preserve our indisputable rights and unequivocal independence."

Fighting was resumed following the breakdown of the Tetuan conference; the Riff forces continued to score decisive victories over Spanish troops. In 1924 the Jabāla tribes, inhabiting the triangle between the Tetuan river,

Anjera, Wadi Lau, and the Tetuan-Sheshuan road, joined the forces of 'Abd al-Karīm and attacked Spanish troops from every direction. Their participation in the liberation movement transformed the war from a localized to a general tribal movement. Their moral as well as material contributions to the war were most potent in hastening the collapse of the various Spanish fronts. The newly augmented forces of 'Abd al-Karīm cut off all communications and transport between Tangier and Tetuan and closed in on Tetuan from all directions.

It was at this juncture that General Primo de Rivera, Dictator of Spain, arrived in Tetuan to take personal charge of the situation. After a conference with his top military aids, martial law was imposed throughout Northern Morocco. Fresh reinforcements of troops were sent from Spain. General Primo de Rivera decided not to attack the interior but to concentrate on defense of the main ports. At the same time he decided to initiate talks with 'Abd al-Karīm.

The Spanish delegates announced the willingness of their country to relinquish the territories from which their troops had been forced out. The Maghrib delegation offered counter-proposals which included the following conditions:

1. That Spain should pay the sum of twenty million pesetas as compensation.

2. That Spain should hand over to the government of the Riff fifteen planes, one hundred rifles, and one hundred and twenty field guns.

3. That Spain should withdraw from Morocco to the borders of Melilla and Ceuta.

4. That if Spain complies with these provisions, negotiations could be started for the repatriation of prisoners of war and the conclusion of peace.

The Spanish delegation rejected these peace terms, and Spanish troops made a general withdrawal from two hundred military posts in accordance with the decision of the higher war council. The uprising of the Anjera tribes behind the Spanish lines, in the area between Tetuan and the borders of Tangier, rendered the position of the Spanish army untenable. It also effectively cut off their sources of supplies and communications.

War with France

The policy of Amir 'Abd al-Karîm had from the outset been designed to keep France aloof from the Riffian war of liberation with Spain. He was convinced that the success of the cause depended upon careful timing and the preservation of correct if not cordial relationships with France until such time as the Spanish had been completely driven out of Northern Morocco. The attitude of the French towards 'Abd al-Karîm was equally reticent. Marshal Lyautey sought to establish ostensibly cordial relationships with him. At the same time he was submitting reports to his government stressing the dangers that might stem from the establishment of a free state in an area of Morocco contiguous to the French. Such a free state, he warned the French Government, would imperil the entire French position in North Africa. Yet he was advising France to play it safe as long as possible in the hope that Spain, alone and unaided, would defeat the Riffians and spare France the losses and expenses of a war with 'Abd al-Karîm.

The French, however, were unable to maintain this wait-and-see attitude for long. Their forces attacked the Wergha tribes along the Riffian border, ostensibly to protect the tribes within their jurisdiction from Riffian encroachments.

'Abd al Karîm has explained to his biographer in writing the reasons that led to the war with France. The Amir stated, among other things: "The French advance on the Wergha valley caused a tremendous furor among the tribes of the Riff. I was then engaged in operations against some of the Jabāla tribes which had remained aloof in our struggle for independence. When I finally succeeded in subduing the recalcitrant tribes of Ghomara and Sinhaja, I resumed military operations against Spanish strongholds. A number of skirmishes occurred along the borders between the French zone and the Riff during the withdrawal of the Spaniards; the direct cause of these skirmishes had been the absence of natural boundaries between the two areas. There was a no man's land of considerable extent to the northeast of Fez, known as the upper Wergha valley. The French claimed that the area was within their jurisdiction under the protecto rate. To this unoccupied strip I sent a force in 1924 which was joined by forces of the local tribes.

"This strip of territory," the Amir went on to explain, "was under the direct control of the Riff when France advanced upon it. It is of no import to me whether Spain or France regarded the strip as falling within her protectorate jurisdiction, considering that the government of the Riff had never accepted or recognized the partition of Morocco into various foreign-held protectorates.

On May 1, 1925 full-fledged war broke out between the Riff forces of liberation and the French. Heavy encounters were fought in the course of which Riffian forces scored important victories over the French. An ever-increasing number of tribes rallied to the banner of 'Abd al-Karīm in a solid demonstration of national unity. The French Government relieved Marshal Lyautey of his duties and appointed M. Steeg in his place. General Naulin was appointed commander-in-chief while Marshal Pétain was sent from Paris on a special inspection tour of the front. Upon completion of his mission in the French zone he proceeded to Ceuta and Tetuan with a view to coordinating military operations with General Primo de Rivera.

The French and the Spanish were puzzled by the extraordinary qualities of tenacity, fortitude, and tactical ability of the Riff forces. The French and the foreign press in general expressed admiration for the heroism of the Maghrib people. There was a mounting public outcry in both Spain and France against the continuation of this costly colonial operation. The labor movements in both countries demanded a cessation of the Riff war and the conclusion of a reasonable settlement with the Moroccans.

In the face of this mounting popular pressure, the French Prime Minister announced that an agreement had been drawn up by the French and the Spanish Governments comprising the terms of peace to be forward to the Riffian leader. In the words of M. Painlevé, the Prime Minister, the French agreed to guarantee the Riff and Jabāla tribes administrative, economic, and political autonomy under the nominal sovereignty of the Sultan and subject to the delegation of the Khalifa. There were provisions concerning the formation and number of the armed forces in these districts. But the Amir was not asked to surrender all his military equipment. The peace terms were unacceptable to 'Abd al-Karīm because they did not recognize the full independence of al-

Maghrib, which was the principal aim of his liberation movement.

The war with France was bitter, though indecisive. It is beyond the scope of this study to recount its many glorious battles. Suffice it here to mention in passing the battles of al-Kīfān and al-Bibān, which shook the Franco-Spanish forces to their foundations and impelled Marshal Pétain to summon from France all available reinforcements on land, sea, and in the air. Little wonder, therefore, that might should have triumphed temporarily over right. The position of the Riff was further weakened as a result of the activities of a group of religious impostors such as 'Abd al-Raḥmān al-Darqāwi and Ḥamīdū al-Wazzāni, who under the guise of religion undermined the morale of their followers. The war of liberation ended on May 25, 1926 with the surrender of 'Abd al-Karīm. The Amir was taken to Fez and later sailed from Casablanca to the island of Réunion, which had, by mutual agreement between the French and Spanish Governments, been chosen as his place of exile. Together with his brother and uncle he remained in exile for twenty-one years.

We have seen how the great leader of the Riff succeeded in mobilizing and activating the moral and spiritual forces of his countrymen in the cause of liberty and independence. The Amir has described to me how the people of the Riff abandoned their quarrels and stayed their vengeful hands during the struggle against France and Spain. Tribes and individuals whose animosity was a byword and whose hatred was proverbial made peace with one another in order to devote themselves completely to the ideal of liberating al-Maghrib and restoring its territorial integrity.

The loyalty accorded to the Amir by his compatriots has become proverbial. The colonial powers made repeated attempts on the life of 'Abd al-Karīm. They were unsuccessful, however, because of the unflinching fidelity of his county men.

As for the religious impostors who chose to serve the foreigner instead of Islam and their nation, they were held under careful surveillance by the Riffian leaders. Some of the more notorious among them were publicly disavowed, but the people had not acquired sufficient immunity to withstand their poison. The Amir did all he could to reform the attitudes and beliefs of his countrymen by encouraging the Salafīyah reform movement. But how can anyone change the mentality of an entire people in a matter of few years?

Abu Laḥyah, a doctor of divinity who held the portfolio of justice in 'Abd al-Karīm's government, informed me that 'Abd al-Karīm insisted that he and the other religious leaders be well versed in the writings of Sheikh Rashīd Riḍā and other religious reformers in the East.

'Abd al-Karīm, in an interview with the military correspondent of "Le Matin", stated: "We Muslims are still in a state of dire ignorance. It is right and proper that we should accept the pleas of the reformers for a return to the fundamental and unadulterated tenets of early Islam and discard the harmful accretions which have drained the strength from the Muslims and Islam and which are completely at variance with true religion."

The French in their publicity have attempted to depict the Riff leader as a mere rebel seeking power. The Amir, however, has never hesitated to declare that his only aim was the liberation of his country and that he had never contemplated disloyalty to the Maghrib dynasty. As soon as the Amir disembarked at Port Said after his long exile, he reiterated his loyalty to His Majesty the King of Morocco. The Amir resents calling his movement a rebellion. I was once talking to him about conditions in North Africa and inadvertently I said, "This took place during the Riff rebellion." The Amir, with a grim look on his face, retorted: "Why do you call it a rebellion? It was nothing less than a war of liberation against the foreigner and in defense of the fatherland."

The Constitution of the Riff Republic

It is gratifying that the Riff liberation movement like its forerunner was democratically oriented and progressive. The proclamation of a republic was not motivated by an aversion to the institution of the monarch. The leaders of the Riff were in fact unable to speak in the name of the King of Morocco, whom circumstances had placed within the French zone of influence. At the same time they were careful not to repeat the mistakes of Mā' al-'Aynayn and his son al-Hibah, who proclaimed themselves kings after a distinguished record of service and loyalty to the crown. The Riff leaders found a compromise solution in the establishment of a provisional regime during which the people would be trained in the art of self-government. When the complete liberation of the entire Maghrib is achieved, the Republic of the Riff would revert to the authority of the rightful sovereign. The Riff leaders did not contemplate asking for more than a constitutional system of government, in the running of which the people would have a voice in the decision-making process.

No sooner had 'Abd al-Karīm achieved his initial victories over the Spanish than he convened a popular convention for deliberations concerning the establishment of a provisional government, capable of carrying on the struggle against foreign troops. Addressing the gathering, the Amir reviewed the history of Spanish-Moroccan relationships since the days of Arab rule in Spain. 'Abd al-Karīm condemned the barbaric acts perpetrated by Spanish troops against the inhabitants and exposed the selfish motives behind Spain's desire for a protectorate over the land. The Amir appealed to the representatives for unity in the struggle ahead. The delegates pledged their full support and approved of the formation of a general council which would serve as the supreme organ of the state. The national government was to be made accountable to this representative body.

The general council was set up and known as the National Assembly. Tribal as well as urban representatives, sheikhs and military commanders took part in it. The Assembly held its inaugural session in 1921. Its first resolution was a declaration of the independence of the Riff and the establishment of a constitutional republic with 'Abd al-Karīm as president in his capacity as leader of the liberation movement.

The National Assembly drew up a draft constitution, based upon recognition of the sovereignty of the people. The constitution, however, failed to make a separation between legislative and executive organs of government in accordance with constitutional practices in democratic states. Instead, the two powers were vested in the National Assembly whose chairman was the president of the republic himself. Each member of the Assembly was bound to accept and carry out the resolutions of the body as a whole. In adopting this principle of unanimity the Assembly was heeding the traditions and customs of the country.

The constitution further provided for the establishment of a four-portfolio government: an assistant to the president (equivalent to prime minister), minister for foreign affairs, minister of finance, and minister of trade. Other government functions such as the interior and the war were retained in the hands of the president.

Members of the government were made responsible to the president, who alone was responsible before the National Assembly. This provision was in conformity to the traditions of the country which held the king directly responsible to the people. The arrangement was also necessitated by the exigencies of the war which impelled the concentration of responsibility in the hands of one leader.

When the Assembly completed the drafting of the constitution it worked on the preparation of a national program behind which the people could rally in their struggle for independence. The National Platform included the following provisions:

1. Refusal to recognize any treaty that prejudices the rights of al-Maghrib and particularly the treaty of 1912.

2. Spanish withdrawal from the territory of the Riff that had not been in the possession of Spain prior to the Franco-Spanish treaty of 1912.

3. Recognition of the unequivocal independence of the Riff Republic (independence from Spain and France).

4. That Spain should compensate the Riffs for the losses sustained by them as a result of the occupation of their country over the previous eleven years.

5. The establishment of cordial relationships with all the states without exception and the conclusion of commercial treaties with them.

Thus, the leaders of the Riff war, while remaining loyal to the territorial integrity of the Maghrib under the 'Alawi dynasty, aimed at the realization of two objectives: independence of the country and its attainment of a constitutional system. These two objectives have remained the goal of all Moroccan nationalists since the beginning of the twentieth century.

The Nationalist Movement after the Occupation

The period between March 31, 1912 and May 16, 1930 was almost entirely taken up by military struggle. The great majority of the people had risen in rebellion following the imposition of the protectorate. The process of pacification required tremendous efforts over a long period of years. With the tightening grip of the occupation, Morocco looked to a new generation of youths, skillful in the techniques of civil resistance, to replace armed resistance which had become no longer feasible as the main instrument of nationalist policy.

This does not mean that Morocco had taken the occupation lying down. The national struggle continued, but it took the form of a spiritual and moral regeneration of the people with a view to preparing them for the new form of struggle, quite different from the sort of struggle that took place when citizens were still in possession of their rifles and when the military hierarchy had not yet disappeared from the organizational setup of the tribes.

One of the important activities during this phase of the national struggle took the form of an intensive publicity campaign for rallying popular support behind the armed resistance which had still been going on in the mountainous regions. Several people were arrested and their houses searched. The authorities seized considerable quantitites of arms which the civilians had been smuggling to their fighting brethren.

Throughout the Riff war posters, placards, and pamphlet prepared by 'Abd al-Karīm's command, were widely distributed in Morocco, calling upon the people to rally behind the Riffian liberation movement. In 1924 the authorities discovered in Casablanca an important center of publicity for the Riffian cause. A considerable amount of literature, advocating an all-out nationalist rebellion, was seized. Many persons implicated in this activity were detained, while a group of youths led by our friend 'Abd al-Qāder al-Tāzi managed to slip away to the stronghold of the Amir 'Abd al-Karīm at Ajdir.

North African workers employed in France staged a number of sympathy demonstrations for the Riffian cause. At a general conference held in 1925 the workers sent a cable to 'Abd al-Karîm expressing solidarity with their fighting brethren against Spanish colonialism.

The capitulation of the Amir 'Abd al-Karîm and the collapse of his movement was received with consternation throughout North Africa. There was an outpour of eulogistic literature by the press, the poets, and the nationalist leaders.

The Islamic Congress at Constantinople

In the treatise on the Tunisian nationalist movement reference was made to the activities within the scope of the Pan-Islamic movement of the exiled Maghrib leaders at Constantinople. It is appropriate to add to the list of those already mentioned the name of Sheikh Muḥammad al-'Atābi, one of the 'Ulemas of Qarawiyîn University and a former official of the Sheriffian Government. He had left Morocco following a quarrel between Sheikh Abi-Shu'ayb al-Dakāli, Minister of Justice, and a number of senior French officials, in the course of which the latter insulted the Minister. Sheikh al-'Atābi was moved by the incident and left the country for Hejaz in 1913. In 1915 he made his way to Constantinople where he was received by 'Ali Bāsh Ḥambah on behalf of Anwar Pasha. He was received in audience by Caliph Muḥammad Rashād V, to whom he described the deplorable situation of the Maghrib people and their forcible conscription in the French army to fight against the Ottoman state. Later he went to Germany where he stayed as guest of the government. In the course of negotiations with the German Government he was unable to accept their vague offers regarding the future of North Africa. For this reason he refused to accompany the Schneider military mission and warned the Germans of the dangers inherent in their attitudes towards the future of North Africa.

On his return to Constantinople Sheikh al-'Atābi joined his fellow delegates at the Islamic Congress. Thanks to his efforts and those of his colleagues, the Caliphate as well as the Party of Union and Progress decided to support the independence of North Africa and to strive for the ejection of France and Spain from its territories. The Maghrib leaders were able to convince the Ottoman Government as well as the Party of Union and Progress of the merits of this program for an independent North Africa, on the basis on their knowledge that Germany had ambitions to replace France in North Africa.

The Islamic Congress decided to send a mission on a publicity tour of the neutral countries such as Sweden, Denmark, and Norway. The neutral governments permitted the delegation to carry on its activities in full freedom. Sheikh al-'Atābi represented Morocco in this delegation, which comprised such eminent men as the Amir Shakīb Arslān, Muḥammad Farīd, 'Ali Bāsh Ḥambah, 'Abd al-'Azīz Jāwīsh, and other leaders of the Islamic movement. Sheikh 'Atābi gave many talks to audiences interested in colonial questions. His speeches were translated into foreign languages and distributed to the press throughout the world, particularly to areas under French control. The French Government and press were greatly perturbed by 'Atābi's activities. He was tried in abstentia by a military court. He was forbidden to return to Morocco and the court ordered confiscation of his property.

In 1917 the Islamic delegates convened a conference at Stockholm which adopted the following resolutions:

1. The complete independence of North Africa, which had never recognized colonial rule.
2. The restoration of Shanqīt (Mauritania) to Morocco.
3. The solicitation of the support of neutral nations for the independence of North Africa.

Simultaneously, 'Atābi and his associates maintained close contacts with the rebellious tribes in southern Morocc Al-'Atābi told me that the Ottoman Government had been anxious all along to help the Morocco resistance movement in arms and soldiers, but it did not find in Mawlay 'Abd al-Ḥafīẓ a sufficient readiness for action. The Ottomans' readiness to assist waned, following the Arab rebellion of Sherif Ḥusayn in the Hejaz and its support in Syria and the Lebanon. The capitulation of Bulgaria and Rumania to the Allies added to the difficulties confronting the Ottomans. When World War I ended al-'Atābi was compelled to leave Constantinople and to take refuge in Egypt wherein the late King Fu'ād accorded him a gracious welcome.

In addition to the armed resistance movement in which the people placed considerable hope, a policy of civil disobedience was pursued and sustained in the face of the tyrannical measures resorted to by the colonial power.

Thus, when Marshal Lyautey attempted to lay down the cornerstone of his future Berber policy in September 1916, the women of the Zammūr al-Shalḥ tribe violently protested this barbaric measure. The measure was designed to resuscitate pre-Islamic customs and practices which would have relegated Berber women to an intolerable status of inferiority. Under the measure, women would be no better than a chattel that could be bought and sold and disinherited. Berber women staged a protest demonstration in al-Khamīsāt. French troops opened fire on the demonstrators, but Marshal Lyautey was forced to suspend implementation of the decree. The measure, he contended, was necessitated by the exigencies of the war and would not outlive the circumstances that had given rise to it.

When the Marshal attempted on another occasion to levy a profit tax, there were widespread popular demonstrations at Rabat where the demonstrators repeated the American slogan, "no taxation without representation". Marshal Lyautey was compelled to use force in quelling the disturbances. A number of leading citizens, including our friend Ḥaj abu Bakr Balkūrah, were exiled outside the country.

The Marshal himself, on yet another occasion, ordered the sequestration of Moroccan property for the benefit of foreign companies. Following a great popular uproar he was forced to withdraw his order. The instigators of the protest movement, however, were sent to exile, including our friend Muḥammad al-Ya'qūbi, who for several months remained in detention in the town of al-Ṣuwayrah.

It is beyond the scope of the present study to give a detailed account of the popular agitation in protest against colonial misrule. What is intended is to show that the people of al-Maghrib had never acquiesced in the protectorate regime imposed against their will. It is imperative, nevertheless, to refer to the fierce and sustained resistance put up by the people against the policy of official colonization and land settlement instituted by M. Steeg, the Resident-General, in the period between 1926 and 1929. The policy led to numerous local uprisings by Moroccan farmers against French colonists and their French guards. M. Steeg resorted to the hangman's rope against citizens who refused to acquiesce in the alienation of their lands for the benfit of French colonists.

M. Steeg, in his book on al-Maghrib, concedes that the Moroccan prefers death to alienation of his land, and that his resistance on account of it is stronger than that of the Algerian or the Tunisian.

The policy of land colonization by the French contributed more than any other single factor to undermine the faith of the Moroccans in the efficacy of pacific resistance; civil resistance soon developed into a terrorist movement, in the course of which the French colonists and officials were harassed, abducted, and killed.

The cause of the resistance was taken up and championed by the royal palace. It was an open secret that a serious conflict over the issue of colonization had arisen between M. Steeg and the late Sultan Mawlay Yūsuf. The King had been greatly perturbed by the colonization program of the Resident. His Majesty sent a communication to the French Government asking for the removal of M. Steeg. The Frenc Government appealed to His Majesty to waive his request for a period of six months in the hope that relations might improve between the Sultan and the Resident-General. Before the six months were over Mawlay Yūsuf passed away. During the King's illness M. Steeg visited the royal palace to pay his respects, but was refused an audience with the ailing King. After the latter's death M. Steeg was removed from his post of Resident-General, in spite of his insistent wish that he be retained in it.

At the conclusion of the Riff war the Resident-General laid down a policy of rapprochement between France and the Moroccan youths. A French-Morocco association was formed under the chairmanship of our friend Aḥmad Barkāsh The attitude of the Moroccan youths at the first meeting of the association convinced the Residency of the Moroccans' unswerving loyalty to independence and the impossibility of cooperating with them on any other basis.

Concurrently with these spontaneous anti-colonial uprisings there had been set in motion a concerted and long-range movement for religious reform and cultural revival, which directly and profoundly influenced the formation of "Kutlat al-'Amal al-Waṭani" (the bloc for national action), progenitor of the contemporary independence movement.

The Salafīyah (Fundamentalist) Movement

It appears that Morocco is predisposed more strongly than any other country to accept reform movements advocating a return to true religion and the tenets of the faith. It also appears that the simplicity characteristic of the fundamental and unadulterated form of religion appeals strongly to the simplicity of Morocco's mystical instincts. No sooner, therefore, had the Wahhabi reform movement been launched that it found a ready and enthusiastic response in the royal circle of Sultan Mawlay Sulayman. Sheikh 'Abdullah al-Senūsi, one of the early religious reformers, had enjoyed the patronage and the support of Mawlay al-Ḥassan in the propagation of his Salafīyah principles. Muḥammad 'Abduh, the eminent Egyptian reformer, had established close contacts with the reform leaders throughout North Africa. He had discussed with them the prevailing popular practices of invoking the intervention of prophets in worldly affairs. He had also been in correspondence with them concerning a number of Salafīyah books which he had written for publication.

All these activities, however, had been of lesser importance than the return to Morocco of the great religious reformer Sheikh Abi Shu'ayb al-Dakāli. The Sheikh had returned imbued with a burning desire to propagate the principles of the Salafīyah reform movement. A group of young enthusiastic supporters gathered around him. They distributed the publications of the Salafīyah movement in Egypt and accompanied him on his tours to pull down trees and shrines which had been made the object of popular veneration.

Mawlay 'Abd al-Ḥafīz deserves the highest praise for propagating and supporting the principles of religious reform, particularly after a group of religious impostors had made themselves the tools of foreign machinations. His Majesty issued a treatise admonishing the Tagant followers. He also ordered the closing down of the Katānīyīn order after the discovery of a plot against the security of the state and its people.

All these activities, however, were only preliminary to the intensive Salafīyah drive, set in motion by our illustrious teacher Muḥammad ibn al-'Arabi al-'Alawi. The qualities of courage, fortitude, and endurance enabled this reformer to achieve considerable success in the mission to which he was dedicated.

When the Riff went to war with France, we were gathered around Ibn al-'Arabi, making our contribution to the success of the movement. The treasonable behavior of some of the sheikhs of the orders during the Riff war intensified our determination to rid the country of them. Ibn al-'Arabi's reform circle at Fez and Sheikh Abi Shu'ayb's group at Rabat carried on an intensive reform campaign through the media of public lectures, exchange of visitors, and articles in the press of Algeria and Tunisia; Morocco did not at that time possess a single newspaper that was not under French influence or control. No sooner had the movement been set in motion than the occupying power began to show misgivings and apprehensions, sensing that it was aimed at its pampered stooges, the sheikhs of the orders. We were summoned to questionings and interrogations and threatened with imprisonment. Our friend Muḥammad Ghāzi, one of the foremost leaders of the Salafīyah, was subsequently thrown into jail.

It is impossible for a historian of the independence movement in Morocco to ignore this crucial phase in the development of popular consciousness in our country. It is right and proper to emphasize that the confluence of the Salafīyah and the nationalist creeds had had the most beneficial effect upon both of them. It is also fair to stress that the manner in which the Salafīyah movement had been conducted in Morocco had secured for it a degree of success unequalled even in the country of Muḥammad 'Abduh and Jamāl al-Dīn, where it originated.

During the year 1925, when the Salafīyah movement was flourishing, our friend M. Emile Dermenghen, author of the "Life of Muḥammad" in French, was visiting Morocco. He wrote a treatise on the Salafīyah, its orientations and objectives, expressing throughout his sympathy with it and hopes for its success. I met him again at his Paris home in 1933, after a royal decree had been issued banning parades by the "orders", and after the people had widely celebrated the final extinction of an institution of superstition that had for long stifled Moroccan progress. M. Dermenghen talked about the "orders", expressing regret at the fate that had befallen them in Morocco. I was astonished and said to him,

"But did you not write articles expressing admiration for our Salafīyah movement?" He replied with a smile on his face, "I had not imagined that you would succeed to this extent or with such speed." Yes, we did succeed to this extent and better, particularly after H.M. Sidi Muḥammad ibn Yūsuf adopted the Salafīyah and exerted his utmost in the fight against impostors, charlatans, and superstitions.

The Salafīyah was not restricted to a negative fight against superstition; it preached the cause of general enlightenment, thoroughgoing reforms, and the abandonment of static and anachronistic modes of living.

When one studies the histories of the great movements of mankind one finds that every constructive revolution has been preceded by probing into the remote past; such a return, which on the surface appears a retrogression, is in fact a mighty liberator from the many harmful accretions of generations past. The removal of those accretions is essential for expediting the march of progress and for orienting it toward sound goals and ideals.

The administration for native affairs in Morocco sent a report in 1939 to the "Comité Mediterrannée", set up by M. Blum in France. The report underlines the brilliant way in which al-Ḥizb al-Waṭani al-Maghribi (the Morocco nationalist party) has combined the most modern revolutionary thought with what it calls the new Salafīyah, which had emerged in the Arab world in the post-war period. The observation is correct and instructive; it is ,therefore, essential to look at the political program of the Salafīyah after World War I, in view of its profound impact upon the orientation of the nationalist movement in Morocco.

The Political Orientation of the New Salafīyah

The aim of the Salafīyah, as propounded by its founder, al-Ḥanbali, was the cleansing of religion from the superstitions that had crept into it and the restoration of its original purity. Its motivational drive was the moulding of the Islamic personality in accordance with the principles of Islam, as the ideal system in religious as well as secular affairs. It is designed to prepare the Muslim nation for pre-eminence in this world. Such pre-eminence, God has ordained, would be attained only by the fittest. The movement, therefore, aimed at the reform of the individual as a prerequisite for the perfection of society. The success of the movement, it was realized, hinges upon the acceptance of an "open mind" towards innovations and their critical evaluation in the light of the general interest. Thus would the Muslims restore the greatness which their virtuous forefathers had attained in the spheres of faith and action. Individual preparation, however, is but a means towards the combining of individuals into the group of Islam, on the basis of Islamic solidarity and human fraternity. Such a program requires considerable tolerance towards non-conformists, while at the same time it advocates a united stand in defense of Islam and the Muslim world in its entirety. Defense of Islam and its peoples naturally requires acceptance of the principles that concede to the individual freedom of belief and of thought. It also concedes to nations the right to self-determination. Freedom of belief carries with it the right of freedom of association in its behalf on the part of both individuals and groups, with the aim of fighting for it by all legitimate means. Self-determination requires freedom of the group to express its views and to choose its own way of life. Both objectives cannot be attained except through modern organizations such as associations, parties, and trade unions.

The goal of freedom, however, must be compatible with the aims of solidarity amongst Muslim nations, within the framework of political unity. This was one of the thorny problems confronting the Salafīyah, and there was considerable hesitation as to whether the form of association envisaged should be a modernized caliphate or a league of Eastern nations. Eventually, the movement accepted the principle of nationality, not on the basis of race or religion but on that of regional ties. In justification of its choice the Salafīyah drew upon Islam's traditions of tolerance, thus striking a balance between the need for common defense of the entire Muslim front and the avoidance of foreign criticisms of Islam on account of alleged religious fanaticism and intolerance towards others.

The principles of nationality envisaged by the Salafīyah, however, should not be so narrow as to preclude or undermine the strongest possible cooperation between the Muslim nations in general and the Arab peoples in particular; other wise it would become racial and be in fundamental conflict with the very basis of Islam.

In order to facilitate cooperation there should be a unification of inter-Islamic cultural patterns; the Arabic language must be made to develop as the effective vernacular of the Muslim world in its entirety.

The Salafīyah believes that Muslims should not discard the laws derived from the Islamic Sharī'ah. With this end in view, Islamic jurisprudence should provide the material for drafting a general civil law. The existing body of Sharī'ah law, however, should not be regarded as the unalterable and final embodiment of legislation. It should be developmental and subject to constant review and interpretation.

These aims cannot be realized within the structure of a Muslim government unless the task of legislation and review is assigned to qualified deputies in a popularly elected assembly, in which is vested supreme power of enactment. A corollary to this is the establishment of a constitutional system, based upon popular sovereignty, to be exercised through competent and elected representatives. The attainment of these objectives, however, is impossible until the Muslim countries have been liberated from foreign control both material and moral; therefore, the struggle for independence is an essential prerequisite for exercising freedom of choice and its concomitant responsibilities.

Above all, the new Salafīyah rejects the idea of a secular state; it assigns to the Islamic state the role of a guardian of the ethics and mores of its people; at the same time it lays upon it the duty of affording to every individual the means for carrying out his duties as an individual and as a member of the group. It should set him an example of upright behavior in his dealings with his family, his countrymen, and the world at large. These, in brief, are the orientations of the Salafīyah movement in the period after World War I. We have seen how it played a leading role in the various phases of our national struggle. Both the National Party and the Istiqlāl Party have given the most attentive consideration to its principles and have been profoundly influenced by them.

Whatever be the degree or intensity of our development towards a secular outlook on life, and whatever be the degree of success we shall attain in the implementation of our program after independence, there is no doubt as to the profound impact which the Salafīyah has exercised upon our spiritual development; upon our belief in a thorough regeneration of all spheres of life and endeavor; upon our striving for liberation and our struggle towards the goal of Arab unity, which is still our ideal and inspiration; and upon the democratic spirit which animates us.

From the Salafīyah to Nationalism

The Moroccan youths found in the Salafīyah movement a field for action and a training center for disciplined service and sacrifice. They formed centers in Fez, Rabat, and Tetuan for participation in public affairs. Opposition to the sheikhs who had benefited from the protectorate regime was foremost in their program of action. Small study groups sprang up for investigating outstanding public issues and enlightening public opinion in regard to them. The Qarawiyīn University at Fez was a meeting place for students from all parts of the land, and we considered it our duty to instill into them the spirit of the Salafīyah and the nationalist creeds. We worked for a reform of university education and the amerlioration of the living conditions of the students. We organized trips and exchange visits for students of the various schools and colleges including those of the interior. In cooperation with a number of my colleagues I started a clandestine monthly magazine by the name of "Um al-Banīn". This forty-page publication was prepared by stencil and distributed secretly in Fez, Rabat, Marrakech Tangier, and Tetuan. At the same time we kept in close touch with a group of our brethren who had gone to France or to the East in pursuit of higher education. They were able to conduct their activities in a healthier and freer atmosphere than the one obtaining in Morocco. In Paris they formed the "Association of North Africa Muslim Students in France" and the "Association of Arabic Culture". During the summer vacations they would establish contacts with leading personages among whom was the Amir Shakīb Arslān. Our colleagues in Cairo were able to participate in the formation of the "Muslim Youth Association" and the "Association for Islamic Guidance". In Morocco itself we tried to form the "Society of Student Friends" and to mobilize support for the cause of Palestine. The authorities, however, refused to grant us permission and prevented us from carrying on our work. In spite of these obstructions, we managed to establish a number of reform schools in various parts of the country which served as a nucleus and a rallying point for local activities. On frequent occasions the authorities closed down these educational centers or imprisoned their staffs, thereby evoking widespread public protests. The reader will be surprised to learn that every move on our part, major or minor, entailed considerable efforts and hardships in the face of French and Spanish obduracy. He will be surprised if I tell him that on one occasion the local administration at Fez was upset because a group of progressive youths had started a modern barber's salon by joint subscription, even though this modest enterprise conformed to all the requirements of the law. The shop was ordered closed and the barber fined. The youths were compelled to send a delegation to the Residency to plead for the reöpening of the shop. The reader will be further surprised to learn that the administration for native affairs in Tetuan had forbidden the distribution of a calendar, prepared by our friend Da'ūd, simply because it carried verses from my poetry and poems of other men of letters in Morocco.

In 1920 the French administration attempted to seize the water supply of Wādi Fass (Fez) spring, which is regarded as the property of all the inhabitants of the city. There were historical and legal records to prove that every house in the city was entitled to that share of the water flow passing through it. The French move had been designed with a view to granting the water concession to a number of French companies. The inhabitants of the city regarded the plan as a flagrant violation of established rights and a spoliation of their property. Widespread demonstrations were held in front of the municipal offices and I made an inflammatory speech inside the municipal buildings which was enthusiastically applauded by the assembled crowds. Later Ḥaj al-Ḥassan abu'Ayād and I prepared a memorandum for submission to the prefect of the Fez area, demanding withdrawal of the scheme and emphasizing the people's right to enjoy their freedoms, including the right of private ownership within the law. Popular gatherings were also held at the Idrīssi mausoleum, the Qarawiyīn University, and other places in town, protesting the administration plan. The movement was successful and the public works department was forced to withdrawn its plan.

These activities and others were pointing the way towards organized political action; but May 16, 1936 marked a new milestone in the history of the nationalist movement.

The Berber Policy

It is essential for an understanding of the spiritual and the intellectual development of the people of Morocco to know what this so-called Berber policy is, as it culminated in the Berber Edict of May 16, 1930. The policy is in reality the latest contrivance of the French mind in its efforts to disrupt the cohesion of the Arab Maghrib and to bring about its assimilation. Since their occupation of Algeria the French have been probing into ways and means that would secure to them permanent possession of North Africa and its colonization by Christian settlers of the Latin race. The unshakable fidelity of the indigenous inhabitants to Islam, to unity, and to Arabism, has been the stumbling block in the way of this French design. At one time the French thought that the indigenous people could be overwhelmed by a policy of unlimited foreign immigration; that by granting the immigrants a stranglehold over the country the native element would be reduced to such a level of misery and impotence as to be rendered incapable of averting utter extinction. They saw in the French colonization of Canada and in the Latin settlement of South America evidences of the efficacy of this policy. Days go by and the indigenous people move farther and farther away from extinction in spite of all the attempts at their annihilation. Foreign immigration could not take place on a sufficiently large scale to achieve numerical superiority. The naturalization of Jews, Algerians, Maltese, and Italians failed likewise to bring about the desired end. Thus, assimilation of the Moroccans, so the French thought, would be the only feasible solution. But the Moroccans refuse to be assimilated by others; they are too proud to accept the nationality of a people whom they regard as despised "Rumis". The feeling of superiority, the French gather, is not the result of a spirit of nationalism as it is understood by Europeans; it seems to emanate from a narrow religious loyalty derived from the all-pervasive influence of Islam. Francization could only be achieved through Christianity, but who would dare an open proselytism of Muslims? The French seek a way out of their predicament and find a promising line of approach, particularly in Morocco, where the majority of the inhabitants are Berber. Those people, according to the French, are only superficially Muslim, though indeed they regard themselves as such; their agreement with the Arabs is based upon the fact of Arab supremacy. If only the Berbers could be separated from the Arabs and from what the Arabs had introduced in language, law, and culture, then the Berbers would be thrown back upon their own inner conscience; they would search for the ancient spirit which Rome introduced to their land. It is not unlikely that they would embrace Christianity, in which case they would become the ardent champions of assimilation with France, which would liberate them from the spiritual as well as the temporal supremacy of the Arabs.

These are in broad outline the ingredients of the Berber policy. We need only consult the minutes of the meetings during which the Berber Edict was worked out to deduce the means and the aims envisaged by the French protectors. The minutes of the committee for studying and organizing the Berber judiciary, at its meeting on October 8, 1924, include the following excerpt: "There is no harm in destroying the unity of the judicial system in the French protectorate; on the contrary, since the aim is the strengthening of the Berber element, as a counterpoise that future exigencies may require, positive political advantages would accrue from such a step."

As regards education, a dissertation prepared by M. Gaudefroy-Demombynes on France's educational work in Morocco declares on page 119: "It is dangerous to allow the formation of a united phalanx of Moroccans having one language. We must utilize to our advantage the old dictum 'divide and rule'. The presence of the Berber race is a useful instrument for counteracting the Arab race; we may even use it against the Mekhzen (Morocco government) itself."

The same author concedes on page 118 that the Arabic language is the prevailing language of commerce, religion, and administration in present-day Morocco, although the Berbers regard it as a higher language. The French language, he urges, should replace Arabic as the common language of life and civilization.

Colonel Marty, one of the staunchest supporters of the Berber policy, writes in his book "Le Maroc de demain": "The French Berber school is French in its instruction and life, Berber in its pupils and environment. Therefore, there is no foreign intermediary; Arabic instruction, intrusions by the 'faqīhs' (Muslim divines), or any other Islamic manifestation, must be resolutely forbidden. Opinion here and elsewhere is agreed on this point." Colonel Marty writes further on: "The diffusion of French will be, at least for this generation, our principal effort. The French language will quickly carve out a large place in Berber society and the teaching of Arabic will not progress at our expense. These Berber schools should be organisms of French policy and instruments of propaganda rather than pedagogical centers properly so-called...that is why the teachers have been invited to consider themselves agents and collaborators of the commandants."

Gaudefroy-Demombynes on page 121 of his book writes: "The curriculum of a Berber school is the same as that of other Beduin schools save as regards teachers; under no circumstances must they be allowed to use the Arabic language, not even in the primary stages of education; further, they most not be permitted to mix with the pupils; where a teacher is unable to use this direct method he must, if he knows Berber, use it in the teaching of his pupils."

M. Mauric le Glay, an official of the Residency-General, in an article entitled "French schools for Berbers" published in 1921 writes: "We must abolish instruction of the Islamic religion and the Arabic language in all Berber schools; the Berber dialects should be written in the Latin alphabet." He concluded his article with the following words: "We must teach the Berbers everything except Islam."

Thus, the Berber policy is designed to Francicize Morocco through the instrumentality of language, politics, and the judiciary. It hopes to do this by causing a schism

between the two principal elements of the population through
suppression of Islamic and Arab culture among the Berber
element, which it imagines is more amenable to France.
It transforms the tribal organizations, whose traditional
functions had been confined to defense of the tribe, management of local affairs, and representation before the king's
valis, into courts of law. It reinstates certain pre-Islamic
customs and usages, which had lingered on, as rules of law;
it goes to the extent of vesting criminal jurisdiction in Berber areas in the French courts themselves. Thus, the
majority of Morocco's citizens are removed from the king's
religious as well as secular authority, as represented in
the Sharî'ah and Mekhzen judiciaries. Further, it closes
down Koranic schools and mosques and prevents religious
divines from instructing people in the tenets of their religion.

This policy was begun in the edict of September 1914,
promulgated by Marshal Lyautey allegedly on account of
respect for Berber traditions. It continued in varying shapes
and manifestations until May 16, 1930 when it took the form
of the so-called "al-Dahîr al-Barbarî" (the Berber edict).

Although the edict is couched in ambiguous terms, it
essentially deprived the Sheriffian Government of its authority
over the Berber tribes and instituted customary courts for
which there is no precedent in the entire history of al-
Maghrib.

The Moroccan People Rebel

It was only to be expected that the youths of the land
would not stand with their hands folded in the face of France's
Berber design. They launched a widespread campaign to
inform public opinion of what was being hatched in the dark
and succeeded in rallying the entire nation in protest against
this policy of proselytism and assimilation. Crowds assembled
in the mosques of Sala, and protest gatherings spread to
Rabat, Fez, and other towns. Developments took an intensive form in the city of Fez, where thousands filled the
Qarawiyîn mosque to overflowing day after day.

On March 15, 1930 large crowds who were assembled in
the mosque poured out into the streets in a great frenzy of
excitement and listened to speeches by youth leaders. When

the demonstrators reached the home of the sheikh of the city they were met by the security forces. Twenty-five youths were arrested and whipped, including my friend 'Abd al-'Azîz ibn Idrîs, al-Hāshimi al-Filāli, and Muḥammad al-Wazzāni. On the evening of the same day I myself was arrested. Earlier, the French authorities had arrested 'Abd al-Latîf al-Ṣabîhi in Sala and 'Abd al-Latîf al-'Atābi in Rabat.

We remained in prison for fourteen days during which time demonstrations did not cease in Fez, Sala, and Rabat. When news of the Edict spread in Berber areas, protest delegations picketed the local administrations but were promptly thrown into jail. The commandant of native affairs in Fez was eventually compelled to issue a statement in which he assured the inhabitants concerning the Islamism of the Berbers. The government move, he declared, was no more than a reorganization of an old judicial system. Our release followed.

The announcement did not completely dissipate public apprehensions, and daily gatherings in the Qarawiyîn mosque continued unabated. A delegation consisting of Muḥammad 'Abd al-Salām al-Ḥulu, Ḥamzah al-Ṭāhiri, Aḥmad Makwa, and Aḥmad abi-'Ayyād was formed to negotiate with the French authorities. When these negotiations proved of no avail, we decided to form an official delegation to communicate our views.

The public was invited to a meeting at the municipal council building in Fez. A twenty-four-man delegation representing 'Ulemas, notables, artisans, laborers, farmer and intellectuals was set up to draft for submission to the higher authorities the demands regarding Berber policy. I took part in the drafting of the memorandum which was subsequently adopted by the committee and supported by popular petitions in all parts of the land. The memorandum comprised the following demands:

1. Abrogation of the Edict of May 16 and all other edicts and resolutions to the same effect.

2. The establishment of a unified judiciary for all Moroccans.

3. All civil and religious officials to be attached to the personal authority of the king.

4. The national religions of al-Maghrib to be Islam and Judaism.

5. The practices of proselytism, resorted to by foreign
missions and the department of education, to be forbidden.
6. The Arabic language to be alone the official language
of the country and therefore the principal medium of education.

When the Residency-General saw that the movement had
taken this organized form, it released an announcement declaring that the protectorate would accept the exclusion of
any tribe choosing the jurisdiction of Sharî'ah law from
jurisdiction of the Edict. The announcement, however, was
merely a blinder because when the tribe of Aayat Yūsa, in
the Safro region, and the tribe of Zamūr in al-Khamîsat,
along with others, sent delegations requesting fulfillment of
the promise, they were promptly arrested.

The Fez delegation left on its mission under the leadership of 'Abd al-Raḥman ibn al-Qurashi, former minister of
justice. My father, 'Abd al-Wāḥid al-Fāsi, acted as secretary for the delegation. The administration of native affairs
at Fez did not permit Ḥaj Omar 'Abd al-Jalîl, Muḥammad
al-Wazzāni, and myself to accompany the delegation, notwithstanding the fact that we had been elected to it.

The delegation was received in audience by His Majesty,
to whom it presented the aforementioned demands. The
leader of the delegation, Ibn al-Qurashi, delivered a moving speech which brought tears to the eyes of the King. The
delegates stayed for a few days in Rabat where the citizens
accorded them a most enthusiastic welcome and expressed
their full support for the cause. Finally, the authorities
ordered the delegation to return to Fez. As soon as it arrived there, Ḥaj Muḥammad ibn 'Abd al-Salām al-Ḥulu, al-
Wazzāni, 'Abd al-'Azîz ibn Idrîs, al-Hāshimi al-Filāli, myself, and several other leaders of the movement were
thrown into jail.

In the face of this provocative challenge to representatives
of the people, the city observed a general strike and violent
demonstrations were staged for ten days on end. Violent
clashes occurred between the demonstrators and the police;
the army occupied the Qarawiyîn, the principal mosques,
and the main streets of the city. A state of emergency was
proclaimed and hundreds of citizens were detained. I was
exiled with seven other friends to the town of Taza; my
colleague Muhammad al-Yazîdi was locked up in the Saraghna

fortress, while 'Abd al-Salām al-Ḥulu was removed to Figig.

When the disturbances subsided two months after our arrest, the President of the French Republic decided to visit Morocco with a view to calming down tension. When he arrived in Rabat we were released from our detention in Taza, while al-Yazīdi remained in his Saraghna detention for several more months.

Repercussions in the Muslim World

The Berber Edict and the events that followed in its wake caused deep indignation throughout the Muslim world. Egypt protested vehemently against this crusading policy. As soon as Ḥaj Ḥassan abu 'Ayyād, representative of the national movement, arrived in Cairo, several important meetings were held in the course of which he exposed the real motives behind the Berber policy. The Muslim Youth Association and the Society for Muslim Guidance sent protests, while the 'Ulemas of al-Azhar University strongly condemned the measure in a memorandum to King Fu'ād I. Various public bodies presented memoranda to foreign embassies, while the Society for Muslim Guidance formed a special committee for the purpose of safeguarding the Islam of the Berbers. The committee succeeded in opening branches in India, Java, and other parts of the Muslim world. In the face of this avalanche of popular protests, the French embassies in Cairo and in Java attempted to camouflage the reality of the case. The two ambassadors claimed that France had done nothing prejudicial to Islam in Morocco. Abu 'Ayyād, however, was quick to answer this denial in the talks he gave at various Arab clubs.

North African students in France did their duty towards this cause; they organized several public gatherings and distributed numerous pamphlets. They also composed two tracts, one entitled 'Āṣifah fi Marākish" (a storm in Morocco) and the other, "Akhtā' al-Siyāsah al-Barbarīyah" (errors of the Berber policy), both of which were later translated into Arabic and published in Cairo by the "Eastern Committee for Defense of al-Maghrib". When the General Islamic Congress was held in Jerusalem, our Kutlah selected al-Makki al-Nāṣiri to represent it. The Kutlah of the North selected Ḥaj Muḥammad Benūnah as its delegate. The two delegates presented to the Congress a report on the colonial situation in Morocco which was later elaborated and published in a book "Faransa wa Siyāsatuha al-Barbarīyah" (France and her Berber policy). The two delegates were elected to membership of the Congress's executive committee.

In short, this battle marked a new milestone in the nationalist struggle both inside and outside the country. The Muslim world was alerted to the cause of the Far Maghrib and was informed of the colonial conspiracies against religion and Arabism. The late Amir Shakīb Arslān played an important part in unveiling this policy before Arab public opinion; as soon as he knew of what was being hatched in Morocco he made a quick visit to the Khalīfīyah Zone [Spanish Morocco]. The French ordered him out of Tangier after forbidding him entry into the Sultānīyah Zone [French Morocco].

Our friend Omar showed a deep understanding of the issues involved in the crisis when he wrote in Maghrib magazine: "In our resistance to the Berber policy we aim to bring closer together and then unite the groups composing the Maghrib nation; we want to fight the Machiavellian principle of division, which the military as well as the religious representatives of France are astutely fomenting; we want to prevent the creation of two blocs having two different cultures and conflicting interests artificially created; we want to secure freedom of conscience and of thought to all our citizens."

Thus, the new liberation movement was begun and Kutlat al-'Amal al-Waṭani (the bloc of national action) came into being.

Chapter IV

THE NATIONAL ACTION BLOC (KUTLAT AL-'AMAL AL-WAṬANI) AND THE NATIONALIST PARTY (AL-ḤIZB AL-WAṬANI)

Neither the widespread popular demonstrations nor the avalanche of protests from all parts of the Muslim world caused France to modify or abandon her Berber policy; on the contrary the French authorities became more obdurate in their resistance to all manifestations of national consciousness among the Moroccan people. The nationalists, therefore, organized themselves into a bloc in order to coordinate and direct the nationalist movement. The "Kutlah" believed that its primary duty should be both to inform public opinion in France and elsewhere and to alert and prepare the people of Morocco for the burden of struggle. Consequently, Morocco witnessed new forms and tactics of nationalist activity hitherto unknown. Pamphlets were posted on the walls or distributed by the thousands in various parts of the country; nationalist songs and slogans were taught in popular forms to the masses; valuable dissertations dealing with the Berbers, their contribution to Islam, their leading historical figures, and their glorious achievements were prepared and published; in addition to this an intensive campaign was launched advocating a boycott of French goods and their replacement by Maghrib and Arab manufactures. The campaign achieved considerable success; local Maghrib textiles which had hitherto lagged behind on the market became the most popular attire; many gave up consumption of tea and sugar because they were imported from France; a wave of austerity spread throughout the nation; the women of Morocco played their full part by preferring the simple dresses of local manufacture to the fancier and more fashionable dresses from France.

The authorities attempted to counteract this nationalist wave by pressure and propaganda, but failed. What disturbed the French most was the spread of the campaign to Berber areas and the manifestly strong awakening of national consciousness even among the shepherds. The Berbers were deeply moved by developments and were making preparations for a showdown in defense of their religion and their convictions.

In 1932 the Kutlah decided to issue a French-language magazine in Paris. The magazine named Maghrib (Morocco) was supervised by Aḥmad Bla Freej (Balāfrīj), presently secretary-general of the Independence Party. He managed to rally support for the magazine particularly from the ranks of liberal French leftists.

The magazine carried articles by Moroccan nationalists as well as by French contributors, expounding the aims of the nationalist movement and the hopes it placed in French democracy. It launched daring attacks against the misdoings of the French authorities in Morocco, giving facts and figures on the policies of racial discrimination pursued by the protectorate regime. It became a meeting place for a number of French deputies and pressmen who soon afterwards called themselves the "friends of Morocco". They were also joined by liberal Spaniards who supported Northern Morocco in its demands upon Spanish colonialism.

The launching of the magazine was received with uneasiness by the Residency-General. An order was issued forbidding its entry into Morocco, but its supporters in Paris were quick to intervene with the French Foreign Ministry for a lifting of the ban.

The Kutlah decided to issue another French-language newspaper in Fez, named "'Amal al-Sha'b" (the people's work), because the tyrants of the protectorate regime had not till then permitted the issuing of an Arabic-language publication. The newspaper, like its counterpart in Paris, gave expression to the views and aims of the Moroccan people. One of its most important campaigns consisted of a series of articles by Omar 'Abd al-Jalīl depicting the horrors of rural colonization and the misery into which the indigenous farmer had been reduced as a result of that policy. The campaign was successful in mitigating the scope and slowing down the rate of land sequestration for the benefit of colonizers. This caused a furor among colonists; they shaved off their heads and demonstrated in Rabat, but their agitation did not succeed in stemming the tide of resistance to their colonial machinations.

At the same time we decided, in cooperation with our brethren in the Northern Zone, to start a number of newspapers in Arabic. Da'ūd founded a magazine by the name of "al-Salām" (peace), devoted to the cause of genuine national awakening while the Kutlah of the North started a newspaper "al-Ḥayāh" (life) to serve as its organ in Arabic.

Naturally, these newspapers tackled the problems of all parts of Morocco; they were widely read in both North and South and received directives from the Kutlah leaders of the two zones.

In addition to organizing these press campaigns, the Kutlah asked me to deliver public talks in the Qarawiyīn mosque (university). My first talk was devoted to an analysis of the life of the Prophet and the early history of Islam. I made a comparison between the condition of the Muslims in the past and their condition in the present, giving the reasons for the greatness of the former and the backwardness of the latter. The lectures were attended not only by students and the cultured elite but also by thousands of ordinary men and women, who found in them a stimulant to reflection, hitherto wanting in the traditional religious sermons.

Without my being presumptuous or boastful, it is fair to state that these lectures achieved a notable success in disseminating a progressive and sound understanding of the nationalist cause among the masses. They also indoctrinated the educated youths in the true principles of nationalism and the Salafīyah.

The administration perceived in these lessons daily political demonstrations which could not be allowed to continue. Several attempts were made to ban the gatherings, but there was always the delicate issue of their religious association and surrounding. The administration, therefore, had to move slowly and with reticence. Since the authorities did not venture an outright ban they searched for a way to achieve their purpose in the name of His Majesty the King, in his capacity as the religious head of Morocco. They made use of their henchmen from among the religious impostors, who wrote a number of petitions accusing me of casting aspersions on their venerated saints and of vilifying some of their Sufi dogmas. The staunch defense put up on my behalf before the higher council of the Qarawiyīn University by Sheikh Muḥammad ibn al-'Arabi al-'Alawi foiled their attempts on no less than twenty-four occasions. His Majesty refused to issue any ban on the lectures in spite of the persistent efforts of the Residency-General and political bureau.

Meanwhile, evidences began to accumulate on the success of our movement. These included a royal decree forbidding all parades by the 'Issāwīyah, the Ḥamdūshīyah, and other Sufi orders. The nation's vitality and desire for development and progress were demonstrated in the popular celebrations which greeted this royal order.

The boycott of French goods was extended to include cigarettes in retaliation against the French tobacco company which had fired hundreds of Moroccan workers on account of their nationalist convictions. The boycott succeeded to such an extent that the company was forced to take back all the dismissed workers. In spite of this conciliatory move and the arrest of one hundred youths who had been advocating this idea to the people, the boycott continued uninterrupted.

During the latter part of August 1933 I made visits to Tangier and to Tetuan. The National Kutlah in Northern Morocco gave a reception for me during which speeches were delivered by my friends 'Abd al-Khāliq al-Tarrīss, Ḥaj Muḥammad Benūnah, and other nationalist leaders. In reply, I delivered an impromptu speech in which I expounded the aims of our movement, namely the liberation of Morocco and the attainment of independence through progress. I pointed out that in the field of internal reforms preference should be given to three things: the school, the factory, and the newspaper.

The Spanish authorities were displeased with the criticisms levelled against them in the course of my speech. They were not happy to see me stand up in Tetuan and declare the unity of purpose for which the nationalists of North and South had been working in concert. Three secret policemen were ordered to follow me wherever I went; three days after the reception I left with my companion Da'ūd on a brief visit to Ceuta, in the hope of returning to Tetuan and thence to Tangier on my way back to Fez to resume my lectures at the Qarawiyīn. On my return the same day, however, I was told by the customs officials that an order had been issued by the Spanish Residency-General banning my entry into the zone under its protectorate. Thereupon, we returned to

Ceuta and thence to Algeciras where we boarded a ship for Tangier. Upon my arrival in Tangier a friend from Fez approached me with a message from our nationalist colleagues in that city.

The message informed me that the Kutlah had intercepted a cable from Paris endorsing my arrest and my detention in a spot to be selected by the Residency-General. The Kutlah, the message added, had met and decided that my arrest would undoubtedly touch off violent demonstrations, which in the circumstances were contrary to the best interests of the cause; therefore, it asked me to proceed to Paris pending further developments. The following morning I left Tangier for Gibraltar and then went to Spain where I was joined by the late Ḥaj 'Abd al-Salām Bennunah and his brother Ḥaj Muḥammad. In Spain we established contacts with various circles and groups and presented a critique of Spanish policies respecting their zone of occupation in Morocco. I also submitted a memorandum to the Morocco department attached to the office of the prime minister, protesting Spain's attitude in my case and the highhanded manner in which Señor Moles, the Resident-General, had turned down the cable of protest sent to him by our brethren in Tetuan. The Spanish Government thereupon relieved the Resident-General of his duties and permitted me to return to the Spanish Zone.

My stay in Paris lasted seven months and was characterized by intensive activity, in cooperation with Bla-Freej and his friends of the "Maghrib" magazine committee and also with the North African Muslim Students' Association headed by Muḥammad al-Fāsi. We organized several conferences and public gatherings, whose protests and resolutions were echoed in the entire French press. The movement was partly instrumental in the removal of the French Resident-General M. Lucien Saint and his replacement by M. Ponsot. It also contributed to a coordination of effort between Tunisia's Dustūr movement, the Etoile Nord Africaine of Algeria, and the Moroccan Kutlah of National Action. I was permitted to return to Morocco to resume my lecturing at Qarawīyīn.

Return Home

After a seven-month sojourn in Paris, the Residency-General notified me, through its office in the French capital and in the presence of Qaddūr ibn Ghibrīṭ, that it no longer objected to my return to Morocco and the resumption of my lecturing at Qarawiyīn. Three days later I left for Madrid where I renewed contacts with Spanish official and non-official circles and particularly with the democrats, who had in the meantime established an Arab center in Madrid in cooperation with Muḥammad al-Fāsi (presently director of Qarawiyīn) and al-Makki al-Nāṣiri. The aim of the center was to work for Spanish-Arab rapprochement. Señor Rico Avello, director of the prime minister's Morocco office, to whom I had submitted my memorandum on my earlier visit to Madrid, informed me that he had been appointed Resident-General for the Khalīfīyah (Spanish) Zone and that he was contemplating a broader and more liberal policy than that of Señor Moles, the outgoing Resident. When news of Señor Moles' removal reached Tetuan, the Kutlah of the North formed a delegation consisting of Ḥaj 'Abd al-Salām Benūnah and 'Abd al-Khāliq al-Ṭarrīs to establish contacts with the new Resident-General in Madrid and to urge upon him the need for a more prudent policy in the interests of both sides.

I returned to Tangier in January 1934, where I found Colonel Benazet, director of native affairs in Morocco, waiting to see me; he informed me that he had been sent in the name of His Majesty the Sultan and of the Resident-General to explore ways and means of reconciling the views of the protectorate and of the nationalists.

The discussions, in which Colonel Truchet, controller of the Mekhzen valis in Tangier participated, lasted for three days, with a six-hour meeting daily. The discussions covered a wide range of subjects concerning the nationalist cause and our demands for reforms; Colonel Truchet referred back every important issue to Rabat for instructions before making any commitments. In the course of the talks he offered me the portfolio of justice in the Sheriffian Government; I declined the offer stating that I could not accept any post so long as Moroccan officials remained mere executive tools, without authority. The policy of M. Ponsot, the then Resident-General, was relatively more appreciative of the nationalist leaders, whose cooperation with the French administration he earnestly sought. As part of the policy, the post of deputy director-general for rural affairs was offered to our friend Ḥaj Omar 'Abd al-Jalīl. He in turn declined the offer.

At the conclusion of the "Platonic" talks, which were merely exploratory in their nature, I returned to Morocco where I found a flourishing nationalist movement.

A few days after my arrival I was invited to an audience with His Majesty the Sultan which lasted for one hour. This was the first time that a nationalist leader had been granted the privilege of a meeting with the King. The audience was intended to disprove reports, circulated by the French, of nationalist opposition to the King and of His Majesty's alleged disapproval of the existing liberation movement. I found in the person of Sidi Muḥammad ibn Yūsuf a great monarch, whose greatness was later to unfold in the desperate struggle he has been maintaining--with courage, fortitude, confidence and nobility of soul--in the cause of his people and the independence of the country. When I explained to His Majesty the aims of our movement, he expressed full support for every endeavor that would enhance the prosperity and the progress of the country. His Majesty added: "The loss of rights we have incurred was caused by the inexperience of the former responsible authorities in the sound methods of statecraft; from now on the country will suffer no further losses and I shall strive to recover what has already been lost."

M. Tardieu had meanwhile formed a new French government with the addition of a new portfolio for what he called "France Overseas". His Majesty informed me that he had protested to the French Foreign Ministry against this cabinet innovation and that as a result of the royal protest the proposed cabinet portfolio had been cancelled.

A Royal Anniversary Feast

I stated earlier that the French had been trying to drive a wedge between the nationalists and the King. When I left for France to escape arrest, they strove to convince the Palace that I had been sent by the National Bloc to negotiate with a view to restoring Mawlay 'Abd al-Ḥafīẓ to the throne of Morocco. Although the King is wiser than to believe such petty intrigues, the Kutlah did not stand with hands folded in the face of this French attempt. It decided to give a practical demonstration of the nationalists' true feelings towards their illustrious King and also to expose the double-dealing of the French in this affair. The Kutlah came forward with a sound idea, namely to set November 18, the day of Sidi Muḥammad's accession to the throne, as a royal anniversary feast. On the assigned day the country celebrated the occasion to the consternation of the Residency-General. The French were anxious to prevent the festival but did not dare to do so. The nationalists did not succeed in making the occasion an official feast although the anniversary was recognized as such in the following year (1934). Thus, the Kutlah's unswerving loyalty to the King was demonstrated beyond any shadow of doubt; it was made apparent to all that the colonial power alone stood in the way of any manifestation of popular sentiment, even in the form of a royal anniversary feast. On May 8, 1934 the King was scheduled to make his annual visit to the city of Fez. The nationalists made preparations to accord him a tumultous welcome in the spiritual capital of his realm. Arches of triumph were erected in the main thoroughfares; lavish decorations were set up, and Moroccan flags and emblems were hoisted in all parts of the city. A special song was composed for the occasion, expressing the nation's high hopes in His Majesty for the attainment of its national aspirations. The newspaper "Amal al-Sha'b" published a special issue carrying the pictures of the King and of the Crown Prince, to whom it gave the title of "Amīr al-Aṭlas" (prince of Atlas). When His Majesty arrived, the vast throngs broke into tumultuous applause joined with national chantings.

The following day His Majesty was scheduled, in accordance with traditions, to pay visits to the Qarawiyīn and to a number of venerated mausoleums. Customarily these royal visits take a purely civil form, that is, without the accompaniment of royal guards, troops, or any other manifestation of militarism, out of deference for the saints and the national heroes to whose mausoleums the visits are made. By established usage the king is accompanied only by his ministers and the staff of the royal palace. Naturally, contact between the people and their king is made much easier under such circumstances; the Fez populace formed large and enthusiastic throngs around the King, reiterating the nation's hopes in His Majesty for restoration of the country's lost rights. These were truly impressive nationalist demonstrations; the King was evidently pleased and his unassuming and democratic bearing endeared him even mor in the hearts of his loyal subjects.

Our French friends, however, saw in these simple popular demonstrations an encroashment upon the rights of Fran and an aspersion on her dignity. They were loathe to see His Majesty for the third time surrounded by his people, openly demanding freedom and independence. The French governor of the Fez area, General Marquis, wished to prevent the King from saying his Friday prayers on May 10 at the Qarawiyīn mosque, in accordance with the royal itinera He claimed that the demonstrators on their way back had passed by his residence shouting anti-French slogans; he also alleged that a youth had assaulted a Jewish shopkeeper for hoisting a French flag and had trampled the flag under his feet. On the evening of May 9 M. Helleu, Deputy Resident-General--M. Ponsot the Resident had been in Paris--came to Fez where he presided over a conference of militar and civil officials. The conferees decided to inform the King of their indignation over the incident and request him to order arrest of the National Bloc leaders. They also requested the King either to cancel his scheduled Friday prayers at the Qarawiyīn or permit the authorities to statior two tight cordons of troops along the way to the mosque.

The Deputy Resident-General, accompanied by the governor of the Fez area, called at the royal palace and communicated to the King certain demands on the occasion of his visit to Fez. His Majesty rejected outright their deman for arrest of the Kutlah leaders while promising to reconsider his scheduled Friday prayers at the Qarawiyīn.

When the French representatives left the palace, the Kin called his Council of Ministers to a meeting to consider the French demands. He was deeply upset and in a determined mood to accept a headlong and final collision with the Frenc The ministers, however, prevailed upon him to leave Fez altogether on Friday morning in protest against the behavio of the French and before completing the official program of the royal visit. This was decided upon because the King could not possibly have cancelled his Friday prayers at Qarawiyīn; if, on the other hand, French troops were permitted to take up positions along the route to the mosque they might seize the opportunity to commit dastardly acts against the inhabitants, as they are all too often prone to do

It was also feared that if the King turned down the proposed stationing of troops the French administration might direct some of its stooges to commit a crime against His Majesty, or some other crime much more serious than the early incidents which had brought about the crisis.

His Majesty returned to Rabat, and the Kutlah sent a cable to the palace expressing its unflinching loyalty to His Majesty and its solidarity with him. The Kutlah also published a special issue of its newspaper "'Amal al-Sha'b" in which it revealed the facts about the events of May 10.

On May 14 His Majesty summoned the Kutlah leaders who had signed the cable to an audience, for talks on a number of important questions. We met with the Council of Ministers in the presence of the chief of the Royal Cabinet; he informed us that the King had authorized him to state that he had not left the city of Fez in anger, as tendentious rumors would have had it; he had left Fez out of concern for the safety of his subjects and lest harm should befall them at the hands of the colonial power. After a broad survey of outstanding public issues, all ministers expressed their support for the country's aspirations. They told us that the cooperation of everyone was essential for the triumph of the cause and the restoration of Morocco's sovereignty.

In the face of this royal attitude, the French authorities did not find a way to retaliate against the Kutlah except by suspension of its paper "Amal al-Sha'b", and by banning the entry into Morocco of its Maghrib magazine published in Paris. The authorities also prohibited circulation of "al-Salām" magazine and "al-Ḥayāh" newspaper, both published by the Kutlah of the North (Spanish Zone).

Thus, the nationalist movement was deprived of all the means for propagating its principles; the movement, however, devised new avenues for expression, foremost of which were the evening lessons, which did not cease during my absence in Paris. The lessons were conducted by my friend Ḥaj Ḥassan abu'Ayyād and 'Abd al-'Azīz ibn Idrīs until an order was issued forbidding their continuation. I resumed the lessons upon my return and the listening audience was greater than ever before; the pressure of the authorities, however, became more intense. The administration for native affairs, not satisfied with its regular spies, directed the clerks of the Sharī'ah courts to attend the meetings officially and to record minutes of the lessons; the minutes had to be endorsed by the cadi (judge) in accordance with procedural law, and the witnesses were summoned to interrogations by the administration. This was a form of censorship which Napoleon had devised to control the work of universities. I submitted repeated protests against this practice and the French eventually requested the Sheriffian Government to order a discontinuation of the lessons. His Majesty the King insisted on refusing to grant the French request. Finally, the French made use of the opportunity presented by the incidents of February 6, 1934, in the course of which clashes occurred between the Croix de Feu and the leftist parties in France, and a military order was telephoned to the Sheikh of the Qarawiyīn forbidding the lessons.

Concurrently with these press campaigns and nationalist agitation, the Kutlah maintained a close watch over the day-to-day activities of the administration; when the French officials struck work demanding better conditions, it utilized the occasion to urge their replacement by competent nationals; it also demanded that the French treasury should be made to bear the extra allowances for French officials in colonial territories; further, it demanded that the Moroccan budget should not be burdened with the costs of the military occupation. In short, the Kutlah maintained a critical and vigilant watch over the financial and economic abuses of the protectorate, based as they are on exploitation and racial discrimination.

Program for Moroccan Reforms

The nationalist movement had turned during this period to the task of criticizing the policies of the protectorate in all their ramifications; at the same time it strove for internal reforms and for betterment of the lot of the people. Naturally, this led to a critical evaluation of France's performance in Morocco against a background of the promises to which she had pledged her honor and reputation. The protectorate, forcibly imposed upon Morocco, had been claiming that its sole purpose was to help Morocco along the road to progress, without prejudice to its unique national attributes and sovereignty, and with full respect for her religion and mores. Lyautey, defining the purposes of the protectorate, declared in 1920 that it was a system whereby the country safeguards its own institutions and manages its own affairs, subject only to European supervision. Such a system, he added, was in contradistinction to a system of direct rule.

The policies pursued by the protectorate, however, were direct rule wholly incompatible with mere supervision and guidance. Thus, it was the primary task of the nationalist movement to remind the French themselves of the need for discontinuing this direct rule, which contravenes the basis of the protectorate itself. Mere criticisms of the policies pursued by the protectorate, however, appeared to many Frenchmen as a negative attitude, reflecting no more than a dissatisfaction with the existing regime; it did not spell out an alternative course of action to replace the old. The French had accused the Moroccan nationalists of fomenting agitation for things they themselves could not define in concrete terms. The Kutlah decided to counteract French accusations by drawing up a reform program for the transition phase prior to independence. We drafted the program for Moroccan reforms, otherwise known as the "Demands of the Maghrib People". The program was submitted to His Majesty the King at his palace in Casablanca, on November 1934, by a Kutlah delegation consisting of Muḥammad Ghāzi, Aḥmad al-Sharqāwi, 'Abd al-'Azīz ibn Idrīs, and Abu Bakr al-Qādiri. A delegation, consisting of 'Alāl al-Fāsi, Muḥammad al-Yazīdi, and Muḥammad al-Duyūri, presented the program to the Residency-General at Rabat, while a third Kutlah delegation, comprised of Omar 'Abd al-Jalīl and Muḥammad al-Wazzāni, submitted the program to the French Foreign Ministry in Paris.

The Kutlah delegation in Paris succeeded in forming a committee of patronage from among friends of "al-Maghrib" magazine and other leftist politicians who had shown sympathy with our program and appreciation of its libertarian and progressive spirit.

The program comprised fifteen sections as follows:

1. Political reforms
2. Individual and public freedoms
3. Maghrib citizenship
4. Judicial reforms
5. Social reforms

6. Islamic waqfs
7. Public health and social relief
8. Labor affairs
9. Economic and financial reforms
10. Colonization and Moroccan agriculture
11. Legislation regarding immovable urban ownership
12. Taxation
13. Miscellaneous reforms
14. Arabic as the official language of the country
15. The Moroccan flag, official feasts, and protocol

Each of these sections detailed numerous provisions for reform of the state apparatus and the nation.

The main outlines of the program were as follows:

1. Application of the protectorate treaty and the abrogation of all manifestations of direct rule.

2. The unification of the administrative and the judicial systems throughout Morocco.

3. The appointment and promotion of Moroccans in all branches of the Maghrib administration.

4. Separation of the powers and jurisdictions vested in the caids and the pashas respectively.

5. The establishment of municipalities, regional council chambers of commerce, and a national assembly comprising Muslim and Jewish deputies.

The program was based on the assumption that the protectorate regime is not intended to preclude Moroccan self-government. Therefore, the Kutlah devoted the preamble to an exposition of this thesis from both the legal and the diplomatic angles. One of the arguments put forward in the preamble, in support of the case for self-government, was derived from a decision of the French court of appeals, handed down on April 13, 1924. The decision stated, in par "The treaty laid down between France and al-Maghrib al-Aqsa pertaining to a French protectorate over the Sheriffian Kingdom does not have the effect of depriving al-Maghrib of self-government."

The reform program was characterized by a democratic orientation based upon respect for individual and public freedoms and an interest in social development for the family and for Maghrib society as a whole.

As regards the constitutional provisions of the program, it must be emphasized that the proposed national assembly was not proposed by the Kutlah as anything more than a preliminary phase towards a genuine constitutional government. Therefore, although the proposed assembly was empowered to present bills, to prepare its own agenda, and to exercise control and supervision over all governmental functions, yet the final power in the assembly was vested in the king. It also retained ministerial responsibility in His Majesty, in accordance with traditional practice. In this sense, it was similar to the constitution drawn up by the National Assembly during the Riff war; but it did not reflect all our aspirations for a full-fledged constitutional system of government. The reason for the dichotomy between program and aspiration is to be found in the belief of the Kutlah that it is necessary to follow a gradualist course in the demand for and the application of democracy. The Kutlah also believed that the people could wrest their rights by a reciprocal developmental process in the relationships between king and people, together with training in the ways of democracy through participation in municipal and regional councils.

Moreover, the question of overriding importance to us in that period was the termination of direct French rule and the restoration of authority to the king and his government; we were convinced that the constitutional issue would be easy to solve once it became a matter between us and our king, devoid of foreign obstructions.

In the preamble to the program the Kutlah declared: "This program is but a reiteration of what the people had demanded on various occasions; it is derived from the collection of petitions and subsidiary complaints submitted on various occasions to His Majesty the Sultan and his government." The preamble added: "Before drafting it in its final form, the Kutlah contacted the various strata of society both in towns and in the countryside with a view to ascertaining the wishes and the views of the people. In addition to that, the Kutlah received numerous messages, expressing the country's urgent need for a sound system capable of preserving the rights and the interests of the Moroccans both as individuals and as a nation, and of leading them along the right path of progress."

The Residency-General succinctly expressed the contents of the program when it stated in its report to the "Mediterranean Committee": "The role of the protectorate should be circumscribed within the sphere of technical assistance, in accordance with the national reform program, until such time as Morocco is able to govern herself."

The reform program was an ingenious strategem to reco cile the existing treaties with the interests of the country. In the economic section, for example, the Kutlah advocates the open-door policy and free trade, in accordance with the resolutions of Algeciras Conference. This platform was de signed to appeal to the support of the left-wing parties in France and to the signatories of the Algeciras international conference; at the same time, it was agreeable to the best interests of Morocco under the circumstances. As long as Morocco did not possess industries capable of competing with foreign goods, the open-door policy was more palatabl than a system of protection because it affords importers a chance to compete for local consumers with the best and cheapest available goods on the world market. This natural lessens the amount of national expenditure needed for purchases from abroad if the open-door were not operative, as is the case in Tunisia. At the same time, the program demanded protection for old Moroccan industries against competition from without as well as from within, where large-scale modern enterprises pose a threat to the survival of these small-scale industries. This limited demand for protection does not conflict with the provisions of Algeciras Treaty; all that the Treaty imposes upon us is the application of the most favored nation clause to all, that is, equality of treatment. By advocating protection for national industries from all foreign competition without discrimination, the program conflicted with neither the letter nor the spirit of the Treaty. The program took cognizance of the fact that protection for local industry could not be maintaine indefinitely; it therefore urged a program for modernizatio of old industries so that they could meet demands of local consumers and carve out a market for their surplus produc abroad.

The reform movement also advocated the nationalization of mines, oil resources, railways, electric power stations, and port installations; this was naturally in the national interest of Moroccans, considering the fact that local capital was inadequate for the exploitation of the country's natural resources to their own benefit. Its seizure by foreign capit would inevitably result in foreign ownership of our national wealth. An outright closed-door policy through nationalization was agreeable to the leftists in France; the protectorate regime could not in good logic reject it, because it was the only way to extricate Morocco from the competition of the foreign states provided for in the Algeciras Treaty; that competition was regarded as anathema by France and a threat to her influence in Morocco. Anyone who studies our program carefully can find many examples of these intricate strategems in the presentation of our demands and the adjustment of our needs.

This method of approach secured us the help of many leading Frenchmen; it also explains the support of the left-wing parties; that support, though exclusively moral, was a help to us in traversing this phase of our movement.

The announcement of the Maghrib people's program had far-reaching repercussions in French and Moroccan circles. The French Government instructed the Residency-General to study the program and give its comments and observations. The Residency in turn assigned the topics to the various competent departments in the administration. We have seen the replies and comments of several of the departments. They highly commended its accurate and imaginative proposals. The department of health, for example, approved of the entire section in the program on health and social relief, commenting that it was the least that should be done for the Moroccans in the field of health. Thus, we were able to place the working of the protectorate regime on the discussion table and to tell the French themselves that there was a sound system of government which they had failed to conceive or did not wish to conceive on account of bad faith. The program remained largely ink on paper, and only a few of its minor provisions were implemented in spite of the laborious studies and the initial favorable reception that greeted its publication.

The real attitude of the protectors was perhaps never better expressed than by M. Girardin, former adviser to His Majesty the Sultan. He said to me: "Your demands consist of three parts: the first part can be implemented now; the second may be implemented, but only after a while; as to the third, it can never be implemented because we have no intention of voluntarily pulling out of Morocco."

The Issue of French Representation

The French do not intend to withdraw from Morocco of their own accord; they want to work diligently for the consolidation of their influence in the country by all possible means. In pursuance of this policy they denied the Moroccans the right to set up a house of representatives with powers of supervision over the administration's handling of financial and economic affairs; at the same time, and in violation of all their obligations and pledges, they establish a system of representation for the French community in Morocco. Although the system was never accepted by the Moroccan people or approved by His Majesty the King, it has remained in being and has been used as a precedent by the French community for demanding a sort of French parliament within Morocco.

A controversy flared up in November 1935 between the Resident-General, M. Ponsot, and the representatives of the third French district, in the course of which the French representatives demanded what they called democratic right for Morocco. Naturally, the national Kutlah came forward once more in defense of Moroccan sovereignty; it demanded a dissolution of these French organizations which have no right to exist in a non-French country. In accordance with its reform program, the Kutlah urged the establishment of a national assembly consisting solely of Moroccans.

The French chambers of commerce and agriculture, together with representatives of the third electoral district, met early in December 1935 and decided by unanimous vote on a policy of non-cooperation with the Residency. The con ferees claimed that the adoption by the administration of important decisions concerning economic and social policie without prior consultation with them, was indicative of the administration's intention to dispense with their participation in the work of the committees and councils.

The conference, therefore, presented the following demands:

1. Convening of the higher councils for trade and agriculture at regular intervals, and the submission to them of all proposed legislation relating to commerce and agricultu

2. Establishment of a higher council for the third electoral district, as is the case for commerce and agriculture, with similar rights and jurisdiction.

3. That the government consultative council (French) should meet at least once every three months after the meetings of the higher councils; that all legislative proposals, other than those pertaining to general policy and sovereignty, should be submitted forthwith to the council, together with all questions still pending before the higher councils.

4. That the purely advisory powers of the government consultative council should be widened to include the right of decision in all that pertains to the budget, save those items which relate to political expenditures and sovereign power.

The French protest conference set up a committee to follow up its demands; it also drafted a program for economic reforms for presentation to the Residency, together with its conditions for resumption of cooperation.

In the face of these developments, the Kutlah cabled on December 14 and 18, 1935 strong protests to His Majesty the Sultan, the Residency, the French Foreign Minister, the President of the Republic, and the chairman of the House and Senate Foreign Relations Committees, against these flagrant encroachments by French colonists upon the natural rights of the Moroccan people. The Kutlah urged dissolution of the French councils in their place; the Kutlah also demanded the formation of a French-Moroccan technical committee to study the proper means for actualizing the demands of the Moroccan people.

The reply of the Foreign Minister to the French committee contained the following declaration: "The French Government is not unmindful of the economic and social conditions of the French residents in Morocco or of the subjects of the Sultan; whereas it has received several proposals through the Residency-General, it is determined to announce in the future, through the Residency, a number of measures designed to give new evidence of France's concern for the well-being of Morocco."

As soon as the Kutlah received the text of the declaration it cabled new protests in January 1936. The Kutlah demanded the realization of the people's demands and condemned the claims of the French councils to speak in the name of the

Moroccan people. The French Government was warned against the adoption of any measures in violation of Moroccan sovereignty.

In the same month of January, the deputy chairman of the Senate Foreign Relations Committee was sent to Morocco in order to investigate for the committee the causes of the existing conflict. A delegation from the Kutlah presented to him the Moroccan case, substantiated by the relevant documentation.

On January 15, 1936 the Foreign Relations Committee of the French House of Representatives [sic] held a lengthy hearing on the dispute, during which representatives of the French community in Morocco as well as of the Kutlah presented their respective cases. At the same time we submitted a second memorandum to His Majesty with a copy to the French adviser. The Ṣadr al-A'zam [prime minister] informed us that the Sheriffian Government was in accord with us that the French had no right to representation in Morocco in whatever form. His Majesty the Sultan asked his French adviser to inform the French Government that acquiescence in the demands of the colonists would constitute a betrayal of France's pledges and obligations. His Majesty made it clear that he could not approve of the colonists' demands and threatened to abdicate the throne if his views were not heeded.

The Moroccan point of view is that the French residents in Morocco, like all other foreign residents, have no claims to rights, which belong solely to Moroccan citizens. The existence of a protectorate does not mean that our country has become French territory. The treaty imposing the protectorate, construed in its broadest connotations, is nothing more than a contract between the Sheriffian state and the French state; relations between the two states have been and should continue to be conducted through ordinary diplomatic channels. The people of Morocco have nothing to do with the French Government, nor do the French people have anything to do with the Government of Morocco. The establishment of French representation on Moroccan councils means usurpation by French citizens of popular sovereignty which is the inalienable right of Moroccans and no one else.

If France had instituted a system of mixed representation in Tunisia and Algeria, she did so over the opposition of the

Tunisian and the Algerians. Moreover, the Tunisian-Algerian experiment is inapplicable in our country since we have rejected it from the very first day of its inception and since our king has consistently refused to endorse it.

France is duty-bound under the provisions of the protectorate to respect the Moroccan constitution and the rights of the people and the sovereign; any act, therefore, which is at variance with these principles constitutes a violation even of the protectorate itself, which had been imposed against our wills.

Even though we are not bound by the provisions of treaties which had usurped our rights and which we had been forced to sign under military and political duress, France is bound by obligations to us voluntarily contracted; she has no right to alter the treaty provisions except in the direction of granting greater independence to Morocco. That is to say, she can waive some of the things she has forcibly obtained, but she cannot acquire rights over and above the treaty provisions.

Marshal Lyautey stressed this fact in a statement in which he declared: "There is another point which we cannot ignore, namely, the underlying principle of the protectorate; I have carried with me from Paris an explicit assurance, made by those most competent to speak, that the fundamental principle of the protectorate must remain outside the realm of controversy; the protectorate regime is not a personal or a local or a French concern; it is a fact embodied in treaties and guaranteed by international agreements, and it is not within the power of any one of us or of the French Government to ignore this. The conclusion to be drawn is that Morocco is an independent state which France protects, but which remains under the sovereignty of the Sultan and has its own independent constitution; one of the primary duties is to safeguard the integrity of this system and to respect this constitution. As a result of this status quo," the Marshal went on to assert, "French political organizations have no legitimacy in Morocco; it is possible for French citizens to set up a number of bodies and a form of technical representation, but it is not possible to accord them political representation; demands and argumentations over this issue are but ink on paper and a waste of time." Lyautey recalled the fact that the constitution of Morocco had been guaranteed by international treaties, and he described demands for French political representation as not only devoid of any practical content but as dangerous in the extreme. The French Government, he concluded, would be the first to resist such overtures.

Marshal Lyautey gave this statement after World War I, when the French demanded representation in Morocco in the face of Mawlay Yūsuf's unequivocal opposition. Lyautey's statement was intended to reassure the people of Morocco and their king of France's fidelity to her pledges. In spite of this, the French did in fact establish representative councils without the approval of the Sultan or of his government. If these councils had not existed, the French would not have been able to cause this great furor in the hope of transforming them into something broader and more powerful. The Moroccan people, however, who had never accepted or recognized the initial step, were no less vehement in their condemnation of the new French encroachment; we shall see that this was not the last time that a violent dispute flared up between ourselves and the French over the issue of French representation.

When the controversy over the issue increased in intensity and M. Ponsot failed either to appease the French or to suppress the Moroccans, the French Government decided to relieve him of his duties as Resident-General and to set the issue aside for the time being (February 1936).

M. Peyrouton

Thus, the French Government decided to appease the French residents of Morocco by the removal of M. Ponsot and his replacement by a more popular colonial figure; this was M. Peyrouton, who as Resident-General in Tunisia has suppressed the Dustūr movement and won the favor of the colonists.

Peyrouton, in cooperation with Colonel Benazet, chief of the native administration, worked out a plan for the suppression of the Moroccan nationalists. Before leaving Marseilles for Casablanca in April 1936, he told pressmen that he was proud of having suppressed the Dustūr Party in Tunisia; he added that he would similarly suppress the National Kutlah in Morocco, and that force and violence should be the motto of French native policy in North Africa. The statement was echoed widely in all the colonial press.

Señor Moles, who was serving a second term as Spanish Resident-General in the Khalīfīyah Zone, summoned press reporters and told them that what M. Peyrouton had said expressed his Moroccan policy also. Experience, he declared, had taught him that a soft policy could merely play into the hands of nationalist agitators. Peyrouton did not content himself with words but proceeded to make a large loan for the Moroccan budget. He granted to the colonists credits which his predecessor had refused, including the sum of six million francs to a number of leading caids.

No sooner had he arrived in Rabat, however, than the government of M. Blum was formed following the victory of the French Popular Front in the May elections of the same year. The Franco revolt in the Khalīfīyah Zone took place in July of the same year. We shall deal with the attitude of the nationalist movement towards both of these events, but let us first complete the story of M. Peyrouton.

We did not wish to comment on M. Peyrouton's statements on policies; instead, we decided to arrange a meeting with him to submit our demands and then decide on the next step. After some hesitation he met us at the end of March as a delegation representing the Kutlah of National Action. In fairness, it must be said that this was the first meeting of its kind to take place between a French Resident-General and the representatives of a national political party in Morocco. Our colleague Ḥaj Omar expressed in brief terms the purpose of the visit, pointing out that it was designed to urge upon the Residency-General a speedy implementation of the people's demands. M. Peyrouton thereupon asked to speak, requesting us not to interrupt until after he had completed what he had to say. Seated on a revolving chair, he went on talking for three hours on end, with his mouth moving to right and to left in the manner of his revolving chair. He spared no foul words in disparaging the Tunisian Dustūr leaders and the leading personages of the French Popular Front; he conceded, however, that we were more sincere in our movement than the others, although he expressed the fear that we might deceive him as the Tunisians had done before.

For our part, we felt that further talk with such a crack-brained and irresponsible person was futile; all we did was to say goodbye and we went away considering how best we could repay him his due. This was an easy thing to do after he had uttered his harangue; we did no more than make a verbatim record of the minutes of the meeting, typed it out, and distributed copies to the press, the deputies, and the leading figures in the French Popular Front against whom he had poured out his vituperation. No sooner had French public opinion been advised of M. Peyrouton's statements than a great furor arose. The democratic and leftist press launched a furious campaign against the Resident-General. Simultaneously, the Kutlah came across the text of a cable, which M. Peyrouton had dispatched to the manager of the Makhzen (government) bank in Tetuan following the fascist revolt of July 1936, instructing him to pay the sum of five hundred thousand francs to the Spanish Falange. The Kutlah published the cable with a castigation of a Resident-General of the Popular Front for supporting Franco's fascism out of Moroccan government funds.

The fact is that the Kutlah decided to do everything possible to secure the removal of M. Peyrouton from his post, in view of the fact that his appointment had been made as a measure of appeasement of the French colonists and in consideration of the heinous acts he had committed against the Tunisians. A policy of solidarity with the Tunisians in opposition to Peyrouton was the only feasible course of action consonant with our national dignity and honor; moreover, we were anxious to demonstrate our ability to cause the removal of a Resident-General so that the power of the colonists would not continue to stand out as the primary threat to any Resident who attempted to curb their excesses. Therefore, we utlized every available opportunity to disparage M. Peyrouton and to depict him as a bigoted reactionary.

During this period preparations were under way for the annual meeting of the students' conference called by the North African Muslim Students' Association of France. The conference was scheduled to convene in Morocco in September 1936. The president of the Association, al-Manja Salīm, presently a member of the Dustūr Party's political bureau and one of Tunisia's most accomplished youths, came to Rabat in connection with the conference. After conferences with the Kutlah it was decided to oppose M. Peyrouton's attempts to place the conference under his patronage. The Resident-General had planned to use the conference as a forum to expound what he called his "working program" in education. After notifying us in writing and before receiving our reply, he announced a program for the conference including the inaugural meeting, the text of his proposed speech, and the reception which he was planning to give for the conferees at the Residency-General. The preparatory committee sent a message to M. Peyrouton signed by its chairman Ibrahim al-Katāni and also by al-Manja Saīm on behalf of the Students' Association, informing him that the African students did not approve of his opening the conference or of delivering the inaugural speech; M. Peyrouton, they pointed out, was a political personage while their association was purely educational and averse to involvement in politics in any way. The committee also notified the Resident that the conferees could not attend his tea party.

M. Peyrouton was incensed by this attitude and decided to disallow the conference. The Kutlah called several protest meetings and sent a cable to the Resident, informing him that his past record in Tunisia and the policies he had embarked upon in Morocco precluded any possibility of a meeting with him around the same tea table.

This was indeed harsh behavior, but it was essential for curbing Peyrouton's conceited and high-handed attitude towards our countrymen. When the French Government saw that the situation had become so tense, it decided to relieve Peyrouton of his duties and appoint General Noguès in his place.

The Spanish Civil War

Two months after the victory of the Popular Front in France and its initiation of a policy of close cooperation with the Spanish Popular Front, the Spanish army in northern Morocco mutinied under the leadership of General Franco. While Señor Moles, the Spanish Resident-General and a member of the Radical Party, was still reiterating his solidarity with M. Peyrouton and continuing his policies of repression and discrimination against the Moroccan people, the civil and military authorities turned their back on him and declared the fascist rebellion for the "liberation of Spain from red enslavement" (July 14, 1936).

The Kutlah of the North had been aware of the conspiracy

that was brewing in the zone against the Spanish Republic. It was fearful that a military coup d'état might undermine still further the rights and interests of the Moroccan people. A delegation was sent to Madrid to warn of the serious situation that was developing and to demand that the Moroccans be accorded the democratic freedoms, which would enable them to organize in self-defense against all threats to their existence and freedom. The Spanish Republic, however, did not heed the warning and thought that it was mere agitation by nationalists, who use every occasion to resist the colonials and to disparage their deeds.

No wonder, then, that one of France's first measures was the arrest of leading labor union leaders and the house-arrest of the nationalist leaders, particularly after His Highness the Khalīfah had protested against this foreign revolt on Moroccan soil the day after it occurred. The Moroccan view was that Spanish ideological conflicts, like French party differences, should not be fought out on a soil foreign to both France and Spain.

In the rest of Morocco the Franco revolt was received with exultation by the French colonists; they envied Spain for the emergence of a savior from the menace of communism, and many looked hopefully to Peyrouton as the would-be Messiah to achieve for France what Franco had been doing for Spain. Delegations from French colonists in Oran, Constantine, and other localities established contacts with Franco with a view to coordinating their activities with his. The French Republicans, alarmed by developments in North Africa and fearful of a fascist revolt by reactionary French colonists, thought that it would be prudent to adopt a new policy of rapprochement towards the Moroccan nationalists with a view to averting the overthrow of democracy. The left-wing parties in France were convinced that only the Kutlah was capable of taking effective action in this regard. Therefore, the Socialists and the Communists sent a delegation to Fez in August 1936 in order to explore the possibilities of cooperation, having obtained adequate assurances of support for whatever arrangements they might conclude from Léon Blum, Vienot, and Pierre Cot. At the same time, a delegation of Spanish Republicans proceeded to Geneva for discussions with the Amir Shakīb Arslān. The Amir advised the delegation to negotiate with the Kutlah, emphasizing that it was the only group competent to take decisive action, provided Morocco's nationalist demands were substantially met.

For our part, we studied the matter with the French and Spanish envoys, after which we submitted a memorandum expressing our readiness to cooperate for the deliverance of Spanish democracy under the following conditions:

1. That the Spanish Republic proclaim the independence of the Khalīfīyah Zone from both Spain and France.

2. That the two governments guarantee this independence and recommend free Morocco to membership in the League of Nations.

3. That Spain conclude with the Sultan's Khalīfah a treaty, embodying the grant of independence and regulating cordial relationships between the two parties.

4. That the Spanish Republic supply us with the necessary arms and equipment.

To facilitate the realization of these objectives we demanded:

1. That France take no action against our military preparations within the zone of occupation.

2. That France expedite the implementation of urgent reforms, particularly those pertaining to public freedoms.

On the other hand, the Kutlah sent a delegation to Barcelona to negotiate with the Spanish Republicans on the basis of the conditions outlined above. The delegation, which arrived in September 1936, was accorded an official and most cordial welcome. In the ensuing negotiations the Spanish Foreign Minister showed the utmost reticence and requested that no final decision be made until after consultations with France. We learned afterwards that the Spanish Foreign Minister had consulted the French Government, which in its turn sought the views of its Resident-General in Morocco, General Noguès. The General rejected the plan outright, while M. Herriot threatened the most serious measures if Spain went ahead with such a plan, which in his view was sheer madness.

The Madrid government communicated orally to our delegation its inability to grant independence in the existing circumstances; it requested the Kutlah delegation to accept the sum of forty million pesetas for publicity on behalf of Spanish democracy, together with a promise that after victory had been achieved the Republic would strive for the well-being of Morocco. Our delegation protested against this mean offer and indignantly withdrew from the conference meeting.

Our Catalonia friends, however, invited our delegation to conclude an agreement with their parties, promising that their minister to Madrid would defend such an agreement before the federal government in Madrid. Thus, an agreement was concluded between the Kutlah and the various Catalonia parties endorsing complete independence for Morocco and providing for mutual cooperation and assistance between Spain and Morocco on a basis of equality. The agreement was free of any provisions permitting Spain to meddle in the affairs of Morocco or to occupy her territory even in wartime. The efforts of Catalonia came to no avail, however, and the agreement remained ink on paper.

The efforts of the Kutlah in those critical circumstances were favorably received in French left-wing circles, and bitter attacks were launched against the French Government and its representatives for refusing to extend a helping hand to the bleeding Spanish democracy. At the same time the Kutlah efforts were instrumental in bringing about a change of policy, more favorable to our friends in the North, on the part of Franco, who was frightened by the nationalist overtures to his opponents, the Republicans.

These overtures were an open secret, and General Franco was impelled to make a countermove to win over the Moroccans. He reversed his earlier policy of repression and sent to Morocco a Spanish envoy who proudly regarded himself as a pupil of Lyautey. This was Señor Beigbeder. The envoy's first contact was with al-Makki al-Nāṣiri, with whom he reviewed the entire situation. Thereafter he instructed the director of native affairs to inform the leaders of the Kutlah in the North that Franco Spain was willing to grant the Moroccans the democratic freedoms which the Republicans had withheld from them. The Residency-General permitted our colleagues to publish a newspaper by the name of "al-Rif," edited and directed by al-Tuhāmā al-Wazzāni, and another newspaper "al-Ḥurrīyah" (freedom) edited by 'Abd al-Khāliq al-Ṭarrīs.

Al-Makki al-Nāṣiri made a trip to Rabat to brief us on developments within the Khalīfīyah Zone. The Kutlah decided to send al-Ḥaj al-Ḥassan abi-'Ayyād to the North in order to deliberate with our colleagues on the future course of action in the light of developments.

In view of the fact that the borders between the two zones of Morocco had been closed, and as a result of the tightening censorship on all messages passing between North and South, it became no longer possible to maintain a centralized organization for the nationalist movement, as had been the case before the Franco revolt. We therefore agreed that the nationalists in the North pursue such policies as they deem appropriate to their circumstances and on their own responsibility, while our Kutlah acts on its own responsibility in the South, with a proviso that both adhere to the following fundamental principles and assumptions:

1. The freedom and independence of Morocco
2. The territorial unity of Morocco under the 'Alawi dynasty
3. Islam and Arabism
4. Loyalty to the 'Alawi throne and to His Majesty Sidi Muḥammad ibn Yūsuf

Thus, the Kutlah of the North continued its activities, which included the founding of "al-Ma' had al-Ḥurr" (the free institute), the convening of an all-Moroccan students conference, and other activities of comparable nature.

A Split in the Kutlah of the North

Hardly a few weeks had passed since Señor Beigbeder initiated his policies when a split occurred within the ranks of the Kutlah in the North. Al-Makki al-Nāṣiri formed a new party, "al-Waḥdah al-Maghribīyah" (Maghrib unity), which launched a widespread publicity campaign for the unification of all parts of Morocco. Al-Makki started an Arabic newspaper carrying the name of his party and another newspaper in Spanish; he also toured towns and villages to mobilize popular support for his movement. On the other hand al-Ṭarrīs and his friends formed a new party by the name of "Ḥizb al-Iṣlāḥ al-Waṭani" (the party of national reform), following the death of Ḥaj 'Abd al-Salām Benūnah, leader of the Kutlah in the North. Although the schism did not arise out of doctrinal differences, it nevertheless led to press recriminations which enabled Spain to play off one group against the other to the detriment of both. In point of fact, both parties found in the policies of Beigbeder an encouragement to go ahead with their plans;

but the Iṣlāḥ (reform) Party soon achieved a considerable lead, when the majority of the nationalists in the zone joined its ranks. The party opened branches throughout the zone and organized a youth movement, along lines of the Spanish Falange, which, however, the authorities disbanded a few months later.

The Sultan's Khalīfah Acts

It was fortunate that the wisdom of His Highness the Sultan's Khalīfah, Mawlay al-Ḥassan, and his aspiration to save his country prompted him to utilize the new era of cordiality, initiated by Señor Beigbeder, for the realization of a number of urgent demands. His Highness was able to announce, at a historic gathering, the independence of the Islamic ministries of justice and waqfs (philanthropic foundations) from the Spanish occupation authorities. He entrusted Ṭarrīs with the waqf portfolio and appointed Da'ūd to the post of inspector of education. A number of students' missions were sent to Cairo and Madrid for advanced studies. No sooner had Ṭarrīs assumed his duties as minister of waqfs, however, than he found himself in headlong collision with the bitter reality: namely, that the administration for native affairs, one of the protectorate's main departments, wished to take back with its left hand what it had granted with its right. It applied its pressure through al-Ṣadr al-A'zam [equivalent of prime minister] who received his instructions from the protectorate. Ṭarrīs was asked to submit to the jurisdiction of the "Ṣadāra" in its capacity as a prime ministership, while in reality it was no more than a subservient department of the protectorate and subject to its instructions in all affairs. In other words, the director of native affairs wished to substitute for his direct orders to the minister of waqfs indirect ones through the so-called prime minister who was still under his control. This led to a controversy between the nationalist and the governmental points of view; the nationalist movement defended the principle of the independence of waqfs from the jurisdiction of any department that was still under control of the protectorate; it emphasized that whatever jurisdiction the protectorate had relinquished or had been forced to concede should revert to the hands of the people themselves and not to the Moroccan administration, which had lost it to the Spaniards in the first place. The only solution, the nationalists declared, was the establishment by election of a higher waqf council, which would supervise the work of the waqf minister and to which he would be made accountable. The Ṣadāra refused to budge from its stand; Ṭarrīs resigned as minister of waqf and resumed leadership of the Iṣlāḥ Party. Da'ūd, still in his position as inspector of education, visited Egypt on a study tour of its educational system. Upon his return home he attempted to carry out an educational reform program; although he succeeded in accomplishing a few reforms, including the enactment of a decree for compulsory education in the zone, he was finally compelled to submit a report to the Khalīfah, informing him of the serious obstacles that the protectorate was placing in his way. Thus, our colleagues discovered for themselves that participation in government under the protectorate regime was a waste of time; moreover it was likely to subvert the consciences of other citizens, who might find in the nationalists' acceptance of office a justification for a headlong run on government posts with every means at their disposal.

Morocco and the French Popular Front

Reference has been made to the cordial relationships between the Kutlah and the left-wing parties in France; the latter had always promised that in the event of their election to power they would implement our demands. When the Popular Front was voted into office in May 1936, we calculated that if we did not obtain all our demands we would at least secure those democratic freedoms which enable us to indoctrinate the people in the aims of the movement and to give expression to our views. With this hope in mind we expeditiously sent a delegation to Paris consisting of Omar 'Abd al-Jalīl and Muḥammad al-Wazzāni. The delegates established contacts with the governing circles--our friends of yesterday; they also carried on a useful publicity campaign. They returned to Morocco with nothing but hopes and promises. The return of the delegation coincided with a mass meeting at Fez, called by the Kutlah and attended by thousands of nationalists. I delivered a long speech on the aims of the Moroccan nationalist movement, after which the petitions of support for the Kutlah, brought by the delegation leaders from all parts of the country, were collected and deposited with the party.

On October 25, 1936 the Kutlah Party met in extraordinary session at the home of al-Ḥafyān al-Sharqāwi in Rabat. In the opening address, I reviewed the past work of the Kutlah and outlined the party's proposed program of action in the future. This included the drawing up of a list of urgent demands, in which the questions of democratic freedoms should occupy a central place so that a propitious atmosphere might be created for conducting a popular campaign on behalf of the urgently needed reforms in all spheres of Moroccan life. After the proposed program had been read and debated paragraph by paragraph, Muḥammad al-Yazīdi outlined the Kutlah's proposed political strategy; the conferees adopted the outline after introducing a number of modifications. The program included the holding of mass meetings in various parts of Morocco, with a view to expounding the aims and programs of the Kutlah, in whole or in part, and enlisting public support by means of petitions to be forwarded to the higher authorities in Rabat and Paris.

As soon as General Noguès arrived in Rabat in October 1936, the Kutlah submitted to him the list of urgent demands together with the resolutions of the conference. He replied that he intended to go to France first, adding that immediately after his return he would strive to meet what could be met, of the Moroccan peoples'demands and aspirations.

The Urgent Demands

The urgent demands comprised the following sections:

1. Democratic freedoms--press, meetings, association education, travel and union organizations.

2. Education--unification of curriculum in all parts of Morocco, increase in the number of primary schools, more adequate system of secondary education, establishment of teacher training colleges.

3. Justice--the appointment of judges by competitive examinations; the guarantee to judges of adequate salaries from the public budget rather than out of fees paid by the litigants; separation of the administrative, judicial, and executive branches; abolition of the high caids' policy.

4. Agriculture--the establishment of a system of inalienable family ownership by distribution of communal land tracts, more generous credit facilities for farmers, equality of taxation between farmer and colonist, protection of farmer against administrative officials, colonists, and money lenders.

5. Workers and craftsmen--the implementation of French labor legislation for Moroccan workers, modernization of Moroccan industry and its protection from foreign competition, unemployment allowances to Moroccan workers.

6. Taxation--abolition of certain taxes and equalization of others for Moroccans and French.

7. Public health--increasing the number of health establishments, distribution of medicines to the needy, a more vigorous campaign against unsanitary homes, combating prostitution both secret and licensed, construction of a sufficient number of centers for the aged and the needy, greater governmental assistance to Moroccan philanthropic societies.

We had been under the illusion that these minimum and sorely-needed reforms would be accepted without much difficulty. We called the first of our public gatherings to publicize the urgent reforms program in the town of Cela; the meeting, attended by a large crowd of Kutlah supporters, was orderly and ended without any incident.

On November 17, 1936 a conference was scheduled to meet in Casablanca pertaining to the problems of the Moroccan press. The agenda of the conference included a mass meeting in one of the city's main halls, to which thousands of supporters as well as French and foreign residents of Casablanca would be invited. The meeting was to have been told of the plight of the Moroccan press resulting from press censorship and the ban on the publication of papers in Arabic. The following day a reception was to have been held for a delegation of the French press and a statement was to have been read to them on the problems of the Moroccan press.

As the time for the opening of the first meeting approached, thousands of Moroccans proceeded to the meeting hall only to find it cordonned off by detachments of armed police and gendarmes. We were having dinner in a neighboring place when a Kutlah youth broke the news to us by telephone; we hastened to the meeting hall where we found representatives of the local authorities--civil and military--surrounded by police, ambulance cars, and all the paraphernalia of a showdown. Khalīfah Pasha, the "muḥāfiẓ" [governor] of Casablanca, informed us orally that the conference had been banned in the name of His Majesty the Sultan, who was then in Casablanca. I replied at once as follows: "His Majesty has decreed an edict pertaining to public gatherings; our conference this evening is in accordance with the provisions of the edict; if you have a special royal order, communicate it to us officially and in writing." The governor conceded that we were in the right and that he would proceed to procure a written order.

We remained on the spot awaiting a written order while the Kutlah youths kept the crowds on the pavements away from the main street in order to forestall the intervention of the authorities, though allegedly to maintain the thoroughfare open to traffic. The period of waiting was an extended one, and we decided to withdraw and not force our way into the heavily guarded meeting hall. The assembled thousands marched away with us, chanting and clamoring for freedom and Moroccan rights. When we arrived at al-Ḥurrīyah (freedom) square, the demonstrators lifted me on their shoulders. I delivered a speech in which I strongly condemned the tyranny of the French administration. I also appealed to the crowds to disperse in an orderly manner and to place their confidence in the Kutlah. The throngs dispersed, voicing their readiness to rally to the call of the Kutlah and make every sacrifice in the cause of freedom. The authorities then arrested me together with Muḥammad al-Yazīdi and Muḥammad al-Wazzāni.

The following day the other leaders of the Kutlah arranged a conference at Casablanca for the French press delegation, which was attended by a hundred and fifty press representatives. Ḥaj Omar 'Abd al-Jalīl gave an address in which he protested against the acts of the administration; he declared that the Kutlah would take decisive action in regard to the arrest of the three leaders. Representatives of the French parties present at the conference strongly condemned in their turn the policy of the protectorate in the suppression of freedoms; they urged release of the arrested leaders and the lifting of the ban on the publication of all the newspapers that the Moroccans wish to publish. The French guests then requested the permission of the Kutlah for intervention with the local authorities, in the hope of dissuading them from their present obdurate stand and with a view to the restoration of peace and the easing of the prevailing tension. A delegation representing the French Popular Front approached M. Orthlieb, the chief administrator of the Casablanca region, to convey to him their views. He was extreme rude and inconsiderate and the delegates withdraw from the meeting in protest.

The Kutlah for its part decided to send Ḥaj Omar 'Abd al-Jalīl to Paris in order to make representations to the government and explain the situation to French public opinion. At the same time, demonstrations of solidarity were called throughout the country.

On the last Friday of November 1936 massive demonstrations were staged in Casablanca, Fez, Rabat, Cela, Taza, and other Moroccan towns and villages. The demonstrators clashed with the police, and as a result many suffered wounds. Several members of the Kutlah executive office as well as hundreds of supporters were arrested. A new executive office was formed on an ad hoc basis consisting of Ḥaj Hassan abi-'Ayyād, Muhammad al-Duyūri, 'Abd al-'Aziz ibn Idrīs, and al-Hāshimi al-Fīlāli. The new executive continued to organize demonstrations and general strikes; it also issued regular bulletins and reports on the progress of the movement.

The detainees conducted themselves with utmost steadfastness, fortitude, and firmness. The authorities learned for the first time of the profound impact of the nationalist training, carried out by the Kutlah, upon the circles of its supporters. They were all clear as to what they stood for; their replies to the French administrators who had questioned them on the reform program astonished the staff of the Residency-General. Their prison sentences ranged from six months to five years.

When Ḥaj Omar arrived in Paris he immediately went into a conference with M. Vienot, Assistant Foreign Minister for North African affairs. The Deputy Minister expressed his indignation over what had happened and attempted to exonerate General Noguès from responsibility for the acts committed by his subordinates. He requested Ḥaj Omar to return to Morocco, in an endeavor to calm down popular tension. The Moroccan envoy replied that tension could not be eased so long as the Kutlah leaders and its supporters remained in jail. Ḥaj Omar opened an office for the Kutlah in Paris and arranged for the regular issuing of a bulletin by the name of "al-Mukhbir al-Maghribi" (Moroccan informer) to replace the French-language magazine "al-Maghrib".

His news items and commentaries disturbed left-wing circles, which felt uneasy that a government of the Popular Front should have begun its term of office in a manner disillusioning to the Moroccans; so the Prime Minister, M. Blum, instructed General Noguès to release the detainees and to alter his inimical policies.

It remained for General Noguès to carry out the instruction of his government without undermining what they call the dignity of the protectorate and its esteem in the eyes of the people. The General at once visited Fez where he met a group of its notables; they expressed to him their solidarity with the Kutlah. Then he conferred with representatives of the Qarawiyīn University; finally he visited the municipal council, where representatives of trades, industries, and workers had been in attendance. The General conferred with them at length on a wide range of subjects. His efforts were directed towards winning them over to piecemeal and immediate solutions to their problems. In reply, the representatives referred him in all outstanding issues, large and small, to the three detained leaders and also the other leaders of the Kutlah. Those men, they told the General, represented the people and could speak in their name. The General left Fez, indignant over the administration for native affairs, which had consistently given him misleading estimates of the Kutlah's popular strength. In Rabat he received a number of delegations and had conferences with His Majesty. Eventually, he began to issue instructions for the gradual release of the internees. When only the three of us remained in detention, the General considered the submission of our case before the high court on charges of advocating and provoking breach of the peace. The case was brought before the court and in spite of the strenuous efforts of the French government attorney, the Moroccan jury, appointed by the president of the court and replaced several times at the behest of the prosecution attorney, returned a verdict of not guilty. We had three defense lawyers including a Frenchman. The attorneys at first approached the Resident-General; when he saw that we were determined to fight the case out and that the trial would give us an opportunity to expound and expose many things, he offered to withdraw the case provided we sign a pledge not to repeat the incident in the future. We naturally turned down the offer and so also did the leaders of the Kutlah in both Fez and Rabat. After considerable hesitation the Resident-General decided to set us free, after we had spent a whole month in detention.

It must be put on record that our colleagues in the Khalīfīyah Zone did all they could to show their solidarity with us; similarly, our friends in Tunisia and Algeria protested vehemently against the acts of the administration towards us. Tawfīq al-Madani, in one of the issues of "al-Shihāb", wrote a brilliant article on the events, underlining their significance relative to the upsurge of national awakening.

The fact is, that the nationalist movement took a great stride forward as a result of these bloody demonstrations; they manifested considerable popular support for and identification with the nationalist movement. Amir Shakīb Arslān sent to me a message of congratulations on the occasion of my release from detention, in which he asserted his view that our movement had become no less advanced than the other Arab nationalist movements in Egypt and the Levant.

General Noguès

The appointment of General Noguès as Resident-General was a disappointment ot the Moroccans. His selection to the post was not made on account of any outstanding qualifications or his alleged understanding of the Moroccan spirit; it was rather a move on the part of Léon Blum to put the colonists in their place, in addition to removing Peyrouton, their most popular Resident. Whatever might be said about Noguès, his main defects, which we discovered in him from the first day and which became all too apparent in his behavior during the last war, stemmed from his weak will, his indecision, and his extreme selfishness. Immediately after his appointment we sent to him a file comprising the documents and records of the Kutlah; he told Muḥammad al-Yazīdi, who presented them to him, that he was determined to implement the demands of the Moroccan people as soon as he took up his duties. While still in Paris, he requested the acting governor of Fez, General Richard, to convey to me the most encouraging assurances as to the intentions of the new Resident-General. No sooner, however, had he arrived in Morocco and engaged in consultations with the administration for native affairs than a complete change overtook him. When he entered Fez in the manner of a conqueror he delivered a speech in which he castigated the Moroccan nationalists. He likened them to pigeons wanting to leave their nests before they had acquired wings, thereby risking fall and injury. When he saw in the practical replies of the Kutlah the errors of his rash underestimation of the nationalists, he attempted to rectify his policies, even thoug temporarily; he reverted to a policy of conciliation, having discovered the futility of repression. We shall see, howeve the extent to which he remained a mere plaything in the grip of whims; we shall see the dire consequences of his unbridl personal selfishness, which finally led him to crack down on the nationalists; this proved his own undoing and did not, as he had hoped, break the nationalist movement or undermine the will of its leaders.

One of his first acts, following our release from jail, wa to try to prevail upon us, through semi-official intermediaries, to meet with him for deliberations on Morocco's demands. Our initial reaction to his overtures was guarded; eventually, we agreed to delegate Ḥaj Omar for exploratory talks, to precede a full-dress conference. Our colleague was received most cordially by the General and his preliminary talks were conducted in a genial and encouraging atmos phere. The General subsequently agreed to receive us as a delegation of the Kutlah of National Action, whereas he had hitherto insisted on receiving us in our personal capacities only. He could not, he had earlier contended, recognize th Kutlah; nor could he concede to the Moroccans the right to form political parties, alleging that the presence of the Sultan in Morocco precluded the establishment of parties. The Sultan only, he had claimed, had the competence to present the demands of Morocco to France and her representatives. This was a fragile argument, and he was force to give it up in the face of Sidi Muḥammad ibn Yūsuf's deter mined stand in defense of his country's rights.

We conferred with General Noguès at a round-table conference during which the list of urgent demands was given the most careful consideration. The General promised to comply with the demands in their entirety. The most important concession that we were able to obtain was a permit to publish an Arabic weekly, by the name of "al-Aṭlas", as an organ of the Kutlah; also, we obtained a permit for a daily newspaper "al-Maghrib", which the late Sa'id Ḥaja, leader of the Kutlah branch at Cela, had requested to publish. We also secured release of the newspaper "'Amal al-Sha'b" which had been suspended by the authorities. It should be noted, however, that all these concessions were within the framework of the Morocco press ordinances of April 27, 1919 and of November 20, 1920; that is to say, they did not imply any extension of freedom for the press.

On the other hand, the French left-wing parties, which had resisted us and had accused us of harboring reactionary views, saw in the widespread demonstrations of the Moroccan people evidence that we were fully representative of the people; consequently, fifteen branches of the Socialist Party came out in support of the Moroccan people's demands and expressed readiness to cooperate with the Kutlah leaders for their achievement.

Split from the Kutlah

The press concessions, together with the support of the French parties in power, created in our opinion a more propitious atmosphere for the reorganization of our movement along the line of major party formations. The Kutlah, therefore, met in plenary session at Fez, and a number of resolutions were adopted, including the opening of new branches and the drafting of a new procedural law for the party, with a view to affording greater rank and file participation in the selection and control of the party leadership. The committee entrusted Wazzāni and myself with the drawing-up of the party's new procedural law. Upon completion of this task we submitted the draft law to a second full-dress meeting of the party. The draft was unanimously adopted in its final form with only minor modifications. The party apparatus, according to the new law, consists of an executive committee, a national council, technical committees and branches. Each of these party organs has its own internal regulations. The Kutlah is a democratic party, the draft law asserts; its leaders are elected by secret ballot at a full-dress conference, in which all branches are represented in proportion to a definite ratio.

The Kutlah then decided to elect an ad hoc executive committee, whose task would be to supervise the opening of new branches and the registration of active members. The committee was to continue in office until circumstances should permit the convening of a general conference, as provided for in the law.

We met in January 1937 for the election of the temporary executive committee. The result of the secret balloting for the committee was as follows:

'Alāl al-Fāsi, chairman
Muḥammad Ḥassan al-Wazzāni, secretary-general
Aḥmad Mikwār, treasurer
Muḥammad al-Yazīdi, member
Omar 'Abd al-Jalīl, member
'Abd al-'Azīz ibn Idrīs, member
Muḥammad Ghāzi, member

When the result of the balloting was announced, Wazzāni announced his resignation from the Kutlah. We do not wish to enter into the details of this split or its consequences; suffice it here to mention that Wazzāni began to work for the enlistment of new supporters, in behalf of a movement by the name of "al-Ḥarakah al-Qawmīyah" (the nationalist movement), while all the other participants in the conference continued their activities within the ranks of the Kutlah.

Dissolution of the Kutlah

The temporary executive committee went ahead with its assigned task; "al-Aṭlas" magazine was its organ in Arabic and "al-'Amal al-Sha'bi" (L'action du peuple) its organ in French. Aḥmad Bla Freej was made secretary-general in place of Wazzāni who had resigned. It opened its headquarters in the city of Fez and undertook the registration of the thousands of applicants for membership from all corners of the land. The Residency-General was not too pleased with this overwhelming triumph; it charged that we were conspiring against the King, because we required applicants for membership to give an oath of allegiance to God, Morocco, and the King, and to pledge to work within the fold of the Kutlah. The Residency-General issued on March 18, 1937 a decree ordering the dissolution of the Kutlah. The following day the authorities closed down the headquarters of the party and issued proclamations to the people announcing the end of the Nationalist Bloc.

The National Movement for the Achievement of Demands

The decision of the Residency to dissolve the Kutlah Party did not dissuade us from our course of action; we continued our national struggle without let and maintained close contacts with our branches and supporters; our magazines and newspapers continued publication and we gave to the movement the temporary name of "al-Ḥarakah al-Waṭanīyah Litaḥqīq al-Maṭālib" (the national movement for the achievement of demands). A few days after the dissolution of the Kutlah we sent a delegation to the Residency-General with a view to discussing with General Noguès the formation of a new party. His chief secretary, however, declined to arrange for a meeting, saying, "You may submit a plan for his approval." We refused to submit a written plan and decided instead to make of our plan an accomplished fact. The aim of the Resident-General and of M. Vienot was to propose to us the formation of a circumscribed association, devoted to research and study of public issues, and limited in membership to a few scores of nationalist intellectuals. In an effort to justify this proposal, M. Vienot acknowledged the valuable contribution made by the Kutlah in its various study projects of public issues; he also praised the scientific method which characterized all our protests and criticisms. This method, he suggested, could render considerable service to our cause without embroilment in disturbances and political entanglements. Naturally we could not accept this proposal, because it would have scuttled one of our great aims, namely, to train the people and to unite the Moroccan masses around the movement in the struggle for our usurped rights. We therefore decided to sever relations with the Residency and send a delegation to Paris.

The delegation, consisting of Ḥaj Omar 'Abd al-Jalīl and Ḥaj Aḥmad Bla Freej, left for Paris to explain to French public opinion the circumstances surrounding the dissolution of the Kutlah. The delegation conveyed to the French Foreign Ministry a comprehensive report concerning General Noguès' blunders and indecision. The Deputy Foreign Minister for North African affairs, M. François de Tessan, who had been a member of the French committee for Moroccan demands and one of the patrons of "al-Maghrib" magazine, expressed to the delegation his condemnation of what he called the vacillation of Noguès and promised a betterment of the situation.

The purpose of the delegation was merely to prepare the French authorities in France and in Morocco to acquiescenc in the formation of the new party. General Noguès was well aware of this and he attempted to entice our delegates to contact him in France, offering to introduce them to personalities other than the ones they already knew. The delegates, however, refused any dealings with General Noguès after he had taken the drastic step of dissolving the Kutlah and threatening to arrest its leaders.

The National Party (al-Ḥizb al-Waṭani)

While the delegation was carrying on its activities in Paris, the nationalist movement convened a conference at Rabat in April 1937, in which representatives of all the Kutlah branches participated. After debating the situation the conferees decided to call the new movement "al-Hizb al-Waṭani li Taḥqīq al-Maṭālib" (the national party for the achiment of demands). The new designation was intended to symbolize the continuity of the Kutlah's principles and its program, which deserved to be taken over and preserved. The following day the formation of the party was announced in a communiqué published in "al-Maghrib" magazine.

A few days later we took up our headquarters in Fez, in the same premises that had been closed down by the authorities following the dissolution of the Kutlah. We also resum registration of new members in the usual manner, but with one modification: we no longer required them to take the oath.

Since it was deemed necessary to give publicity for the new party, we utilized the opportunity of His Majesty's return from France, towards the end of April, to send cables in the name of the National Party from all parts of the kingdom; these were published in the press.

This moved the administration to action, and General Bl the governor of the Fez region, summoned me to his office.

At the government house I met the General, in the prese of Colonel Noël, chief of the political section, the pasha [governor] of the city, Muḥammad al-Tāzi, and the chief of the translation bureau. The General opened the discussion as follows: "On the occasion of His Majesty's return to his capital, we read in the papers several congratulatory cables addressed to him in the name of al-Ḥizb al-Waṭani; these included a cable in the name of the party's headquarters and signed by you. This means that you have re-established a proscribed party."

In reply I pointed out that al-Ḥizb al-Waṭani was technically not the same as the Kutlah of National Action. I explained that the order of prohibition could not be applied to a party formed afterwards. The General retorted that the headquarters of the two parties was the same, that the supporters were the same, and he wanted to know what differences if any existed between one and the other.

In reply I said: "The headquarters, the leader, the supporters, all these do not alter the fact that the new party is called "al-Ḥizb al-Waṭani" (the nationalist party) while the other carried the name of "Kutlat al-'Amal al-Waṭani" (the bloc for national action). I pointed out that there was considerable difference between the two; at any rate, I added, we had sought a meeting with General Noguès to obtain his approval of the new formation, but his chief secretary had advised us to submit the request in writing. I submit herewith," I said in conclusion, "the application in writing relative to the national party and its organizational setup; if you have any observations or comments to make I shall be ready to study them." The General expressed the view that this was not a new plan but a resumption of an illicit one. I took exception to his view, stressing that we had observed the prohibition of our own accord and were now launching a new party. As to his repeated inquiries concerning differences between old and new, I said: "Do not forget, Your Excellency, that a considerable difference does exist on account of the deletion of the oath requirement in membership of the new party. Was not the oath requirement the ground upon which you had justified the outlawry of the Kutlah?" When the General again conceded that he could not really find considerable difference, I turned to Colonel Noël and asked, "Did you not regard the oath requirement as the substantial ground for proscribing the Kutlah?" The Colonel answered in the affirmative, conceding that the oath requirement constituted a substantial difference but not a sufficient one. The General, supplementing the Colonel's remark, declared: "The prestige of the state has now been aspersed because the people see its order flouted without its taking any action relative thereto; therefore, the new center must be closed down. I am as you know a military commander whose duty is to carry out the orders issued to me from Rabat." When he had finished, I said: "Admittedly you are a military man, but at the same time you are governor of an important province; it is your duty to impress upon the Residency-General that we shall not accept this time the closing down of our headquarters without demonstrations that would inevitably cause a disturbance of public security. If your concern is solely on account of prestige I am willing to resolve it satisfactorily." The General asked what solution I had in mind and I replied: "Since it appears to me that you object to the existence of the new party's headquarte in the same premises that had been occupied by the Kutlah, I shall be willing to move the headquarters somewhere else. Such a transfer is sufficient to demonstrate a difference and to maintain the prestige of the state."

There was a pause of silence, after which the General said that he would consult with the political administration at Rabat which alone was competent to make a decision. The General immediately telephoned Rabat; they answered that they wanted an hour to deliberate on the matter. After about one hour and a half the telephone rang and the Residency-General informed the General of its approval of my suggestic namely the transfer of the headquarters to some other place, as a condition for the authorities' recognition of the National Party.

I have given a résumé of the meeting between the General and myself in order to acquaint the reader with one example of the sort of political methods that are conducted in our country and to impress upon him the deviousness characterizing relationships between the Moroccans and the French. We had in fact been well aware that the Residency could not possibly let the party alone without taking some action, if only for the sake of principles, as they are prone to say. Thus we had decided beforehand on a change of headquarter premises; when I went to see the General we had already prepared new premises to serve as our headquarters. This illustrates our understanding of the French mentality and ou insight into what I always call the "French philosophy".

The National Party continued its activities, taking within

its fold all the former members of the Kutlah and its supporters. It also continued to enlist new members and to open new branches throughout Morocco. "Al-Aṭlas" newspaper, published by our friend Muḥammad al-Yazīdi, continued to be its official organ. Several new papers were issued in French but were successively suppressed by the Residency-General. The Party adopted "Maṭālib al-Sha'b al-Maghribi" (the demands of the Moroccan people) as its own program; thus the party placed the goal of independence first and reforms and rejuvenation second. It continued, however, in the policy of the Kutlah as regards timing; that is to say, to strive for the implementation of the new protectorate as the first step towards independence. It is the policy of gradualism whose utter futility we were later to discover. Perhaps it was necessary that our movement should have gone through that experiment, which revealed to us the mentality of the colonials and their unwillingness to arrive at any understanding as long as they could remain evasive and gain time for continuance of the status quo.

<u>The Struggle of al-Ḥizb al-Waṭani</u>

The most distinguishing feature of the National Party was its struggle to the death on behalf of democratic freedoms and its fight in defense of the underpriviliged classes of the people. Its contribution was not restricted to acts of political defense but entailed tremendous exertions in the organization and the training of the masses, as well as the orientation of the Moroccan community towards modern life. The pillars upon which the party built up its program for modernization and orientation of the people are:

1. <u>Morocco is a Country Inextricably Attached to Islam</u>.

The modernization of the political and economic system is in no way incompatible with religious precepts. Islam addresses the individual primarily as a member of the group; therefore, it is interested in and devoted to the needs and problems of community life, which the generations have overburdened with rigidities and restrictions from which it must be freed. And so, the separation of powers, the people's participation in elections and the management of government, their equality in rights and obligations--all these principles are not innovations for Muslims; they are doctrines embodied in the Koran and reiterated in the Sunnah.

2. Morocco is Loyal to a Royalist Regime

Morocco over the past fourteen centuries has not known a form of government besides the monarchy; the throne has remained a symbol of its unity and a legacy of its past, and will in the future be the pillar of its social stability. This, however, does not in any way mean that a royalist regime may not develop into a constitutional monarchy along the lines of what is happening in England and in some of the Islamic countries today.

Thus, Moroccan nationalism was crystalized into a clear-cut doctrine, which is the liberation of the Maghrib within the fold of its religion and in loyalty to its illustrious monarchy. In order to propagate this concept, which is no more than a reflection of the people's beliefs and aspiration we organized a program of popular lessons and lectures, in schools, mosques, and private gatherings,which I supervise in person and contributed to with my best efforts. The National Party achieved such success and popularity as to frighten the colonials in all parts of the country.

The National Party followed in its organizational setup the plan of its progenitor the Kutlah; it had an executive committee, a national council, branches and party cells; the executive committee had a number of technical committees, whose job it was to study and supervise implementation of the tasks assigned to it. These technical committee had sub-committees in each of the party branches, accountable to the central committees. The most important of the committees were:

1. Committee for education
2. Committee on religions and social reforms
3. Committee for national relief
4. Committee for moral guidance
5. Press committee
6. Committee for publications and publicity
7. Committee for the national youths
8. Committee for defense of Palestine and the Holy Pla
9. Committee for economic affairs.

Each of these committees performed its assigned task within the short interval afforded by the authorities to the National Party. Our principal aim in the formation of thes committees was to help develop specialists in the various spheres of national endeavor who could handle the problem submitted to them competently and on the basis of knowledge. We also aimed to afford the young and active intellectuals a field in which to exert their energies and develop their capabilities. Further, it had been--and still is--my conviction that our party should permeate all spheres of activity in the country, so that it may be able to direct the nation towards what it deems to be the right path and prepare the ground for the implementation of its national program after independence;and this without opposition or resistance on the part of the masses, which will have been made ready for its acceptance.

The committee on education established a number of schools in towns and villages, in spite of the difficulties that usually stand in the way of the establishment of such schools. It also exerted its utmost towards a reorganization of the Qarawiyīn University and the mobilization of its students in support of a progressive orientation in this ancient religious institution. It also succeeded in the establishment or the rehabilitation of a number of religious institutes at Oujda, Fadhālah, and other places. The committee also carried on an intensive publicity campaign for the education of females; it urged the sending of student missions to Egypt and elsewhere by appeals to the well-to-do and to the parents of promising students. It assisted the Association of North African Muslim Students in France by material and moral support; it also helped in the organization and convening of the association's conferences at regular intervals. At the committee's behest, a number of alumni associations were formed for graduates of Arab and French schools as well as of the Qarawiyīn University. The protectorate, however, consistently refused to license the formation of these associations. The committee attempted to form "Jam'īyat Aṣdiqā' al-Ṭalabah" (the association of students' friends); educationalists were enlisted and a program of action laid down. No sooner, however, had the association begun its activities than the authorities issued an interdiction against it. The obliteration of illiteracy occupied an important place in the committee's devotion and work; evening classes were opened at various centers, particularly in Fez and Marrakech, where attendence reached very high proportions. Students from Berber schools were enrolled for courses in the Arabic language, the teaching of which had been prohibited in the curriculum of Berber schools. In September 1937, the committee mobilized public opinion in defense of the students who had been persecuted by the authorities at al-Khumīsāt and other towns; it spurred the students of Qarawiyīn to a strike in support of their essential demands. It established student houses at Fez, Rabat, Cela, Oujda, and other places, as centers of debates and discussions in which students of Arab and French schools participated.

The committee on religious and social reforms undertook the task of consolidating the Salafīyah movement, of resisti the impostors of "taṣawwuf" (mysticism), and of cleansing minds of superstitions. A special committee was formed to organize religious instruction and to advocate reforms. Sermons were written in modern form and attempts were made to appoint educated and reform-animated youths in religious posts; it paid particular attention to the societies dedicated to the preservation of the Koran; they were broug together and organized in committees affiliated to the centr reform committee. These societies were instrumental in unifying the various readings and chantings of the Koran in all mosques; they supplied the reading centers in Morocco with copies of the Koran in sufficient numbers; they also played an important role in propagating the nationalist cree and enhancing the prestige of the nationalists in the midst o our God-fearing people. They published many articles and studies on family and social problems, urging a return to the spirit of the early founders while simultaneously advoca ing the adoption of a modernist and progressive educational program.

Improvements were introduced in the celebration protoc observed on the anniversary of the Prophet's birthday; the reformed protocol was made worthy of this great occasion; celebrations were also arranged on the anniversary of the Hegira; religious chantings were made to fit the spirit of the time; attempts were made to curtail many of the deforn ties that had crept into the observance of lofty anniversarie such as supplications at the mausoleums of saints, a practi contrary to religion. The nation was given a sound orienta which, while preserving the spirit of respect and veneratio for the nation's heroes and saints, liberated it from the superstitious accretions of ages past.

In the field of social affairs the committee conducted a

heroic struggle to gain for the workers minimum rights, including an eight-hour day and increased wages. It also advocated strongly a weekly holiday for workers, in spite of the obstacles that were placed in its way by the government and by reactionary circles. It succeeded in making the city of Fez and a number of other towns close down on Fridays, as a step in social progress and as a manifestation of social solidarity.

We did all we could to establish a full-fledged trade-union movement. The workers responded wholeheartedly to our call and struggled for the attainment of their rights by means of petitions, demonstrations, and strikes. The administration, however, adopted repressive measures at all times, neither permitting the workers to defend their interests nor complying with them of its own accord. French workers in Morocco succeeded in obtaining permission to open branches for the Conféderation Générale du Travail of France. The administration would not grant Moroccan workers the right to form their own confederation and the refusal persists to the present day. This confronted Moroccan workers and ourselves with a dual struggle: in the first place, we struggled against the government ban on the right of Moroccan workers to found their own labor unions; in the second place, we resisted the establishment of a foreign labor confederation in Morocco, which aims at the organization and the mobilization of all Moroccan workers in support of objectives that are not our own and of interests that are not on all occasions identical with our interests. Our attempts to exclude Moroccan workers from the orbit of the French C.G.T. brought us into a bitter conflict with its representatives. In fact, however, the latter were inadvertently supported by the Residency-General, which had resisted all our demands for trade union organization while at the same time conceding that the French unions had no right to enlist Moroccans. Political considerations, so the Residency alleged, compelled it to delay recognition of the Moroccans' right to their own trade unions.

Our point of view was that Moroccan as well as other workers in Morocco should establish Moroccan trade unions which would combine within a general Moroccan confederation along lines of the C.G.T. in France, but not as part of it. Such a Moroccan confederation could then join the World

Federation of Trade Unions as the C.G.T. has done. More over, the Moroccan confederation should keep out of political and religious issues, so that all workers could join together in the common bond of work. The French, on the other hand, were striving to strengthen the left-dominated C.G.T. in order to utilize Moroccan workers in support of leftist activities in France. It is evidently unreasonable that the C.G.T. in Paris should issue orders, motivated by purely local considerations, and expect their implementa tion in a country which is foreign to France and must remai outside influences generated by purely internal French considerations. When the government persisted in its resistance to our trade-union demands, we attempted to establish instead cooperative societies for Moroccan workers. Cooperatives for Moroccan auto drivers and for a number of other trades were actually formed but again permission by the authorities was withheld. In spite of all we continued tc work within the fold of unrecognized committees, whose principal aim was to spur the workers to struggle in defens of their rights and to orient them towards sound objectives. We shall see later on that the right to union organization is still being denied to Moroccan workers at the present day.

The committee also devoted attention to the condition of Moroccan industry, spurring its leaders to the creation of a cooperative spirit and the founding of a more vigorous or ganization. On behalf of the committee I submitted a repor to the government, outlining the form of organization most conclusive to a revitalization and development of Moroccan industry; I made a distinction between the organization of labor in large-scale industrial plants and that in the traditional small-scale crafts. In general, I aimed at one objective, namely, the narrowing-down of class differences as a step towards their final elimination.

The committee expended considerable efforts in its figh to win recognition for a system of inalienable property ownership and the protection of farmers from the exactions o caids, controllers, Sufi impostors, and money-lenders.

The country had been in the grip of an economic depression resulting from the poverty of the farmers and craftsmen and a general slackening in business activity; it had been further accentuated by the drought that befell the coun in 1936 and afterwards. The committee for national relief organized numerous aid societies for feeding the hungry and sheltering the refugees. The headquarters of the committee in Fez offered 3,500 meals every day and the branches did likewise throughout Morocco. A publicity campaign for relief of those in distress was got under way, in which community leaders and writers depicted the distress of the Moroccan masses, calling the attention of the people and the administration to the seriousness of the situation. The protectorate did not view with favor these purely philanthropic efforts and obstructed them all along the way. Nonetheless, the committee for religious and social reforms, in cooperation with the relief committee, did a most commendable job; attention was devoted to a number of major problems such as the plight of the "tin cities" and the urgency for their replacement by new living quarters; the well-to-do citizens were urged to construct cheap housing for rent to the poor; the authorities were urged to drop taxes on the unemployed and to launch work projects for their employment, and so forth. Attention was also devoted to such minor problems as aid for circumcision of the sons of the poor, improvement of public baths, and the like. The relief committee had another important task in the critical circumstances then prevailing; this was to provide assistance for the families of the victims in the nationalist struggle, families whose breadwinner had been either imprisoned, banished, or killed. The committee continued its work after our arrest and its services to the cause will long be remembered.

The committee for moral guidance consisted of students from Qarawiyīn and the secondary school at Fez. It had branches comprising students of both religious and secular institutions throughout Morocco. The aim of the committee was to combat immoral behavior in youth circles and in other strata of society by means of public lectures, gatherings, and press articles. Still more important, members of the committee used to frequent public places, urging upon the people to desist from alcoholic beverages and narcotics; they also succeeded in closing down bars in Islamic quarters. The campaign had a profound impact upon the participants in the campaign as well as on others; members of the committee felt the need for training themselves in habits of self-discipline so that they might serve as a good example to others; at the same time they convinced many people of the harmful effects of their violating the moral codes. Of even greater importance is the close contact they had established with the common folk, which afforded them an opportunity to study at close range the ills and the needs of their fellow countrymen. Their experience stood them in good stead in the days ahead and many of them are working today within the fold of the Istiqlāl (independence) Party for the good of their country.

The press committee undertook the task of coordinating and orienting the work of the national press, of defending its interests, and establishing for it working relationships with the foreign press. Along side it, the committee for publicity and information carried on a widespread campaign for the nationalist cause at home and abroad. It issued the party communiqués and releases; it counteracted publicity hostile to the party; it organized public gatherings and party conferences. Furthermore, it supervised the extension of party formations and branches; it investigated the work of the party apparatus both at the central as well as the local level; it kept a close watch on the currents of popular and foreign opinions. The committee was also in charge of special party publications and bulletins other than those appearing in the press. It is now recognized, on the basis of the available records, that the committee for publicity and information made a valuable contribution to the National Party; its chairman, al-Hāshimi al-Fīlāli, deserves the highest tribute for the committee's achievements.

The national youth committee devoted its utmost towards organizing the Moroccan youths in sport and scout associations, after the authorities had withheld permission for the establishment of special party youth formations, as had been originally planned. But even these sport and scout associations failed to secure government approval; we kept them going, however, by submitting one application after another, each of which remained pending with the governme for at least two months; the applications were, as expected turned down; in the meantime the associations continued in being. In spite of all these obstructions we instilled in the youth a love of sports and trained them in sound ways of scouting. The youth movement outlived the dissolution of the National Party and the arrest of its leaders; it has now attained its full flowering under the auspices of the Istiqlāl Party, as we shall indicate later on. It has never been accorded official recognition, however, save for the encouragement and the patronage which His Majesty has bestowed upon it, as he has done upon every other reform movement.

The committee must also be credited with the establishment of "Jam'īyat al-Shubbān al-Muslimīn" (the Muslim youth association), "al-Hidāya al-Islāmīyah" (Muslim guidance), and other associations, in the face of relentless governmental opposition.

The committee for the defense of Palestine and the Holy Places made strenuous efforts towards alerting Moroccan public opinion to the dangers which Zionism poses to the Arab world; statements of the Palestine Arab Higher Committee were given widespread publicity; subscriptions were collected, and each year, a day was observed as "Palestine day". Thus we joined the Arab and the Muslim worlds in their manifold demonstrations and activities in support of the Palestinian cause. We succeeded in disseminating anti-Zionist propaganda, even in Moroccan Jewish circles; the campaign was so effective that they joined with us in sending a memorandum to the British Foreign Office in protest against the 1937 Royal Commission's report, which had recommended the partition of Palestine into three zones. Our cordial relationships with the French Socialists had their influence upon the attitude of France when the Commission's plan was submitted to the League of Nations. Both we and the Amir Shakīb Arslān contacted the French Government and prevailed upon it to adopt a favorable policy towards the Arabs in the interests of both parties.

The committee for economic affairs submitted several memoranda to the government in connection with fiscal and agricultural policies. It supported the union of small porters in their demands for better working conditions; it demanded the holding of agricultural and industrial exhibitions; it launched a widespread publicity campaign in support of the establishment of stockholding companies and cooperative societies. Although it did not achieve a degree of success comparable to its contemporary counterpoint in the Istiqlāl Party, it nevertheless laid-down sound policies which are being built upon today.

It is not our aim to desecribe exhaustively the achievements of these temporary committees during the few months of their existence; we have not, for example, touched upon the literary, musical, and stage festivals organized under the auspices of the party. Our aim has been merely to depic in this brief summary, examples of the manifold and diverse forms of resistance organized by a people aspiring to life and liberty, as well as the reaction of a cowardly and a niggardly colonial regime to these stirring and aspirations. Supervising all these activities, in addition to its heavy political responsibilities, was the National Party's executive committee. Perhaps its most notable achievement was its vigorous publicity campaign, both at home and abroad, in support of the Moroccan reform program. In pursuance of this objective it succeeded in rallying the entire nation, both Muslims and Jews, behind it. The Jews of Morocco had bee lukewarm towards the nationalist movement; they were unde the influence of Tunisian and Algerian Jews in demanding assimilation or some other formula, and thus were placed outside the national fold. The executive committee, therefore, expended tremendous efforts to convince them that the were citizens and should not seek solutions to their problem outside the common Moroccan fold. I asked Lord Lockash, chairman of the international league for resistance to anti-Semitism, which comprises more than seven hundred thousand Jewish or pro-Jewish members, to hold on the spot an investigation into the conditions of Moroccan Jews. Hearing were held in Rabat to which our party sent Aḥmad Bla Freej and Muḥammad al-Yazīdi as observers. The conferees adopted a resolution stipulating that the Moroccan reform program was identical with the program of the league itself for the benefit of Moroccan Jews. Moroccan representative of the Jewish faith declared their unshakable attachment to the citizenship of the land, their loyalty to His Majesty the King, and their support for the demands of the Moroccan people and the National Party movement for their realizatio

At the same time, the committee obtained the recognitio of the French left-wing parties for the Moroccan reform pr gram, as being the program of the Moroccan working class of the underprivileged strata of society. Thus representativ of the French Socialist and Communist Parties in Morocco adopted a resolution endorsing our program and supporting demands. When the general Socialist conference met at Ma seilles in July 1937, a report based entirely upon our progr was submitted to the conference. The conference was attended by Ḥaj Omar 'Abd al-Jalīl and Ḥaj Aḥmad Bla Freej as observers.

The party also established the closest ties of cooperation with the Liberal Constitutional Party of Tunisia, the Algerian People's Party, the Society of Muslim 'Ulemas, and other organizations, with a view to strengthening the solidarity of North Africa in its common struggle against foreign imperialism. The support of the Arab and the Muslim worlds had been strengthened by the efforts of Moroccan students in the East, as well as by the moral support extended to our movement by the late Amir Shakīb Arslān and his active friends, such as Muḥammad 'Ali al-Ṭāhir, who dedicated his paper "al-Shūra" and later "al-Shabāb" to exposing the horrors of colonialism and to commending the struggle of the Arab movement's faithful leaders.

The National Party was firm in its resistance to the reactionary rulers and in its support of public freedoms; one of its foremost campaigns was conducted against the caids (the influential chieftans) who allowed themselves to be the henchmen and the tools of colonialism. Perhaps the most deadly struggle was fought against Glaoui (al-Jallawi) Pasha and his misdeeds in the south; the struggle liberated the inhabitants of the Moroccan town from the "house levy" which Glaoui had exacted from them for a long period of time; it also protected them from the "licentious city", which Glaoui had planned to found in league with a number of foreign companies. The struggle restored to these down-trodden inhabitants their feeling of self-respect and gave them an opportunity to break loose from the bondage of a tyrannical rule. The party also showed the people how to bring to account those entrusted with the management of their affairs, as in its campaign against the managers of the philanthropic society or against the municipal authorities. Our colleagues in the south expended tremendous efforts in defense of the party principles and the underprivileged in their region, who had been enslaved and cowed down by their oppressive rulers. We must pay tribute to the struggle of our friends al-Mukhtār al-Sūsi, and to the hero the late Muḥammad al-Mallākh; we must also cite with admiration the contributions of 'Abdullah Ibrāhīm and 'Abd al-Qādir Ḥassan. If we were to record every valuable contribution made by our movement during this period, we should need a long time for painstaking research and we do not have such today. But we cannot gloss over a number of important events, typical of many others, in order to bring out the dynamic spirit which had animated our movement. We shall confine the narrative to three important cases: defense of the farmer, the combat against misery, and defense of religion.

Defense of the Farmer

The struggle of the party in the cause of the farmer took different shapes and manifestations, as was pointed out in the section on the committee of religious and social reforms; it included defense of his land and resistance to its sequestration for the benefit of the colonists. We succeeded in defeating the edict that would have brought considerable tracts unde public domain. The National Party made a heroic stand in its desperate defense of the 200,000 hectares of the Tadla lands; these had been earmarked for sequestration for a long time, but implementation had been delayed in the face of our resistance. General Noguès made an attempt to revive the scheme. The National Party thereupon mobilized the entire tribe in defense of its rights. The agitation resulted in the arrest of many Tadla nationalists, but the plan of the Residency was suspended and some of the disputed land was actually distributed to Moroccan farmers only.

On another occasion the colonists, taking advantage of inadequate rainfall, attempted to exploit the farmers of Wādi Imūr, near Marrakech. The tribe made repeated complaints but to no avail. The nationalist movement came to its support, organizing a big demonstration before the government house in the area. In spite of the attempts of Glaoui and of the French commandant to resolve the dispute in favor of the colonists, the tribe determined to fight for its rights, come what may. The dispute was finally resolved with a partial satisfaction of the farmers' demands; it guaranteed the watering of their land from the wadi flow and allocated certain days of the week to watering the lands of the colonists.

The tribe of Banī Yazighah, near the town of Safro in the province of Fez, had been subjected to the authoritarian and arbitrary rule of the local administration. A number of colonists and rich Jews succeeded in taking possession of the water sources in the upper valley upon which the entire tribe depends for its water requirements. They withheld th water from the tribe whenever it suited them to do so. The National Party had established a strong branch in the area which stood in strong opposition to the tribal chieftain al-Bazāri who had been a willing instrument of the colonials. General Blanc, the governor of the Fez province, could not reconcile himself to the spread of the nationalist movement in the tribal areas in the way it had spread in the urban centers. He resisted the nationalists by all possible means including the tampering with their water supply. The colonists, who owned the water supply, complied with his request and withheld the water flow. The farmers complained to the local authorities but were turned back. They sent a delegation to the Residency-General, which upon its return was arrested. A demonstration organized by their compatriots was dispersed by the police. The branch of the National Party decided on a policy of civil disobedience. The authorities sent summons to the party branch leaders, but they refsued to present themselves. The commandant, with a detachment of cavalary troops, proceeded to their headquarters where they had locked themselves up. The commandant opened fire, provoking them to retaliation; an engagement ensued in the course of which the commandant and several of his men suffered wounds.

General Blanc, governor of the province, was shaken by the incident and so also was General Noguès. In his capacity as supreme commander of the army, he ordered the eighth cavalry battalion in Fez to proceed on a punitive expedition against the unarmed tribe of Banī Yāzighah. Unspeakable acts of savagery were inflicted on the unarmed Moroccans; they killed the men, violated the women, and plundered livestock; they even destroyed household furnitures and other articles. The cavalry force remained in the abode of the tribe for ten days on end, living on its food provisions and arresting those who had escaped death. When we submitted our strong protests, demanding releases of the internees and payment of compensation to the tribe for the losses it had incurred as a result of plundering and destruction by the troops, the General issued a communiqué commending the performance of the eighth battalion at Banī Yāzighah, and citing it as an example of courage and discipline.

On August 30, 1937 the department of public works,

affiliated to the Residency-General, issued an order for re-channelling the flow of abi-Fakrān river, upon which the city of Meknes and its environs depend for their drinking water and the watering of their lands. The plan was intended to change the course of the river in favor of four French colonists. At first the authorities alleged that the river was state-owned; the inhabitants submitted documentary evidence that it was the property of the inhabitants of Meknes; a system of distribution had been observed by custom for ages. In yet another move, the authorities claimed that the water was Islamic waqf property and that the waqf administration had agreed to forgoe it against payment of monetary compensation by the municipality of Meknes. The Sharī'ah court, however, had ruled that the river was not waqf property. There remained one course of action open to the authorities: the use of force to dispossess the inhabitants of their established rights. The city protested by all peaceful means; we wrote articles in "Aṭlas", "Maghrib", and "al-'Amal al-Sha'bi" newspapers, expounding the true facts of the case and requesting the protectorate to act equitably in the solution of the problem. The protectorate, however, refused to consider our demands and turned down our protest

On the first of September a crowd of Meknes citizens assembled before the municipal building to register their protests against the proposed deflection of the river flow. Many demonstrators were arrested. The following day an even greater throng, estimated at ten thousand, assembled to express their solidarity with those arrested in the demonstration of the previous day. Anti-colonial slogans were shouted demanding the eviction of the colonists. The governor of the province summoned a large force of French and Foreign Legion troops to engage the demonstrators. The troops opened fire on the people, who replied by stone-throwing. Fifteen Moroccans were killed and one hundred from both sides suffered wounds. Tension and demonstrations continue unabated, while our press organs launched a campaign demanding investigation and punishment of those responsible for the violent clash.

The following day a delegation of the National Party called on the director of the political department at the Residency to demand release of the Meknes internees, return of the wadi to its rightful owners, and punishment of those responsible for the violent clash.

The following day a delegation of the National Party called on the director of the political department at the Residency to demand release of the Meknes internees, return of the wadi to its rightful owners, and punishment of those responsible for shooting down the demonstrators. In spite of the cordial reception accorded the delegation, the position of the Residency remained vague. A second demonstration was staged and a general strike called in Meknes on November 8; General Noguès decided to proceed to Meknes in person for talks with town representatives. After an investigation on the spot the General promised to act promptly on their demands.

In the meantime the National Party organized demonstrations of solidarity throughout Morocco. A general one-day strike was observed in protest against the policy of repression in Meknes; special prayers were said in the mosques of Morocco in memory of the martyrs. The national press intensified its anti-government campaign, with the result that the Residency suspended "al-'Amal al-Sha'bi" (the people's action) newspaper and confiscated the issues of the "Aṭlas" and "Maghrib" papers. The Residency also used the prevailing tension as a pretext for banning the conference of the North African Muslim Students' Association, which had been scheduled to convene in Morocco this year also.

In the Khalīfīyah Zone the municipality of Tetuan attempted to seize a number of water springs for the benefit of colonists also. Moroccans whose rights would have been infringed protested and three national youths were arrested in the process. The Islāḥ (reform) Party organized a large-scale demonstration which led the Spanish Residency-General to retreat from its position and set free the three arrested youths.

All these events and others likewise demonstrated the profound concern of the nationalist movement for the rights of Moroccans as individuals and as groups; the farmers who had suffered most from exploitation by the French and their henchmen claimed our particular attention. The chain of local events eventually compelled the Residency-General to give consideration to our repeated demands for the adoption of a sound water policy, based upon regulating and damming the water supplies of Moroccan rivers and canals. General Noguès made a start along these lines in the area of Tadla in the south; but so far the plan has not been brought to fruition, although it is the only way to overcome the vagaries of rainfall and the attendant droughts which afflict the country.

Combating Misery

The National Party did not stop at the point of direct relief work organized by its relief committee but carried on a ceaseless campaign against the plight of the underprivileged and of those in distress. There was hardly one issue of "Aṭlas" that did not carry an article depicting the abject poverty of the Moroccan masses and demanding amelioration of their conditions. We expressed and defended the view that economic distress could only be overcome by providing employment or private means to the needy classes; that a people could not live on hand-outs and philanthropy; that every citizen had the right to expect a basic minimum; and finally, that the government must provide the means whereby every citizen is able to earn this basic minimum in an honorable way and without losing his human dignity and self-esteem.

As the economic depression deepened, the Residency-General became ashamed and was fearful of public opinion in France and elsewhere. In the face of its attempts to cover up the realities of the situation, the party published numerous photographs depicting the prevailing misery. When M. Ramadier, Minister of Public Works, visited Marrakech on September 24, 1937, accompanied by General Juin, the Residency arranged an impressive welcome designed to convey a rose-colored picture of the situation and to cover up all manifestations of mass distress. The branch of the National Party in the city immediately organized a countermove; it assembled more than five thousand of the city's hungry and unclad men, women, and children. They shouted slogans against the protectorate regime, which had deprived them of their land and had placed them under the oppression of the colonists. The crowd closed in on the French Minister and he had no alternative but to withdraw from the scene in the company of the Resident-General. The throng, however, followed in his trail, demanding that he acquaint himself with the realities of the situation from the common folk and not from Glaoui and his associates. The Minister finally made his way to the government house after leaving with the demonstrators pieces of his mauled garment. The crowds continued their demonstration, shouting anti-colonial slogans, and demanding bread and freedom. Hundreds of demonstrators were arrested in this incident.

On September 26 demonstrations were resumed in the city of Marrakech under the leadership of party members in the city. Large crowds, drawn from all classes of society, marched in a demonstration of solidarity with their compatriots in distress. The troops opened fire on the crowds wounding several scores, while several hundred others were locked up in jail. The authorities also arrested five party leaders in the south and banished them to the town of Tarudant for detention at hard labor.

The party organized several public gatherings to express solidarity with the struggle of the citizens of Marrakech. One of the most important of these gatherings was held at Casablanca where thousands of citizens participated; the conferees sent cables of protest to the French Foreign Ministry and to the Residency. The headquarters of the party at Fez called a conference in which representatives from all parts of Morocco took part. The conferees protested against the French policy of perpetuating poverty and ignorance. After the conference an orderly demonstration was staged in which large throngs took part. The "Aṭlas" and the "Maghrib" were again confiscated on account of their articles and news coverage of the demonstrations.

Defense of Religion

In its struggle to secure human freedoms for Moroccans as individuals and in their collectivity, the National Party addressed its attention to the principle of religious freedom, which France's Berber policy had attempted to subvert. The party seized on every opportunity to dissuade the administration from its policy, and to leave the Berber Muslims unhindered in the enjoyment of their religious freedom and the spiritual contentment which they had found only in their Islamic faith. The authorities planned to institute an official pilgrimage to the town of al-Khumīsat in honor of St. Theresa, patroness of the Catholic Church. Al-Khumīsat, as we have said earlier, is a Berber town which had been chosen by the authors of the Berber Edict as the testing ground for the implementation of their policy. It is a well-known fact that up to the present day it does not have a single Christian among its inhabitants. The proposed pilgrimage to this missionary church was, therefore, only another demonstration of France's Berber policy. The National Party submitted an official protest to the Residency-General. At the same time the local authorities made matters worse, when they banned a traditional Muslim festival, organized in November of every year by teachers at the Koranic schools, for the tribes of Zamūr and Zāyān. When the teachers protested, the French controller informed them that he would permit their gathering only if they restricted it to mere festivities and excluded a mass recital of the Koran in the traditional manner.

In the face of this decision, the National Party's branch at al-Khumīsāt decided to hold a mass demonstration in protest against this new manifestation of the Berber policy; thousands of demonstrators from the Zamūr tribe jammed the great mosque in the town, where they listened to an address by 'Abd al-Ḥamīd al-Zamūri, chairman of the party branch and an alumnus of Azūr school. After prayers were said the crowds marched through the streets of this Berber town. The controller summoned troop reinforcements from Rabat and General Noguès himself arrived by plane. In the clash that ensued between the army and the demonstrators several persons lost their lives and many more sustained injuries. The authorities arrested members of the party branch as well as hundreds of Berbers. Nevertheless, the proposed pilgrimage for St. Theresa was abandoned in the manner originally envisaged.

The October 13 Celebration at Fez

As a counterpoise to the missionary demonstration organized by the Residency, the nationalists in the city of Fez held unprecedented celebrations on October 13 to mark the anniversary of al-Mawla Idrīs, patron of the city and the son of Idrīs the Great, founder of the first independent Arab Muslim state in Maghrib. The crowds assembled at the Idrīsi mausoleum said prayers for the martyrs of the events in Meknes, al-Khumīsāt, Banī Yāzighah, and other places in Morocco. It was the general view of the celebrants that the task of the nationalist movement was no longer solely one of resistance to French tyranny and of a demand for political and social freedoms; it had become rather a questic of defending Islam against foreign encroachments and of resuscitating the independent Moroccan state, first founded by Idrīs the Great.

The sequence of events was so disconcerting to General Noguès and his associates that they lost all sense of balance and prudence. Attacks against the nationalists were intensified throughout Morocco, and the civil controllers indulged in a sort of a race to arrest party members and supporters. This was particularly the case in the Berber mountainous regions, where the French could not bring themselves to acquiesce in the organization of the inhabitants within the fold of a firmly established Moroccan party. Extensive arrests were carried out in Banī Majild and Ayat Yūsa, while hundreds of nationalists were tortured in Banī Warayn. In spite of these severe measures the prisoners refused to sign statements that they were quitting the National Party. By the middle of October the number of internees exceeded ten thousand. The authorities also showed increasing impatience towards the national press; several issues were confiscated and finally the "Aṭlas", mouthpiece of the National Party, was suspended. The authorities also considered the imposition of press censorship, but the national press preferred to cease publication altogether rather than submit to press curtailment.

The National Party's General Conference

It became no longer possible for the leaders of the National Party to remain content with the issuing of directives to active participants in the movement, nor could they watch with hands folded the wave of arrests that was sweeping the country from one end to the other. The executive committee of the party decided, therefore, to convene an extraordinary conference of the party, with a view to studying the situation and obtaining its mandate for a policy of open hostility to the protectorate. The conference was held at Rabat on October 13, 1937 in the residence of Aḥmad al-Sharqāwi, member of the party's national council and leader of the Rabat branch. I opened the conference with a speech, in which I dwelt on the protectorate's intensified wave of persecutions and requested the delegates to study the Moroccan situation in the light of these developments. Omar 'Abd al-Jalīl, member of the executive, also reviewed the position of the nationalist movement in the prevailing critical conditions. After a general debate in which representatives of all regions participated, Muḥammad Yazīdi read the draft of a covenant, drawn up by the executive committee, for discussion and adoption by the conference, so that the party could continue in its effective resistance to the hideous policies of the protectorate. The conference adopted the final draft as follows:

The National Covenant

The conferees, assembled in the house of the brother Aḥmad al-Sharqāwi, the evening of Wednesday the seventh of Sha'ban 1356 A.H. (October 13, 1937), representing the branches of the party in the regions of Oujda, Taza, Burkan, Fez, Meknes, Wazān, Sidi Qāsim, Sidi Yeḥya, Qunayṭera, Cela, Rabat, Casablanca, Jadīdah, Āsifi, Suwayrah, Settat, and Marrakech--

In view of the material and the moral crises through which our Moroccan land is passing at the present time and which have resulted from the policy of discrimination and oppression pursued by the Residency-General;

Whereas the protectorate had failed to live up to its promises, made on many occasions, concerning the implementation of Morocco's urgent demands, in spite of the country's dire need for action in the fields of relief, social welfare, and justice;

In view of the painful events in Meknes, in the course of which the blood of freedom-loving martyrs was spilled, fire was opened on the unarmed crowds, and many an innocent person was arrested for trial before military tribunals, their only guilt being their solidarity with the prisoners who had resisted the spoliation of their water rights;

In view of the persecutions, resorted to by the authorities, in the Bawādi [tribal areas] of Morocco against anyone who joins or contacts our movement, and where hundreds have been imprisoned, tortured, and bound in iron chains, where livestock was let loose and house holdings were destroyed; and whereas the administration had let loose a regular cavalry force upon the abode of Maṭarnāgha of Bani Yāzagha where they committed the most heinous crimes including the destruction of tents, the plundering of properties and livestock, the raping of women, and the torturing of the innocent.

Whereas the authorities had given a free hand to Bayyāz, Glaoui, and their associates, to oppress Moroccans by means of imprisonment, exile, torture, flogging, iron chains, and rape; whereas their attacks extended to the 'Ulemas of the Sharī'ah law and other religious dignataries, the closing down of Koranic schools, the banishment of their teachers, the desecration of their books, the confiscation of the national press, and the imposition of punishment and fines upon those who read them;

Whereas the responsible authorities had permitted a missionary pilgrimage to the church of St. Theresa, as patroness of the missionaries at al-Khumīsāt, and had forbidden students of Âyat Urbīl of the Zamūr tribe to hold their annual Koranic celebration, except on condition that they refrained from reciting the Koran and from including in their prayers solicitations for His Majesty the Sultan; whereas previous to that they had banned celebrations in Marrakech, on the anniversary of the Prophet's birthday, which proves that the spirit of the Berber policy still dominates the administration of the protectorate;

Whereas the Moroccan press has been choked by censorship, suspension, and confiscation;

Whereas the government has turned down all applications for the establishment of various societies and associations;

Whereas the hired pro-colonial press has been levelling accusations and depicting our movement in a manner contrary to facts; --and having listened to the statements of the National Party pertaining to the aforementioned, and having studied the situation in all its ramifications, the conferees have resolved:

1. To condemn in the name of the Moroccan people all the dastardly persecutions committed in Meknes, Marrakech, Bani Yazāgha, and the Moroccan Bawādi; to protest against these barbarous acts, which represent the spirit of the Dark Ages, and to demand the release of all internees and the expeditious payment of compensation to all the victims and their families for the losses inflicted upon them.

2. To protest in the strongest terms against the persecution of the Moroccan press and resolve to combat all measures and attempts designed to suspend, confiscate, or censor the press; to demand for the Moroccan press the same rights that are accorded to the foreign press in Morocco.

3. To condemn the persistent refusal of the Residency to concede to Moroccans the right to form associations whatever be their aims.

4. To place responsibility for this policy upon the reactionary spirit which permeates the protectorate circles and which had in the past stirred the indignation of Morocco and the Muslim world.

5. To pledge themselves to resist these iniquitous policies by all effective and legitimate means, and leave decision as to methods and timing to the responsible leaders of the party.

6. To condemn all the false accusations and the tendentious fabrications attributed to our movement by reactionary circles and the colonial press; and to declare that the movement has no connection with any foreign element and should not be regarded as responsible except for what emanates from those responsible in the National Party.

7. To resolve that no understanding with the government is possible so long as liberties are suppressed and persecutions persists and so long as the urgent demands of Morocco have not been met; to consider His Majesty the King's patronage of his people and the sympathetic attitude of the libertarians in the French democratic camp as facilitating the attainment of these objectives.

8. To pledge God to carry out the contents of this Covenant and declare their readiness to offer the necessary sacrifices with a view to this end.

Thus, the conference decided upon direct action in resistance to the policy of General Noguès and in defense of Moroccan freedoms. The executive committee directed Muḥammad al-Yazīdi to communicate the text of the Covenant to the Residency-General. As soon as the chief secretary read the text he was perturbed; two hours later he flew to Paris on a mission for the Resident-General. Earlier,

Glaoui Pasha had flown to Paris to join with the Residency-General in impressing upon the French authorities the seriousness of the nationalist menace.

Thus, reactionary feudalism united with colonialism in resistance to modernism and national liberation. On October 20, Commandant Couget contacted me in the name of the Residency-General and the governor of Fez, with a view to exploring a way out of the dilemma, or, to put it more correctly, to threaten me with the impending disaster. I refused, however, to meet with him except in his office. He agreed, and we met in the presence of 'Abd al-Jalīl al-Wazāni, one of the administration supporters, whose presence Couget evidently thought would serve as witness that the protectorate had exerted all possible efforts towards appeasing us before taking its final decision of banishment. But I was not in a situation that permitted me to accept the slightest friendly overtures or artificial congeniality, so my talk with him was one of firmness and anger, filled with accusations against the Residency-General and the protectorate, and a condemnation of their acts against religion, the country, and humanity.

On October 25 the Resident-General issued an order for my arrest together with Muḥammad al-Yazīdi, Omar 'Abd al-Jalīl, and Aḥmad Mikwār. We were moved to the town of Midlet where we spent the night together. In the morning, we were taken to the military fortress at Qaṣr al-Sūq and placed in solitary confinement under the surveillance of French troops.

On November 3, I was flown in a special plan from Qaṣr al-Sūq to the desert, and thence to Gabon in Equatorial Africa, as I shall narrate later on, while my colleagues were taken to various places in the Moroccan desert.

The National Rebellion

These tyrannical measures caused intense revulsion in the hearts of all Moroccans; no sooner had the news of our arrest become known than widespread demonstrations occurred throughout the towns and villages of Morocco from Marrakech to Oujda. The demonstrators expressed their strongest solidarity with the party's arrested leaders and their loyalty to the cause for which they had been detained.

The authorities arrested hundreds of demonstrators in all parts of Morocco. A violent clash occurred in Qunayṭera on October 27 between the nationalists and the police, as a result of which fourteen were killed and scores of Moroccans were injured. Following the clash, our friend Muḥammad al-Duyūri, leader of the Qunayṭera party branch, was arrested and sentenced to two years imprisonment. The arrest was followed by further strikes and clashes. The arms depot in the town was blown up by unknown persons, causing considerable losses.

In Fez, the intellectual capital of Morocco and the headquarters of the National Party, demonstrations reached the peak of intensity. The supreme military command instructed General Blanc, governor of the province, to occupy and defend the city. Violent encounters between the army and the civilians continued for days, during which the General issued military communiqués on the progress of the operations against nationalist concentrations in Fez. After a bitter struggle, in the course of which many were killed and wounded, the General succeeded in occupying the headquarters of the party, located in the Nawā'iriyīn quarter; the center is still under military occupation almost ten years after this encounter.

After the siege and occupation of the city the demonstrators were left with only one center, the Qarawīyīn mosque, in which to assemble in thousands to express their solidarity with the leaders. The government thereupon issued an order closing down all the mosques in Morocco. The nationalists continued, nonetheless, to assemble in the Qarawiyīn, using all means to reach it. The army drove them forcibly out of the mosque and into the street, where other detachments of troops stood ready for them. Bloody battles ensued, following which 1,150 nationalists were jailed. 'Abd al-'Azīz ibn Idrīs, al-Hāshimi al-Fīlāli, and other distinguished leaders of the movement were also arrested.

On October 29 the administration summoned Muhammad Ḥassan al-Wazāni for an inquiry into his attitude towards the events; when he expressed his solidarity with the National Party, he also was thrown into jail. At the same time, Ḥaj al-Ḥassan abi'Ayyād, member of the party's national council, and Ibrahim al-Kattāni were arrested also. Demonstrations continued throughout Morocco for several weeks on end, during which the authorities behaved with the utmost brutality. The wave of demonstrations was followed by a series of terrorist acts by unknown persons, which included attacks upon the offices of some foreign newspapers and the petroleum reservoir, along with similar manifestations of popular disaffection.

The internees in the various military and civilian prisons were treated like ordinary criminals; a considerable number of their intellectuals and leaders were banished to Būthnīb and other localities in the remote desert, where they were forced to work at hard labor, which crippled their health and cost many of them their lives. It is not our intention to record here what our colleagues in the movement suffered on account of their solidarity with us. A special 150-page book has been prepared by a number of those colleagues depicting in detail the treatment meted out to the nationalists in October 1937.

General Noguès thought that he had taken his revenge and had finally destroyed the Moroccan nationalist movement. He visited Fez on October 31 while blood was still flowing, and there he told the pressmen, "I shall never close my eyes on the acts of the nationalists." The General added: "I know well that now I can count upon the support of all French parties, which have realized the extent of the danger and have seen the gradual unfolding of the revolutionary program. Launched in the name of the National Party, it has in one month stirred the entire country from one end to the other. In order to destroy the plans of the nationalists it has been necessary to use the force of our army; this is a case of public security; we have therefore done our duty; we have used force, and will continue to use it.

The General had thus testified to the strength and the pervasiveness of the nationalist rebellion under the leadership of the National Party. The party had successfully mobilized the entire nation under one banner in defense of national rights and the freedoms of the citizens.

Solidarity of the Khalīfīyah Zone

The demonstrations of solidarity were not restricted to the French Zone of occupation but went beyond it to the International and the Spanish Zones. Since October 29 Tetuan had been the scene of massive demonstrations in support of freedom, the unity of Morocco under the common crown, and the struggle of the arrested leaders. The crowds had responded to the call of 'Abd al-Khāliq al-Ṭarrīs and al-Makki al-Nāṣiri for a general strike and public gatherings.

In the town of 'Arāish several thousands representing all the tribes of the Khalīfīyah Zone assembled in a conference which was addressed by al-Makki al-Nāṣiri. The conferees cabledprotests to the President of the French Republic, to the Foreign Minister, and to General Noguès, expressing the determination of the Moroccan tribes to rally to the support of the nationalist movement, with all possible means, for the achievement of its sacred goals. The conferees also cabled their loyalty to His Majesty the Sultan.

The press in the Khalīfīyah Zone gave full coverage to the events, with editorials deploring the behavior of the French authorities and demanding release of the nationalist leaders and party supporters.

Expressions of solidarity with the Moroccan people were made in both Algeria and Tunisia, in spite of the fact that the policy of repression had been extended to Algeria herself. The conference of the Tunisian Dustūr Party, meeting at the palace of Hilāl, declared absolute solidarity with the Moroccan nationalists; a general strike was called for three days, and strong protests were addressed to the authorities.

In the Arab East and throughout the Muslim world generally, thepress gave full publicity to the struggle of Morocco, expressing their solidarity and admiration, while the various parties and organizations conveyed their protests and indignation to French diplomatic representatives.

The Moroccan rebellion was also echoed widely in the foreign press and broadcasting stations; it became the subject of a bitter war of nerves between French broadcasts on the one hand and the broadcasting stations of Italy, Germany and the Arab countries on the other, which gave full play to the atrocious acts of the French authorities.

The secretary general of the party, Ḥaj Aḥmad Bla Freej conducted a propaganda campaign in France and Switzerland, in spite of the French parties' unanimous support for and solidarity with General Noguès. His activities led the Residency-General to petition the French Government for his extradition, but the request was turned down. He continued his activities until he was afflicted with a serious illness which would have cost him his life had it not been for a successful operation.

It is fair to acknowledge the protest which Professor Massignon and a group of his colleagues at the Sorbonne and the Collège de France had submitted against my banishment to Equatorial Africa, in spite of the hostile public opinion in France towards our movement.

The Struggle Continues

Despite the severity of French repression, and despite the closing down and occupation of the National Party headquarters by armed troops, the party cells continued to function quietly but nonetheless effectively. The nationalists became known in Moroccan circles as the Ḥizbīyīn (the partisans). They regained mastery of the situation in 1938, following the release of al-Yazīdi, who led the movement with great discretion and foresight and succeeded in revitalizing the party's manifold activities.

The work of publicity and organization did not cease for one moment in the city of Fez; many of the party youths deserve warm tribute for keeping alive the spirit of the movement and preserving its orientation. Of these we mention the name of Muḥammad al-Sa'dāni, who succeeded in winning the friendship and respect of his colleagues and in rallying them behind the movement.

The Residency-General was not unaware of these activities, and arrests of active party members were carried out at various intervals. The year 1939 witnessed a number of important events and public gatherings in protest against the Residency-General; it also witnessed mounting resistance to Moroccan collaborators with the French.

General Noguès attempted a number of friendly overtures towards certain nationalist elements; he extended a cooperative hand to the alumni associations, which he regarded as moderate and non-partisan. The associations accepted his overtures and submitted to him several memoranda pertaining to educational, judicial, and other vital reforms. They were soon afterwards convinced, however, that the protectorate did not want reforms, and contacts with the General waned.

The policies of the nationalist movement were always dictated by prudent and passion-free calculations of the national interest; thus, when Fascist Italy submitted her demands pertaining to the exploitation of Moroccan phosphate deposits and referred her case to the Permanent Court of

International Justice at the Hague, the nationalists acted promptly, declaring their opposition to the seizure of Morocco's natural resources by Italy, France, or any other state. They reiterated the nationalist standpoint, enunciated by the National Party, in favor of the nationalization of the country's basic resources.

In confluence with the political movement were the societies for the preservation of the Holy Koran, which played an important role in consolidating the movement during the absence in exile of the leaders. When we consider that these societies had been the only ones in the country permitted to carry on their work in the open, we are able to gauge the extent of their contribution in religious and social instruction as well as in the gatherings which they were able to arrange and which were attended by many party supporters. Party members, however, did not cease activities of their own, despite the reign of iron and fire; anniversaries and party observances continued as before; statements, speeches, protests, and demonstrations continued to emanate from the party at home and abroad. Moroccan students in France formed the "Hay'at al-Difāʿ 'an al-Maghrib al-Aqṣā" (the organization for defense of Morocco) and continued the struggle for the principles of the party; they availed themselves of every conference and gathering to raise the voice of Morocco and condemn the atrocities of the colonial regime.

The National Party's student mission to Egypt did a most commendable job; it resuscitated the Moroccan cause in the East, which had lain dormant and was forgotten, through press releases, articles, lectures, and other media of communication.

In the Khalīfīyah Zone

In 1938 the Party of "al-Iṣlāḥ al-Waṭani" (national reform in the Khalīfīyah Zone decided to draw up a program for national reforms along lines of our program of 1933. The central committee of the party adopted the Moroccan People' Demands as the platform of the reform party, after introducing minor changes to suit the peculiar circumstances of the zone. The preamble reads in part:

> The Moroccans are conscious of their independent entity and the need for preserving it; the main attributes

of our country are: Islam, Arabism, and Maghribism; therefore, we wish to state in this preamble that we are Maghrib Muslims, our religion is Islam, our official language is Arabic, and our nationality is Arab Muslim nationality, oriented towards cooperation with the Muslim states; that the Maghrib in all its zones is a unity indivisible; that our fundamental concept of government is a Muslim monarchical system based upon "shūra" (consultation) and the precepts of the Islamic Sharī'ah, together with those aspects of the modern system whose application has attested to their suitability for the human society. We do not forget the notable services made by the noble 'Alawīyah family in Morocco; we are, therefore, strongly attached to the exalted 'Alawi dynasty. Formerly, in our capacity as the National Kutlah of the North, and latterly, as the Party of National Reform, we have consistently defended the unity of Morocco and have supported unity of action in the common struggle for its betterment. We had been acquainted with the "Demands of the Moroccan People" before their submission officially to His Majesty the Sultan and to the French Government; we had supported the demands and had defended them on many occasions in the pages of the then mouthpiece of our movement, "al-Ḥayāh", because the "Demands of the Moroccan People" in the South are in reality the needs of Northern Maghrib.

Yes, there have been a number of modifications in the "Demands of the Moroccan People", but these modifications have been necessitated by conditions in this zone and by its new legislative enactments, which on occasion have been at variance with the enactments in the Sultānīyah Zone.

The demands were submitted to His Highness the Sultan's Khalīfah and to representatives of the Spanish protectorate. They were printed in a special booklet by the Mahdīyah press and distributed to the people by the Reform Party with appeals for its support.

While the nationalists were preparing their demands, the Spanish community had been conspiring against His Highness the Khalīfah, who had adopted a sound nationalist attitude and had succeeded in securing a number of rights and concessions for the people, to which reference has been made earlier. The Spanish community started an agitation for depriving the Khalīfah of his powers and for a return to the policy of repression, which had been pursued before the appointment of Beigbeder as Resident. The Franco regime heeded the complaints of the Spanish community and removed Beigbeder from his post in 1938, appointing General Asensio in his place. The community submitted its demands to the General and he accepted them on condition that they be implemented in gradual stages. A series of extraordinary decrees were promulgated and the Residency tightened the grip on the Khalīfah government and on the nationalist movement.

Before we conclude this chapter, it is necessary to indicate that Morocco remained until the declaration of World War II under a system of arbitrary and oppressive government, just to please a group of rulers who are averse to any form of accountability or control.

The protectorate did not carry out any of the urgent demands submitted by the nationalist movement in 1936 as a follow-up to the reform program. The ministers of the right as well as those of the extreme left in the Third Republic were in collusion on the maintenance of things as they are. Naturally this convinced the Moroccan nationalists that it was futile to seek cooperation with a regime which had withheld its hand from them and had flouted even the provisions of the 1912 agreement.

During World War II

In spite of all the hardships to which Moroccan nationalism had been subjected, and in spite of the Residency-General's persistence in its reign of oppression and terror, the National Party decided to demonstrate once more its goodwill. A delegation was sent to the Residency-General to convey the solidarity of the Moroccan nationalists with His Majesty the Sultan in his desire that nothing should happen that might hinder the war effort and prejudice final victory.

Indeed, the attitude of His Majesty the King had profoundl influenced the orientation of the nationalist movement during the war. His Majesty had expressed his genuine desire that

Morocco should assume the role of a faithful ally. He did not wish the Moroccan army to be a mere fighting unit in the ranks of the other forces; his wish was that Morocco should be considered as a belligerent state, fighting against racialism and the persecution of peoples, so that he might be able to press national demands in the name of these principles after the war. His Majesty's personality appeared in all its greatness in the face of all the trepidations and vicissitudes of the period. He utilized every opportunity to press forward the demands of Morocco. This was the case at the beginning of the war, during the Vichy armistice, and after the Allied landings in North Africa. He was unperturbed by defeat or adversity and unmoved by success; the succession of various regimes and powers did not take him aback. His Majesty declared on more than one occasion that Morocco was ready to go to war if either Germany or Italy decided on an invasion of the country. He also resisted the racial decrees, which General Noguès had attempted to enforce against Moroccan Jews, requiring them to vacate their residences in the European quarters. When the Resident-General requested him to leave Rabat after the Allied landing, he refused his request, stating that he should set an example to all Moroccans and that he could not leave the capital of his kingdom, come what may. He remained in his palace while bombs were thundering from one end of the city to the other.

The Germans attempted to enlist collaborators from among the National Party ranks but did not find a single member willing to cooperate. They intensified their direct propaganda campaign, harping on the theme of an impending German victory which would enable Morocco to attain greater freedom and justice; the nationalists, however, were not taken in by their promises. They had been able to uncover the real intentions of the Germans through party supporters in Paris and in other European capitals; this was the founding of a German empire based upon the racial superiority of Aryans. The secretary-general of the National Party, Aḥmad Bla Freej, went in person for the purpose of ascertaining Axis intentions; he was not deceived by the attitude of certain Arab leaders or beguiled by the avalanche of foreign propaganda; he sent reports to his colleagues warning them to beware of Axis intrigues and enticements. Thus, the National Party was able to steer its course amidst conflicting currents and ideologies and to adopt an attitude of support for the principles of democracy, while at the same time defending the rights and freedoms of Morocco. It was also getting ready for its great stride forward, which we shall describe later on.

In 1940 there were intensive probings in nationalists circles for a way of deliverance from the protectorate regime and liberation from foreign bondage. They had been pondering the atrocities of French rule and the unrepentance of France, in spite of all that had befallen her and in forgetfulness of Morocco's sacrifices in blood for her cause.

The policies of General Noguès during the war consisted entirely of repression, marshal law, and wild accusations against the innocent. The General had been apprehensive of the King's farsighted policies and of the exemplary manner in which the National Party had pursued its aims.

If we add to this the General's lack of moral courage and his vacillations, which were always exhibited most pitiably in emergencies despite his high office, we shall be able to understand the deep contempt in which the Moroccan people held a regime headed by people like Noguès, ruling over the destinies of a brave country.

If the Residency-General had justified its persecution of the National Party on account of its extremism and its methods for achieving the national aims, its attitude towards the alumni associations, which comprise alumni of French institutions and in which General Noguès had at one time placed confidence, unveiled the true face of the protectorate and its men. These associations are established in accordance with the stipulations of the Residency itself and function under the surveillance of French technical advisers, who receive instructions from the Residency. Notwithstanding all this, the associations failed to obtain even the most trivial of their demands for reforms; their reports to the Residency-General, pertaining to a reorganization of Moroccan courts and education, for example, did not receive the slightest consideration on the part of the protectorate. This led the alumni to refuse participation in the so-called "government consultative council"; they refused to act as dummies, whose views were not solicited even on such vital war-time problems as food, housing, and the necessities of life.

The protectorate persisted in its repressive policies even after the Allied landings in North Africa; it could not care less what the hundreds of thousands of Europeans and Americans felt after witnessing the sorrowful plight of the Moroccan people; on the contrary, the presence of those foreigners was used by the Residency as a spur for renewed oppressions, to prove perhaps that it did not fear anyone and that it could continue its tyranny regardless of all considerations, in order to dim in the hearts of the people all hopes of assistance from the democratic camp.

It is no wonder then that the Moroccan people should have decided on a sound new course of action; it is no wonder that the National Party should have declared its abandonment of the policy of gradualism in favor of a policy of unequivocal and expeditious independence.

The Vichy Armistice

The policies of the Residency-General in Morocco did not undergo any changes as a result of the German occupation of Paris and Marshal Pétain's seizure of power. All that had happened was a visit to Morocco by the armistice commission. The commission did not meet with any response from the nationalist circles. His Majesty the King continued his efforts in defense of Moroccan rights, as has been stated earlier. All the while, however, the idea of launching a new movement was gaining in momentum, and nationalist circles were awaiting an opportune moment for making their voice heard.

In this year (1940) Spain occupied the International Zone of Tangier and there were demonstrations by the Spanish Fascists throughout Spain demanding the military occupation of the French Zone in Morocco. Franco responded to the demands of his compatriots; he permitted the Germans to undergo military training in the Khalīfīyah Zone and to occupy a number of Moroccan ports. Nationalist sentiment in Tangier, as in the rest of Morocco, was averse to the Spanish step. The Moroccan nationalists were incensed by the expulsion of the Sultan's representative to Tangier and the taking over of his palace for the German embassy. There was a sharpening of national consciousness and of the desire for independence from both France and Spain so that the country might be spared their disastrous competition for hegemony.

When the Allies landed in Morocco on November 8, 1943, anxieties arising from Spanish expansion and German occupation were relieved. The nationalists intensified their activities in the face of French obduracy and ill-treatment. The National Party reorganized its branches and was joined by many government employees who had hitherto refrained from active participation in politics. The party issued a magazine by the name of "Risālat al-Maghrib" (the mission of Morocco) which gave renewed expression to the views of nationalist literary writers and intellectuals. It also strove to rally the entire people behind a new orientation, which in fact became prevalent a year later.

The Delegation of the National Party to the East

In 1937 a student mission, consisting of 'Abd al-Karīm ibn Thābit, 'Abd al-Majīd ibn Jallūn, Aḥmad ibn al-Malīh, 'Abd al-Karīm Ghallāb, and al-'Arabi al-Banāni, proceeded to Egypt for advanced study at the Egyptian University. Upon graduating from the faculty of arts, members of the mission formed themselves into a delegation for propagating the Moroccan cause. They rendered considerable services in the critical circumstances that followed the Moroccan rebellion of 1937.

In 1943 the delegation decided that it was in the best interests of the cause to ask the other Moroccan groups in Egypt to join them in one unified organization. Representatives of the other Moroccan groups agreed, and a new organization came into being by the name of "Rābiṭat al-Difā' 'an Marrakesh fī Miṣr" (the league for defense of Morocco in Egypt).

The organization drew up and adopted the following platform:

1. To demand the independence of Morocco under the reign of His Majesty the King.

2. To safeguard in toto the territorial integrity of Morocco.

3. To achieve membership of the Arab League.

4. To propagate Morocco's nationalist cause and submit its case to Arab public opinion, to Arab governments, and to the Allied Powers.

5. To defend the nationalists in Morocco and demand the immediate return of the exiles and the release of detainees.

Thus, the delegation of the National Party in Egypt arrivat a program that was identical with the party's program in Morocco herself, in spite of the war exigencies that had cut off one from the other.

The League made valuable contributions to the cause since its founding in 1943; it established various publicity centers, distributed pamphlets, prepared booklets, and maintained contacts with the various Arab governments and their representatives.

The League utilized the presence in Egypt of delegations from the Arab states for discussions on Arab unity. At the invitation of Naḥas Pasha, it conveyed the aspirations of Morocco for freedom and independence. Memoranda and statements were presented, and marked success was achieved in winning for Morocco the sympathy and the active support of the Arab states.

Scores of refugees had also arrived in Cairo representing the Tunisian Dustūr, the Algerian People's Party, and the Society of Muslim 'Ulemas in Algeria. At first, each of these delegations worked separately; later, they all agreed to join the North African Front, set up in 1944 under the chairmanship of Sheikh Muḥammad al-Khadr ibn al-Ḥussein, one of the Zaytūnah 'Ulemas who had taken up refuge in Egypt after World War I. The organization was strengthened by the arrival of al-Ḥabīb abu Raqībah, and it continued to represent the concerted efforts of all the delegations until the convening of the Arab Maghrib conference, as we shall relate.

When the disturbances touched off in Morocco by the Istiqlāl Party occurred, they were able to echo them widely and more effectively than would have been the case if they had not been so compactly organized in one Moroccan phalanx.

All the while delegations from the National Party, and later from the Istiqlāl, had been arriving in Cairo since the resumption of the pilgrimage to the East. This bolstered up their morale and enabled them to coordinate their activities with those of their colleagues at home, even though the forced separation resulting from the war had proved the complete identity of views between members of the National Party both at home and abroad.

The Efforts in Exile

The developments in the views and orientations of my colleagues in Morocco were identical with those I had experienced in my remote exile in Gabon, and later in the Congo of French Equatorial Africa; despite the rigid control under which I had been placed, and despite the fact that I had been completely cut off from all contacts with the rest of the world and forbidden to meet with people, to read the papers or to listen to the radio, throughout the period of my exile; despite all this, my spiritual communion with the developments in the national consciousness of Morocco remained strong and unimpaired. I had been coming to the view that the Moroccan movement, after having awakened national consciousness in the masses of the people, should henceforth struggle with all its might for the achievement of independence. Even more, it should concentrate on this one objective to the exclusion of all else; for independence alone affords the opportunity to awaken our nation and to liberate it from the poverty, the ignorance, and the sickness into which it had relapsed. I used to ponder the record of the protectorate only to feel that its system had been naught but the stumbling block in the way of Morocco's progress and popular awakening, which began sixty years ago. In the midst of my inauspicious surroundings, therefore, I spent my time seeking some way that would enable me to express my views and cause the movement to leap forward to completion and success.

General Noguès had calculated for every contingency, but he had not thought that the exile of Gabon or the Congo would be a new battleground for further activity on behalf of the liberation movement. He had sent me to this remote exile in the belief that he had buried me, at least for a long time. It did not occur to him that I would find a way of working for my country, at a time when his oppression had weighed heavily upon the nationalists and had prevented them from any open activity for their country's cause.

As a matter of fact, from the moment of my banishment until the de Gaulle rebellion, it had not been possible for me to do anything except to protest against my ill-treatment and demand the rights of a political prisoner. The Vichy armistice, however, and the rebellion of General de Gaulle afforded me an opportunity to express the views of Morocco and to make a modest contribution to its cause.

In July 1940 the forces of General de Gaulle occupied the village of Muellah in the south of Gabon, where I had been detained between November 1937 and June 1941, on their march upon Libreville, the capital of Gabon. The Governorate-General appointed Commandant Rouget, a French militarist well-versed in Islamic affairs, as chief prefect. Contacts with Morocco and the rest of North Africa had been severed because the local French authorities had remained loyal to Marshal Pétain. Equatorial Africa had been a rallying center for the Free French; Brazzaville had been used as a temporary capital and a refuge for General de Gaulle whenever his relations with the British and the Allies in London became strained.

It had been the policy of the French colonial authorities in Equatorial Africa to enlist the support of the European inhabitants for de Gaulle, or failing that, to detain Vichy sympathizers in special camps. Commandant Rouget invited me one day for a discussion on the current situation; he emphasized that the situation would alter for the better and that the de Gaulle movement could fundamentally change France's colonial policy. He invited me to submit my views in writing to the Governorate-General; I discreetly evaded his request and told him that he could write to the officials himself and inform them that in my capacity as leader of the National Party I would not depart from the aims and aspirations of the party for progress and liberation. A few days passed during which Commandant Rouget wrote to the Governorate-General and made a trip to Brazzaville; when he returned, I gathered from his talk that he had not found in the local authorities the readiness or the resilience to serve France in the manner of Lyautey, to use his expression.

We had a lengthy discussion on the overall international situation, after which he asked me quite frankly to write a message to General de Gaulle; he even handed me a draft text similar to that submitted to the French residents in soliciting their support. I replied that the question of the dispute between Vichy and de Gaulle was a purely French concern and that neither I nor my other Moroccan colleagues had the right to meddle with it. "As regards resistance to the Germans," I added, "I can assure you that no Moroccan wishes to fall under the governance of Germany or Italy; moreover, it is only logical that since it is France that had entered the war in the first place, so long as it is in her power to continue resistance she should not be disloyal to her allies or betray them to the enemy. As regards the Moroccan case," I went on to say, "I consider it as my own, in my capacity as representative of the National Party; I am ready to cooperate with General de Gaulle provided he is willing to realize the aspirations of the Moroccan people. Therefore," I added, "my acquaintance with the policies of the Gaullist rebellion in regard to France is not enough. It is essential that I know his Moroccan policy as well; only then would I be able to act in the light of my evaluations and findings." I explained to the Commandant the plight of the Moroccan people and the efforts of the National Party to arrive at a working compromise between the needs of the country and friendship with France. He expressed his approval of my case and asked me to embody it in a special message which he undertook to deliver in person to General de Gaulle on the occasion of the latter's visit to Brazzaville in May. General de Larminat had been the supreme commander of French forces and High Commissioner in Equatorial Africa, while General Sicé had been director-general of the health department and was regarded in Equatorial circles as being chiefly instrumental in the Congo's siding with de Gaulle. Felix Eboue, Governor-General of Tchad, and chief administrator Laurency had been instrumental in swaying over the territory of Tchad to the Free French movement. Considerable competition had existed between de Larminat and de Gaulle with the latter enjoying by far the greater support.

I wrote a message to General de Gaulle through General Sicé, on the basis of the discussions I had had with Commandant Rouget. In the message I said, among other things

> Morocco, which is being forced to continue under a system of the Middle Ages, and which is desirous of progressing to a status similar to that attained by Egypt and Iraq, could not accept a new occupation by Germany or Italy. It believes that a true government of real France is worthy of giving satisfaction to its national aspirations.

I do not intend to outline in this message our demands; however, I do wish to emphasize that I do not seek any personal fortune, my sole aim being the welfare of my country and the realization of its rights.

The leader of the National Party, exiled since five years, wants only to know the new policy which you intend to launch as regards Morocco.

I do not represent anything in myself; my worth is solely in the confidence which my people have placed in me and in what I shall convey to them on the result of your official acts.

Lyautey, whom you respect, did not commit the mistakes which Noguès and his like have committed; he expressed his repentance for many of the policies which he himself had pursued.

Many Frenchmen have supported our movement, and if the policy of Your Excellency is in agreement with ours, then it would be possible for me to act.

Commandant Rouget carried this message to Brazzaville where he handed it over to General Sicé; the latter delivered it in person to General de Gaulle, who promised to study it with General Catroux in Syria, to which country he was proceeding to proclaim her independence. Rouget returned to his headquarters and informed me that he was optimistic regarding the attitude of de Gaulle and pessimistic as regards de Larminat and his clique. He assured me, however, that General Sicé would replace de Larminat and that the situation would thereby improve. General Sicé did in fact accompany the de Gaulle entourage to Syria, later to return to Brazzaville as Commissioner-General for the Union of Equatorial Africa.

Several days passed following which Rouget was summoned to Brazzaville; his assistant informed me that the case was proceeding satisfactorily and that Rouget's visit to Brazzaville had been undertaken in connection with it. When Rouget returned he invited me to his home where he spoke with the utmost liberality; his talks evoked in me considerable hopes, although I was well aware that the French do not change their position even in the face of the most trying vicissitudes, that they are conservative in their thinking, and that it is difficult for them to accept change as easily as is sometimes thought.

Later, a special envoy, naval lieutenant de Legrand, arrived in Muella on a mission for the department of political affairs in Equatorial Africa. He was an Arabist who had worked in Syria with M. Ponsot and had been condemned to death by the Germans for his activities on behalf of de Gaulle. We had several meetings together during which we discussed the current situation at length. He informed me that the Governorate-General had authorized him to negotiate with me, in the name of Free France, on the affairs of Morocco and the rest of North Africa. He pointed out that the Free French movement was anxious to placate the people of North Africa with a view to securing their assistance in forestalling a German occupation of North Africa, and also in accomplishing the eventual liberation of France. I expressed to him my readiness to mediate between Free France and the nationalists of Tunisia and Algeria; as regards Morocco I assured him of my readiness, along with the National Party, to work for the deliverance of the country from German pressure, in cooperation with the Free French; but I made this cooperation contingent upon one condition, namely an explicit and immediate declaration by de Gaulle pledging Morocco's independence. After the liberation, I suggested, His Majesty the Sultan would form a national government, which would conclude with France a treaty of alliance and friendship. Our talks lasted for three days during which I expounded my views on the future of Morocco and on the democratic regime that we envisaged after the declaration of independence; I suggested that the controversial points be deferred for future official negotiations over the conclusion of a treaty of alliance. We finally agreed that the Lieutenant address a cable to the Free French government summing up the results of the talks. He thereupon sent the following cable: "I have negotiated with M. 'Alāl al-Fāsi. He agrees to cooperate with Free France for the liberation of North Africa from Axis pressure, conditional upon the expeditious recognition of Morocco's independence. M. 'Alā is candid and talks sincerely and clearly; in addition to his influence in Morocco he enjoys the confidence of many Arab leaders."

The following day he received a cable, asking me to proceed to Brazzaville; upon our arrival we conferred with M. Laurency, secretary-general at the Governorate-Genera and a person who had won the confidence of M. Pleven, Minister for the Colonies, and General de Gaulle himself. The talks took place in his home, in the presence of the director of political affairs in Equatorial Africa. They lasted for three hours and were conducted in a quiet atmosphere. The theme of my talk centered around the urgency of declaring the independence of Morocco as a prerequisite for regaining confidence in France; I expressed the view that the de Gaulle movement should be at the same time a revolution for the liberation of Morocco, under the 'Alawi crown, from the existing colonial regime.

My stay in Brazzaville lasted for seven months, during which I had occasions to meet with various official personages who had been frequenting the Congo capital. I defended with the utmost zeal the nationalist cause for which I had been exiled; I also expounded to them, to the best of my ability, the Arab points of view on Tunisia, Algeria, Syria, and the Lebanon.

In July 1941 the Governorate-General received a cable from General de Gaulle in which he said: "I have studied the case of al-Fāsi and Morocco; I shall bring the file with me to Brazzaville."

The General arrived in Brazzaville to mark the first anniversary of Equatorial Africa's association with his movement, or the "memorial of the three glorious days" as they call it. He was accompanied by the Ambassador of Free France to Ethiopia, who was formerly an official of the native administration and the Residency-General in Morocco and an adjutant of Marshal Lyautey on Moroccan affairs. I met the Colonel at the home of M. Laurency; he told me that General de Gaulle had talked about me in the plane and had asked him to negotiate with me. I reiterated to him clearly and explicitly the demand for independence. I understood from his talk that he was not agreeable to independence, but was in favor of a policy of constructive and practical reforms.

Later I had a meeting with General Sicé in his office at the High Commission with M. Laurency being present also. I discerned in his talk a certain reluctance, which was at variance with what Commandant Rouget had informed me about him. He attempted to convince me of the need for a continuance of French assistance to Morocco; Morocco, he expressed the view, had not fully matured for independence. I pleaded for two hours urging the need for independence and stressing that it was the only solution for the Moroccan question.

Thus, I found myself in the confused atmosphere of Brazzaville, in the position of an exile under continuous surveillance; French official circles were split into two conflicting factions over my case; one faction consisted of the Governor-General and his chief secretary, who were in favor of cooperating with me and the National Party and utlizing our moral force, even though they did not see eye to eye on my plan for independence. Their plan was for a more liberal protectorate, which would accord partial independence agreeable to the Moroccans and at the same time safeguard the interests of France. The other faction was led by M. Giraud, chief administrator for the High Commission, who succeeded in swaying over General Sicé to his side. His view was that the nationalists should be left aside and that no help should be sought from them, because it would impose unnecessary sacrifices upon France.

It was natural that these conflicting approaches should have led to conflicting policies, which at times worked in my favor and at others found me its chief sufferer. At any rate, the conflict saved me from the life of tedious quiet and plunged me right into the midst of intense struggle. M. Giraud went so far as to forge a message, which he alleged I had sent to Marshal Pétain, assuring him that Morocco's hopes were placed in him. I must in fairness acknowledge M. Laurency's noble stand on my behalf; he put up a heroic defense emphatically declaring his faith in my probity, honor, and forthright conduct, which had been attested to by all those who had been placed in charge of me in exile. The conflict went so far that the High Commissioner would issue instructions to his employees, only to be countermanded or contradicted by Laurency. Finally, M. Laurency was summoned before an administrative tribunal but he emerged victorious.

The French National Committee headed by de Gaulle was perturbed by the widening conflict between the High Commission, and the Governorate General over all questions, including the Moroccan one. It dispatched Professor Cassin the Free French commissioner on education and justice, to Brazzaville for a general investigation of the situation. The professor invited me to present my views on the Moroccan question. M. Laurency also presented to him a report on Morocco, in the name of the Governorate, which as he told me later on was largely in accord with my views. The report, as I gathered from M. Laurency, urged the granting of partial self-government, together with the expeditious implementation of a number of vital social and economic reforms. The underlying purpose was to substitute for France's complete protectorate a kind of moral influence over the Sheriffian government, whose friendship with France would be assured by the latter's sincere help and support.

M. Cassin also sought the views of the British consul in the Congo, who was well-versed in North African affairs. The consul, as a senior staff member of the governorate informed me, suggested the urgency of granting partial independence to Morocco.

If what M. Laurency had told me--after the Allied landings in North Africa and following my protests against the ill-treatment meted out to me since my arrival to the Congo --if what he had told me was true, then both the British Foreign Office and the State Department had officially requested General de Gaulle to release me and allow me to return to North Africa with the Allied armies on the basis of my conditions for independence. M. Laurency then uttered the following words, and I quote them verbatim: "General de Gaulle is angry like yourself; he had intended to work out a solution for the Moroccan case in agreement with you; however, the request of the British and the Americans for your release and for declaring the independence of Morocco had evoked his apprehensions and had challenged the spirit of a man who does not like to work under duress."

Whatever be the case, General de Gaulle did not make any declarations on Morocco; my efforts were no more than an attempt to advance the Moroccan cause to the point it was later to reach, thanks to the efforts of my colleagues in Morocco. If my endeavors and my candidness in defense of my points of view had delayed my release for at least three years, and if they had placed me under an even more rigid control than during the first years of detention, I had at least satisfied my conscience by making a contribution in an exile from which, I must confess, I despaired of ever returning. The attempt had, moreover, fully convinced me that the colonials, whatever their differences and their circumstances, were in agreement respecting their fear of independence and their intention to retain the colonies. Even though they permit themselves and their henchmen to use the term independence on frequent occasions, their real aim is oriented solely towards assimilation or something very much like it. When the Allies landed in North Africa I realized that the role of Free France had come to an end and that circumstances would undoubtedly permit my brethren to resume their struggle. I was also convinced that my duty in communicating the voice of Morocco to the Free French had been accomplished, and that it was better to leave the field to those in Morocco to say their word. The French, I thought, would find out for themselves the truth of my predictions concerning the maturing of national consciousness in all Morocco. I therefore informed all responsible officials that any negotiations should henceforth be conducted with representatives of the National Party in Morocco and that I was in full accord with what they might say or do.

Chapter V

THE INDEPENDENCE PARTY (HIZB AL-ISTIQLAL)

We have seen how the experiences of the previous years under the protectorate and the disillusionment of the nationalist leaders in the policy of gradualism had evoked in the nationalists, inside and outside the country, the impelling need for decisive action and a frank confrontation of realities. It was no longer natural for the movement to continue in a policy of cordiality towards those who for the sake of colonialism disregard all considerations and accept no limitations. It had become obvious since 1937 that an irrevocable divorce had occurred between the people on the one hand and the protectorate regime on the other; that the Moroccans had come to see in the policies of the protectorate an outright enslavement which could no longer be masked by the charlatanism of the administration for native affairs, or by the affected smile which Lyautey had bequeathed in the manner of a sacred legacy to his successors.

It is futile to deny the impact of the war, the Atlantic Charter, the Allied landings in North Africa, and the declaration of the independence of Syria and the Lebanon--it is futile to deny the impact of all these events upon the nationalists and the encouragement they had derived from them in coming out for a forthright policy of independence. But without minimizing the influence of all these events, it must be said that the real driving force behind the new approach had been the bitter experiences of the nationalist movement. That movement had consented with considerable misgivings and reluctance to the policy of cordiality and gradualism. It is only fair to confess that it had consented to such policies with a guilty conscience, whose tantalizing prickings it could only evade by making a distinction between methods on the one hand and fundamental principles and aims on the other, with the consideration that by making the most out of the existing reality it was contributing to its ultimate ideal. Its bitter experiences, however, had caused it thoroughly to despair of the protectorate rulers, who would receive all its sincere offers for cooperation with disdainful colonial arrogance and even refuse to recognize the nobility of purpose for which it strives.

At any rate, there was general agreement on the need for abandoning a policy doomed to failure in favor of a forthright and unequivocal policy of independence--independence before all else. His Majesty the King marked the beginning of this new phase by the statements he gave on various occasions to representatives of France and of the Allied Power The statements emphasized that Morocco, which had remained steadfast during the war and had sacrificed in the cause of human freedom, should also receive her rightful share of such freedom. "You know," His Majesty declared in one of these statements, "that Morocco's shouldering of all her duties has given her an added reason for expediting the attainment of all her rights."

In order to attain these rights in their entirety and to reiterate the statement made by the people's foremost representative, the Istiqlāl (independence) Party was formed.

The National Party itself deserves most of the credit for the establishment of the new party; its executive committee had decided in favor of this sound orientation, and in order to ascertain that it was in practical accord with the wishes of the people, a general conference was called to which representatives of all shades of opinion in the country were invited to participate. The conference met at Rabat on January 11, 1944, where it gave birth to the Istiqlal as a party whose primary aim is national liberation.

The Istiqlal Party comprised the following groups:

1. The National Party, representing the overwhelming majority of farmers, craftsmen, workers, merchants, and a majority of the intellectuals in the land.

2. The presidents and members of the executive committees of the alumni associations in the cities of Rabat, Fez, Meknes, Cela, Marrakech, Azro, Oujda, and Aāsifi. These associations exercised considerable influence upon the orientation of students and had been accorded official representation on the so-called government consultative council.

3. Many leading personages in the "al-Ḥarakah al-Qawmīyah" (the nationalist movement).

4. Many leading Moroccan personages such as muftis, Sharī'ah court judges, senior officials of the Mekhzen [national] administration, lecturers at the Qarawiyīn and other leading institutions, and teachers at secondary and primary schools both state and private.

Thus, the whole nation grouped together within this party and set to work for the achievement of its aims. On January 11, 1944 the party presented a charter to His Majesty the King of Morocco and to representatives of France and the Allies. This we shall analyze before quoting in full:

1. The protectorate is a regime imposed by force upon the Moroccan people under exceptional circumstances; no better proof of this fact can be given than the record of military resistance maintained by the nation from 1907 to 1934.

2. The imposed protectorate treaty has been violated all along, in the spirit and the letter, by those who had officially pledged themselves to respect it, with the result that Moroccan sovereignty has been wiped out.

3. The policies of the protectorate have been designed to enhance the interests of European colonists and to retard or obstruct the progress of the Moroccans.

4. The recognition of the people's right to self-determination, as underlined by various Allied statements during the war, and particularly in the Atlantic Charter, as well as the presence of Moroccan armies on the Western Front; all these considerations entitle the Moroccans to the right of a free existence.

For all these reasons, the Istiqlal Party, expressing the wishes of the people, demands the following:

1. Independence and complete unity for all the Moroccan zones.

2. The establishment of a democratic system of government, similar to that obtaining in the various Islamic states, which would safeguard the rights of all elements and classes composing the Moroccan nation.

Charter of January 11, 1944
The Official Text

The Istiqlal Party comprising members of the former National Party and independent personages--

Whereas the Moroccan state had always enjoyed its freedom and national sovereignty and had preserved its independence for thirteen centuries until the protectorate regime was imposed under exceptional circumstances;

Whereas the purpose of this regime and the rationale for its existence are the introduction of reforms, needed by Morocco, in the fields of administration, the judiciary, education, economy, finance, and the military, without prejudice to the historic sovereignty of the Moroccan people and the authority of His Majesty;

Whereas the protectorate authorities had substituted for this a system based upon direct and oppressive rule, in the benefit of the French community, including the army of government employees, of which only a minor portion is Moroccan, and had not attempted to reconcile the interests of the various elements in the country;

Whereas the French community had been able through this system to take possession of the government and to monopolize the resources of the country to the exclusion of its people;

Whereas this regime had attempted by various means to disrupt Moroccan unity, to exclude Moroccans from effective participation in the management of the affairs of their country, and to divest them of all freedoms private and public;

Whereas the circumstances through which the world is now passing are different from those in which the protectorate was established;

Whereas Morocco has participated effectively in the world wars on the side of the Allies, and Moroccan soldiers have lately accomplished feats on the battlegrounds of France, Tunisia, Sicily, Corsica, and Italy which earned them the admiration of all; further, they are expected to participate on a larger scale in other fields, and particularly in the liberation of France;

Whereas the Allies, who are expending their blood in the cause of freedom, have recognized in the Atlantic Charter the right of people to govern themselves, and have at the recent Teheran conference declared their abhorrence of a system whereby the strong claim the right to dominate the weak;

Whereas the Allies have on various occasions expressed their sympathy with the Islamic peoples and have granted independence to other peoples, including some whose past and present are inferior to our own;

Whereas the Moroccan nation, which forms a coordinate unity, is conscious of its rights and obligations, at home as well as abroad, under the guidance of its beloved king, and accords full recognition to the democratic freedoms, which are in essence conformable to the precepts of our illustrious religion and have been the basis of the systems of government in the Islamic sister countries;

Resolves:

I. Pertaining to general policy--

a. To demand the independence of Morocco and its territorial integrity under the crown of His Majesty, our beloved King Muḥammad ibn Mawlana Yūsuf, may God grant him victory.

b. To request His Majesty to make representations to the interested powers, with a view to obtaining their recognition and guarantees of this independence.

c. To demand Morocco's affiliation with the signatory states of the Atlantic Charter and also participation in the peace conference.

II. Pertaining to internal policy--

d. To request His Majesty to take under his patronage the reform movement upon which the fate of Morocco hinges.

The Istiqlal Party as a Doctrine and a Faith

1. The Party Seeks Independence

The essential prerequisite for the progress of Morocco is independence, because a country that does not enjoy its national sovereignty will inevitably fall a prey to the enslavement of those who stand to gain from its seizure.

Such independence naturally requires the unity and the liberation of all Moroccan areas.

2. The Party Supports Freedom

The activities of the individual in social life require that he possess full freedom, which knows no limit save that of preserving the freedoms of others or the reasonable interests of the group as a whole. (Freedom alone enables a person to appreciate freedom.)

3. Form of Government: a Constitution

The question of the form of government does not arise in

Morocco; this is because there is a royal family, beloved by the people, who owe allegiance to the crown and to His Majesty the present reigning sovereign, Muḥammad ibn Yūsuf. His Majesty will make of the system a pillar for the unity and the cohesion of the nation.

In accordance with the principles of Islam, which are essentially in harmony with democratic precepts, Morocco should be regarded as one of the free and progressive Islamic and Eastern nations.

The Istiqlal Party, nonetheless, demands the promulgation of a democratic constitution which recognizes the rights of man and the citizen and which would take cognizance of the needs of the Moroccan people.

The constitution should provide that the Arabic language is the official language of the land and that Islam is the official religion of the Moroccan state, but with safeguards for freedom of belief and of thought for all.

All Moroccans should enjoy equality before the law; they should enjoy equal rights and assume equal obligations, without discrimination on account of religion or race.

The Jewish question is non-existent in Morocco because the Jews of the country are members of the Moroccan family as are the Copts in respect to Egypt; they would continue to enjoy, as before, their religious freedoms, and particularly those pertaining to the jurisdiction of religious courts, as is the case with other Moroccans.

4. Education and Democratic Revival

The Istiqlal Party stands for constitutional monarchy and for democratic principles. But democracy is not something new to Morocco; it is an established feature of many of our popular institutions since ages past. Therefore, the party urges a revival and a reorganization of democratic institutions such as the tribal organizations, whose functions and purport the protectorate had subverted from one of municipal councils to courts of customs and usages.

But what the party seeks is democracy in the sense understood in the great democracies of the West; it is not sufficient to revive and reinstate the old forms; the party considers it its duty to carry on a continuous training campaign in the ways of democracy for all the citizenry; it also demands a system of compulsory education in urban as well as tribal regions for children of both sexes; further, the party seeks to accustom the nation to constitutional life through the various institutions that foster its growth, and to help it acquire an appreciation for and an attachment to the aims of a democratic regime, which would be gradually adopted in the country.

5. The Question of the Cadre

The Istiqlal Party is not unaware of the fact that Morocco cannot organize unaided a government and a people on the basis of the most up-to-date Western institutions; but the party places responsibility for Morocco's lack of an adequate cadre upon the policies of the protectorate, which has arrested the country's development and the training of its citizenry; the protectorate has also adopted the French language as the medium of communication in all the important departments of government, thereby excluding from office the country's elite whose education is in Arabic.

The situation can be remedied by the restoration of Arabic as the official language, not only in principle but in fact, because it would all but remove the deficiencies in the cadre, particularly in the fields of administration, the judiciary, education, and finance. This means that the old cadre would be retained after some shakedown, while a new cadre was being prepared to replace gradually the old.

As regards technical matters, Morocco would enlist the help of foreign technical advisers in departments where no qualified Moroccans were available. At all events, the party does not subscribe to the view that the question of the cadre is an impediment in the way of Morocco's expeditious attainment of independence; the party regards it as an internal question which can be solved by a national government in a manner conducive to the welfare and progress of the country. Morocco must become independent and carry on, even with an old cadre, so as to be able to set up a modern machinery of government; otherwise she will never be able to attain her aspirations; the three generations of the protectorate are ample proof that a system run by the foreigner could not lead to the desired progress in conformity with the national and social aspirations of the country.

6. The Judiciary

Morocco should adopt a unified judicial system; the country has pursued for a long time the dual system of Mekhzen and Sharī'ah courts of law. The party, therefore, demands the drafting of a unified code, derived from the sources of the Islamic Sharī'ah and taking into account the special needs of Morocco as well as the advances achieved in the legal systems of foreign countries. In pursuance of this objective, the courts of law envisaged in the plan should be established forthwith and the judges trained in the performance of their duties. At any rate, there is no room in Morocco for foreign or mixed courts; all must be subject to the jurisdiction of Moroccan laws and Moroccan courts, and all traces of foreig extraterritorial rights must be erased.

7. Social Policy: Education and Relief

The party holds that social legislation should be enacted in Morocco, with a view to raising the material, the moral, and the mental level of the Moroccan masses; it should also improve the conditions of the working people in towns and villages, afford them adequate training, and bring them up in such a way as would inspire in them a feeling of the dignity, the worth, and the inviolability of their humanity.

Since the class of small craftsmen in towns and villages will continue to constitute an important factor in social stability for a not inconsiderable time, it is a duty to assist them, to afford them protection, to organize their ranks, and to guide them towards a cooperative system.

The distressful problem is the condition of the rural proletariat. The party holds that it can be solved through an equitable division of Morocco's land resources; this would enable villagers to obtain small and medium size farm holdings.

Free and compulsory education must be provided for all children of both sexes in their school age, in towns as well as in the countryside; public lessons should also be provided free of charge with a view to combating illiteracy.

For the benefit of all, the country must be industrialized and launched upon sound economic policies; the party advocates the nationalization of public services and the basic resources of the country.

It is the duty of the independent Moroccan government to place in the forefront of its aims programs for social relief, particularly with a view to protecting women and children and safeguarding public health.

8. National Defense and Internal Security

Irrespective of what certain prejudiced writers have

alleged regarding public security in Morocco, our country has never been in the throes of chaos; if in the beginning of the twentieth century our military establishment was inadequate for the needs and the exigencies of the time, we nonetheless had sustained vital military stations and tribal posts, which had proved adequate for the maintenance of internal and external security for many generations on end. They had even extended the benefits of Moroccan peace to remote areas along the periphery of Morocco's borders in the north, south, and east; these establishments, however, had become inadequate for the needs of the modern era and were incapable of withstanding the intrigues and the onslaughts of foreign powers, which had been lying in wait to fall upon our country. A reform of the military establishment, therefore, is vital.

The protectorate has claimed that it established public security and devised the most efficacious means for its sustenance. But we may ask what sort of security is this which knows naught but force and indiscriminate oppression? The security achieved by the protectorate has been at the expense of right and justice, and not only that, for it has deployed all its tools and techniques in the defense of an exploiting and monopolistic class of foreign capitalists and colonial usurpers.

Furthermore, it has been used as a ready instrument for political suppression and for the protection of a regime imposed upon the country in the face of continuous uprisings which lasted for thirty-eight years after its inception. The Istiqlal Party visualizes an equitable system more simple and less complicated; as regards external defense, Morocco must subscribe fully to international collective security in accordance with whatever arrangement the United Nations will adopt.

As regards internal security, a force should be established, devoted solely to the needs of maintaining order, and without the slightest power over political currents and movements; Morocco does not need a huge army such as the one maintained by the protectorate, particularly after implementation of social and educational reforms by the national government; what it needs is a mobile force which inspires public confidence in the vigilance and efficiency of the security forces. In addition, detachments of rural guards would be formed here and there, on state and common lands, to assist in the maintenance of peace, if necessary, and to instruct farmers in modern agricultural methods.

9. Economic and Financial Policy

The policy of the open door and equality of treatment for all foreign states in economic matters, as laid down in the treaty of Algeciras, will for some time be retained as the economic policy of the country. The party, however, deems it necessary to introduce certain modifications. The policy of the open door, for instance, should be made conditional upon a reciprocal treatment for Morocco; moreover, it will be necessary to resort to certain fiscal measures, particularly as regards raising tariff duties, but without prejudice to the principle of the most-favored-nation clause, granting equality of treatment for all.

The easy taxation policy of the protectorate has attracted substantial foreign capital to Morocco. But this facilitation to foreign capital has been at the expense of the consumers, who have been made to bear the brunt of the budget deficit by indirect taxation. One of the foremost duties is to relieve the consumers of their heavy burden, by taxing those who should be taxed.

Equality of taxation must be re-established and the policy of discrimination between French colonists and Moroccan farmers abolished.

The Istiqlal Party believes that the exploitation of the country's mineral resources, which are state-owned and inalienable, should be carried out directly by the state, or by means of a dual system of state and private enterprise, so that the country's needs respecting such basic resources could be met as inexpensively as possible. The party also advocates the nationalization of many public utilities and services in pursuance of the same objective.

For the maintenance of the state's financial well-being, the government should pursue vigorous anti-inflation policies and should stabilize its currency within the framework of international monetary agreements; it should also bring about the independence of the Moroccan franc from its link to the French franc.

In general, the party does not in its economic and financia policies adopt any of the well-known economic doctrines, nor does it champion any one social class. It does, however, devote particular attention to the poorer classes, whose material and moral standards must be lifted to the level where they occupy a respectable place within the Moroccan social structure.

10. Foreign Policy

Although Morocco has of late been forced into isolation, and has been preoccupied with a struggle to regain freedom, she has throughout her history pursued policies of close and friendly relations with the rest of the world.

The hospitality meted out to the Jewish expellees from Spain testifies to the liberality of the Moroccan people. These Jews were permitted to preserve their religious beliefs, their properties, and their separate religious courts; they were accorded Moroccan citizenship which enabled them on occasion to rise to the highest positions in the state. This should disprove all allegations of religious or racial intolerance and attests to the willingness of Moroccans to cooperate sincerely with other states and communities.

It is the view of the Istiqlal Party, however, that such cooperation and solidarity are possible only after the rights of Morocco have been fully recognized, according to the principles of such international documents as the Atlantic Charter and the decisions of the United Nations.

The party believes that Morocco should establish particularly strong and intimate relations with the Arab states, to which we are bound by innumerable historic, cultural, and racial ties. Such a relationship should eventuate in a federation joining together all the Arab states in one greater family which would participate in the establishment of world peace and bring into being a humane system for the benefit of the entire world.

Demanding Independence

These are the principles of the Istiqlal Party embodying the legacy of the National Party and the movements that preceded it; the party marched forward, supported by the entire nation's irrevocable demand for recognition of Morocco's effective independence.

On January 11, 1944 the party submitted the Istiqlal Covenant to His Majesty the King; copies were also presented to the French Resident-General and to representatives of the great powers.

The rulers of the protectorate were astounded, but they did not take any countermoves until they were assured of the hands-off attitude of the Allied armies stationed in the country.

His Majesty the King called a meeting of the Council of Ministers on January 13, to which leading citizens and notabl[es] were invited, particularly district leaders, religious dignataries, civil and Sharī'ah judges, and prominent members of the royal family. The King opened the meeting by summarizing the Covenant submitted by the Istiqlal Party and inviting their opinions and comments. The conferees expressed their unanimous endorsement of the Covenant and their deep indignation over the policies of the protectorate, which had failed to reconcile the wishes of the people with those of France.

The conferees then decided to form a committee comprising two ministers and the chief of protocol at the royal palace, with a view to contacting the executive of the party and of exploring ways and means of achieving the goal of independence. The committee was also entrusted with the task of attempting to win over the Residency-General to the plan, with a view to averting a serious clash with the French

The committee held meetings with the party leaders during which all were agreed on the need for annulling the protectorate; they also explored possible ways of reconciling the goal of independence with the state of French-Moroccan relationship. Discussions with the Residency-General continued for three days, after which a spokesman for the Residency declared that the protectorate would accept no modifications in the provisions of the 1912 Treaty but that it was willing to implement satisfactory political and social reform[s]. Naturally, representatives of the party and of the royal conference refused to desist from their demand for independenc[e]; the Residency thereupon discontinued the talks and asked for a dissolution of the committee.

The Istiqlal Covenant remained intact, and the Council of Ministers held another meeting on January 18 to explore ways of giving effect to it.

During this period there was an unending stream of popular delegations from all parts of Morocco to submit petitions in support of the demand for independence. All social classe[s] from the highest judges of the Islamic Sharī'ah to the most humble secret servicemen participated in this demonstration of popular solidarity. A wave of independence consciousness swept through the country from one end to the other.

It is significant that among the delegations which had petitioned the King in support of independence was one representing the academic council of the Qarawiyīn and the religious institutes; the importance of this council in the public life of Morocco is very considerable.

We should also make mention of the various women's delegations that had come out in support of the party and had expressed their readiness to sacrifice in the cause of independence.

The French administration behaved with utmost reticence throughout the entire week, which had been devoted to expressions of solidarity and support for independence; it took no measures to prevent the ceaseless stream of delegations from reaching the royal palace in Rabat.

On January 18 the Resident-General, M. Gabriel Puaux, called at the royal palace, just before the augmented Council of Ministers had been scheduled to meet, and asked for an audience with the King pertaining to an urgent business. M. Puaux informed His Majesty that he had received a communication from the French National Committee for Liberation, which had had its headquarters in Algeria, instructing him not to enter into any negotiations which had as their basis the alteration of the protectorate regime. He alleged that France alone had the right to propose reforms as she deemed necessary and that the liberation committee was actively studying such reforms. The Resident added that he would submit the proposed reforms for His Majesty's approval as soon as the liberation committee completed its study. The French Government, he concluded, would not tolerate any discussion on the question of the protectorate treaty.

His Majesty conveyed to the Council of Ministers the decision of the French Government; after reiterating his continued adherence to the demand for independence, the King asked the council to adjourn its meeting to some other day. Thus, the committee formed at the royal conference, on January 13, was unable to present to the Council of Ministers the memoranda of the party on ways and means of furthering the program.

As soon as the party learned of the Residency-General's communication it issued a statement stressing that the demand for independence did not in any way imply hostility to France or to any one else. The statement emphasized that the party did not contemplate the attainment of its objective save by legitimate means.

French Reaction

The following day the French authorities ordered the many leading members of the party who had come to Rabat to leave the capital at once and return to their various localities.

On January 22 the Residency-General issued an official communiqué, which was published in the French press, announcing an agreement with His Majesty the King for the implementation of many reforms, designed to further the progress and the prosperity of Morocco within the framework of French-Moroccan friendship.

Local French administrators in the meantime summoned leading citizens and notables in their areas and admonished them for their solidarity with the party in the demand for independence. In the course of thse meetings, many persons were arrested in Marrakech, Aāsifi and Oujda; in spite of this, the people remained quiet.

There was general expectation that a wave of repression would be set in motion; but all were waiting in a state of anxiety and expectation to see what pretexts the protectorate would put forward in justification of such action; all the demonstrations had already taken place in a most orderly manner during the presentation of the Covenant.

French colonialism, however, can always contrive some excuse; it alleged that the independence movement was supported and encouraged by the Axis, with a view to creating difficulties for the Allied armies. Thus, a few hours after M. Massigli of the French Foreign Ministry had announced in a broadcast from Algiers approval by the French National Committee for Liberation of a speedy reform program for Morocco, French commandants, on the evening of January 28, were rounding up eighteen leaders of the independence movement on charges of contact with the enemy. Foremost of those arrested was Ḥaj Aḥmad Bla Freej, secretary general of the Istiqlal Party, and Muḥammad al-Yazīdi, member of the executive committee.

In the early morning hours of January 19, news of the

arrest of the secretary general and other leading party members spread throughout Morocco. There was widespread indignation and a general strike was observed in all Moroccan cities.

In the city of Rabat throngs gathered in the courtyard of the royal palace to protest against these measures and demand release of the party leaders. When the French director of political affairs had failed to disperse the crowds, he released Muḥammad al-Yazīdi and permitted him to enter the royal palace for talks with the King. Al-Yazīdi then requested the crowds to disperse, assuring them of the King's interest in the case. The demonstrators complied with the appeal of al-Yazīdi, who was only expressing the party's policy of not giving to the French authorities a pretext for the perpetration of dastardly acts against the people.

Despite this, a European was killed near the entrance to the palace by a number of demonstrators who had been incensed by a disparaging remark uttered against the Moroccans.

When the demonstrators arrived at Bab al-Madīna they were engaged by a detachment of gendarmes which was later reinforced by detachments of regular troops. The demonstrators turned back from Dār al-Makhzen Street and headed in the direction of the Residency-General's quarter; the army again attacked and the demonstrators turned towards Bāb Būybah and Bāb Shālah; the military authorities ordered the Bāb Shālah gendarme force to join in the encounter. The demonstrators, finding themselves encircled, were compelled to defend themselves; they hurled an avalanche of stones and succeeded in breaking through the army cordon. The inspector of police then charged with his men; the crowds seized him, snatched his revolver, and killed him with it. The secretary of the French chamber of commerce, M. Deperetti, was also hit by a stone in the course of the encounter.

At 3:30 p.m. of the same day, the Residency-General dispatched a further reinforcement of cavalry troops which succeeded, after a violent two-hour fight, in occupying the Bāb al-Madīnah.

French losses were three killed (two civilian employees of the administration and a police inspector), three officers seriously wounded, and four army officers and three gendarmes who suffered stone injuries in the head.

Six of the Moroccan demonstrators were killed and sixty others wounded.

On the evening of that day the entire city assembled in solemnity and grief for burial of the nationalist martyrs; Moroccan women participated in force in these nationalist demonstrations.

While the city slumbered in the quiet of the night, the French authorities were busy amassing large army forces for a siege of Islamic quarters and even more drastic acts of repression. When the inhabitants woke up in the morning they saw artillery and armored cars throwing a cordon around all important roads, cutting off one from the other, and imposing a strict curfew upon the inhabitants. The city went on strike as popular tension mounted. The authorities were forced to summon a number of leaders, who had not been arrested, and to use their influence in calming down the people; at the same time, the military siege was lifted but only to be reimposed a little while later. The troops spread out in the narrow streets rounding up the crowds en bloc; bystanders of all groups and ages, men, women, children, adults and the aged, were indiscriminately assaulted. Eight hundred persons were summarily and without trial sentenced to jail for periods ranging from three months to two years. The prisoners were subjected to the utmost cruelty and scores of them died as a result.

The troops were let loose upon the city to plunder and assault; not a sūq (market place) or a café or a Moroccan establishment escaped their wrath.

Under a pretext of searching for criminals and caches of arms, which the authorities alleged had been stored by the nationalists, the troops broke into houses, plundering what they could lay hands on.

During all these operations telephone communications were severed and telephone sets removed from the homes of citizens known for their nationalist sympathies; the homes of leading members of the movement were placed under siege and cut off from all contacts with the outside world.

This situation lasted for three days and only came to an end by an accident: a youth employed by the American consulate general in Rabat was arrested by the troops, beaten-up, and his official papers torn up; the American representa tive protested against the incident, and the French were compelled to issue orders to their troops to cease their indiscriminate assaults.

In Fez, the intellectual center of Morocco, large-scale demonstrations were staged in protest against the arrest of the leaders and the repressive measures that followed. The demonstrations of January 29 were orderly and passed off without any incident; the following day, however, the authorities arrested all the leading members of the movement, mostly teachers, lawyers, and doctors. The people resumed demonstrations on a more intensive scale, but the full-fledged clash between demonstrators and army troops occurred only on January 31, in the course of which sixty nationalists were killed and one hundred others wounded, while two thousand were thrown into jail. The nationalists had attacked the citadel of Tamdart, in which the Senegalese army was stationed, and also Ḥawmat al-Dawḥ.

On the first of February a fierce encounter occurred between the nationalists and the Senegalese army, which had been making unsuccessful attempts to break through the Bāb abi al-Junūd leading to the Islamic quarters. On the evening of the same day the demonstrators killed a Senegalese soldier. The incident led to more intensive fighting. In another incident, the nationalists assembled in the Qarawiyīn mosque killed a Moroccan spy who had the insolence to take down the names of speakers inside the mosque. An unknown person slew him with a knife. The authorities were enraged and intensified their already drastic measures; the intensification, however, served only to embolden the Fez nationalists. Resistance and clashes between the people of Fez and the army continued for two weeks, after which the French administration besieged the native quarters and cut them off from electricity, water, and food rations; thus the Moroccans were bereft of all the necessities of life.

The vigilant defenders of Moroccan freedom did not succumb; these atrocious measures only evoked the spirit of solidarity permeating all classes of the population. Party members soon formed a relief committee at whose disposal the rich placed all their food stores and supplies; the committee undertook the distribution of the available food supplies to the more needy class. Since all the quarters were occupied by the army and cut off from one another, the distribution was carried out by an airlift--the roofs of the city of Fez were ideally suited for the purpose at hand. Naturally, this spirit of solidarity only heightened the nervousness of the French. General Suffren, governor of the Fez region, addressed a final ultimatum to the inhabitants, warning them to discontinue the disturbances which had lasted for two weeks and threatening to instruct his troops not to respect the inviolability of the holy places. The people, fearing for the inviolability of their holy places, decided to call off the strike.

On February 4 the committee of 'Ulemas, which had been endeavoring to calm down popular tension, informed the General of its solidarity with the arrested leaders and demanded before all else release of the internees. The stand taken by Sheikh Muḥammad ibn 'Abd al-Raḥman al-'Irāqi on this occasion deserves the highest tribute and admiration. Several members of this committee as well as a number of Qarawiyīn 'Ulemas and students were arrested.

On February 8 three hundred demonstrators were arrested in the mosque of Raṣīf.

During the earlier incidents which took place on January 31, and while the nationalists were making arrangements for the burial of the victims, General Suffren ordered a siege of the public cemetery, with a view to preventing burial of the victims, lest their tombs should become a national pilgrimage shrine and a visible symbol of French colonial atrocities. The Fez nationalists refused to heed the orders of the army and went on digging the graves. The General, accompanied by a colonel, mounted an armoured car and went to the scene in person. He ordered his troops to close the tombs and to place the bodies of the victims in the Andalus mosque under military guard. This, however, did not defeat the heroes of Moroccan resistance; national scouts infiltrated by night through the roof into the interior of the mosque and removed the bodies of the martyrs, carrying them across from one roof to the other; before an hour had passed the bodies of the victims were laid to rest in their tombs. This remained a tightly-held secret, unknown to the French intelligence.

While the struggle was at its peak, the publicity committee of the Istiqlal Party carried on a pamphleteering campaign in the European quarters to bring to the notice of foreign public opinion the atrocious acts perpetrated by the protectorate. One such pamphlet was distributed on February 1, describing the situation and defending the Moroccan stand; on February 9 it distributed a pamphlet entitled "Civilization or Savagery?" depicting the atrocities of French troops; on March 1 a third pamphlet was distributed contrasting the misdeeds of the French authorities with the solemn pledges which France had taken upon herself towards Morocco.

Events in the town of Cela were similar to those in Rabat and Fez, resulting in eleven persons killed and scores of others injured while three hundred more were thrown into jail. A lycée student seventeen years of age was executed.

In Rabat a French penal court sentenced fourteen persons to death, of whom four were executed on March 7; the executions marred the celebration on the occasion of the Prophet's birthday.

In Casablanca a general strike which included dock workers was observed on January 30. Army troops took up positions throughout the city using tanks, armored cars, and other deadly weapons. The troops opened fire on the unarmed Moroccans killing a man in the seventies and wounding three youths; many persons were arrested and released a few days laters; some of them almost lost their lives as a result of the torture to which they had been subjected while in jail. Moroccan students of the French lycée, who had participated in the strike, were expelled from school.

Thus, terrorism swept across the entire country and a state of war prevailed in the main Moroccan towns. The administration went so far as to close down all Moroccan primary schools, and three out of the four Islamic secondary schools that exist in the country. The Jassūs institute, a private school founded by Aḥmad Bla Freej, was also closed down and occupied by army troops; the young pupils were detained without food for two days before they were gradually sent back to their families. Students of French lycées and of Ma'had al-Durūs al-'Ulyā al-Maghribīyah (the institute of higher Moroccan studies) were also expelled. As for the secondary school, established in 'Azur as a laboratory for implementation of the Berber policy, it was also closed down, and most of its students were jailed for their solidarity with their brethren and their practical demonstration of the failure of the Berber policy. In Ifrān the Moroccan headmaster of the school was removed from his job and sent to prison. Lastly, the Qarawiyīn University was closed down; its director together with three members of its higher academic council were imprisoned and then exiled. Studies at the Qarawiyīn University remained irregular for three years.

In the sphere of Moroccan administration, we must cite the forced resignation of His Excellency the Minister of Justice and the great reformer, Muḥammad ibn al-'Arabi al-'Alawi, who was banished to a solitary detention in the desert; the Minister of Education and former pasha of Azmūr Aḥmad Barkāsh, who was placed under house arrest; and the pasha [governor] of Rabat and his immediate successor, who were also placed under surveillance.

At the same time, all the employees who had signified their solidarity with the Istiqlal Covenant were removed or suspended for varying periods. They included lecturers at the royal institute, two judges of the supreme court, four members of the Sheriffian secretariat, and many other employees of the treasury, the Mekhzen state domains, education, communications, the police, and other departments.

In southern Morocco, three Moroccan caids were fired for supporting the independence move; in Fez, twenty leading craftsmen were accused of complicity in the slaying of the spy and sentenced to hang; the sentence was later commuted to life imprisonment at hard labor. Five of them have so far died of torture in their Qunayṭera prison.

As for those nationalists who had been falsely accused of foreign contacts, the most heinous atrocities were inflicted upon them; the indescribable horrors to which they had been subjected were unmatched even by the German Gestapo. In spite of this, the courts could not indict them. It was later revealed that their case had been mapped out by the French administration, acting in conjunction with the military commandants. The courts sought some evidence to substantiate the charges, and when none was forthcoming was compelled to acquit them. They were all released with the exception of Bla Freej, who was banished to the island of Corsica.

We must in fairness pay tribute to the endurance, fortitude, and courage displayed by Aḥmad Mikwār, 'Abd al-'Azīz ibn Idrīs, al-Hāshimi al-Faylāli, Ibrāhīm al-Kattāni, and Rashīd al-Darqāwi; their behavior earned them the gratitude of their country and the admiration of their countrymen.

Towards the end of December 1944 the department of education notified the parents of students in French Arabic schools that all students would be referred to disciplinary councils as a preliminary to expelling all those who had participated in the events of January and thereafter. The students in all Moroccan schools organized a well-knit resistance through a hierarchy of local committees leading to a central council in Rabat. They issued statements, distributed pamphlets, submitted protests, and launched strikes; their actions eventually compelled the administration to abandon its plan and to reopen the schools without further ado.

Thus, the Istiqlal Party succeeded in advancing the nationalist movement a big stride forward and in awakening national consciousness to an extent that has earned for it the admiration of all.

We cannot give an exhaustive description of the results of the incidents which occurred in those glorious days; but we can sum up the events in the following points:

1. Tens of nationalists lost their lives during the demonstrations.

2. More than five thousand were imprisoned; of this number those detained in Jarniyear and Shāsur were subjected to torture no less heinous than that meted out to prisoners of the Gestapo in occupied Europe.

3. Scores of youths were sentenced to death and some were executed on the morning of the Prophet's birthday; tens of nationalists were sentenced to life at hard labor.

4. Secondary schools remained closed for a whole year, while primary schools in many towns and cities were kept closed for three months. Studies at Qarawiyīn University, whose rector and many of whose faculty had been banished, remained disorganized for three years.

5. Scores of Moroccan intellectuals were arbitrarily jailed for several months in the military prison of Burj al-Nūr and later at Tatwīb bi al-'Adhar (near Jadidah).

6. Two Moroccan ministers were removed from office and placed under house arrest.

7. Scores of government employees were fired from their jobs without trial or investigation of any sort, and so forth.

In conclusion, the events which followed January 11, and the great sacrifices which the people had willingly offered in the cause of independence, clearly attest to the popular strength of the Istiqlal Party. Moreover, the drastic measures resorted to by the Residency against the citizens had destroyed to a considerable extent the reputation of France, not only in Morocco but throughout the Arab world. In contradistinction, all the charges which the French administration had levelled against the Istiqlal leaders went astray and they emerged unscathed. The French themselves were compelled to acknowledge the nobility of purpose that had animated the National Party and later of the Istiqlal, whose leaders' sole aim is the liberation of their country and the happiness of its sons in peace, plenty, and liberty.

Even though the party had emerged from this battle somewhat weary, it had nonetheless achieved a decisive success inasmuch as the movement had attained a degree of diffusion and publicity surpassing by far anything that had preceded it. Moreover, the martyrs who had fallen in battle in all parts of the land had vividly brought home to the people the meaning of true sacrifice and the pleasurable taste of struggle in the cause of their cherished independence. The intensity of government pressure, the strict controls, the crowded prisons, and the numerousness of the victims--all these did not break the party's will to continued activity.

One of its foremost acts had been a reorganization of the party along the lines of its progenitor, the National Party, with a few minor exceptions, pertaining to the qualifications of voters and candidates for the pivotal party organs. The National Party had given the right to elect and be elected to every member of the party; the Istiqlal Party, for its part, has divided joiners into two categories: the active members who enjoy the right to elect and be elected and in whom certain special qualifications are required, and the supporters who constitute all the rest. Every supporter may be promoted to active membership if his competence and readiness to work are ascertained. The "national council" was renamed "the higher council of the party". A new body, affiliated to the executive committee, was introduced, to supervise the orientation and indoctrination of party supporters in the nationalist cause; it was made responsible for morale in the party ranks.

The exceptional conditions prevailing in the country, and the perpetual state of oppression, prevent us from adopting a stable democratic system in the full sense of the term. But the Istiqlal people recognize the difficulties of the situation and work in a spirit of solidarity and responsibility, in the firm belief that the loyalty of all and the identity of their faiths would compensate for many of the formalities which our special circumstances do not permit us to observe.

In the field of social work the party continued its activities, devoting particular attention to education, as we shall see later on; in this task it was aiding the efforts of His Majesty the King, the foremost champion of the educational renaissance which has been making considerable headway under His Majesty's patronage.

Opposition to the Policy of Reforms

Since the launching of the Istiqlal Party, the policy of the nationalist movement had become opposed to the so-called reforms of the Residency-General; or, to put it more clearly, the party had become fully opposed to the policy of cooperation with the Residency on anything falling within the aegis of the protectorate and under its sponsorship.

Indeed, experience had taught us that all reforms proposed by the Residency were entirely chimerical and had no basis in reality. In a more profound and subtle sense, they had been merely new attempts to usurp the little that had remained of Moroccan sovereignty. The party believes that the differences with France are basic and are beyond merely trivial differences as to attitudes and policies. The party holds that there is an essential prerequisite for the effectuation of any genuine reforms: it is nationalist control over the direction of such reforms. As long as direction and control remain in the hands of the occupying power, so long will they be conceived and based upon its own basic concept, namely to steer Morocco towards integration with France, or at least in the direction of self-government within the French Union. This is at complete variance with the concepts of the nationalists towards which they are orienting their fellow countrymen, namely, complete independence, affiliation to the Arab League, and the placing of solidarity with the Arab peoples above any other loyalty.

This, however, does not in any way mean that the party opposes reforms per se; it merely considers reforms as an internal question concerning only the Moroccan people and their government. Thus it was that the Istiqlal Covenant had requested His Majesty to place the reform movement under his patronage. When His Majesty succeeds in extracting some of Morocco's rights and asks the party for technical assistance in the implementation of reforms, the party members will unquestionably heed the call of their King, as indeed they had done in the royal commission which drew up the charter on Moroccan education.

The party regards the claims of the Residency-General --as having the exclusive right to propose whatever reforms it deems fit for Morocco, under the aegis of the protectorate--as being an aggression against the sovereign rights of Morocco. Therefore, the party rejects any cooperation with the Residency under the existing regime. At the same time, it will not reject those reforms, proposed to His Majesty, which in their essence and their manner of presentation do not infringe upon such sovereignty, even though it will never concede the Residency's alleged right to present such reforms.

Finally, the party believes that it is a waste of time to expend its efforts in making minor requests of the protectorate; the party prefers to exert its efforts and to offer sacrifices in the cause of basic issues, wherein lies the key to the solution and success of all the subsidiary ones. We shall see that the party's approach to reforms is the direct and practical one of establishing as many schools, institutes companies, and relief centers as it can, and the implementation of all other measures that are conducive to the goal of progress and reforms.

This policy of the party is the most positive and efficacious one for the realization of the people's wishes and aspirations the policy of gradualism and negotiation over subsidiary issues has by experience been shown to be negative and sterile It has been barren of all substantive achievement, not only in Morocco but in Tunisia and Algeria as well. Therefore, it is futile, nay criminal, to pursue it any further.

Reforms of Gabriel Puaux

A few days after the events touched off by the Istiqlal Party, M. Gabriel Puaux, French Resident-General in

Morocco, announced his determination to introduce profound reforms in the country. The commission for foreign affairs in the French Committee for National Liberation paid a visit to Rabat to assure His Majesty of France's acceptance of these reforms.

On March 22, 1944 the Resident-General presided over a meeting of the advisory council for administrative affairs; on March 24 he presided over the committee on social insurance, rural affairs, and labor; on March 25 he presided over the committee on the judiciary. The Ṣadr al-A'zam was present at the meetings of all these committees.

The committee on rural affairs adopted a resolution in favor of inalienable family ownership, while the committee on administration decided to offer equality between Moroccans and French in government posts and jobs.

In the committee on the judiciary an acrimonious debate took place between the Moroccan and French members. The latter had proposed to bring Moroccans under the jurisdiction of French courts; the Moroccan members, including representatives of the Sheriffian Government, unanimously rejected the proposal.

The committee on education decided that the French language should continue to be taught along with Arabic; it also decided to admit Muslim pupils to French lycées, as well as to open an adequate number of elementary schools to the Moroccan population.

M. Puaux summed up the work of the advisory council in his final address when he said: "On this day when Moroccans are celebrating the 'Id al-Adhha (Bairam feast), I consider myself happy to announce that at the suggestion of the Government of the French Republic, His Majesty the King has approved a series of measures that will have a historic impact upon the development of the Sheriffian Kingdom." After paying tribute to the work of the various technical committees, he added: "The attention of the government of the protectorate has been devoted to three issues:

1. To enable Morocco to achieve a form of government comparable to that enjoyed by modern states.

2. To give Morocco an elite capable of sustaining this progress.

3. To raise the living conditions of the entire people, particularly the farmers, who constitute the overwhelming majority of the people."

The Resident then spelled out the details of the proposed reforms. He explained that the question of the judiciary had raised some serious difficulties because, he alleged, the separation of powers was a European creation difficult to apply in Islamic countries all at once; therefore, a transition period was necessary, and even the modest reform itself, envisaged in the plan, would at first be experimentally applied in the main cities only. In pursuance of the reform plan, he announced, the Liberation Committee had drawn up a penal code.

The Resident warned that modern courts required the preparation of modern judges; the protectorate, therefore, had given careful consideration to employing increasing numbers of educated Moroccans in such European-run departments as finance, public works, and economy. It had also decreed the equalization of their salaries with those of their French opposite numbers. (Reference here is to basic salaries; the colonial additional allowances remain untouched.) The augmentation of such an elite, the Resident pointed out, hinged upon its training in sufficient numbers; therefore, the facilitation of educational opportunities and an increase in the number of schools were essential for the achievement of the Residency's objectives.

In conclusion, the Resident stressed the need for improving the condition of the farmer, and for the adoption of inalienable family holdings and the creation of a higher council for rural economy, which would be entrusted with implementation of the "Baysānah" program.

These are the reforms designed by the Residency-General to mitigate the pressure of Moroccan resistance. Before explaining the attitude of the people towards them, we might mention that they were never implemented at all; the little that had been implemented suffered such grievous mutilation as to become worthless; the penal code, for example, has not yet been issued or even drafted; the law pertaining to inalienable family holdings has been so deflected in application as to render it of little or no benefit at all.

The Istiqlal Party Replies to M. Puaux

The Istiqlal Party found itself compelled to reiterate in detail what the Moroccan people had demanded since January 11, 1944, pointing out that the sine qua non for any understanding was the freedom of Moroccans to exercise their own sovereignty, and that any cooperation before this condition had been conceded was unacceptable.

The party announced its reply to the claims of the Resident-General in a statement distributed to the people. The statement reads in part:

> The Residency-General had announced, in the aftermath of the tragic incidents, the formation of four committees on March 16, 1944. Unfortunately, however, if we gloss over the beguiling sentences contained in the announcement, together with the numerous reservations that circumscribe these statements and render them ineffectual, we find that they are barren of direct applicability; they are not so much concerned with a basic solution of the Moroccan crisis as they are with the creation of a confused atmosphere, conducive to a perpetuation of the policy of lulling and pacification which has been pursued until the present day.
>
> Consequently, the enlightened class in Morocco has not attached the slightest importance to the decision of the Resident-General of March 16, 1944, because it knows by experience that nothing of importance could come out of official committees, which are the traditional instrument for burying all programs of genuine reforms.
>
> But in view of the fact that these reforms had been the result of six months of study, it is our duty to examine and criticize them in all sincerity.
>
> Judiciary
>
> The organization of the Sherifian judiciary, as part of the general administration, exhibits the following dual features: the lingering on of an antiquated system, which has been emptied of all content and changed in form, and the abject silence before the French governor or controller, who rules willy-nilly under the façade of a Moroccan puppet, usually chosen from among greedy illiterates who only accept this fiction of authority in order to extort the people who come under this sway.
>
> The political authority that might have strengthened the hand of the Moroccan judge and enabled him to perform his duties is sacrificed to the French controller, in exchange for the latter's silence concerning his acts of extortion and self-seeking pursuits. The abject obedience of these judges is increased by the lack of a penal code,

which leaves the controller free to govern as he wishes.

Every pasha and every caid enjoys absolute power over his subordinates; it is natural, therefore, that he should rule arbitrarily and without any restraint. He is not obliged to make inquiries or to study any files, nor is he duty-bound to accept pleadings or grant the freedom to summon defense attorneys. Everything that pertains to justice can be destroyed by a message from the French governor or by a telephone call, and how many times did judges evade their duties under pretext of implementing the orders of the higher authorities!

The sum total of this state of affairs should have been the proper object of study by the committee on the judiciary, with a view to introducing the much-needed reforms.

Two more points must be mentioned:

1. The law committee had been formed for the purpose of drafting a penal code; it is our duty to record that since the Residency's decision to set it up, the committee has met only once and that was the occasion on which it came into being.

2. The advisory committee on the judiciary had been assigned the task of studying the principle of the separation of powers, whose existence in the Islamic Sharī'ah, we can emphatically assert, had preceded its recognition by European lawmakers, in contradiction to the claim of the Residency. The fact is that the body of Islamic law provides that a judge derives his authority directly from the Sharī'ah and enjoys complete independence from the executive branch save in the instance of his appointment.

The committee, however, has restricted the separation of powers to civil and commercial matters and has confined its application to the main towns; the jursidictions of the pasha and the caid, which constitute the most heinous features of the present regime, are left intact. These restrictions divest the reforms of all significance, because a judge who can do to a person what he likes can always oppress such a person. As the great de Montesquieu has said: "Again there is no liberty if the judiciary power be not separated from the legislative and the executive. Were it joined with the legislative, the life and liberty of the subject would be exposed to arbitrary control; for the judge would then be the legislator. Were it joined to the executive power, the judge might behave with violence and oppression."

The aims of the formulators of the Residency's program are therefore obvious: they are more interested in the preservation of the means, which facilitate the continuance of the regime by force and compulsion, than in a reform of the Moroccan judiciary. Therefore, the avoidance of arbitrary rule by limitations on the authority of the judge, the protection of the latter from the pressures and encroachment of the executive, the protection of individuals from every Gestapo capable of throwing them into jail at any time or of ill-treating them without the slightest restraint, save that of an irresponsible administration--all such reforms, the formulators of the plan allege, would undermine the basis of order and public security!

But what does a recognition of the authority, independence, and dignity of the judiciary amount to unless the freedom of the people is also recognized, and unless man's exploitation of his fellowmen ends and the principle of colonialism is defeated? It is easy, as some journalists have said, for the strong to resist the weak, but not for the weak to resist the strong. However, when the interests of the ruled are sacrificed and the balance is upset in favor of brute force, the people are left with only one of two alternatives: enslavement or revolution; most often, the balance is gravely upset either demonstrably or under the guise of allegedly vital interests. Thus oppressors emerge and thus revolutions occur.

Public Administration

We can sum up the proposed measures pertaining to the public administration as follows: the granting of some posts to the Moroccan elite, and in order to secure their acceptance, the equalization of their pay with that of their French opposite numbers of equal competence and rank.

It was unnecessary, however, to set up a full committee in order to arrive at this conclusion; the question of employing the Moroccan elite in the rejuvenated Sherifian administration had been settled by the Edict of 1938. The question of equal pay, moreover, had been under discussion since the early phase of the protectorate regime, and all those concerned had submitted their views and demands on the subject. The union of government employees suggested a solution which the Resident-General might do well to approve today. At any rate, the Residency's proposed ameliorations would give no comfort to Moroccan employees because they are so limited in scope. The benefits envisaged in the scheme would accrue only to employees of special cadres equivalent to French cadres, such as translators, police inspectors, tax assessors, the government's central clerks, judges of the Sheriffian supreme court, pasha assistants, and so forth. Discrimination and inequality would still remain where Moroccans did not possess qualifications equal to those of the French. Such is the ruling notwithstanding the fact that the majority of Moroccans are not specialists and have no skills which the French themselves could not acquire. But, we may ask, does not a Moroccan judge hand down decisions? Does not a clerk of al-Ṣadr al-Aʿzam perform the duties of a secretary? Or in other words, are not the graduates of purely Arabic institutions entitled to recognition and consideration in a country where Arabic has been the official language at all times?

Similarly, is it not unjust to perpetuate inequalities as regards living allowances to this category of employee Have not these allowances been devised to assist employees in the support of their families or to encourage them to have families, regardless of all considerations of technical competence?

They have blamed the inadequacy of the Moroccan cadre, but who is responsible for it?

Is it not painful that a protected country, after thirty-three years of the protectorate, should still be unable to provide the necessary cadre for its development? It is impossible to support the claim that when the protectorat was set up it had come upon a complete vacuum, and that it had not been possible to fill that vacuum in a short time In a report to the French Government on December 3, 1920, Lyautey said: "We have found here a state and a people; they are indeed in a crisis of chaos, but this crisis is of a recent duration and is more governmental than social; if the Mekhzen had been reduced to a mere semblance, it had at least remained in existence. We can look a little backwards to find in it an effective government represented in the world by ministers of state and ambassadors, who had been in touch with European statesman, and some of whom are still alive right at the present day. If we set aside the Mekhzen, we find before us viable organizations,varying according to regions, but representing concrete realities." Morocco, therefore, was not backward as some would like to claim; on the contrary, it was ready to develop into a modern government. If it had not done so, it is because it did not receive any assistance from the protectorate, which instead veered it towards a system of direct rule.

As regards the real public administration, which is the source of the present crisis, the Residency-General's measures have been nil.

It should have been the duty of the committee to recognize this fact and do something to remedy it; at any rate, if the educated Moroccans have shied away from Moroccan jobs, it is because they are well aware that they will be called upon to perform only minor duties; they are also convinced that the regime for which they are asked to work is nothing more than an assortment of institutions based upon vagaries, favoritism, irresponsibility, and injustice, and that their aim is not the guidance of the Moroccan people but their enslavement.

It is instructive to quote the following excerpt from Lyautey's same report, concerning the basic weaknesses of the regime. He stated: "All administrative measures are promulgated in his name [meaning the Sultan's]; he signs the edicts, but in reality has no local authority and no connections save with the Sultan's adviser who sees him daily; his opinion is not solicited except as a formality. As for the Ṣadr al-Aʻzam and the rest of the ministers, they do not participate in any deliberations pertaining to important issues, which are studied far away from them in the French departments. There is no relationship between the heads of these departments and the ministers of the "Mekhzen", which enjoys the rapturous delight of slumber. It is easy to discern that the monopolization of legislative power by the French administrators has made them the sole executers of their own decisions; this has resulted in a confusion of authorities and a complete absence of ministerial responsibility."

René Vanland, the well-known publicist, writing in a Paris newspaper, observed: "The least perceptive of people will realize that a country would exhaust itself if five hundred millions out of its total budget of one billion francs was spent for the upkeep of the administration and three hundred million for payment of interest on debts; such is the situation of Morocco.

"A government with ten thousand employees in a country whose population is eight millions! This is something strange. There are sixty-three different items of extra allowances to employees in Morocco; these are responsible for the inflated figures which the budget has to bear."

Education

How can the problem of education be solved in the French colonies and protectorates? The answer to this was given by the experts on native policy: "Education must not be made widespread among the people, in view of the danger that it might awaken in them political hopes and aspirations which would one day destroy the authority of the occupation power itself. Education must not be distributed generously like a piece of medication; it should be granted the Muslims as a reward and an honor, and should be limited to a native aristocracy. It is understood by the conquering nation that the school youths, selected from the sons of the notables, should be trained to fill government jobs or to assist our administration." This is what the author of the "Manuel de politique musulmane" (Mūjaz al-Siyāsah al-Islamīyah) said in his publication printed by the Bossard press in Paris in 1925.

"Education here is not an end in itself; it is but a means for the attainment of moral conquest, which is the supreme goal of a native school." This is an excerpt from a booklet published by the director general of education in 1930.

A circular (no. 25, 1920) issued by the department of education defined the aims of the school in the following words: "A school must be oriented towards raising the professional competence of the native; it is a factor for wealth, peace, and work. Politics, in the modern

European sense of the word, is at variance with the progressive work which we are undertaking here; therefore, it should not be included in the instruction of Moroccan citizens or in the emancipation of women."

Education in Morocco, therefore, has been entirely subordinated to the interests of French colonialism. This is so true that the administration, in its efforts to divide the country and to obstruct its cultural progress, has been fighting relentlessly against a system of unified shools such as obtains in the other countries of the world. Moroccans have found themselves compelled to send their children to various types of schools, such as the French Arabic school, Berber school, school for sons of notables, industrial school, village school for Arab areas, village school for Berber areas, Islamic school for daughters of notables, and Islamic school for girls.

It is certain that this diversity will persist or even grow worse as a result of the reform outlined by the Resident-General.

The record of the protectorate after thirty-three years is in keeping with its aims outlined earlier. It had graduated a total of three doctors, six lawyers, and six agricultural engineers. Thus, it is futile to expect the French program, based upon such principles, to prepare in a short while the cadre upon which the future of Morocco hinges merely by making a slight increase in the number of schools.

Furthermore, the slight increase envisaged in the program provides for the establishment over a number of years of no more than two hundred classes yearly with a total capacity for ten thousand pupils; against that there are approximately one million children of school age of whom only thirty thousand find accomodation in existing schools.

If we consider that a population normally doubles itself every twenty-five years, we shall find ourselves confronted by an ever-increasing rise in the number of neglected children.

The administration of the protectorate pleads on some occasions the lack of funds, and on others, war-shortages in construction materials. The administration, however, is always able to overcome these difficulties when it comes to satisfying the demands of the European inhabitants, whose contribution does not exceed a fifth of the Moroccan budget.

Rural System

In the economic field the Residency's reform program has been silent concerning the deplorable conditions of the workers and the city craftsmen. It does, however, deal with questions pertaining to the farmer. The committee on rural affairs has been forced to recognize that the progress of the agricultural workers is a prerequisite for the development of the country as a whole. This is true in a country where the village constitutes sixty per cent of the people.

The methods devised by the committee for the amelioration of rural living conditions, however, are ineffectual; it is restricted to the setting up of a higher council for rural affairs, the creation of collective farming for areas of over two thousand hectares, and the initiation of inalienable family holdings.

Our experiences with administrative methods have taught us that the establishment of a council is tantamount to shelving action for an indefinite period. Thus, our farmers should not expect any concrete or rapid results from the higher council, whose task in any case does not exceed the study and drafting of a code to regularize the status of "al-Khumās" [twenty per cent share-croppers].

Few people know that the proposed scheme for collective farming will be restricted to no more than two thousand hectares. This is a very limited thing indeed. In contradistinction to that, if the principle of inalienable family holding were carefully applied, a portion of our villages would be insured against distress, and satisfaction would be given to all those who have been demanding its application since ten years ago, when the farmer was still in possession of the most valuable of his inalienable holdings.

Moreover, to grant the Moroccan farmer a piece of land is not everything; the condition of the farmer calls for deeper and more daring solutions. The more immediate steps should have in view the restoration of his human dignity and the improvement of his moral as well as material existence, by destroying feudal priviliges, guaranteeing the safety of his person and property, and assuring him of deliverance from sickness, poverty, and ignorance.

The intelligent Bedouins of Morocco have not achieved any progress over the past thirty-three years. Not only have they remained in the deplorable condition in which they had been before; they have also become an army of slaves serving the Moroccan administrator, the French controller, the colonist, the revenue collector, officials of the water department, the forestry, and so forth.

The authorities, whose duty should have been to protect the farmer from his ignorance and unaffected simplicity, have not only failed to do so but have encouraged his exploiters and oppressors and participated directly or indirectly in his degradation.

More than that, when the authorities saw that an opportunity had presented itself to the farmer to regain some of his lost inheritance, they strictly prohibited his purchase of holdings submitted for sale by the Europeans in 1941.

Moreover, the farmer has been so neglected that he still ploughs his land according to the antiquated methods of farming. The upshot of all this is, that any reform which is not designed to create a Moroccan technical cadre to supervise the modernization of agricultural methods is doomed to failure.

Defending the Sovereignty of the People

The continuance of this systematic struggle against the policies and methods of the Residency-General did not exhaust the activities of the Moroccan Istiqlal movement; the party found itself compelled to resist the efforts made by Frenchmen of all parties and orientations to usurp Morocco's popular sovereignty. The resistance began in the era of the Kutlah Party and has continued ever since. The fact is, that an acquiescence in the demands of the French residents in Morocco would have constituted the most serious step towards the Francization of Morocco or its assimilation within the family of the French Union.

The National Kutlah, it will be recalled, had resisted the attempts of the French to constitute themselves as Moroccan councils with powers to criticize the work of the government;

General Noguès had attempted to revive these demands, but the National Party warned him, in the most unequivocal terms, that it was opposed to any such plans and would resist their implementation even to the extent of rebellion and bloodshed.

The entry of General de Gaulle into North Africa, however, with his repeated appeals to the French community for support against pro-Vichy elements, as well as French aspirations for the creation of a new regime in place of the defunct Third Republic, upon which they laid all blame for their defeat in war and their failures in diplomacy--all these evoked in the French a strong awareness of empire and colonialism, within which they viewed France, the colonies, and the protectorates as an invisible whole. They began, therefore, to demand a voice in everything pertaining to the fate of France and her affairs. This attitude became manifest in two moves:

1. A demand that they be represented by deputies of their own choosing in the French Parliament.

2. The enrollment of Moroccans in the various French political parties.

The party took the strongest exception to these two moves in defense of the Moroccan people's rights and sovereignty.

When the election campaign began for the French constituent assembly, the French section of the so-called government consultative council decided at the closing session to press for French participation in the elections. Muḥammad al-Yazīdi submitted protests on behalf of the party's executive committee to His Majesty the King and to the Residency General. It might be useful to quote the following summary of the protest:

> The Istiqlal Party, disconcerted by the claims of the French community for political rights in Morocco, and having considered the decision adopted by the French section of the government consultative council to this effect, and having considered that the French council of ministers had decided on steps for implementation of the decision, and that the Residency-General had issued a resolution to this effect on August 4, 1945--
>
> Whereas the only right to which the French and other foreigners in Morocco are entitled pertains to personal

status in accordance with the Edict of August 19, 1915;

Whereas it is impossible to disregard Morocco's sovereignty, guaranteed even by the existing treaties, particularly the Treaty of Algeciras;

Whereas the treaties imposed upon Morocco have, in spite of their usurpation of Morocco's diplomatic rights, recognized Morocco as a self-governing country whose territory is alien to France;

Whereas numerous decisions handed down by the highest French tribunals have asserted this fact and have interpreted the purport of the imposed protectorate;

Whereas these interpretations, upon which political as well as judicial rules are based, have asserted that French political organizations should have no place in Morocco, being a foreign land, and that the enjoyment of political rights is inextricably connected with the nationality of the territory; and whereas in a speech delivered at Rabat on November 24, 1918 Marshal Lyautey declared that the French were wasting their time in demanding political rights in Morocco and that they could not possibly be accorded any political representation;

Whereas the granting to the French community of the right to participate in the elections for the constituent assembly is an act of the French Government in violation of all pledges and obligations;

Whereas silence over this affair is tantamount to complicity in the crime of despoilment and assimilation of the fatherland;

The party resolves:

1. To protest vehemently and with the assurance derived from the established right, against the decision of the French Government, which violates existing treaties and which had been made without the slightest consultation with Moroccans.

2. To condemn the demands of the French community, which constitute a threat to the Moroccan state and people.

3. To draw the attention of His Majesty to the menace threatening Moroccan sovereignty, whose faithful guardian he is.

4. To urge the French Government to abrogate its decisions in this regard, or any other decision that

refers in any way to the policy of integration and assimilation.

Rabat, on September 18, 1945

The memorandum was effective; His Majesty the King protested against the French move and demanded an abrogation of the arrangements made by the Residency-General in this connection.

The Resident-General was compelled to issue a communiqué, in which he asserted that the French in Morocco would not enjoy voting rights for the French Parliament; their participation in the elections for a constituent assembly, he explained, was a non-repeating case and had been necessitated by their extraordinary interest in the fate of France. Thus, the nationalist movement succeeded in warding off a new aggression against popular sovereignty, thanks to the decisive support of our sovereign, may God grant him success.

This, however, did not prevent French political parties from persisting in their demands and their attempts at the enrollment of Moroccans within their ranks, ostensibly out of concern for equality between Moroccans and French. The party was therefore impelled to launch an intensive campaign in resistance to this new danger. It succeeded once more in prevailing upon the majority of French parties to refuse admission of Moroccans. It also succeeded in alerting the masses of Morocco to the dangers inherent in the affiliation of citizens to foreign parties which could not possibly defend any Moroccan cause, save at the expense of the most sacred national rights of Morocco.

At the present moment, only one French party--the Communist--has been able to continue its activities under a Moroccan label. But the fact that the French constitute the overwhelming majority of its leadership and membership impells us to withhold recognition from it as a Moroccan party. The Istiqlal Party, therefore, has turned down the repeated appeals of this party for the formation of a national front. At the same time, the Istiqlal Party is continuing its efforts to safeguard the Moroccan people from the propaganda of any foreign party, whatever its form. This is being done by training and organizing the masses and explaining to them the dangers that would accrue from the spiritual colonization which undermines the nationalist creed. We must make mention here of the facilities which the Residency-General is according to the Communists in the country, for no reason save to join with them in resisting our indomitable party; but neither the machinations of the colonials nor the defection of traitors will undermine the party so long as it enjoys the confidence of the entire people and the sympathy of its beloved King.

The Policy of M. Erik Labonne

M. Gabriel Puaux departed, following his manifest failure to implement his plans, whether by terrorism or allurements. M. Erik Labonne, one of the distinguished French diplomats, was appointed to succeed him.

M. Labonne was not a stranger to Morocco or the Moroccans; he had previously held the post of chief secretary at the Residency, in which post he had shown undeniable administrative competence; he had also devoted considerable activity to economic questions and financial policy. In addition to that, he was well known for his balanced and penetrating judgment. His appointment as Resident-General came at the most crucial phase in French-Moroccan relations. It was, therefore, assumed that he would introduce to the country a more liberal policy than the antiquated traditions of the protectorate, and that he would bring about a profound change in the regime imposed upon Morocco. This was what the people thought, or at least what French propaganda had made them believe.

When M. Labonne arrived in Morocco, one of his first public acts was to do away with the pompous receptions which his predecessors had been fond of staging in order to domineer over the people and match the ceremonials that should more properly have been reserved for the representative of Moroccan sovereignty, the King. He also cultivated the most cordial relationship with the Palace and gave sweet promises to His Majesty, particularly in regard to education, the judiciary, and other reforms to which the King was particularly devoted.

As an expression of his good intentions and in compliance with the frequently repeated wishes of His Majesty the Sultan and his people, he ordered my return from the remote exile in Equatorial Africa, to which I had been banished for nine whole years; he also released my friend Aḥmad Bla Freej, secretary-general of the party, from his exile in Corsica. Muḥammad Ḥassan al-Wazzāni, who had been placed under detention in the village of Itzar in the vicinity of Fez, was also permitted to return to Fez.

The secretary-general of the party returned to Rabat before me, and the release of al-Wazzāni took place at the same time.

Then the higher council of the Istiqlal Party met and decided to send Dr. al-Fāṭimi al-Fāsi to accompany me on my return trip from the Congo to Rabat. I do not wish to describe the joy which the arrival of my Fāsi compatriot evoked in me, or the exhilaration that permeated me when he reported the details of the nationalist movement in its later phase, of which I had been totally uninformed.

I should also leave it to others to describe the welcome that greeted my release and my arrival in the country--it is not my right to do so myself. However, I cannot but refer to one of those ecstatic moments of spiritual communion which we experienced with our friends and supporters: it was the moment when Moroccan delegations from every corner of the land, including branch representatives, party committees, and leaders, assembled at the spacious home of the Fez notable Ibn Jallūn. I gave an impromptu speech which issued straight from my heart and thus penetrated to the innermost depths of my hearers; the atmosphere was filled with tears of joy, with shouts of rejoicing, and with rapture at the thought of our comradeship in the struggle for freedom. Indeed, the mood was such that my colleague Ḥaj Ḥassan abu 'Ayyād was overwhelmed with emotion and fell unconscious from his chair. The gathering reiterated the pledge of loyalty to the king and country and of readiness to bear every sacrifice in the struggle for liberation.

These spontaneous expressions by the Moroccan people on the occasion of the return of one of their active men were not very acceptable in the eyes of the sages of the protectorate; they worked feverishly, systematically, and through every conceivable channel, to poison the atmosphere between us and the Palace. But the astuteness of our King, his sound judgment, his faith, and his long experience with the methods of the protectorate, made him ignore their tendentious promptings and intrigues.

His Majesty graciously received me in audience the day following my arrival to the country. I expressed to His Majesty what he already knew of my lasting loyalty to the crown. He talked about the developments that followed the presentation of the independence petition and the considerable efforts he had expended for its furtherance. He made no secret of his readiness to sacrifice all he possessed, including the throne itself, on behalf of the Moroccan cause. I emerged from this audience with the firm conviction that Morocco will achieve its rights and aspirations as long as it has at the helm a great king and hero like Sidi Muḥammad, may God grant him victory.

The release of the exiled leaders evoked considerable hopes, and a sense of expectancy as to the next step of the new Resident-General. M. Labonne had conferred repeatedly with the secretary-general of the party together with members of the executive. The deliberations were conducted in an atmosphere of mutual understanding and appreciation, although they always bogged down as a result of the conflicting views of the two sides on basic political orientations. Thus, while the party pressed for a profound change entailing the substitution of effective independence for the existing protectorate regime, the attitude of the French representative towards reforms was determined in the light of the colonial creed; the Resident-General attempted by various means to win over our representatives to the policy of reforms, without sacrificing in principle the demand for independence. He went so far as to request that a certain wing of the party cooperate with him, even though the leaders maintained their stand, which he regarded as negative. Naturally, the leaders could not lend their support to such a solution. It is perfectly legitimate for them to pursue whatever methods they deem advantageous to the cause, but they cannot permit themselves to pursue methods which the protectorate itself directs them to adopt.

Our colleagues were able to obtain from the Resident-General permission to issue newspapers in Arabic, which permission had been withheld since the national rebellion of October 1937, even though censorship has remained in force until the present day. Thus the party started publication of an Arabic daily "al-'Alam" (flag) and a weekly magazine "Ra'y al-Sha'b" (people's view) in French.

On July 22 the French section of the so-called government consultative council met. The Resident-General delivered an elaborate speech in which he disclosed his political program as well as his entire reform program. It became manifest to all, as a result of the speech, that colonialism was one and the same; that the policy which others had tried to forge by iron and fire was the same policy which M. Labonne had been endeavoring to carry through by cordiality and kindness.

The reaction of the Moroccan people to the speech of the Resident was one of great astonishment and disappointment --the disappointment of a nation aspiring to freedom and far-reaching developments.

In his speech the Resident-General dwelt upon a wide range of Moroccan issues, but the political and economic overtone of the speech was in the tradition of colonial policy. It also showed that M. Labonne was still in the grip of reactionary elements in both France and Morocco. His entire approach indicated that he still thought within the closed circle of the protectorate regime, whose shortcomings had been shown to be the principal cause of Morocco's misfortunes.

The Resident-General, however, was not addressing himself to the Moroccan people, who had never been consulted as to their fate and who had been deprived of the most elementary democratic freedoms of expression. When he talked about the necessity of maintaining the international framework in the implementation of his proposed reforms, he intended to remind certain foreign powers that Morocco had an international status which could not be made subject to a new international review.

But what is this framework? Is it not the Treaty of Algeciras, whose signatories had recognized the independence of Morocco? Was the protectorate treaty itself designed to maintain this framework or to implement the international trusteeship stipulated in the Treaty of Algeciras?

Did the treaty of 1912 introduce a new international status for Morocco? Whatever might be said about its legality or illegality, was it anything other than a contract between a strong state, France, and a weak one, Morocco? Therefore it was an attempt to establish a new relationship between France and Morocco, on the basis of genuine cooperation, in which the good faith of the strong power and its fidelity to its obligations were to be tested.

But has the experiment succeeded? The mere fact that the Resident-General and not the Ṣadr al-A'zam should have given a speech that falls within the competence of the latter --a speech given before a council whose French members the Resident regards as true representatives of Morocco, is the best proof of the deterioration of the protectorate into a system of direct rule, in disregard of the people's authority and the king's sovereignty.

The Resident talks about public opinion in Morocco only to portray the reports of the police and the architects of native policy, who see in the Moroccan people a conglomeration of elements, varying in origin, religion, and traditions. Naturally, such views are addressed only to foreigners; we are sure of our own unity, and the French themselves are equally sure that we form one nation whose language is Arabic; the multiplicity of elements in the composition of a nation does not vitiate its nationhood.

Even more astonishing is the fact that the Resident based his political postulates upon the alleged existence of racial differences. This was an attempt to institute administrative systems varying from one region to another, in a country which had been and still is a united kingdom whose administration is concentrated in the hands of the Sheriffian Government and whose spiritual ingredients are derived from its common Islamic religion, Arab culture, and the continuous contact with the civilizations of the Mediterranean.

The Resident talked about the regional councils without spelling out any details. He emphasized the necessity of introducing decentralization, which would have done away with the administration for political affairs only to create miniature administrations to replace it in every region. The Resident declared that he was anxious to give greater latitude to the local Moroccan caids, without, so he thought, undermining the authority of the central Sheriffian Government! Yes, he wanted to do that in order to enable the French commandants to usurp the little that remained of the king's authority and of the rights of the Moroccan people.

A careful reading of M. Labonne's speech would show that French policy had not departed from its colonial basis; this is particularly the case in Morocco where, far from conforming to the international framework, as the Resident had claimed, it has been keyed to the traditional policy of imperialism which aims to divide the indigenous races and elements, to confuse their outlook, and to create psychological differences injurious to their solidarity. It is designed to convince the people that their nationalist experiment had failed and that the only national loyalty which could place them under the banner of freedom, without discrimination on account of religion or race, is the nationality of the conquering nation and the union of its manifold peoples.

The Resident-General in his reform program maintained silence on the question of basic freedoms, such as freedom of the press, of meetings, of associations, and others.

As for trade unions, the Resident did not promise more than to permit the establishment of special unions, for a category of skilled workers and within the confines of factories only. (The promise has not so far been honored in practice.) The Bādiyah [tribal areas] and its workers, along with the class of unskilled workers, would have no right to combine in defense of their interests.

The political program of the Resident can be summed up in the following two aims:

1. To create a new feudalism by means of instituting a system of decentralization for the benefit of commandants and French colonists.

2. To orient the Moroccan government and administration towards the method of direct cooperation, namely, a mixed system of government.

This means that the strategy of integrating the Moroccans by means of assimilation, the granting to French residents as well as to the people of Morocco the rights of the French citizen and likewise the privilege of participation in the French Parliament, had been abandoned in favor of the integration of the French themselves within the Moroccan family, on the basis of the co-existence of two equal races--the indigenous Moroccans and French Moroccans--under the common crown of the Moroccan Sultan and with the French representative as chief of government; the transformed Moroccan nation would thus be prepared to live as an active member of the French Union.

What claimed the principal attention of the Resident, however, was not the political but the economic program. M.

Labonne was convinced that Morocco would undoubtedly attain its independence and that, in spite of all procrastinations, France would one day have to grant and recognize this independence. Thus, he saw the need to implant economic interests which would subjugate Morocco to France even after the attainment of political independence. He was fond of telling his friends that he aspired to be the "economic Lyautey" of Morocco, meaning that he wanted to establish an economic dominion for France in Morocco as Marshal Lyautey had established political dominion.

M. Labonne was not reputed to be a supporter of free enterprise, but was a French socialist, loyal to French socialist governments. His economic program, therefore, as outlined in his speech, envisioned the handing over to the French Government (and not to the Moroccan) of an important part of Morocco's national resources by granting to it a monopoly of certain Moroccan raw materials. This is one of the most ingenious devices in the vocabulary of modern colonialism. At the same time, he promised to encourage the flow of foreign capital into Morocco, although he could not have been unaware of the serious effects of such an unregulated flow upon inflation and the high cost of living.

In an attempt to implement his program, the Resident formed a coal mining company in which the French and Sheriffian Governments were assigned a third of the shares each, while the remaining one-third was floated for foreign and Moroccan capital; the Sheriffian Government's subscription was to be met through a loan from France. The Resident-General appealed to Moroccan financiers to participate in his economic projects and to cooperate in the implementation of this program, which he claimed was beneficial to both Morocco and France.

Opposition to the Policy of Labonne

No sooner had the speech of the Resident-General been released than the higher council of the Istiqlal Party was called to a meeting in Rabat. This was the first meeting of the council after my return from exile. After a careful study of the Resident's speech the council resolved upon the following measures:

1. The presentation of a memorandum to His Majesty, expressing the party's opposition to the Resident's political program and rejecting the form of the proposed reforms,

particularly those pertaining to decentralization and mixed councils. The memorandum was to emphasize the party's continued adherence to the principles enunciated by the National Party and the Kutlah, in rejecting French claims to any of the rights of Moroccan citizens.

2. The release of a public statement to this effect.

3. The presentation of a memorandum to His Majesty, stressing the dangers to Morocco of M. Labonne's economic program, and requesting His Majesty to withhold approval of any proposed enactment designed to usurp Moroccan natural wealth or parts thereof.

4. The address of an appeal in the name of the party to Moroccan financiers, requesting them to refuse the economic cooperation requested by the Resident and to refrain from subscription to companies under French colonial direction.

5. The establishment of an economic ways and means committee, affiliated to the party executive committee, whose task would be to suggest new Moroccan enterprises and direct them in opposition to the projects of the Residency.

6. The declaration of the determination of the party to lead the people in a supreme sacrifice if the Residency-General attempted to implement its program by force.

A party delegation called at the royal palace to present these memoranda. His Majesty assured the delegates of his support for every Moroccan right and interest. The executive committee published and distributed to the public the statements decided upon by the higher council.

The Resident-General summoned members of the executive committee in connection with their views on his proposa[l]. He expressed the view that the attitude of the party was prejudicial to the Moroccan cause; then he offered Ḥaj Aḥmad Bla Freej, secretary-general of the party, the post of chairman of the board of directors to one of these companies, and agreed to the appointment of party nominees to the boards of directors of the most important of the companies. The secretary-general told the Resident that in compliance with the resolutions of the party's higher council, neither he nor any other member of the Istiqlal could accept cooperation with the Residency-General within the framework of the protectorate and on the basis outlined in the Resident's speech.

The Residency-General repeated the offer to party members and supporters other than members of the executive;

Muḥammad al-Zaghāri, al-Ḥamyāni, and others were invited to join the board of directors for these companies, but they declined, as did the rest of the national youths, in response to the appeal of the party.

The Moroccan financiers also refrained from purchasing the shares of the companies in spite of the insistent requests of M. Labonne and representatives of the protectorate in the various provinces. The boycott demonstrated the extent of the Istiqlal Party's moral influence throughout Morocco.

But the party was well aware that the boycott could not be maintained unless alternative opportunities for Moroccan investments were provided; therefore, it formed the economic ways and means committee, referred to earlier, to explore such possibilities, and its contribution to Moroccan enterprises was considerable.

The Resident-General had formed an aviation company, whereupon national financiers formed "al-Nujūm" (the stars) company for civilian air transport; when the Resident-General established a motion picture industry, the nationalists were quick to form their own "Maghrib Studio". Thus, in spite of their meagre resources and the pressure to which they had been subjected, the Moroccans succeeded in standing steadfast behind His Majesty the King and in responding to the call of the party, thus causing the projects of M. Labonne to fail beyond all expectations.

The principal credit for this achievement, however, is due to His Majesty the King, who categorically refused to endorse the various edicts pertaining to the coal mining and other companies, through which M. Labonne had hoped to nationalize Moroccan wealth in favor of French concerns.

The viewpoints of the King and of the Moroccan people may be summed up in their belief that Morocco's basic resources should be retained for Moroccans, and that they can best be safeguarded under the present circumstances by Moroccan nationalization, whereby the government undertakes development either directly or by means of granting concessions involving government participation in capital and profits.

The Istiqlal Party Delegation to Paris

While M. Labonne was witnessing the failure of his Moroccan policy, both he and his supporters were creating the impression in France, through colonial propaganda organs, that he was in agreement with His Majesty the King concerning his program of action. His aim was to secure support for his program, which had been meeting with opposition on the part of French capitalists, who objected to nationalization even though it would place the resources of another nation in the hands of their own government; he was also anxious to belittle in the eyes of the French public the real strength of the nationalist movement.

The Istiqlal Party, sensing this vulnerable spot, decided to send a delegation to Paris in order to explain to the French Government and people the reality of the situation, so that they would no longer have an excuse to persist in a policy doomed to extinction by Moroccan and world developments.

The delegation consisted of Ḥaj Omar 'Abd al-Jalīl as chairman, 'Abd al-Karīm ibn Jallūn, a former judge of the supreme court in Rabat, and Aḥmad al-Ḥamyāni, an advocate from Fez; the three are members of the Istiqlal Party's higher council.

The delegation performed a most commendable job; contacts were established with leading French statesmen and the Moroccan cause was given eloquent expression in various French circles. One of its most important statements was given at a press conference attended by one hundred and fifty French and foreign pressmen; the leader of the delegation gave a detailed description of the true situation in Morocco, expounded the demands of the Moroccan people, and told how the party proposed to realize them. He also replied to the many questions addressed to him by the journalists.

French newspapers gave widespread coverage to the statements made at the conference. Though comments differed from one newspaper to another, there was a general appreciation of the urgency of the situation and the need for decisive and quick action.

The delegates did not restrict their activities to publicity in French circles; they organized Moroccan nationalists in France, opened a permanent office for the party, and organized the Istiqlal student body, establishing for them a committee for orientation and guidance.

The "office of information and publicity" of the Istiqlal Party published with the direction and help of the party delegates a treatise entitled "Tārikh al-Ḥarakah al-Waṭanīyah bi al-Maghrib al-Aqṣā" (the history of the national movement in Morocco). It also printed the statement and minutes of the press conference and published a collection of Istiqlal Party documents in a special booklet in French, which was translated and printed in English also.

The presence of the delegation in Paris coincided with a visit to the French capital of ʻAbd al-Raḥmān ʻAzzām Pasha, Secretary-General of the Arab League. He conferred at length with members of the delegation, and subsequently made statements in which he expressed the Arab League's official support for the peoples of North Africa in their demands for freedom, independence, and membership in the Arab League.

On November 8, 1946 the delegation gave a large reception on the anniversary of the King's accession to the throne. The reception was attended by a considerable number of European and Arab personages, including His Highness the Amir ʻAbdullah Sayf al-Islam, son of the late King Yeḥya of the Yemen. Several addresses were made, including one by the distinguished French scholar Massignon and another by Sheikh Darrāz. The speakers expressed their admiration for His Majesty the King and their support for the Moroccan cause.

On the official level, the delegates conferred at length with the Deputy Foreign Minister on possible solutions for the Moroccan question. The discussions revealed that the French Foreign Ministry had been contemplating the appointment of a special official envoy for negotiations with His Majesty the King on the future of Morocco, while the Resident-General continued in his post as head of the protectorate. If negotiations were brought to a successful conclusion, the French Government would announce the end of the existing regime and would take steps to implement what had been decided upon in the new agreement.

The party was of the opinion that this was a mere method of approach, with no real significance in itself; what really mattered was the content of the offer to be made to His Majesty by the special envoy. We gathered from the reports of the delegation that the French contemplated a solution within the orbit of the French Union regardless of the continuance or abrogation of the protectorate.

Naturally, the Istiqlal Party was at no time a supporter of the French Union, in which it perceived an even more onerous form of enslavement than the protectorate itself. This became more manifest when the special council of the Union announced in its charter that the President of the French Republic would be regarded as head of all the countries joined or associated with the Union. This circumstance renders the difference between us and the French Foreign Ministry so deep as to preclude the possibility of any practical agreement, save by the retreat of one of the two parties from the basic stand to which it adheres.

The party has been adamant in its refusal to compromise on this point; it therefore worked hard in an effort to convince the French Government to budge from its stand, more particularly so since the French were aware that the protectorate treaty itself did not accord them the right to bring Morocco into the fold of a union of which it disapproves and which runs counter to its nationalist aspirations.

Although the delegation was accorded a warm reception by French official circles, the press, and public opinion, it did not succeed in bringing about a modification of the Fren Government's attitude and plans.

Despite this, the party continued to express its good will by addressing French public opinion. A second delegation was sent to Paris led by Aḥmad Bla Freej, secretary-general of the party.

The secretary-general continued the efforts of his prede cessors in establishing strong contacts and conducting an intensive publicity campaign. His statements had importan repercussions in French official circles.

While in Paris he organized a general conference for all Moroccan students in France, which was instrumental in rallying the student body behind the party.

But the exertions of the party did not meet with the appreciation which the Moroccans had expected from a nation like the French; French policy towards Morocco has not changed, nor have colonial methods been modified. The hostility of the colonials to the nationalist movement inside Morocco is becoming ever more intense. Despite such con siderations, the party decided not to set out on a new cours of action before addressing a final warning; it decided to send me to France with authorization to conduct the movem in accordance with the prescriptions which it has followed since my departure to the East.

Before describing my visit to France and then to Egypt, it is necessary to complete the survey of this important phase in the history of the movement by a narration of the Casablanca events and the royal visit to Tangier.

The Tragedy of Casablanca, April 7, 1947

While Morocco was festive in anticipation of His Majesty's visit to Tangier, the diplomatic capital of his kingdom, and while towns and villages along the royal route were making preparations to accord a triumphant welcome to His Majesty on his impending visit to a city that neither he nor his father had been permitted to frequent, colonial circles were working themselves up to a boiling point over the King's refusal to heed their opposition to the visit. These circles had been well aware that the visit would constitute an impressive demonstration of Moroccan unity and would afford nationalism an opportunity to express solidarity in opposition to French, Spanish, and international colonialism.

In spite of the wild charges levelled by the colonial press against the King, the Moroccan people, and their leaders; in spite of extraordinary military movements by the French; and notwithstanding the deluge of rumors that General de Gaulle and his associates would seize upon the occasion of the royal visit to declare their nationalist rebellion from Casablanca to Paris, and that the French Communists were contemplating a railway strike to tie up services along the royal route--in spite of these and other rumors and much vituperation, Moroccan nationalists controlled their nerves in order to facilitate the royal visit, which they regarded as a great triumph for the Moroccan cause, and to foil the policy of provocation, to which the French colonials resort whenever they face the rising tide of Moroccan nationalism.

What shocked the Moroccan public, however, was the tragedy of Casablanca, which occurred on the very eve of the royal tour.

While a number of children were playing in "Ibn Massīk" quarter of the workers' town in Casablanca, three Senegalese soldiers passed by. One of the children asked them for a little gift; the Senegalese reviled the boy and slashed him with a whip which they carried with them. This incensed the child's playmates who set out in pursuit of the three soldiers, throwing gravel and grains of sand. The Senegalese withdrew to a nearby camp only to return with a detachment of Senegalese troops armed with rifles and machine-guns and accompanied by French officers. As soon as they arrived at the quarter, the officers gave permission to the troops to open fire on the unarmed inhabitants; they closed in on the native quarters from all directions, occupied the streets, killed and mutilated the bystanders; then they broke into one house after another murdering whomever they came across--men, women, and children, and plundering or destroying whatever they could not carry away; even chickens did not escape their wrath.

An additional detachment of Senegalese cavalary troops, also led by French officers, arrived on the scene. The ensuing battle extended a distance of ten kilometers; in the course of the fighting the Senegalese turned into savage beasts; they chopped off the heads of the victims and mutilated their bodies. Not even the children were spared these unspeakable acts of savagery; the Senegalese killed and mutilated them in the sight of their mothers, and having done that, turned upon the mothers themselves.

Another detachment of Senegalese troops occupied the rooftops of buildings and directed their machine-gun fire against anyone who dared cross the streets or perchance happened to be passing by.

The French civil authorities did not intervene to stop the aggression, which lasted for more than ten hours, during which the police force was conspicuous in its absence; in fact, the city guards whose job it is to guard the city were forbidden by their military commanders to intervene for the protection of the inhabitants. A delegation of leading Istiqlal Party members called at a nearby French military camp known as the headquarters for protection of the city, of which the entire soldiery is Moroccan though led by French officers. The delegation notified the commandant of what was going on and requested him to obtain the general's approval for calling our Moroccan troops with a view to restoring order. The commandant of the camp asked the delegation to wait for a while during which he communicated with the colonel; a few minutes later he returned only to issue instructions that all the troops be locked up inside the camp.

On the following day the authorities amassed French and foreign armies in all the quarters of the city and along the roads leading from Casablanca to Rabat; they did not include a single Moroccan soldier. Later investigations revealed that all Moroccan troops and police had been disarmed one day before the incident, which goes to prove that the tragedy had been premeditated behind the scenes.

The total of Moroccan dead and wounded in this vengeful act, perpetrated by the French army against national consciousness, amounted to two thousand innocent persons.

The tragedy had a profound effect upon His Majesty the King, as upon every other Moroccan. His Majesty proceeded to Casablanca in person to supervise the investigation, from which he learned the true facts of the tragedy; he conveyed his sympathy to the families of the bereaved and gave assistance to the wounded.

The youth and scout formations of the Istiqlal Party conducted themselves with the utmost heroism. They rescued at considerable peril to themselves the bodies of the victims, counted their numbers, and identified their names; they carried the wounded to hospitals, searched for missing relatives, and conducted a thorough investigation into the events. Their exploit is deserving of the highest tribute.

The Moroccan people as a whole expressed their strong condemnation of the events by a general strike, which was observed throughout Morocco, and by the strong message of protest which various public organizations addressed to the authorities; there was also a general subscription in aid of the victims. The Istiqlal Party demanded withdrawal of Senegalese troops from Morocco, and it has always persisted in the demand for such a withdrawal.

The feminine organization in Casablanca, known as "Sayyīdat wa Fatayāt Ḥizb al-Istiqlāl" (the ladies and girls of the Istiqlal party), performed a most commendable job in caring for the families of the victims; a home and school was established for the orphans of the tragedy and was aptly named "April 7".

The French authorities, for their part, did not show any great interest in the affair; all they did was to condemn it, alleging that it had been committed by the Senegalese acting on their own. Several cadet officers whom the nationalists had implicated in the crimes were arrested but were soon after released. The authorities took advantage of the Tangier journey and later, of the appointment of General Juin, to divert Moroccan public opinion from the Casablanca tragedy.

The memory of the martyrs of April 7, nonetheless, fills the heart and the spirit of every Moroccan. The high-handed attitude of the French army in this encounter, and the indifference of the protectorate authorities, can never be forgotten by the Moroccan people, who have become seasoned in patience but not in forgetting crimes or forgiving criminals. If the French should come up against the ardent zeal of the Moroccans in demanding liberation from their rule, and if they should hear in the future of the violence of Moroccan vengeance, and if they should read that the Moroccans are no longer able to tolerate their oppressio or to heed the call to peace, even from their leaders, they should not be surprised, and they should not complain of Moroccan fanaticism and intransigence. They must rememb that their armies did not bring to us security and peace; they brought to us the savagery of the blacks protected by th flag of the Republic, which should have protected only freedo equality, and fraternity.

The French should remember that our sacrifices in the cause of their liberation from the heavy hand of the Germans during the First and Second World Wars did not meet with any gratitude on their part. On the contrary, the end of the First World War was the signal for a series of military expeditions against our country, which had rebelled against the protectorate and its regime, while the close of the Secon World War heralded a wave of armed persecutions against our unarmed people and youths, who want nothing but peace and security in freedom.

The Royal Visit to Tangier

Before the Journey

Since the return of Tangier to its international status, His Majesty the King had been considering a visit to Tangier the diplomatic capital of his Kingdom, as a sequel to his great tours inside the Sheriffian Kingdom. He had expresse his wish to M. Erik Labonne, who at first saw something alarming in the idea. In spite of the procrastinations and the pleas of the Resident-General for an abandonment of a trip so disquieting to the protectorate, His Majesty insisted on his projected visit. Following protracted negotiations between the Palace and the Residency, the question assumed important international ramifications; the protectorate expressed approval in principle as regards France, but claimed that the powers participating in the Tangier international setup should be notified. Later, the Residency informed His Sheriffian Majesty that both England and the United States were not agreeable to the plan for fear that it might lead to political and diplomatic disturbances. His Majesty replied that he was determined to move around in his country and that if any state had objections to his legitimate right it should present them in writing to him, adding that he would know how to deal with any foreign claim restricting his sovereign rights over all parts of Morocco. The Residency took up the issue again, this time alleging that the Anglo-Saxons were fearful lest the Russians should take advantage of the royal visit to dispatch units of their fleet to the Mediterranean, as a demonstration of their might and their right to bring them over to these waters which Britain claims to control. His Majesty rejected these pretexts also and released a communiqué fixing the date of the Tangier visit, thereby confronting the Residency-General and the powers behind it with an accomplished fact. Resident Labonne thereupon conveyed to His Majesty France's wish that the visit be put off pending completion of diplomatic procedures in this regard. The King reluctantly agreed to postpone the trip for a few more weeks. Finally, M. Labonne informed him that France, England, and the United States had approved of the plan. He suggested, however, that the voyage be made by sea to avoid passage through the Khalifiyah Zone, which is under a Spanish protectorate. The King refused this suggestion, stating that he wished to pass through this zone of his Sheriffian Kingdom, and that if Spain had any objections it should present them to him. The Spanish authorities informed His Majesty that they had no objection to his visit to a part of his Kingdom; on the contrary, they thought that was a natural thing to do. However, they stipulated a number of reservations, foremost of which was the French Resident-

General should not accompany His Majesty inside the Khalifiyah Zone; they suggested that the French Resident stop at 'Arbāwah, from which spot the Spanish Resident would accompany the King instead. They also demanded that Khalifiyah troops and not French should provide escort inside their zone during the visit. A special Spanish committee arrived in Rabat to negotiate with the French Residency concerning arrangements for the royal visit. There was agreement on the reservations requested by Spain.

His Majesty had planned to stay in a special encampment to be set up in the town of Aṣila. The Spanish proposed that His Majesty stay in the "Raysūli Palace" which had become Spanish property. The King turned down the Spanish offer and refused to continue discussions of various Spanish proposals regarding his movements inside their Moroccan territory; instead, he asked His Highness the Khalifah to send a special mission to receive His Majesty's instructions on the itinerary of the visit. The instructions included His Majesty's insistence on staying in a special encampment at Aṣila, where he would have luncheon with the Khalifah and with all the caids and pashas from every part of the zone.

This done, the French Residency-General requested His Majesty to notify the International Commission in Tangier of his impending visit. The King refused to make such a formal notification because it was tantamount to seeking its permission.

As a prelude to his visit to Tangier, the King introduced electoral reforms for Moroccan representation in the legislative assembly, whereby deputies would be elected instead of appointed to the assembly. Although this was a modest reform, the French controllers in Tangier obstructed its implementation. Lastly, M. Labonne presented to His Majesty the following demands in the name of France:

1. That the Residency accompany the King and attend all his receptions in Tangier.

2. That the French Resident-General undertake the task of introducing the foreign diplomatic representatives to the King.

3. That the Resident-General should have prior acquaintance with the speeches of His Majesty, the Crown Prince, and Princess 'Ā'ishah.

4. That His Majesty refrain from issuing any statements during his sojourn in Tangier.

The King accepted the first demand but categorically turned down the second; Tangier was not under French or Spanish protection, so there was no justification for the Resident-General's assumption of duties pertaining to foreign affairs. His Majesty decided that his Sheriffian representative in the International Zone should introduce the diplomatic missions and others. As for the speeches, His Majesty did not object to showing them to the Resident on a personal and extraordinary basis. On the fourth point, regarding statements, His Majesty replied that he did not contemplate the issuing of any unusual statement.

When the Resident-General read the texts of the speeches he proposed that His Majesty insert in his official address an expression of the value which His Majesty attaches to French-Moroccan cooperation. The King promised to think the matter over, and eventually a sentence was inserted towards the close of the speech, advising the citizens to benefit from the experiences of the West and particularly of the French. His Majesty, however, deleted this sentence at the last moment, on account of his deep grief over the tragic events of Casablanca.

Before the beginning of the journey, His Majesty received invitations from the ambassadors of the United States, Portugal, and other states for a dinner to be given in his honor. His Majesty apologized, stating that he would be in his own country and that it would be unreasonable that he be a guest; instead, he intended to invite his foreign guests to a royal banquet as an expression of the esteem in which he holds them and the states they represent.

The municipality of Tangier allocated the sum of five million francs to meet the expenses of the visit. The inhabitants, for their part, set up lavish decorations in celebration of this most auspicious occasion in their life.

The Istiqlal Party made full arrangements for participation in the popular celebrations; a special issue of its newspaper "al-'Alam" was devoted to Tangier, its pivotal location, and the significance of the royal visit. The paper was distributed without charge upon the arrival of the royal train to the "Bride of the Mediterranean". The party branch in Tangier and the Ḥassanīyah scouts of the party supervised the massive national celebrations. The party's office of information and publicity issued daily bulletins in French which were the only source of news coverage for the entire world press. Its headquarters at the Manzah Hotel served as the meeting place of all pressmen, who later expressed their gratitude for its help and assistance. The party's motion picture representative, 'Abd al-Kabīr al-Fāsi, made a comprehensive film coverage of the royal journey which was developed by the Maghrib studio.

There had been world-wide interest in this historic journey, and journalists and photographers arrived in Tangier from all parts of the world. The Egyptian press was represented by Ibrahim Mūsa, correspondent of "al-Miṣri" newspaper, who was also the only Arab representative in this great national demonstration.

His Majesty Leaves Rabat

Large throngs crowded the embellished streets of Rabat to bid farewell to His Majesty the King on his departure for Tangier. At 7:50 a.m. on Wednesday April 9, 1947 the railway station resounded with the applause of the assembled crowd as the royal convoy approached the station. In the forefront of the convoy was the "Prince of Atlas", Crown Prince Mawlay al-Ḥassan, Her Highness Princess 'Ā'ishah, and Prince Mawlay 'Abdullah. His Majesty stepped out of the car accompanied by the Crown Prince. He was greeted by the Resident-General, the chief secretary to the protectorate, and the supreme commander of the army. The royal anthem was played as the King walked into the lavishly decorated railway station. On hand to bid farewell were member of the cabinet, pashas, senior commanders, and notables of Rabat and Cela. The royal entourage which accompanied the King on the journey consisted of sixty-five persons, representing all strata of the people.

When the royal train arrived at 'Arbāwah (the artificial boundary between the two zones of Morocco), thousands of our Moroccan brethren broke into a tumultous ovation for their great King. Mawlay Muḥammad, brother of the Khalifah, stepped forward to greet the King and was followed by the minister of justice in the Khalifiyah Zone, the chief of protocol, the commanding general, the director of native affairs, the Spanish minister, and the chief of the Resident-General's office. They boarded the train with His Majesty on the way to the town of Aṣīla, which was reached at 1:10 p.m.

The Loyalty of the Khalifiyah Zone

On arrival at Aṣīla His Majesty was greeted by His Highness the Khalifah, his son Mawlay al-Mahdi, the Spanish Resident-General, M. Erik Labonne, French Resident-General, and delegations from various towns and tribal areas. His Highness the Khalifah gave a luncheon party in honor of the King, which was attended by a larger gathering of senior Mekhzen officials in the zone.

After the luncheon His Majesty received representatives of the Arabic and the foreign press and gave them the following statement: "You have seen that Morocco is one nation, nay, one family, and that the aspiration of the Moroccan nation, which with God's help will be realized, is the aspiration of all the Arab peoples, for they constitute one nation."

In the afternoon the royal party attended a tea party at which Ibrahim al-Ilghi recited a poem before the King. A closing address was delivered by His Highness the Khalifah in which he said: "Our country has a glorious past, and the Commander of the Faithful in his wisdom will achieve the noble aim of restoring its past glory; Morocco is one nation which recognizes but one sovereign, in whose reign it will ascend to summits of progress; we pray God to help Your Majesty in all your endeavors."

The King then left Aṣīla for the station, where the Khalifah, Moroccan and Spanish officials, as well as M. Labonne, bade him farewell.

The Loyalty of United Morocco

The royal train left the station at 4 p.m., arriving in Tangier at five. As soon as the train came to a halt, three Portuguese warships fired one hundred and one salvos, signalling the arrival of the royal party. The representative of the Sultan boarded the train where he presented to His Majesty the representative of the United States, the British minister--who was also chairman of the international control commission--members of the commission, and the Portuguese governor of the city.

Huge crowds lined the main streets and roof tops of Tangier to greet the royal visitor; their deafening cheers mingled with the thundering guns as the fifty-car royal convoy tried to make headway in the face of these surging human masses, and through the arches of triumph which had been erected along the main thoroughfares.

In short, the Moroccan inhabitants of Tangier gave a shining demonstration of their loyalty to the Moroccan crown and its great sovereign; in the evening an impressive display of fireworks was staged by the municipality.

Audiences

The morning of Thursday, April 10 was set for audiences with the King. His Majesty first received the Ambassador of the United States of America, Mr. Allen, who expressed the friendly feelings of his people towards Morocco. When the Ambassador told His Majesty that he had been appointed Ambassador to Syria, His Majesty replied that whether in Tangier or in Damascus he would be in an Arab country; the King expressed the hope that the Ambassador would be the best representative of democratic America's sympathy with the Arabs. The King then received the representative of England, to whom he recalled the old friendship which had existed between England and Morocco. The King expressed the hope that Morocco, which was striving to achieve its aspirations, would in the future establish the same friendly relations with England that had existed in the past. The Ambassador assured the King that England would maintain the traditional friendship with Morocco. The following audience was given to the Spanish Ambassador, to whom His Majesty expressed appreciation for the great reception which had greeted his passage across the zone. The King took the opportunity to remind the Ambassador that Morocco was one country. The Spanish Ambassador stressed the traditional friendship that has existed between the two countries for many centuries.

Later, the King received the Ambassador of France, to whom he declared: "It gives me pleasure while in this Moroccan city, where all friendly states are represented, to recall French-Moroccan friendship which has been demonstrated in the most trying and perilous circumstances. Morocco, which has contributed to the war effort, is anxious to obtain her share of the peace by enjoying the rights for which she aspires and which she will attain thanks to her friendship with France."

Thereafter, our sovereign made his appearance before his people, and with him were the Crown Prince Mawlay al-Ḥassan and Prince Mawlay al-Mahdi, son of the Khalifah in Tetuan. He gave his historic speech, whose every paragraph was interrupted by loud cheers and applause.

Later, His Majesty granted audiences to a delegation of the Iṣlaḥ (reform) Party, to the secretary-general of the Istiqlal Party who was accompanied by Ḥaj Omar 'Abd al-Jalīl, to members of the Istiqlal branch in Tangier, to al-Makki al-Nāṣiri representing al-Wiḥdah al-Maghribīyah (Moroccan unity), and to other city notables and delegations.

At two in the afternoon the Crown Prince visited the Arabic-French Marshān school and the industrial school.

At three o'clock the same afternoon the Crown Prince deputized for his father in the inauguration of a school founded by Abdullah Jannūn.

At four p.m. the Muslim scouts gave a tea party for His Highness the Crown Prince in his capacity as the first scout.

At four-thirty the Crown Prince visited Mawlay al-Madhi school.

In all these visits the Crown Prince delivered addresses which evoked the enthusiasm and the ovation of the audiences.

Her Royal Highness Princess 'Ā'ishah visited the girls' school at Qaṣabah, where a large welcoming crowd assembled, which included diplomats and representatives of the foreign communities. Her Highness gave a speech in Arabic, and then in French and English, in which she defended her progressive and liberalist views to which she had dedicated her youth. The Princess paid warm tribute to the Arab renascence movements in Egypt and the East generally, emphasizing the attachment of the Moroccan woman to the ideals for which all Arabs are striving. The speech made a profound impression upon all those present and emphasized the determination of the royal family to lead the nation towards progress and a better life.

The Reformer-King at the Grand Mosque

On Friday, April 11 His Majesty proceeded to the grand mosque for the Friday noon prayers. The King led the prayers in person and then delivered the Friday sermon, thus reviving a tradition of the Orthodox Caliphs, which had been in abeyance for a long time.

In his sermon the sovereign pointed out the secret behind the success of the virtuous forbears; he declared that it was on account of their attachment to the precepts of their orthodox religion that they had been able to deliver the world from the claws of ignorance and tyranny and to teach humanity the worth of individual liberty and human rights in general. He related how the Prophet, upon whom be peace, had embraced all the most trying hardships with unflinching determination, steadfastness, and endurance until the triumph of truth had been assured. The King then declared that the Islamic nation cannot achieve her aspirations or live in dignity and strength except through unity and adherence to the teachings of the glorious Koran. He concluded his sermon with a prayer for all the Muslim kings and presidents.

Thus, after asserting his temporal suzerainty over the Moroccan city of Tangier, His Majesty reaffirmed his spiritual leadership in this part of his Arab Muslim Kingdom

In all this, His Majesty was only giving expression to the popular wishes of his people for a comprehensive rejuvenation of all aspects of life, spiritual as well as material.

Gifts of the People to Their King

Following the Friday prayers, the royal procession made its way to the Barrāni sūq, where the traditional gift-presentation ceremony was to be held. The Muslim inhabitants of Tangier presented to His Majesty a sword with a gold and china hilt, on which were inscribed the words: "fidelity and loyalty". Precious gifts were also presented to the Crown Prince, to Princess 'Ā'ishah, and to Mawlay Abdullah.

The Israeli community in Tangier presented a complete sterling silver tea set with expressions of loyalty to the 'Alawi royal house and to His Majesty.

The gift of the inhabitants of Tetuan was symbolical; it consisted of a silver-made map of united Morocco with gold inscriptions, and a gold case filled with soil drawn from the mountain earth of the region with the following inscription: "On the occasion of the King's visit to Tangier, the inhabitants of Tetuan present this soil mixed with the blood of the martyred heroes as a symbol of Morocco's unity under the illustrious 'Alawi crown."

'Abd al-Khāliq al-Ṭarrīs declared amid the cheering crowds: "To the protector of the nation and religion, in the name of this generation which is irrevocably attached to your blessed Kingdom, we express our respects, admiration, and loyalty to the Commander of the Faithful, in the hope that our sovereign will accept this modest gift as a symbol of our love and fidelity to the throne of your immortal ancestors. Your Majesty, we shall faithfully follow your lead and your example."

In short, the demonstrations of Tangier highlighted Morocco's deep-rooted unity, and her striving for complete liberation and independence under the adroit and progressive leadership of the King.

On the morning of Saturday, April 12, the King visited the Muṣalla public school where a large crowd assembled to greet His Majesty; after addresses by the King's secretary and by the Crown Prince, the King laid the cornerstone for the new building, the expenses of which had been raised by public subscriptions.

At noon the United States Ambassador, Mr. Allen, the French Resident-General in Morocco, M. Labonne, and the British consul general had luncheon with His Majesty. A press delegation asked for an audience with the King. The Chief of the Royal Cabinet asked for the questions in writing, promising to give the answers later in the evening. The text of the royal statement, delivered to the journalists by the Chief of the Royal Cabinet, reads:

> Before we leave Tangier, the diplomatic capital of Morocco, it gives us pleasure to address our thanks to all the inhabitants for their expressions of fidelity and loyalty; in the reception accorded to us, Tangier has fulfilled our confidence in her as a Moroccan city staunchly attached to the throne of her king. She has thus proved that Morocco is a unity whose symbol is the crown; may this journey expedite a solution of the question of Tangier.
>
> Morocco is anxious to maintain good relations in the future with all the states that have struggled for freedom and still continue to support it; she is most anxious to attain her full rights.
>
> Needless to say, Morocco is an Arab country closely attached to the Arab East; it is natural, therefore, that these ties grow closer and stronger, particularly so since the Arab League has become an organization playing an important role in world politics.
>
> We are convinced that the role of culture is important in the achievement of closer ties; therefore, we are endeavoring to promote the enlightenment of the Moroccan people, principally through the establishment of educational institutions having identical curricula with those of the

educational colleges of Egypt, Syria, Lebanon, and Iraq; we have also endeavored since our accession to the throne to accord our subjects the democratic rights, and we are confident of achieving all our aspirations.

Return to Rabat

On Sunday morning the royal party left Tangier on the way back to the capital. Upon arrival at 'Arbāwa the King, accompanied by the Khalīfah, laid the cornerstone for the new 'Arbāwa mosque; in the afternoon His Majesty inaugurated the Sūq Arbi'ā' al-Gharb school, amid massive popular demonstrations in which the Ṭāriq ibn Ziyād scouts of the Istiqlal Party branch participated. At 6:50 p.m. His Majesty arrived back in Rabat.

The Tangier Speeches

We shall describe later the special significance of this royal visit to the "diplomatic capital of Morocco", as His Majesty has called it in his speech; but it is necessary now to consider the speech and the statements of His Majesty, together with the speeches of the Crown Prince and of Princess 'Ā'ishah, which in fact reflect the views of their adroit father.

The public speeches of the king are invariably couched in the manner of a religious sermon in order to underline the king's dual position as suzerain temporal and spiritual. They recall the glorious past of the early Muslims in contrast to the sad and ineffectual condition of contemporary Muslims, as shown by the partitioning of this Muslim country, Morocco. They probe into the reasons which had enabled the early Muslims to assume leadership in the world, and into the causes which had sapped the moral fiber of the later generations, thus bringing about their lapse into the present state of degradation. His Majesty repeatedly emphasized the urgency of adhering to the true principles of Islam, cleansed of all superstition and idle practices, with a view to restoring the sound outlook of the virtuous forebears, an outlook based upon knowledge, reason, and investigation. His Majesty is optimistic over the prevailing orientation and trends in the Arab world, which have resulted in the formation of the Arab League; he asserts that Morocco is an Arab country, animated by the same ideals that imbue all Arabs and Muslims. His efforts in the field of education and enlightenment are directed to the long-range goal of achieving unity of outlook between Moroccans and their Arab brethren elsewhere, with a view to ensuring that Morocco will neither fall back and be outpaced nor be moulded in a non-Arab orientation and outlook. His Majesty feels that the achievement of these goals is not possible unless Morocco attains her freedom; thus, he reiterates his determination to spare no effort in defense of his people's rights and their attainment of a worthy place as an Arab Muslim nation.

In his statement to the press, His Majesty emphasizes his profound desire to accord his people the democratic rights and freedoms. Thus, we may sum up the royal views in the following points:

1. The affirmation of the purely Arab character of Morocco.
2. The need to achieve unification of the country by an integration of its various zones.
3. The attainment of cultural and religious unity with the rest of the Muslim and Arab countries.
4. The achievement of the other national aspirations of Morocco.
5. The need to reorganize the Moroccan Government on a democratic basis.

By delivering the Friday sermon at the grand mosque and leading the worshippers in prayer, His Majesty underlined the importance he attaches to the religious rejuvenation in Morocco and to a modernization in the contents and methods of religious instruction and moral guidance; this became evident when His Majesty ordered that loud speakers be installed in the mosques to enable worshippers to hear distinctly the sermon and the Koran reading. In his Friday sermon the King urged the adoption of modern forms of cooperation, particularly in the economic field, by the formation of stock-holding companies and the encouragement of competitive enterprise. This is perhaps the best answer to the policy of economic monopolization propounded by M. Labonne. His Majesty did not neglect the material aspects of the struggle; he merely wanted religion to be a driving force in fulfilling God's wish for the reclamation and development of the earth and the preservation of rights against all manner of usurpation. The King's speech did not substitute religious forms of energy for the kilowatts proposed by the Resident-General, as some French magazines have interpreted it; all that he wished was that these kilowatts be developed by the Moroccans themselves and for the benefit of their country. The Moroccans, in doing this, would be performing a national as well as a religious duty. Moreover, His Majesty wished to remind his fellow citizens of the moral worth of man, as a fundamental precept in the legacy of Morocco and a principle in her striving for a better human existence in the years to come; if she failed to live up to it she would be deserving of perdition and would be overcome by reformers from other nations. But Morocco cannot assume this responsibility unless she is freed from the shackles of foreign colonization and enslavement; all efforts, therefore, should be directed to the overriding goal of national liberation.

His Majesty, as was stated earlier, deleted from his speech the sentence proposed by the Resident-General; French commentators saw in this act not only a slight to France and a disregard of her achievements, but also a questioning of M. Labonne's competence as a foreign minister to His Majesty and an assertion of the King's independence from the control of the Resident-General. As a matter of fact, His Majesty could have included in his speech a reference to French-Moroccan cooperation, as indeed he had done during the audience granted to France's representative to Tangier. The circumstances of the Casablanca incidents, however, left no room for such mention, more particularly so since the speech was addressed to the Moroccan public as a sort of a discourse, in which a plea for cooperation with France or any other state would have been out of order.

The view that the advice of the foreign ministry should be heeded is only applicable in a democratic system of government; when M. Labonne submitted his remarks to the King, he did so as a representative of France and not as a Moroccan minister. At any rate, there is no stipulation in the Moroccan constitution that a Resident-General has the capacity of a foreign minister. Not even the protectorate treaty, which recognizes the French representative as the sole intermediary between the king and foreign states, requires that His Majesty appoint him as foreign minister, or for that matter, have a foreign minister at all.

There is an even more basic fallacy in this whole affair.

The city of Tangier has a status independent of the French protectorate; it is not to be expected, therefore, that His Majesty should confine his cooperation to France and to Spain, to the exclusion of other states represented on the control commission.

The references made by the Crown Prince to his grandfather Sultan Mawlay al-Ḥassan were intended to symbolize the struggle which this heroic King had put up in the face of foreign diplomatic intrigues; in that struggle, the Sultan succeeded in warding off all foreign attacks for more than twenty years; at the same time his achievements at home were brilliant. It was a reminder of the era of independence in which the country enjoyed unity, dignity, and security, as against foreign colonization, which has since torn Morocco asunder.

The speech of Princess 'Ā'ishah surveyed the history of the Arab renascence and its future orientation; it was an assertion of the ideals and aspirations that animate and unite all the Arab peoples.

Significance of the Royal Visit

For half a century Tangier had not been visited by the legitimate king of the land. International policy had consistently prevented any such visit, or even passage across the Khalifiyah Zone. All the trips of His Majesty to France and other parts of Europe had been made via the port of Casablanca; whenever a ship on which the King was travelling anchored off Tangier, the local officials hurried on board to greet His Majesty.

As a result of the partition of Morocco between France and Spain and the ceding of the southernmost portions of Morocco to West Africa, Tangier was placed under an international regime for the benefit of the participating states. The king retained only nominal authority, symbolized by the presence of a Mekhzen representative, whose sole function is to affix his official signature to decisions and decrees submitted to him by the commission. England had consistently striven to whittle down even this nominal Moroccan authority. In 1926 France herself defended the rights of Morocco against the claims of the other states. Spain for her part missed no opportunity in pressing for the annexation of Tangier to her zone of occupation. Immediately after the defeat of France in 1940, Spain calculated that the propitious moment had arrived; her troops occupied the international city and annexed it to her zone of the protectorate. The representative of His Sheriffian Majesty was expelled and his palace handed over to the German Ambassador. England tentatively approved this Spanish act, while the Moroccans persisted in their demand for the territorial unity and liberation of Morocco.

With the victory of the Allies, Tangier reverted to her former international status; Allied spokesmen declared that the arrangement was provisional and that a better system would be devised in a few months. The King again sent a representative, to the profound satisfaction of the inhabitants. Later, when the King expressed his desire to visit the city in person, his aim was to assert the sovereign right of the Moroccan people over all parts of their land and to emphasize the rights of the Moroccans to determine their own fate.

Since Tangier is not included in either the French or the Spanish protectorate, it should be possible to accord it the status of a free city, under the suzerainty of the King, and in accordance with an administrative and fiscal system devised by His Majesty. The profound significance of the royal visit may be gauged in the light of this diplomatic wrangle over the disposition of the Tangier zone.

French diplomacy had been anxious to make political capital out of the Resident-General's accompanying of the King on his visit to Tangier; the fact, however, that the Mekhzen representative was made to introduce the ambassadors of the foreign states gave a practical demonstration that France's influence does not exceed the usual limits, and that notwithstanding Morocco's present status she is an entity independent of France; this means that the Moroccan question cannot be resolved by a bilateral agreement with France. The international ramifications of the Moroccan issue go beyond the matrix of French, Spanish, or international zones of occupation; the core of the question lies in the general treaties which had brought about the present state of affairs.

Finally, the events of Tangier had decisively dispelled any illusions concerning the adherence of Morocco to a French or a Spanish union; the King, voicing the wishes of the people, declared categorically that the development, liberation, and independence of Morocco could only be contemplated within the framework of an Arab united family of nations. I wish to conclude this section by quoting the testimony of the special correspondent for the Paris daily "Le Monde", who said: "The Sultan's visit to Tangier was without any question a solid victory for Moroccan nationalism and its independence movement."

The Effect of the Royal Vist on French Official Quarters

The statements of the King in the course of the Tangier journey had a disconcerting effect on French official circles, and particularly on M. Ramadier, the Prime Minister, and M. Labonne, the Resident-General. The Prime Minister attempted to construe the royal statements in a manner totally at variance with their true purpose.

He declared that His Majesty the Sultan was a descendant of the family of the Prophet, adding that Morocco had never recognized the Ottoman Caliphate; therefore, the Prime Minister explained, it was his right to address his subjects as a Muslim Caliph; if he had not as yet claimed his right to the Caliphate, his noble descent gave him authority to speak in its behalf.

It will be recalled that during World War I certain French circles had dallied with the idea of proclaiming His Majesty Sultan Yūsuf as a Caliph over what they called French Islam. Was this what M. Ramadier had in mind when he deliberately misinterpeted the noble aims of the King?

Or, could it be that the King's salutatory references to the Arab League and his inclusion of Morocco within its fold had evoked in M. Ramadier the desire to sow the seeds of discord among the Arab kings, who might view with disfavor the claims of any one to the Caliphate?

Whatever may have been the motive of the French Premier, the traditional prayer uttered towards the end of the sermon was for all the Muslim kings and heads of state and not to his person; moreover, the Arab kings, presidents, and people are wiser than to be taken in by such foolish talk, to which even the French press paid little attention.

As for M. Labonne, he delivered a speech before the French community of Tangier in which he said: "Everyone in Morocco, from the King to all those in responsible places, knows that the primary condition for progress lies in order and development; anything that takes place outside orderly processes would merely lead to disintegration, sufferings, delays, or perdition. Cooperation between France and Morocco is reflected in the understanding and fraternity which have been our motto in this country, and which completely harmonize with the work, the intelligence, and the other virtues of the Moroccan people; all the nations of the earth approve and recognize this fact, and there is no one who does not acknowledge it or does not hope for its continuance."

In contrast, the main theme in the King's speech was related to the unity and liberation of Morocco and adherence to her Arab-Islamic character.

We should not, however, be misled by the attempt of M. Labonne to reconcile what he had to say with what he should have said; he was merely playing for time until he could make a trip to Paris to report his vexation and resentment over the events of Tangier.

When he left Morocco, following the appointment of General Juin, he did not even pay the customary courtesy to His Majesty the Sultan, as had been the practice of his predecessors at the Residency.

Press Comments

The French and the foreign press in general gave prominence to the news of the royal visit; they commented widely on its significance and implications, stressing that it had been a notable success for the Moroccan nationalist movement.

The French press continued for two months to carry articles describing the impact of the visit upon the Moroccan people and the foreign residents, and voicing deep misgivings over the deterioration of Moroccan-French relations. The rightist press vigorously attacked M. Labonne, accusing him of weakness and indecision; they admonished him for permitting himself to be duped by the astute tactics of the Sultan. They were unanimous in deploring the failure of the King to make any reference to France; a number of newspapers had the temerity to attack the King in person and to remind him of his indebtedness to France's protection and assistance.

The French press also devoted considerable attention to the Arab League and its impact upon the Moroccan leaders; there was an attempt to explore ways and means of harmonizing it with the claims of the French Union; the impact of internal French politics upon the orientation of Moroccan leaders was not overlooked. Thus, the Tangier visit continued to claim the attention of the French press until the appointment of General Juin as Resident-General in Morocco.

Nationalist Activity in the Khalifiyah Zone

With the victory of the Allies and the ejection of Spain from Tangier, there was a general feeling that Spanish policy would undergo some modifications; the new Resident-General, Varela, persisted, however, in following the footsteps of his predecessors. In fact, he opened the gates of the zone even wider to the influx of Spanish colonists. His Highness the Khalifah attempted at first to resist the policy on the spot; however, the persistence of the Resident in his colonial policy, and his disregard for the jurisdiction of the Khalifah himself, prompted His Highness to proceed to Madrid in the hope of bringing about a modification of the policy of unlimited immigration. The visit convinced the Khalifah that the policy had the approval of General Franco himself, and that the Resident was merely complying with the instructions of the Madrid Government.

It was natural that the Khalifah should turn to the Arab League for support; he expressed to the Egyptian minister his desire to send representatives from the Khalifiyah Zone to the Arab League; his request met with the enthusiastic approval of the League.

The delegation, consisting of Muḥammad ibn ʻAbbūd and Muḥammad al-Fāsi, arrived in Cairo on February 7, 1946 and were received in audience by His Majesty King Faruq. The delegates presented memoranda and reports on the situation in Morocco to the conference of Arab kings and presidents at Inshāṣ, to the Bludan conference of the Arab states, and to the council of the Arab League.

The release of the exiled leaders in the Sultaniyah Zone was received with exhilaration throughout the Khalifiyah Zone; demonstrations and celebrations were held, principally at the various clubs of the Iṣlāḥ (reform) Party and at al-Waḥdah al-Maghribīyah (Moroccan unity) house. Several delegations visited Southern Morocco to congratulate their released colleagues and renew contacts with them.

The Iṣlaḥ Party resumed its activities by the publication of statements urging a cessation of immigration, the sequestration of land in favor of Spanish colonists, and the financial subsidies paid to the Catholic Church out of the Moroccan budget. The statement demanded the recognition of public liberties and the setting up of a strong provisional government to prepare the country for independence.

On August 28 the Iṣlaḥ organized peaceful demonstrations throughout Northern Morocco to back up their urgent demands. The military authorities intervened and a violent encounter with the demonstrators ensued. The Khalifiyah Government protested against the intervention of the Spanish army and warned that serious consequences might follow the use of force.

In September 1946 the Iṣlaḥ Party sent a delegation to Rabat, led by al-Ṭayid Benūnah, its secretary-general. After an audience with the King, the delegation held a conference with the higher council of the Istiqlal Party, during which agreement was reached on the coordination of the policies of the two parties in the struggle for independence and unity under the 'Alawi royal house. The delegation also agreed to abandon in their zone the policy of gradualism, and to reject the deceptive promises of reform held out by the colonials. Upon the return of the delegation to Tetuan, al-Ṭarrīs gave a speech in which he declared: "The Iṣlaḥ Party in the North and the Istiqlal Party in the South have resolved and have pledged God and the nation to work for the realization of this objective and to accept no alternative to the independence and unity of Morocco." Turning to the agreement of solidarity just concluded at Rabat, the leader of the Iṣlaḥ declared: "Just as there should be no cleavage between Northern and Southern Morocco, or between His Majesty the King and his Khalifah, so also there must be none in the orientation and policies of the Iṣlaḥ and the Istiqlal Parties."

The Two Parties Oppose the Resident's Reforms

In the wake of this renewed nationalist activity in the Khalifiyah Zone, and on the occasion of the Muslim festivals, the Spanish Resident told a gathering of Muslim notables, who had called on the Khalifah to pay their respects, that he planned to submit for the approval of the Khalifah a reform scheme which would provide for the creation of a number of ministerial portfolios. The Iṣlaḥ issued a statement reiterating the refusal of the party to participate in government, and stressing the conviction of Moroccans that the reform proposals of the protectorate were distorted and merely designed to serve the aims of colonial policy. Simultaneously, the Istiqlal Party issued a statement to the same effect; it stressed the solidarity of Moroccan nationalism in North and South as regards both aims and tactics. The statement warned the citizens not to be duped by the sweet utterances of the colonials, which merely serve as a facade for their intrigues against Moroccan sovereignty.

The Spanish protectorate attempted to crush this movement by force; it also tightened up press censorship, having earlier suspended "al-Waḥdah al-Maghribīyah" (Moroccan unity) newspaper. In the face of these measures, the Iṣlaḥ Party submitted a memorandum to the United Nations Secretariat, with copies to the Arab League Secretariat and to the member states, demanding the abrogation of the protectorate and the declaration of the country's independence. In retaliation, the Spanish Residency-General took more stringent measures against the nationalists; the homes of nationalists were searched, the newspaper "al-Ḥurrīyah" (liberty), mouthpiece of the Iṣlaḥ, was suspended, and a heavy fine was imposed upon the party. Tension continued and finally erupted in the events of January, as we shall explain later on.

The Conference of the Arab Maghrib in Cairo

The League for Defense of Morocco continued its activities in Cairo, while representatives of the Istiqlal Party obtained a mandate from the Iṣlaḥ Party to speak on its behalf, following the concord to which reference has been made earlier. Their activities gained added strength from the presence in Cairo of an official Khalifah delegation to the Arab League. There was a growing feeling in favor of coordinating the activities, not only of the Moroccan organizations, but of all the North African parties as well. It was known that the Istiqlal Party had taken steps on the home-front with a view to this end. The Moroccans, therefore, agreed with the representative of the Algerian People's Party in Cairo, al-Shāthili al-Makki, and with representatives of the Tunisian Dustur Party, to convene a general conference, with a view to agreeing on a common strategy and of coordinating the work of their various offices abroad.

The conference continued in session between February 15 and 22, 1947, during which outstanding problems were studied and appropriate decisions made.

The organizers of the conference were careful to invite the participation of all existing movements in North Africa; thus, Tunisia was represented by the Dustur branches in Damascus and Cairo, and Algeria by the office of the People's Party in Cairo, while Morocco was represented by the League for Defense of Morocco along with the Moroccan delegation to the Arab League.

The inaugural session was held on Saturday evening, February 15, 1947 at the headquarters of the Muslim Youth Association, under the honorary chairmanship of 'Abd al-Raḥmān 'Azzām Pasha, Secretary-General of the Arab League, and was attended by a large gathering of Arab and Eastern leaders. The speakers included 'Azzām Pasha and 'Abd al-Karīm Ghallāb, secretary to the conference. The conferees adopted the following resolutions:

1. To declare that the protectorate treaties imposed upon Tunisia and Morocco are null and void and to refuse recognition of any French rights in Algeria.
2. To demand that the Maghrib governments and nationalist organizations declare the independence of North Africa.
3. To demand the evacuation of foreign troops from all parts of al-Maghrib.
4. To reject membership in the French Union in any form whatsoever.
5. To observe May 5 (occupation of Algeria), May 12 (imposition of the protectorate over Tunisia), and March 30 (imposition of the protectorate over Morocco) as days of national mourning throughout North Africa.
6. To intensify the struggle both at home and abroad for the achievement of independence and the withdrawal of foreign troops.

The following resolutions were adopted in regard to the coordination of the nationalist movement inside North Africa:

1. To urge agreement among the various nationalist parties within each country.
2. To establish closer ties among the nationalist movements of the three countries.

With a view to this end, the conference recommends:

a. Agreement on a common objective, namely, independence and withdrawal of foreign troops.

b. The setting up of a permanent committee whose task would be to coordinate strategy and tactics for a common struggle.

c. Working for the unification of the workers' movements as well as the social, cultural, and economic organizations in the three countries, and their orientation along nationalist lines.

d. Urging that the three countries form a common front when a crisis breaks out in any one of them.

The conference adopted the following resolutions relating to North Africa and the Arab League:

1. To request the Arab League:

a. To declare the protectorate treaties over Tunisia and Morocco null and void, as well as the occupation of Algeria; to determine upon the independence of these countries and the admission of their representatives to the Arab League Council.

b. To submit the North African cause before international organizations and to assist the countries of North Africa with all means at its disposal towards the achievement of their full independence.

c. To send commissions of inquiry to North Africa.

d. To ask the member states to appoint representatives in North Africa.

2. To submit the cultural problems of North Africa for the consideration of the Arab League Council, with a view to promoting Arab culture throughout the Arab Maghrib; to assist North African students seeking education at Arab colleges and institutes in the East.

3. To thank the Arab League for its continuing efforts on behalf of North Africa.

At its fourth session, the conference considered the submission of the question of North Africa before international forums, and adopted the following resolutions:

1. To submit to one of the Arab states documentary evidence showing how France and Spain had violated in their colonial policies all the resolutions and ideals of the United Nations, and to request that the question be raised before the United Nations.

2. To urge that the North African parties submit a memorandum to the United Nations describing the aggression of France and Spain against the rights and freedoms of the North African peoples.

3. To submit a memorandum to the United Nations Economic and Social Council and to the Commission on Human Rights showing how France and Spain had violated the economic and social rights of the peoples of North Africa.

The last topic on the agenda pertained to the coordination of the work of the various North African offices in Cairo. The conference decided that the League for the Defense of Morocco in Egypt, the Moroccan delegation to the Arab League committees, the office of the Algerian People's Party, and the office of the Tunisian Dustur form a united office to be known as "Maktab al-Maghrib al-'Arabi" (the office of the Arab Maghrib).

The conferees adopted at their closing session the following general resolutions:

1. To thank His Majesty the King of Egypt for all his countless services to the cause of North Africa and Arabism.

2. To thank His Majesty the King of Morocco for his gallant stand in support of the nationalist cause, and to express the conference's loyalty to His Majesty and its gratitude to His Highness the Khalifah in the Northern Zone for his sympathy with the nationalist movement.

3. To support the Bey of Tunisia, al-Munṣif, and to protest against his detention and forced abdication from the throne.

4. To support the Egyptian cause, and the unity of Egypt and the Sudan.

5. To support Arab Palestine and demand her liberation.

6. To support Libya in her demand for unity and independence.

7. To support Indo-China in her struggle against oppressive colonialism.

8. To address the salutations of the conference to all the leader of the North African parties.

On the evening of February 24 a reception was given at the Shepheard's Hotel for the press and leading personages. The secretary of the conference gave a speech, in which he expressed satisfaction at the success of the conference and paid tribute to the Arab leaders and the press for their support and encouragement.

The office of the conference received a deluge of calls and messages from all parts of the Arab East and expressions of solidarity from the various leaders and organizations in North Africa. These showed that the conference had been timely and that it had performed an essential task in the circumstances of the moment.

The Office of the Arab Maghrib

As soon as the conference was over, representatives of the Istiqlal, al-Sha'b, and Dustur Parties moved to a new headquarters in Cairo, in accordance with the recommendations of the conference. The new headquarters, known as Maktab al-Maghrib al-'Arabi (the office of the Arab Maghrib) consisted of three sections: the Moroccan section, comprising the Istiqlal and the Iṣlaḥ Parties; the Tunisian section, represented by the Neo-Dustur Party; and the Algerian section, supervised by al-Sha'b Party. The Office has a director general elected for a period of one year by representatives of all the parties meeting in plenary session. It also has several technical committees.

The Office has published several important publications on North Africa in addition to issuing regular news bulletins and commentaries on current events in North Africa.

The library of the Office has a continually expanding collection of books and publications dealing with North Africa. Arabic and foreign press extracts on North Africa are being kept in special files, and an annual count is made to register increases and decreases in the volume of items published concerning North Africa and the reasons therefor. The Office gives receptions on various occasions and holds press conferences whenever the need arises.

The Office of the Arab Maghrib in Cairo has indeed become the focal point for all those interested in North African affairs. To North African writers it is a pilgrimage center, particularly after it became the meeting place of North Africa's leaders, and after Morocco's hero, 'Abd al-Karīm, and his gallant brother arrived in Egypt.

The French magazine, "La France," observed in a special issue devoted to North Africa that the Arab Maghrib Office had become an extension of the Arab League or a complement of it. This is indeed true, for without this Office North African representation in Cairo--center of Arab activities--would have been woefully deficient.

In France

In the charged atmosphere following the Casablanca inci- dents, the royal visit to Tangier, the virulent press campaign in France against Moroccan nationalism, the special French cabinet meeting on Morocco, and the recall of M. Labonne to Paris, for consultation or castigation--against this background the party decided that I should proceed to Paris in order to continue the efforts of the two previous delegations and convey a final warning to French diplomacy In truth, my assignment was a most difficult one; the atmosphere had been extremely tense, particularly in French official circles, which were still unable to put up with the Tangier incidents and were growing increasingly impatient in the face of the mounting wave of national consciousness in Morocco. The atmosphere had been still further inflame by tendentious reports, accusing the Moroccans of pro-American leanings or dependence on Americans for support My instructions had been to avoid the use of strong language and not to utter any threats; the situation required that I go about my task in a manner that would not be repellent to French psychology and would enable me to carry out my mission to the satisfaction of my conscience.

Upon my arrival at the Paris airport, I was greeted by a large gathering of Moroccan students, merchants, and workers. When I alighted from the plane, the airport resounded with the anthem of the Istiqlal Party and other national songs. To the press correspondents who had been waiting at the airport I gave the following brief statement: "I have come to France to continue the efforts begun by my colleagues before me; I shall contact all French circles fro which I hope to obtain attention and support." I was visited at the Lutetia, the party's hotel suite in Paris, by many press reporters, to whom I gave various statements. It might be worth while to reproduce a summary of my interview with the correspondent of "Franc-Tireur" because it gives an outline of our policies in an independent Morocco:

"What is your policy and program for the Morocco of tomorrow?"

"We shall organize the government and the people in the independent Morocco along western democratic lines while preserving our spiritual and moral legacy; we believe in equality and fraternity among all Moroccan citizens, the abolition of class differences, the education of women and their participation in all fields of endeavor; we support economic planning within a national framework, but are opposed to monopolization as well as to stifling restrictions on private initiative and enterprise."

"Do you have a social program?"

"We envisage a reorganization of the economic system, with a view to a more efficient development of the national resources. This includes nationalization of such basic resources as credit facilities, minerals, and so forth; initiation of rural reforms; widespread instruction and education for all sections of the people, with a view to imbuing the Moroccan masses with the outlook of modern citizens who know their duties as well as their rights; and finally, the promotion of social institutions and services, such as unions, social relief, social security, child welfare, sports, and recreation."

"What is your attitude towards His Majesty the Sultan?"

"He is our beloved sovereign and we are all behind him; we believe that Morocco will live in an era of happiness and prosperity under his reign. His Majesty works only for his people, and he has stated on more than one occasion, and particularly in Tangier, that all his efforts would be oriented towards according his people a free and democratic system of government."

"What are your relationships with the Arab League at present and in the future?"

"At present we are following with considerable interest the efforts of the Arab League for the revival of the Arab world; its efforts should be supported by all the Mediterranean peoples, because Arab civilization is a great ingredient in the composite of Mediterranean civilization. We are firmly convinced that the Arab world will play an important role in bringing about close cooperation with the peoples of this important sea; we also believe that an independent Morocco will play anew her historic role as a link between the two great elements of the Mediterranean."

"How do you visualize your relationships with France in the present and in the future, and your relationships with the other states?"

"If the protectorate treaty is replaced by a treaty of alliance with France, Morocco will honor her pledges; France will then see that the Moroccans who had stood by her side in the most critical moments over the past thirty-five years will not turn their back on their ally France.

"As regards the present, all our efforts are devoted to convincing the French Government of the need to give more serious attention to the disaffection that has prevailed in Morocco for a third of a century and is daily becoming more serious. We believe that there are no difficulties which cannot be ironed out; but the situation must be dealt with firmly, with a view to working out a solution satisfactor to Morocco's national aspirations while preserving legitimate French interests; an equitable deal would make the best of friends.

"We do not forget that a part of the settlement should be the solution of the question of Northern Morocco, a portion of which France had given as a sub-lease to Spain, while another had been placed under an international regime We depend on the support of France for the achievement of the territorial unity of Morocco; but it is evident that such a unity cannot be achieved without the prior independence of all Moroccan zones. The great act we want France to carry out for the benefit of the Moroccan people is to take the lead in recognizing the independence of the zone under her occupation."

"And the other nations, the United States of America for example?"

"Our relations with the other foreign nations will be in accord with the interests of Morocco."

The Moroccan community gave a large reception for me at the Claridge Hotel, to which many French and Arab personages were invited. Speeches were delivered by representatives from the Arab countries, following which I gave a speech in French and then in Arabic. The speeches stressed Morocco's principal aim of independence and her Arabism.

Another reception was given to me by the "Maison de la Pensée Française", to which many literary men of the French resistance were invited. I delivered a speech on the civilization of the Mediterranean and the aversion of the people to all forms of oppression and injustice. Several French speakers spoke in support of freedom for Morocco. Professor Massignon praised the love of justice which animates the people of Morocco, adding that France should imitate this noble quality by restoring right and justice.

My statements in France were intended to convince the French of the need to grant Morocco her freedom and independence. They recalled the rights of man proclaimed by the French Revolution; they emphasized that the best empire was the one established in the minds and hearts of people and not in time and space; they attempted to impress upon them that the liberation of Morocco was in fact a liberation for France from the sin of oppressive colonialism, which would only end in obliterating the love of freedom in France herself.

My activities were not restricted to contacts with French circles; I continued the work, begun by my predecessors, of organizing the Moroccans in France. I gave an address to a gathering of fifteen thousand Moroccan and Algerian workers, in which I urged the organization and emancipation of workers, and supported their legitimate right to combine in unions for the defense of their common interests. I also visited the city of Lyon where I met North Africa's merchant community.

In Paris I maintained close touch with North African student organizations. In addition to the permanent headquarters of the party, we decided to establish an office for the party branch in Paris, whose executives would be elected by party members from among merchants, students, and workers. The office was instrumental, not only in organizing the Moroccan residents, but also in coordinating their activities with those of their Algerian, Tunisian, and other Arab brethren in France. A coordinating committee was set up, comprising representatives of the Istiqlal Party, the Tunisian Dustur Party and the Algerian People's Party, with a view to coordinating the activities of the three major North African parties in France.

The Foreign Minister did not respond to my request for a meeting with him; I was contacted instead by a number of pro-Moroccan Frenchmen close to the Minister, who assured me that the Foreign Ministry was ready to receive me and to consider a solution of the Moroccan question; but, they pointed out, the question required the clarification of certain ambiguous points before any positive steps could be initiated. The points, as I gathered from these semi-official sources, may be summed up as follows:

1. France is not ready to grant independence to Morocco outside the French Union.

2. France is ready to abrogate the protectorate treaty and accord self-government to Morocco within the French Union.

3. Any solution for the Moroccan question should take into account what is called "diplomatic and military solidarity" between France and Morocco.

4. France is willing to regard Morocco as the principal state among the members provided she agrees to join the French Union.

5. The French community in Morocco must be accorded the rights of Moroccan citizenship.

6. The French language should be retained along with Arabic in the administration, commerce, and education.

The French justify these demands on the ground that Morocco is a rich country, having an important strategic position in the Mediterranean which they could not afford to give up. The abandonment of Morocco by France would, they claim, inevitably expose her to American or Russian occupation, both of which endanger her and France.

I made a considerable effort trying to convince responsible circles of the fallacy of this reasoning, and stressing that if Morocco obtained her independence she would safeguard it not only vis-à-vis Russia, America, and other big powers, but even against the Arab and Islamic states themselves. I pointed out that the independence we sought was not independence from France only, but from every other state in the world. As a matter of fact, many intelligent Frenchmen are convinced that Morocco seeks genuine independence; that she would not substitute one occupation for another; and that the question can only be solved if France places her confidence in Morocco and in the pledges she would undertake on attaining independence.

I had occasion to meet with representatives of the major French parties and shades of opinion; there was unanimous condemnation of the colonial policies pursued in North Afric But, it must be said, I did not find among them anyone in favor of independence outside the framework of the French Union. In view of the fundamental conflict on major premis my efforts were entirely devoted to convincing them of the need for exploring a solution outside the framework of the

French Union. In the absence of a modus vivendi, it was natural that our discussions should have bogged down in a whirlpool of repetitive and endless argumentation. This explains our decision not to engage in any negotiations until our independence had been conceded; because the first step can be taken only by those who have control over our country. As long as France refused to recognize the principle of independence, negotiations and meetings would go on in a void and end in dismal failure.

During my visit to France the internal political situation was in a state of utter confusion; the Communists had been threatening strikes and withdrawal from the government; General de Gaulle had resumed his activities in opposition to the existing regime; he had called a rally of the French people for a regeneration of French life and for resistance to the Communists, whom he regarded as endangering the future glory of France. The government of M. Ramadier had become weary of General de Gaulle and his movement, and there was the suspicion that he had the backing of the United States, which was unalterably opposed to the spread of Russia's moral influence over the peoples of Western Europe. In addition to that, the European, American, and Eastern press had been launching vigorous campaigns against French policies in North Africa, and the impact of these campaigns upon all sections of the French press had been profound. Rightly or wrongly, M. Ramadier believed that America's aim was to exert pressure on France; he considered, therefore, that France's best interests would be served by a shift in policy towards full cooperation with the United States. By ejecting the Communists from government and by easing tariff restrictions on American imports to France and her colonies, he hoped to give satisfaction to the United States in exchange for a free hand in Morocco and the rest of North Africa. M. Bidault approved of this plan; the Socialist government decided to turn out the Communists from its ranks and to relieve M. Labonne of his duties as Resident-General in Morocco. He was appointed adviser to the President of the Republic on matters pertaining to the French Union.

M. Labonne had not been popular with French capitalists, on account of his socialism and his support for the French Government's nationalization of major colonial enterprises.

His opponents took advantage of the royal visit to Tangier to accuse him of weakness unbecoming to a Resident-Genera in Morocco. M. Labonne himself had always placed the blame upon the French Foreign Ministry, accusing it of obstructing all his plans, good and bad. It is a fact that M. Bidault had never viewed his appointment with favor and would have preferred the post to go to a candidate from the Mouvement Républicain Populaire. It was at his insistence that the Resident was recalled.

When M. Labonne arrived in France, ostensibly for consultations with the government, he was kept waiting fifteen days for an appointment with M. Bidault. The Foreign Ministry's displeasure with him was equalled only by his own anger with His Majesty the King, who he alleged had let him down by the deletion of the sentence on Moroccan-French cooperation from the Tangier speech.

While in Paris I learned that the Foreign Ministry had offered the post of Resident-General to several important persons including M. Ponsot and M. de Jouvenel; they declined the offer, however, because they were unwilling to add a new link to the series of failures which had marked French diplomacy in Morocco, and which were bound to continue as long as the government declined to work out a final settlement for the question of Morocco.

Thus, General Juin was appointed to the post; he was the most senior of French generals and had been born in North Africa; moreover, he was not a supporter of General de Gaulle and could, therefore, be depended upon to counteract any moves by General Leclerc, the chief of staff to the French armies in North Africa.

The appointment of General Juin was applauded in most French circles; the appointment was regarded as a step towards adopting a decisive policy against the nationalist movement in Morocco. Many French political organizations in North Africa addressed to him messages of congratulation and admiration. The left-wing parties, however, regarded the appointment as a political mistake which was more likely to complicate the situation than to resolve it. The executive committee of the French Socialist Party protested against the decision of the government, notwithstanding the fact that the Prime Minister, M. Ramadier, was himself a Socialist.

"Le Populaire", mouthpiece of the French Socialist Party

commented: "We do not believe that the appointment of a general, and particularly this general, would be viewed by the people of Morocco as a step towards pacification and conciliation."

"L'Humanité", mouthpiece of the Communist Party, wrote: "The appointment of General Juin would be regarded by the Moroccans as a threat leading to the fall of the Residency-General into the grip of the French right."

The entire left-wing press criticized the appointment as a step designed to further the stranglehold of French capitalists over the inhabitants and resources of Morocco.

The colonial and the pro-government press, however, harped on their favorite tune that force was the only way to deal with the Moroccans. Their enthusiasm carried them to the point of threatening the King as well as the people, and of describing the Moroccans as a primitive people who could only be impressed by the glittering luster on a general's uniform. We might cite as an illustration the comment that appeared in the newspaper "Epoch", which reads in part: "It is not a secret that he [the Sultan] will henceforth be put to slumber; he will be asked politely but firmly to cease obstructing our work and to affix his signature to all the decrees from which he has withheld it since April 10. These decrees, for the political and economic organization of Morocco, will be submitted to him by General Juin; in case he does not adopt a more elastic policy, we shall not hesitate to replace him by someone else."

In Morocco herself the appointment of General Juin caused a furor among all Moroccans; the King sent a cable to the Foreign Minister, urging him not to appoint a military man for the Residency, in the interests of French-Moroccan friendship. The French Government, nonetheless, insisted on the appointment, challenging the King, his people, and the opposition in France herself, in the hope that General Juin would clip the enthusiasm of the Moroccan nationalists and force the Sultan to sign decrees of which he disapproved. We shall see that General Juin succeeded only in complicating the situation and in driving Moroccan nationalists to meet challenge with challenge.

The Nationalist Movement Stiffens

The appointment of General Juin, therefore, was intended merely as a challenge and a threat to the Moroccan people. There was no room left for conciliation, and we felt that further effort to convince the French authorities of our good intentions were futile, so long as the French semi-official press spoke disparagingly about the first citizen of Morocco as though he were an ordinary official who could be replace by someone else in case of insubordination to the Residency. How can we, therefore, expect them to understand our overtures or believe in our good intention?

It had been our policy that the King should remain as a link between the Moroccan people and the representatives of France; for we were the bearers of the popular struggle, which by its nature blows hot and cold as exigencies require The representatives of France adopt whatever policies for o against us that their national interests dictate. His Majesty the King, however, is above parties and disputes, and his official as well as his personal standing entitle him to act as a conciliator between the Moroccan and the French points of view, and to obtain gradually the rights and national aspirations of his people for independence and reforms. French diplomacy, however, refused to accept this noble role, and pursued an antagonistic policy to the King for no reason othe than his adoption of his people's cause, and in spite of his full endorsement of French-Moroccan friendship. The French failed to realize that the conciliatory role of the King was the best safeguard against the occurrence of serious disturbances, and at the same time a face-saving device for what they call the honor of France. They refused to understand that the implementation of Morocco's aspirations through a King who had steadfastly supported France in the most critical times of her modern history would not be regarded as a submission to pressure or as a retreat in the face of force and duress.

If we add to this my conviction, that France was determined to persist in the policy of suppression and was unalterably opposed to the independence of Morocco, nay, eve to those democratic freedoms which would enable the Moroc can people to give expression to their aspirations, it will become perfectly clear why I had availed myself of the discretionary powers, given to me by the higher council of the party, to proceed to Cairo, thereby heralding the new and stiffer attitude of our movement, with its motto of "no negotiations before independence". One of the manifestations of the new strategy was the conversion of the party's permanent center in Paris into an office for information and publicity. The executive committee appointed 'Abd al-Raḥīm ibn abi 'Ubayd as a local delegate in charge of directing the independence movement in France.

I arrived in Cairo on May 25, 1947 and went straight to the Office of the Arab Maghrib, without having notified my colleagues there--not even by cable--of my impending arrival. My arrival coincided with one of the regular news conferences which the Office holds for Arab and foreign journalists. The conference was devoted to a discussion of Spanish policy by 'Abd al-Khāliq al-Ṭarrīs. When he had concluded his address, the pressmen requested me to speak on the latest developments in Morocco, following the King's visit to Tangier. I gave an impromptu talk in which I explained the circumstances that had prompted me to choose Egypt for my destination. I asked the journalists to warn the Arab world that France had chosen to become an appendage of America in her foreign policy, and that in order to maintain the colonies she would concede economic and military rights to the United States in Africa as well as in France herself.

My work during this first year of sojourn in Cairo has followed a circular course where, as Ḥaj Omar has aptly put it, its beginning resembles its end. It did not go beyond meetings with statesmen, lectures in various associations and clubs, articles for the press, participation in conferences and popular gatherings, contacts with the Arab League and with the delegates from the Arab states, participation in the activities of the Office or with the Liberation Committee, and the coordination of the activities of the Maghrib liberation movements in the East.

We shall not attempt an exhaustive description of these activities; we shall, however, highlight some of the important events that have influenced the orientation and the activities of the North African movement. At this point, I must pay tribute to the work of the League for the Defense of Morocco, whose members had laid the ground-work upon which all those who came after them have been able to build.

Closer Moroccan-Egyptian Ties

Perhaps one of the most important events has been the consolidation of ties between Morocco on the one hand, and Egypt and the Arab world on the other. Even though Arabism, religion, historic relationships, and common aspirations and sufferings had united our countries, and even though the establishment of the Arab League had given a strong demonstration of such unity, Morocco had been kept out of active participation, let alone official representation on inter-Arab organizations. In fact, the statesmen of the Arab League had continued to doubt the strength of the Maghrib movement and the degree of dependability that could be placed upon it. The Secretary-General of the Arab League said something to this effect to a delegation of the Istiqlal Party in Paris, not only in connection with Morocco, but as regards Tunisia and Algeria as well. The King's visit to Tangier, however, and his statements of all-out support for the Arab League, convinced our Arab brethren of the advanced stage of national consciousness in our country and encouraged them to devote serious attention to the Maghrib cause. One of my foremost tasks was to acquaint the Arabs with the realities of the situation in Morocco and with the extent of the struggle that was being waged; I stressed the notable stand of His Majesty the King in support of his people's rights and aspirations, and his staunch friendship towards Egypt and the rest of the Arab world. I exposed the machinations of French policy and its intrigues against His Majesty's legitimate rights. My efforts met with a receptiv hearing, and the feelings of respect and admiration which th Egyptians and the Arabs generally cherish towards His Majesty will stand in good stead as solid foundation for the closest and most intimate fellowship which we aspire to establish in our future relationships.

As soon as 'Azzām Pasha, who had been in the United States, was informed by telephone from Cairo of the circumstances through which Morocco and her valiant King were passing, he launched a spirited defense of His Majesty, which was echoed widely in the American and European pres During several meetings of the Arab League Council, the name of our King was mentioned with respect and admiratio The exchange of cables between Their Majesties the Kings of Egypt and Morocco is indicative of the mutual feelings of friendship between the two illustrious Arab Kings.

The Egyptian Foreign Ministry made representations with a view to appointing an Egyptian representative in Tangier, but the French Foreign Ministry opposed the move, according to press reports. When Egypt refused to budge from her stand, France conceded to Egypt's consul in Marseilles the right to look after Egyptian interests in North Africa. This was regarded as a preliminary step towards the establishment of official diplomatic ties with the Arab Maghrib.

In the field of education, the Egyptian Ministry of Education decided to recognize the certificates of Maghrib secondary classes (at the Qarawiyīn and the Zaytūnah) for admission of their holders to Dar al-'Ulūm and the department of Arabic studies at the university.

There was also an upsurge of interest taken by Egyptian cultural circles in the problems of North Africa; foremost among the hundreds of articles, written by leading literary men and scholars, was a study by Aḥmad Ramzi, published in the weekly literary magazine, "al-Risālah", and another by 'Abd al-Jabbār Jūmard, the Iraqi writer in the "Thaqāfah" magazine. All the articles stressed the importance of North Africa as an integral part of the Arab world.

If a somewhat greater latitude were permitted our colleagues for an intensification of their activities in this field, the results would be remarkable; new and great horizons would be opened up for cooperation between the two parts of the Arab world, thereby making an effective contribution to the cause of Arab unity and its great league.

The Hero 'Abd al-Karīm

This was not the first time that the Moroccan nationalist movement had worked for the deliverance of the hero 'Abd al-Karīm from captivity; on more than one occasion it had exerted its utmost with the French Government in order to secure the release of the victimized hero and his suffering kinsmen. The Kutlah of National Action worked for his release in 1936, and was assisted by the late Amir Shakīb Arslān in a spirited press campaign which he launched in the East and in North Africa. Many people addressed friendly appeals to France, urging release of these honorable opponents. There was an exchange of correspondence between me and the late Amir Omar Ṭūsūn, who had been one of the strongest sympathizers with the Moroccan hero and had expressed his full readiness to lead any movement designed to secure his liberation.

In 1937 the National Party stepped up its agitation for the release of 'Abd al-Karīm. A number of French senators we won over and they submitted a motion for his release to the Senate Foreign Relations Committee. Although the committee adopted the motion, the French Foreign Ministry claime that the measure was premature.

In the course of my contacts with the Free French in exil to which I alluded to in a previous section, I took up the cause of 'Abd al-Karīm with the utmost vigor and urgency. I assured the Free French of the falsity of Vichy press reports concerning 'Abd al-Karīm's alleged support for Marshal Pétain, stressing that the Moroccan hero would not permit himself to interfere in purely French affairs.

In 1947 the representatives of the Moroccan Independence Movement in Cairo raised the question with the Arab League The Secretary-General of the League thereupon made repre sentations to the French Foreign Ministry, requesting the release of 'Abd al-Karīm and his return to Morocco.

In his repeated pleas with the French for the release of the detained leaders, His Majesty the King used to single out the case of the Riff leader for special mention.

Finally, the French Government decided to transfer the hero of the Maghrib and his colleagues to France, where they would continue to live in forced detention and under colonial surveillance. At the same time, the French press dropped hints that France was contriving to use the Amir, or his brother, as a threat to the King, in order to coerce him into joining the French Union. Although the speculation had no basis in fact, yet the Amir's decision to take refuge in Egypt put an end to French designs, and saved his honor and glory from the mischievous tamperings of colonialism; even more than that, for it permitted the Amir to become once more the symbol of the liberation movement for the whole of North Africa.

The French and foreign press placed the most indiscriminate and conflicting interpretations upon the Amir's refuge in Egypt, taking the most serious view of the event; but in fact nothing could have been more natural than for Egypt to accept a political refugee who had requested the protectic of her King; more particularly so when the refugee is a world hero of the stature of 'Abd al-Karīm. It is only fair to record that his decision to take sanctuary in Egypt was entirely his own; it was not made at the behest of His Majesty King Faruq, or at the insistence of the Maghrib nationalists. All that we did was to facilitate the realization of his own wish to take refuge in Egypt.

The Amir had disembarked at Aden where he was greeted by the Arab inhabitants of the city. At his request, cables were sent to many distinguished leaders including Muḥammad 'Ali al-Ṭāhir, the proprietor of "al-Shūra" magazine, and to Sheikh al-Khudair ibn al-Ḥussein, president of the Society for Muslim Guidance. The former, a distinguished Palestinian known for his strong sympathies with the cause of North Africa, promptly showed us the cable as he had done to others. The cable mentioned the arrival of the ship off the port of Aden, the date of its sailing, the ports at which it was scheduled to call, and the date of its arrival at Suez and Port Said.

We held a meeting with members of the Istiqlal and the Iṣlaḥ Parties in Cairo, at which we decided to send a delegation, consisting of Aḥmad ibn al-Malīh for the Istiqlal, and Muḥammad ibn 'Abbūd for the Iṣlaḥ, to greet the Amir, his uncle the Amir 'Abd al-Salām, and his brother the Amir Muḥammad in the name of Morocco and to put themselves at his disposal. The delegates went to Suez and were permitted to board the ship to greet the Amir, who later told press reporters that if he were given the choice, he would choose to remain in Egypt. The Amir and his brother expressed to the delegates their desire to visit Egypt and greet her King. Then the Amir asked the delegates to convey a message to the Chief of the Royal Cabinet. The message addressed to His Majesty King Faruq reads:

> I take the happy opportunity of my presence in the territorial waters of Egypt--leader of Arabism and Islam--to submit to Your Majesty my most respectful salutations and gratitude for your efforts in behalf of the glory of Arabism and its great future; I express to Your Majesty my profound joy on account of my presence in this Arab land, after an absence of twenty years in exile, away from my homeland which constitutes an integral part of the Arab world. I have felt while here that I was truly in my home.
>
> The peace and blessings of God be upon you.

The following day I proceeded to Port Said, with a delegation representing the Arab Maghrib Office, to greet the Amir upon his arrival to the city. We boarded the ship together with representatives of the Egyptian authorities, political parties, journalists, and leading citizens of the city. The Amir expressed to his visitors his admiration for Egypt and her efforts on behalf of the Arab cause. He also expressed his unflinching loyalty to the Moroccan crowr and to His Majesty Sidi Muḥammad. He declared that his struggle was not a rebellion but a war of defense against foreign colonialism. In the meantime, the Amir Muḥammad intimated to us the desire of ʻAbd al-Karīm to remain in Egypt. The latter had meanwhile asked to go on shore for a stroll, and he went straight to the governorate, where the governor conveyed to him the greetings of King Faruq and his thanks for the message which he had addressed to the King on the occasion of his passage through Egyptian territorial waters. Thereupon the Amir told the representative of the King to the city of his desire to seek the sanctuary of the King, in order to escape from French captivity and afford his children education in the Arabic language. The governor promised to convey his request to the King and to the Egyptian Government. After a tour of the city, in the company of his family, the Amir returned to the ship for the night.

At 10 o'clock the following day, the Amir went on shore for the second time and headed straight for the governorate. The governor informed him in the name of the King of the granting of his request for sanctuary; Fu'ād Shirīn Pasha kissed him in the name of the King and asked him to regard himself and his family as royal guests. The Amir was introduced to an official of the royal palace, Muḥammad Ḥilm Bey, whom the King had delegated to look after the Amir an his family.

It is difficult to put in words our elation at the news of King Faruq's action, an elation equaled only by the joy with which the Egyptian people in their entirety greeted the event

We returned to Cairo late in the afternoon; in the evenin the Amir, his brother, and a number of his relatives arrive at the Egyptian capital in a royal car. The Amir called at the palace to register his name in the royal call book and to convey his profound gratitude. He was received at the pala by Karīm Thābit Bey, press adviser to the King, Muḥammad Ḥilmi Bey, and Saif al-Nasr Bey, chief of protocol. Later, he visited the Arab Maghrib Office where representatives of North Africa, pressmen, and hundreds of other personages had assembled to greet him. Speeches and poems were read, to which the Amir replied briefly. He then proceeded to Inshāṣ palace to stay as guest of the King, while the Amir Muḥammad, his uncles, and members of the family stayed in the homes of North African leaders.

On Friday, June 5 the Amir was guest of King Faruq for lunch. The King listened attentively to the Amir's description of the Riff war, and in the course of the luncheon told his guests that in giving sanctuary to the Amir, he had no political motives whatsoever; his sole aim was to give protection to an Arab fighter who had sacrificed in the cause of his country. The King expressed his profound respect for His Majesty the Sultan of Morocco and his gratification at the receipt of a congratulatory cable from the Sultan on the anniversary of his accession to the throne. He expressed his hopes for a renewal of close contacts between North Africa and the Arab East.

The King observed that the Amir was somewhat fatigued, and he asked him to spend several weeks at the Fu'ād I Hospital in Alexandria; he also told him that the government was arranging proper accommodation for him and his family.

The Amir Muḥammad and the rest of his family remained at the Office of the Arab Maghrib to receive the greetings of the hundreds of callers, who included ministers, ambassadors, political leaders, and prominent citizens.

The Egyptian press, and the Arab press in general, continued to carry articles on the Amir and on the cause of North Africa for almost two months, thereby assisting our liberation movement. It is our duty on this happy occasion to express, on behalf of the people of North Africa, our deep gratitude to His Majesty King Faruq, the government of Nuqrāshi Pasha, the press, and the Arab League, for their devoted attention to our cause and for the liberation of the foremost captive in the cause of our homeland; his liberation has permitted our movement to draw upon his glory, his experience, and his world-wide reputation.

Repercussion in Morocco

The liberation of the Amir and his colleagues from

captivity had the most profound repercussions in Morocco as well as in the rest of North Africa. The headquarters of the Istiqlal Party in Rabat overflowed with a deluge of congratulatory cables and messages. The secretary-general of the party in Rabat reported to us the deep satisfaction of the Moroccan people at this happy surprise, stating that it had been the best consolation for the shock which the people had sustained on account of the appointment of General Juin as Resident-General. Congratulatory messages were also received from Tunisia and Algeria, as well as from Muslims in all parts of the world.

Reaction in French Government Circles

Reaction to the incident in French government circles was vehement; a Reuter's report on March 31 quoted a French Foreign Ministry spokesman as saying that the landing of ʿAbd al-Karīm in Port Said had caused great astonish ment in French government circles. He added that he coulc not go into a discussion of possible diplomatic action until the Cabinet had received fuller information on the subject.

Describing the treatment meted out to ʿAbd al-Karīm in exile, the spokesman declared: "ʿAbd al-Karīm surrendere to France in 1926 and pledged to remain under French rule. His conduct was always good, and we had always accepted and respected his word of honor. The step he has taken today, after his honorable conduct in the custody of France, has caused us great astonishment." The government spoke man explained that when ʿAbd al-Karīm surrendered to France in 1926, agreement was reached with the Spanish Gc ernment as to his custody, for fear of another rebellion in North Africa. When the spokesman was asked whether he thought the action of ʿAbd al-Karīm would evoke official reaction from the Spanish Government, he expressed his belief that Spain would in all likelihood send a protest to the Egyptian Government, and would ask the French Government for an explanation.

As things turned out, the Spanish Government maintaine silence; it neither protested to Egypt nor asked for explana tions from France.

In France herself a deputy from the M.R.P. queried the government on the action of ʿAbd al-Karīm. The Foreign Minister explained, that the government had recalled its ar bassador in Egypt and the governor of the island of Réunior where the Amir had been detained, for consultations before taking further steps. The French Cabinet met on the same day to hear reports from the Foreign Minister and from the Minister for the Colonies. The two ministers stressed their belief that 'Abd al-Karīm's landing in Egypt had occurred at the instigation of the Egyptian Government. When the Minister of Information was asked about the fate of French-Egyptian relations on account of the incident, he replied that for the moment a severance of diplomatic relations was not contemplated, and that a final decision must await the collection of more thorough information. The Minister also disclosed that a series of precautionary measures would be taken in North Africa, but he did not divulge the nature of those measures.

On June 2 Reuter carried reports that the French Foreign Minister, M. Bidault, had delivered a strongly-worded protest to the Egyptian Ambassador in Paris concerning what M. Bidault described as the conspiracy of the Egyptian Government in the escape of 'Abd al-Karīm. M. Bidault was reported to have told the Egyptian Ambassador that he was in possession of documentary evidence implicating Egypt in the case. The Egyptian Ambassador reiterated the point of view of his government that Egypt was within her right in granting sanctuary to a political refugee who had sought her protection.

The Egyptian Ambassador also issued a denial of French press reports alleging that 'Abd al-Karīm had landed in Egypt in response to an invitation from King Faruq or of his government. The Prime Minister, Nuqrāshi Pasha, reiterated in Cairo that it was 'Abd al-Karīm himself who had requested the governor of Port Said to convey to the Egyptian Government his wish to remain in Egypt. It was his duty as prime minister, Nuqrāshi Pasha added, to observe Egyptian traditions by granting sanctuary to the Amir, after requesting him to abstain from political activity.

In general, the French press expressed the view that the Arab League had singled out France for its hostile activities, having given satisfaction to England on all questions save that of Palestine.

"Le Figaro" succinctly expressed the prevailing feeling in France when it commented: "French public opinion feels a deep sense of shame on account of the insult that has befallen France; it feels that a country which has accepted so many sacrifices in the common cause of victory deserves a more generous treatment at the hands of the great nation [England] whose friendship France has always maintained with fidelity and selfless devotion.

Prominence was also given to the event in the English and the American press. 'Azzām Pasha took advantage of the lively interest aroused by the event to condemn French policies in North Africa.

The Muslim press in India, China, and Turkey expresse solidarity with Egypt, bringing into relief the points of weak-ness in French policies. The newspaper "Waqt" (time) com-mented: "Did 'Abd al-Karīm decide on this course in order to live a life of tranquility within the Arab League, or was it rather a part of a program, organized by the leaders of the Maghrib in Egypt? There is no doubt that the second possibility is the source of all French apprehensions. But, the newspaper added, "The legal position of France is un-tenable in the extreme; for is there a French law that com-pells 'Abd al-Karīm to reside in France after a decision ha been made to set him free? We believe that it would be in the best interests of France to control her nerves and to de-vise a solution that will have the quality of permanence. If France fails to heed this advice, she will find herself con-fronting numerous difficulties of which she already has enough."

Naturally, the vehement wave that spread through govern-ment and press circles in France gradually subsided, for the French Government realized the weakness of its positio The Foreign Minister did no more than declare before the French National Assembly that 'Abd al-Karīm had violated a pledge to which he was duty-bound by Islamic precepts an traditions. The Riff hero, however, has stated on more than one occasion that he had never committed himself to a pledge, because his captivity had not been voluntary.

Indeed, it was improper on the part of France to adopt such a violent attitude towards the Egyptian Government, which had done no more than observe the dictates of reason religion, and traditions towards an Arab hero who had sought its protection. The heads of state at the present time, no less than in the past, have competed in the releas of captives, in the aid of victims, and in granting sanctuar to refugees; Christian traditions on this score have been no less firm than Islamic traditions.

A glance at the recent past will show that France herself has flung her doors wide open to the many political refugees from Russia, Spain, Italy, and other countries; that the French have boasted of this fact on every occasion; and that their Constitution recognizes the inviolable right of asylum in territories hoisting the French flag. If the colonial spirit and the desire to deny the colonial peoples every manifestation of freedom had impelled many French statesmen to disregard their country's own laws and traditions, it was an even more grievous disservice to the honor of France that her government and assembly should have come out officially against an act which French principles regard as praiseworthy and noble. If heroes of France like de Gaulle, Giraud, and other leaders of the resistance boast of their success in breaking loose from German bondage, how could they accuse 'Abd al-Karîm of treachery, simply because he refused to continue in a captivity to which he had been forced for twenty-one years?

If M. Bidault had given a little more thought to the circumstance of 'Abd al-Karim's surrender, he would have recognized that it was the French colonials who had violated their pledges; for the surrender came only after negotiations between 'Abd al-Karîm and the military and civil representatives of France, in consequence of which the French Government granted him categorical assurances of "amān" (guarantees of safety), both for his person and his family. In those negotiations France was claiming to give effect to the wishes of the Sultan of Morocco, in whose name she had fought 'Abd al-Karîm for insubordination and rebellion. Therefore, France should have respected the military traditions of Morocco pertaining to "amān" by refraining from the arrest of a person to whom it had been granted, and by his release as soon as he had laid down his arms. Our traditions provide that a person whose surrender is obtained on condition of safety is exonerated thereby from any liability to the state; only when surrender is unconditional may punishment be meted out or pardon granted as the king sees fit and proper.

'Abd al-Karîm's surrender was conditional upon "amān", as official documents testify; that is why he had always complained of France's failure to live up to her pledges. At all events, it is utterly inhuman to blame a person for seeking deliverance from captivity; we know that a bird will not remain in a cage if the doors are opened before him.

Liberation Committee for North Africa

The twenty-one years of captivity in the uncomfortable heat of Réunion and under the tight grip of colonialism did not blunt the determination of the Maghrib hero or of his gallant brother; rather, they had emerged from exile with a greater determination and readiness for work. They had been encouraged by the presence in Cairo of representatives of all independence movements in North Africa to seek a coordination of activities and a pooling of efforts. The trend towards such coordination had earlier culminated in the establishment of the Arab Maghrib Office; the Office had manifested the strong desire of North Africans to cooperate for the liberation of their three countries, united by the manifold ties of language, religion, race, history, geograph and common sufferings under colonialism and aspirations for liberation from its yoke. The Arab Maghrib conference in Cairo, it will be recalled, had recommended in article II the establishment of a permanent committee, whose task should be to coordinate strategy and activities for a commor struggle. I had taken a step in this direction during my stay in Paris, when a liaison committee was set up from representatives of the Istiqlal, the Dustur, and the Peoples' Parties. When the Riff hero arrived in Cairo, we all looked forward to the implementation of this recommendation on an expanded scale, under the leadership of North Africa's foremost leader and fighter. The invitation addressed by 'Abd al-Karīm to the Moroccan parties made the realization of this hope a feasible goal; every loyal patriot expressed readness to respond to this noble call.

The question, however, required the expenditure of efforts towards achieving a common outlook as regards the strategy of the various parties at home and abroad. The Istiqlal Party insisted upon a prior agreement concerning the goal of independence in accordance with its party platform. After extended deliberations, we reached agreement on the establishment of "Lajnat Taḥrīr al-Maghrib al-'Arab (the committee for the liberation of the Arab Maghrib), to include representatives from all parties that subscribe to our principles and strategy.

On December 9, 1947 the basic law of the committee was adopted and a temporary office set up with the following officials:

Muḥammad 'Abd al-Karīm al-Khattābi....chairman

Muḥammad ibn 'Abd al-Karīm al-Khattābi....vice-chairman

Al-Ḥabīb abu Raqībah (Dustur)....secretary-general

Muḥammad ibn 'Abbūd (Iṣlaḥ)....treasurer

The chairman and vice-chairman were elected for a permanent tenure, the secretary-general and the treasurer for a period of three months. The chairman informed all North African parties of the establishment of the Committee, requesting their endorsement and the appointment of representatives.

On January 5, 1948 the Amir 'Abd al-Karīm formally announced the establishment of the Committee and distributed the liberation manifesto to the Arabic and the foreign press. At the same time, the secretary-general of the Istiqlal Party issued a statement on the formation of the Committee and its objectives, which was published in the press throughout North Africa. Following is the text of the Amir 'Abd al-Karīm's statement:

> Since God had granted us deliverance from captivity, in the sanctuary of the great King Faruq, we have not ceased striving for the unity of the leaders and the realization of a coalition among the independence parties in Morocco, Algeria, and Tunisia, with a view to carrying on the struggle in a phalanx for deliverance of the country from the yoke of colonialism.
>
> At this time, when all peoples are working for the security of their future, and when leaders of the Arab Maghrib are aspiring to the restoration of their country's usurped independence and alienated freedom, it is imperative for all leaders of the Maghrib to unite and for all independence parties to coalesce; this is the only way that will enable us to achieve our goals and aspirations.
>
> If the colonial powers in their misguided pursuits require solidarity and mutual help for the consolidation of their colonial control, how much greater is our need for such unity, in order to restore justice and pull down the foundations of tyrannical colonialism, which had wrought catastrophe upon us, divided our counsel, partitioned our

country, plundered our resources, seized the management of our affairs, stood in the way of our progress and development, and then striven by all means to destroy all our values as an Arab Muslim nation.

It pleases me to announce that all those to whom I have spoken on this matter--leaders of Moroccan parties and their delegates in Cairo--have expressed agreement with this appeal and a willingness to respond to it.

The phase we have traversed towards unity portends well for our country; for agreement has been reached with leaders and delegates of the parties on the formation of the Committee for the Liberation of the Arab Maghrib, comprising all independence parties in Tunisia, Algeria, and Morocco, on the basis of the following charter:

1. The Arab Maghrib has lived by Islam, and will continue to live by and for Islam in the future.

2. Al-Maghrib is an integral part of the lands of Arabism; her cooperation with the rest of the Arab countries, on equal footing and within the framework of the Arab League, is both natural and imperative.

3. The independence, visualized for the Arab Maghrib, is complete independence for the three constituent countries--Tunisia, Algeria, and Morocco.

4. No objective shall be sought before independence.

5. No negotiations shall be conducted with the colonial powers on subsidiary issues within the existing regime.

6. No negotiations shall be conducted until after the declaration of independence.

7. The member parties in the Liberation Committee may enter into negotiations with representatives of the French and of the Spanish Governments, on condition that the committee be kept fully informed concerning the progress of such talks.

8. The attainment of complete independence by any one of the three countries does not exonerate the Committee from its obligation to carry on the struggle for the liberation of the rest.

This is the charter according to which we have pledged ourselves to work; both my brother Muḥammad and I have approved of it, as have the leaders and representatives of the following Maghrib parties:

The (liberal) Tunisian Dustur Party

The (liberal) Tunisian Neo-Dustur Party
The Algerian People's Party
The Maghrib Unity Party
The National Iṣlaḥ Party
The Shūra and Istiqlal Party
The Istiqlal Party

We have written to the other parties requesting their final approval for the formation of the Committee, the endorsement of its charter, and the appointment of official representatives to it. As of now, our cause will be entering a decisive phase in its history. We shall confront the usurpers as a strong phalanx, comprising twenty-five million persons, unanimously agreed on one word and striving for one aim, namely, complete independence for all countries of the Arab Maghrib.

We shall work for the realization of this objective by all possible means at our disposal, at home and abroad. The colonial powers will not, after today, find a breach through which to undermine our determination, cause dissension in our ranks, and exploit the multiplicity of parties and divided counsel for our enslavement and the consolidation of their hold upon our land.

We, in our three countries, regard our cause as one and indivisible, and confront colonialism in unity and solidarity; we shall not accept any solution short of unequivocal independence and full sovereignty. We hope, however, that the French and the Spanish will find their way to an equitable solution, without driving us to bloodshed; we also hope that they have learned from their experiences that dependence on force and oppression, for perpetuating the colonization of our country and silencing our pleas for freedom and independence, will avail them nothing, and that it would be better for them to unlock the chains by mutual understanding and appreciation of the interests of both parties.

If they refuse to pursue this path, however, they would be responsible for a change of strategy on our part because we shall not hesitate, if we despaired of restoring our independence by understanding, to restore it by sacrifice of life.

In announcing the establishment of the Arab Maghrib Liberation Committee, I address my salutations to the peoples of North Africa, praying to God the Almighty to grant them strength, unity, and success in the struggle ahead.

I also address my salutations and gratitude to the Arab peoples and states for their support of the Arab Maghrib. I have no doubt they will receive the formation of this Committee with approval and support.

In conclusion, it gives me pleasure to salute our brethren the fighters of the sister country, Palestine; I pray for their victory and assure them of the solidarity of the countries of North Africa, and their determination to help in every possible way towards the salvation of their country and the preservation of her Arabism and unity.

The Committee devoted the first few months of its existence to organizational work; it also associated itself with the committees for the defense of North Africa in Damascus and Beirut. Contacts were established with the Arab League on all questions pertaining to North Africa, and memoranda were submitted to the United Nations. Efforts were also made in support of the Palestinian cause.

On May 10, 1948 the Committee met in plenary session to hear progress reports by members of the temporary office, following which elections were held for the current year. The results of the elections were as follows:

'Alāl al-Fāsi....secretary-general

Al-Ḥabīb Thāmer....treasurer

The Amir 'Abd al-Karīm and his brother Muḥammad, it will be recalled, had been elected permanent chairman and vice-chairman respectively, in accordance with the basic law of the Committee.

The Policy of General Juin

The events that accompanied the appointment of General Juin in Morocco, particularly, the landing of 'Abd al-Karīm in Egypt, hampered the program which the General had intended to carry out in Morocco. The surge of press interest in 'Abd al-Karīm had drawn the attention of the world towards Morocco. A number of my colleagues in Paris wrote to me that the succession of events had upset the equipoise of

French officials in charge of Moroccan affairs. This is true to some extent, because when General Juin proceeded to Morocco he was compelled to move slowly and with reticence, pending a clarification of the situation that had been beclouded by events in Cairo. The arrival of the General at Casablanca, and his call on His Majesty the Sultan, did not cause anything unusual, save for the symbolic exchanges, which passed between him and the sovereign regarding the legitimacy or the illegitimacy of Morocco's aspirations, as the Resident preferred to call them. The attitude of the Moroccan people was one of reserve; the nationalists did not show the slightest inclination to meet with him, despite the efforts of a number of our French friends--who apparently came specially from Paris--to persuade the executive committee of the Istiqlal Party to get in touch with the General and to place confidence in his good intentions.

The tone of the General's speeches and statements was one of plain threats. If we wish to analyze the aims of the Resident-General from the sum-total of his statements and acts, we find the following:

1. To endeavor to press home the legitimacy of the French protectorate.

2. To consolidate and enhance the power and prestige of French authority.

3. To separate Morocco from the Arab East and orient her towards the West, that is, towards France, as a countermove to the Tangier declarations.

4. To resist Moroccan nationalism and endeavor to exploit human frailty towards enlisting a group of collaborators.

5. To promise an overhaul of the Moroccan administration with the allurement of superficial reforms.

The first two points seem to have been uppermost in the General's mind, as his speech on June 30, 1948 indicates. The speech stated, in part:

> There is a treaty, signed here, between the two countries; this treaty must be respected because it is still in force. It lays upon us the duty of carrying out reforms and of leading Morocco towards social and material progress, with a view to expediting the happy termination of her development. The protectorate, as I have often repeated and am not afraid to repeat again,

is a legal form which must develop quietly, reticently, wisely, and within orderly processes.

Morocco is not at crossroads; in spite of the variety of ideas and opinions, she is following essentially a single path: the road which had been marked out by my revered teacher Lyautey thirty-five years ago. There are only minor differences between us; some have followed in his path while others have held back; but it is our duty to pool our strength and proceed together. The protectorate is no more than a legal form which had been applied to Morocco at a time when it was in the throes of chaos; but it must be transformed, little by little, into a social and a human endeavor and a loving relationship between the two peoples.

To achieve this objective, we must carry out the reforms which it is my duty to propose, but which could only be implemented by the approval of His Majesty the Sultan. This would lead us smoothly towards a second contract, but with caution and wisdom and always within an orderly framework.

Thus, the protectorate according to General Juin is a legitimate arrangement though not a permanent one; to transform it into a new contract, it must first be consummated through the instrumentality of reforms, suggested by him and approved by the King. But what is this new contract, towards which we are advancing? This is what General Juin did not spell out, although he had on more than one occasion visualized the development of Morocco as a state within the French Union. Thus we see that the path envisaged for Morocco by the General is not the path of eclecticism; it is, moreover, not the one of our own choosing. It is Lyautey's concept for the amalgamation of the two peoples within a French community. Our path leads towards complete liberation and unequivocal independence.

Furthermore, the program of the protectorate is at variance with that of the Sheriffian Government also; for this government has itself adopted the independence movement, and its King, who must approve the proposed French reforms, has taken upon himself the orientation of reforms in the direction advocated by the nationalists. This direction does not lead to Rome or to Paris but to Mecca and

Cairo; this is what General Juin complained of in his speech of July 1947. He said:

> In the political field, following the tensions that had been caused by several political demonstrations (meaning the events of Tangier), we must remove all ambiguities and reiterate the legitimacy of the protectorate treaty, which constitutes the basis of any French-Moroccan relationship. But it is strange that the Sheriffian Government, in order to give the appearance of strength before some agitators, should have pursued a distorted and reproachful course--reproachful on account of the interpretation placed on the mission that France had undertaken in this country, thereby straying from a true preception of living realities in the Western world, which determine the development of Morocco, nay, even her very existence.
>
> Morocco has found the way marked out by Marshal Lyautey; it will advance without delay, behind the crown, towards the glorious and tranquil future promised her.

At this point the General was courageous enough to hint at the prospect of a contractual partnership but without explicitly advocating membership in the French Union. He declared:

> But Morocco must know that at the end of her development, which I hope will be rapid, though cautious and sound, she will remain linked to France, which will give her the best she has, through a solid partnership that does not ignore the common interests and benefits.

The nationalists kept up their campaign against the speeches and statements of the General, while the Istiqlal Party stood solidly behind the King in his rejection of all reforms that are incompatible with the Moroccan aim of liberation. The Resident-General became aware that Moroccan nationalism was something solid, and the the nationalists were not a mere handful, as he had imagined. The suppression of the movement was not an easy task, requiring no more than sweet promises, the arrest of several hundred libertarians, and the shooting down of innocent people. Moreover, French public opinion itself was not going to accept indefinitely a policy whose only result would be to rally the Moroccan people behind a King advocating liberation. The Resident-General had warned the King in his previous speech; now it was the turn of the nationalists, in whose ranks he hoped to create dissension, by differentiating between what he called moderates and extremists. Let us read what he had to say on July 1, 1947:

> They talk about Moroccan nationalism. I am not an enemy of this orientation; but there are types of nationalism. There is a reasonable nationalism that faces the future through development, which is the task of France in Morocco by virtue of an existing contract. It is a task that must be emphasized; but there is a limit to this contract, and it would be foolish to believe that the protectorate will not end. On the day when Morocco will have acquired her technicians and administrators, a new contract will replace the Treaty of 1912; it will be in the form of a partnership, meaning a treaty based upon interests. No useful purpose would be served if we separated before development had taken its full course; otherwise, the country would revert to the chaos in which we found it.

Thus, the nationalism deserving of the General's sympath is not the one that demands effective independence and refuses cooperation on any other basis. It is the moderate nationalism that recognizes the "civilizing" mission of France and proceeds in the path traversed by Lyautey, so that one day we should be able to enjoy participation in the family of the French Union and take from France the best she has; this best is the French spirit and the consciousness of French citizenship. Thus we shall have lost our most cherished possession: Moroccan loyalty and the consciousne and pride in Moroccan citizenship.

In his attempts to carry out his program, General Juin exerted pressure on the King and on the people, with a view to securing the passage of the decrees that had been suspended. The French had regarded the suspensions and the observations of the Sultan as being in the nature of a strike, to which they had not been accustomed before the maturing of national consciousness to its present extent.

The most important of the suspended bills was the draft budget for the fiscal year 1947-1948. Hitherto, the procedure had been for the Ṣadr al-A'zam to approve the budget and then pass it on to the King for signature. This time, the King instructed his Prime Minister not to endorse the budget until His Majesty had studied it in detail. The Residency-General was astonished at the refusal of Prime Minister Muqari to sign the budget, a thing he had not done since the beginning of the protectorate. In his observations on the budget estimate, the King urged the setting up of a Moroccan committee to study the budget before its adoption; this amounted to a non-recognition of the budget committee, ordinarily formed by the Residency-General.

M. Labonne had left the issue pending and the government had been run on an ad hoc budgetary basis. When General Juin arrived in Rabat, his first act was to submit the budget anew to the Palace. His Majesty the King did not await the Residency-General's approval for his proposed Moroccan committee; he appointed it and presided in person over its meetings at the royal palace. The committee ascertained that there was nothing unusual in the proposed budget, particularly as regards items pertaining to the companies which M. Labonne had established without royal approval. The King had been anxious to make sure that the budget did not involve recognition of those companies; nonetheless the King approved the proposed budget with reservations relating to safeguarding the country's mineral resources.

The other Residency schemes, pertaining to municipal councils and a consultative assembly, were also submitted to His Majesty, but failed to obtain royal approval, as we shall explain later on. Thus, General Juin failed in his program, and he made no secret of that failure when he declared in a speech at Marrakech, the same month of June, that if he did not succeed in his policies he would resign.

In the face of the King's steadfast stand, the protectorate launched a campaign of vilification against the person of the King in an attempt to discredit his great religious and social reforms in the eyes of the public. The protectorate also removed five Moroccan caids who had been loyal to the King, appointing nonentities in their place, despite the opposition of the King and of his subjects. These appointments soon led to violent clashes between the protectorate and the people; suffice it here to mention one example: the incidents of Zāwiyat Sīdi al-Sheikh.

Incidents of Zāwiyat Sīdi al-Sheikh

The French authorities appointed as caid over the tribes of Zāwiyat Sīdi al-Sheikh a person of no importance or qualifications, from among the "chaouch" [doorkeepers] of the native administration, who had been accustomed to servility to their French superiors. The entire locality protested against this appointment, but the controller did no more than promise to refer complaints to the higher authorities. At the same time, the newly-appointed caid was encouraged to plunder the vicinity and exact forced labor (with no remuneration to the tribesmen) for his own benefit and that of the French control. He did not hesitate to confiscate the building material which the people had bought for the construction of a school and a mosque in the village, and to use the confiscated material for building a private house for himself.

The inhabitants of the locality sent a delegation to Rabat in order to lodge a complaint with the higher authorities.

In June 1947 the control summoned the members of the village council for deliberations. After a long wait they wer ushered before a panel of French officers, including Colonel Darsimol, the commissioner of the Khunayfirah district. The control also summoned the four tribal Sheikhs as well as the committee for the construction of the mosque and the school. One of the officers told the villagers that permissio had been received for the construction of the mosque. The villagers replied that the question of the mosque was no longer the paramount issue; their main concern was for the removal of the caid from his post, in view of his lack of qualifications and integrity, and considering that his appoint ment had not been approved by the King. The representative then explained the prevailing disaffection in the locality on account of the administration's policies. The French officer asked the villagers to select five representatives from each of the tribal clans for further deliberations on this matter. The tribal representatives expressed by an overwhelming majority their opposition to the caid. The French proposed the appointment of the chaouch of the control office as temporary caid, pending a final decision on their complaint. The representatives retorted that they did not wish to see one chaouch replacing another, whereupon the meeting was ordered adjourned.

When the representatives left the control building, they headed towards the crowd which had assembled before the building in a demonstration of solidarity. As they were talking with their folk, a military detachment came upon the scene and arrested five of the representatives. The crowd attempted to oppose the passage of the transport car in which the five representatives had been detained, whereupon fire was opened on the demonstrators by administration supporters, killing four and wounding ten others seriously.

The commanding colonel then ordered his Moroccan troops to engage the demonstrators, but they refused. Clashes in the locality continued for several weeks, resulting in many dead and wounded. The commander found out for himself that the "Qawm" [Moroccan troops], who had obeyed his orders in the mountains of Italy, were unwilling to go along with him in shooting down their own brethren and in fighting the "unreasonable nationalism", to use General Juin's description.

Attempt to Divide the People

Attempts were made by General Juin to resuscitate the Sufi orders, which had been all but destroyed by the religious reform movement. His chief instrument was Sheikh 'Abd al-Ḥay al-Kattāni, whose blatant disloyalty to his people, his country, his religion, and his King, had been the principal cause for the failure of the entire Sufi movement. The King, it will be recalled, had issued a decree forbidding the establishment of new orders, or demonstrations by the old ones without his special permission. The decree had also empowered His Majesty to dissolve any Sufi order considered inimical to religion and the public interest. The Residency-General had withheld approval of this decree and had refused its publication in the Official Gazette. The General, desirous of opposing the King, summoned al-Kattāni and his associates and informed them that the protectorate had no objections to their propagation of the Sufi movement, whenever and wherever they wished to do so. He told them that France was a champion of freedom of thought and of belief. This group of hirelings now went roaming through the country, without royal permission, but with the encouragement of the French control administrations. His Majesty, supported by the people, protested vigorously to the Resident-General. Several protest demonstrations were held, including one within the Zamūr tribe, which had been considered as one of the principal strongholds of the Kattānīyah order. Sheikh Kattāni eventually retreated in defeat to Fez and then fled the country, going to Tunisia and Algeria, where the Salafīyah reform movement had not as yet achieved a success comparable to that in Morocco.

Dismayed by the solid opposition of Moroccans to his poli cies, General Juin and the native administration set to work new intrigues: pamphlets, allegedly emanating from a new "Islamic Unity Party", were distributed, attacking the Istiqlal and the King's policies towards France. As I pointed ou in an article in the Cairo daily, "al-Kutlah", there is no suc thing as an Islamic Unity Party. The native administration sank to a new low, when it fabricated pamphlets smearing th King and the royal family as we shall explain later on.

It appears that the Residency-General had realized the futility of endeavoring to divide the people by fomenting a conflict between the Salafīyah and the reactionaries. The religious impostors had fallen in utter disgrace on account of their blatant treason, and the people had become aware that the nationalists were the true defenders of religion. Masquerading in the guise of Sufism and religion, these impostors had been the willing tools of the colonial power, from which they derive support and through which they plunder the people and enslave their souls. If they had had one iota of faith, they would not have remained neutral, much less have aided in the implementation of the Berber policy when it closed down the Sharī'ah courts and attempted to obliterate Islam in large portions of Morocco.

Having sensed the futility of fomenting religions dissension, the Residency pursued a new program: to contact moderate nationalists and encourage them to adopt policies at variance with the principles to which they had previously subscribed in league with the Istiqlal Party. We shall give a brief description of some of these attempts, without alluding to either persons or organizations.

Opposition to the French Union

In spite of all these attempts, Morocco stood like one man in solid opposition to participation in the French Union. His Majesty the King has made it clear, in his private as well as his public utterances, that the destiny of the Sherifian Kingdom was the destiny of all the free Arab peoples, and that its future lay within the fold of the Arab League and peoples. All Moroccan parties have reiterated their unflinching opposition to any steps that would prejudice the future of Morocco as a free and independent state within the Arab League. The statement made to the French press by the Ṣadr al-A'zam, Ḥaj Muḥammad al-Muqari, during his visit to Paris in July 1947, is an unequivocal proof that there is not one person in Morocco who contemplates acceptance of the French Union; for al-Muqari is well known to the French as a staunch friend, and as one of the foremost architects of the protectorate. Moreover, he has borne responsibility for all the enactments and legislation adopted by the protectorate during thirty-five years. Al-Muqari had been replying to questions addressed to him by pressmen concerning the French Union. He said: "What is this French Union about which there is so much talk but so little knowledge? My opinion is that the participation of Morocco is impossible, because she is a state having unique attributes and characteristics that do not lend themselves to her participation in such a vague union." In reply to another question on current conditions in Morocco, al-Muqari declared: "I do not recollect--having been Prime Minister throughout the period of the French protectorate--that Moroccan-French relations had ever reached an impasse comparable to the current crisis."

Thus, the record of General Juin testifies to the failure of French militant diplomacy to win over the Moroccan people to the scheme of French unity.

Opposition to the Reforms of General Juin

General Juin's barrage of statements, speeches, threats, and cajoleries eventually boiled down to the submission of a scheme to His Majesty the Sultan for a reorganization of the government, or the reform of the Mekhzen, as he called it. After extended exchanges and deliberations between the Palace and the Residency, the King signed three decrees providing for a reorganization of the governmental system; modifications in the higher echelons of the local administration; and the appointment of five assistants to the prime minister, with the status of under-secretaries, to supervise the work of the important departments, namely, finance, agriculture, commerce, public works, industrial production, mines, postal services, telegraphs, telephones, social welfare, and public health; they also provided for the appointment of a legal adviser, whose task should be to study and scrutinize proposed laws and decrees before they are submitted to His Majesty for signature.

The scheme provides for a convening of the Council of Ministers, under the chairmanship of His Majesty, whenever such a meeting is deemed necessary, while members of the Cabinet shall meet with French directors of departments once every month, with the Prime Minister in the chair, to consider important public issues.

The Associated Press correspondent had the following comment to make: "The decision is the first of the important reforms which will be introduced in the future; the Cabinet will comprise ten Moroccans and ten Frenchmen, while France will retain responsibility for foreign affairs and defense. A spokesman for the French Foreign Ministry declared: "It is not certain that a parliament will be established in Morocco in the near future; but this will happen one day, and France is anxious to transform Morocco into a modern democratic state and to increase the responsibilities and powers of the Moroccans."

The French news agency carried this report, and the French press depicted the scheme as a genuine reform, which would gradually lead Morocco towards self-government. In order to correct such a mistaken impression, I gave a press statement the day following the promulgation of the decrees, in which I said:

> At a time when Morocco is swamped by troops, when caids are removed from their posts and public-spirited citizens are arrested throughout the land, when fire is being opened on the protesting tribesmen, General Juin increases his talk on the participation of the people in government, and on the democratic orientation which the French protectorate should pursue in Morocco. To prove his sincerity the General secures the passage of a decree, providing for the appointment of a number of employees, in departments that were and still are within the jurisdiction of the Ṣadr al-A'zam. In other words, the prograr entails no more than a designation of these employees as deputies to the Ṣadr al-A'zam.

Those acquainted with the realities of the Moroccan administration will readily admit that all departments of the administration are branch organizations of the Residency-General; all questions are prepared and studied by the French directors of departments and then passed on to the Moroccan administration, where they are translated and submitted to the various secretaries of the Ṣadr al-A'zam. This arrangement has not been altered.

It is also known that all files and documents are kept in the Residency-General and in the Sheriffian administration, which is headed by a Frenchman, and not in the Mekhzen. The Sheriffian administration acts as a liaison between the Residency-General and the Mekhzen. The appointment of five employees in new posts, therefore, is merely intended to beguile. Moreover, the A.P. correspondent has described the program as a prelude to the formation of a Franco-Arab government, comprising ten Moroccans and ten Frenchmen. Such a mixed government has been rejected repeatedly by the Istiqlal Party, on account of its incompatibility not only with Moroccan sovereignty, but also with the protectorate system itself, which recognizes Morocco's separate and unique status.

It is pertinent to mention that this program, with its concomitant idea of a mixed cabinet, had been presented to us by M. Labonne, the former Resident-General; but we turned it down because it is in reality a form of direct rule in the spirit of the colonial policy in Morocco. The Istiqlal Party is adamant in its rejection of the plan and regards it as a step towards the formation of a mixed consultative council, half French and half Moroccan, as well as mixed municipal and regional councils. I told the former Resident-General, in the presence of one of the party executives and the secretary-general of the Residency, that we shall never recognize the claims of the French community to participation in administration or consultation; for they are foreigners in our country, and we could not possibly accord them any of the rights of Moroccan citizens so long as they retain their French nationality.

The policy of the new Resident, therefore, is designed to usurp what little has remained of our independent existence and attributes, and it could only meet with our unflinching opposition and resistance. As for the enticement of democracy, neither we nor any loyal Moroccan will be deceived or blinded to the concrete realities of the situation in Morocco.

The Istiqlal Party will not accept any solution that is not based on a recognition of effective independence and the liberation of the people from foreign interference.

While I was giving this statement in Cairo, the executive committee of the party was distributing a statement to the same effect in Morocco. This ended as follows: "In conclusion, any act which is implemented within the framework of the protectorate will not bring about the desired progress; a genuine reform would be the abrogation of the protectorate and the establishment of a provisional government to supervise free and general elections for a national assembly, which would draw up a constitution for the country."

The executive committee called an extraordinary meeting of the party's higher council to study current developments. The council considered the statement issued by the French Foreign Ministry to the press on July 5, 1947, together with General Juin's statements before the government consultative council and in various towns of Morocco. The council was convinced that the French Government, which had been violating the protectorate by its system of direct rule, was now planning to give it legal form. Although the decrees, published in the Official Gazette on July 4, provide for only minor changes in the Mekhzen setup, and for the appointment of assistants whose task is confined to liaison work, and although they do not accord the monthly meetings between the ministers and the French directors the status of a cabinet, yet the communiqué of the Foreign Ministry regards this mixed body as a council of ministers, in which the French and the Moroccans enjoy equal participation. No one will doubt that the French had, and will continue to have within the new body, the real power of decision.

The higher council was also convinced that the aim of the French Government and its Residency in Rabat is to lead Morocco in stages towards the French Union, with a view to destroying Morocco's exclusive entity and of preventing the restoration of her independence.

The council, therefore, passed the following resolutions:

1. To alert Moroccan public opinion to the fact that genuine reforms can only be introduced by a free Moroccan government, in the confidence of the King, and deriving its powers from the people through a truly representative assembly. The council warns of the devious and beguiling methods of French policy, designed to deflect Morocco from the sound orientation laid down by His Majesty the King in his address and statements on every occasion. Needless to say, our being duped into the French plan would be tantamount to an act of suicide and would result in our perdition as a nation.

2. To condemn the French administration's suppression of public liberties, the denial of union rights for Moroccan workers, the tightening of press censorship, the restrictions on travel and movement, the continuous and inciting display of force, as well as the violent and provocative statements addressed to an unarmed people, who are defending their right to life by legitimate means.

3. To protest strongly against the policies of the French Government, which ignore the will and aspirations of the Moroccan people, do not follow the course of world progress, and violate international charters to which France had pledged herself to adhere; the council regards these policies as incompatible, not only with Morocco's international status, but also with the fading protectorate regime to which the French Government clings. The protectorate does not entitle France, under the guise of reforms, to destroy the essence of Morocco's national existence and the structure of the Sheriffian state, after having pledged to respect them.

The council also protests against the derogatory references to His Majesty the King and to the Moroccan people made by representatives of the French Government.

In the name of the Istiqlal Party, the higher council reiterates, before world public opinion, that Morocco is an Arab Islamic country, fully determined to obtain her rights and independence and to restore her position in the family of nations.

The statements of the French Prime Minister and the Foreign Minister regarding the participation of French directors in the Moroccan Cabinet caused deep anxiety and concern in Moroccan public opinion. On July 28, 1947 representatives of the national press called at the royal palace and handed to the King's private secretary the following memorandum for submission to His Majesty:

> Following the publication, on June 21, 1947, of the decree pertaining to a reorganization of the Mekhzen, the French Foreign Minister issued a communiqué on July 5, 1947, and a statement was made by M. Ramadier, the Prime Minister. Both the communiqué and the statement are at variance with the provisions of the aforementioned decrees. Whereas the decrees provide that the assistants shall be representatives of the Ṣadr al-A'zam and in no way imply the promotion of the French directors to the status of ministers, the statements of the Foreign Ministry and of M. Ramadier, as reported in the press, regard the directors as being ministers in the complete meaning of the term, and the assistants as being subordinate to them.
>
> Considering that this interpretation has caused widespread speculation and deep anxiety, we petition Your Majesty for a clarification, with a view to allaying public apprehensions.

In reply to this memorandum, the special secretariat of His Majesty the King issued a communiqué dated July 31, 1947, which said:

> In such matters, textual provisions only are authoritative and valid; the letter and the spirit of the decrees pertaining to governmental reorganization are perfectly clear. We have been astonished, no less than has Moroccan public opinion, by the French interpretation of the decrees, the more so as we know that clarity and adherence to logic are characteristic of the French.
>
> The three decrees leave no room for equivocal interpretations; we can best describe the purport of the decrees by an analysis of the texts which provide:
>
> 1. For an increase in the number of assistants to our minister the Ṣadr al-A'zam.
>
> 2. For meetings of our ministers under our chairmanship, whenever we deem necessary.
>
> 3. For monthly meetings between our ministers and the French technical directors of our Sheriffian departments under the chairmanship of the Ṣadr al-A'zam.

Therefore, the French directors continue as before, as technical employees of our Sheriffian Government; it goes without saying that the assistants will act as representatives of the Ṣadr al-A'zam and not as aids to the technical directors.

Let our loyal people be reassured and calmed; for we are diligently watching over their interests with the help of God, and we shall not rest until the day when our people shall occupy a worthy place amongst the nations. May God lead us to the path of righteousness.

Thus, His Majesty put an end to the maneuvers of French military diplomacy, in its attempts to drag the country towards the objective in which M. Labonne had earlier failed, namely, the establishment of a mixed government.

But even these minor and fragmentary reforms remained ink on paper; the assistants did not participate in any substantive work, but remained as they were before, as the Istiqlal Party had predicted, an inconsequential group. Unlimited powers remained in the hands of French administrators. This fact has been attested to by one of those assistants, 'Abd al-Salām al-Fāsi, who was in charge of education. In an interview with the correspondent of "Le Figaro" he said: "There is no significance to the post which I now hold; the decrees for ministerial reform have been issued, but no steps have been taken to carry them out; we shall have to await what will be done in the future."

For our part, we can assert, one full year after the passage of the alleged reforms, that the situation remains unchanged and that the Moroccan Government is still as powerless and as impotent as before. Schools founded by the department of education are still liable to punitive measures and suspension by the French control administration; employees removed from office by the Ṣadr al-A'zam are being reappointed by the Residency-General. In spite of all this, it is claimed that General Juin's mission in Morocco is to modernize the Sheriffian Government and to guide its development towards a staunch democratic government.

The second reform, presented to His Majesty the King by General Juin, relates to the establishment of a mixed consultative council, half Moroccan and half French, to be elected directly by the French voters, and in two degrees by the Moroccans.

It is known that the so-called government consultative council whose establishment had never been approved by the Sheriffian Government, consisted of three sections: a French section, comprising representatives of public services, chambers of commerce, agriculture, and industry; a second section, elected by members of the French community; and a Moroccan section, appointed exclusively by the government. The new plan provides for the establishment of a mixed council, whose Moroccan half is appointed by the government and the chambers of commerce, while the French half is elected directly by members of the French community in Morocco. This is the plan which we had previously rejected and which the King had refused to endorse when it was submitted by the former Resident-General, M. Labonne. It was not to be expected that General Juin would succeed where his predecessors had failed. The King, therefore, refused to accord the French residents electoral rights, demanding that such rights be given to Moroccans only. He also refused to sanction a mixed council in any form, because the French community had no business to meddle in Moroccan internal affairs.

French circles attempted to exploit His Majesty's opposition to the plan of the Residency-General, alleging that the King was averse to the development of the country towards a democratic form of government. French newspapers carried reports and commentaries, claiming that His Majesty was opposed to granting Moroccans electoral rights. To refute these allegations, the royal secretariat issued the following statement:

> His Majesty the King has read with considerable astonishment the commentary that appeared in the local French newspaper, "La Vigie Marocaine", on September 24, claiming that His Majesty was opposed to granting Moroccans electoral rights. This is contrary to the facts. His Majesty, far from denying electoral rights to his loyal citizens, has never ceased demanding such rights for his people, but in a manner that would secure full equality among them.
>
> His Majesty attaches considerable importance to granting Moroccans electoral rights, conformable in every sense to those enjoyed by free peoples.

The censorship department, a branch of the Residency-General, prohibited the publication or broadcast of the royal statement, whereupon the Istiqlal Party's office of information in Paris undertook the distribution of the statement to the press and the news agencies.

The upshot of this struggle was the abandonment, or at least the shelving, of the Residency-General's scheme; at the same time a royal decree was issued providing for the institution of Moroccan chambers of commerce, industry, and agriculture, independently of the French chambers, and on an elective basis.

Following the promulgation of this decree, the French authorities launched a campaign against the Istiqlal Party through the French-controlled broadcasting station in Rabat. The party, however, while refusing to cooperate in any reform measures devised by the protectorate, or to participate officially in the elections for the new Moroccan chambers of commerce, permitted its supporters to run in the elections on the platform of the party. Although the French administration had disfranchised a majority of merchants, craftsmen and farmers, and although pressures had been exercized and allurements resorted to in order to keep opponents of its policies away from the polls, ninety-eight per cent of the voters cast their ballots for the pro-Istiqlal nominees. The French were astounded by the nation's solid support for this indomitable party.

The new Moroccan chambers initiated their activities by demanding the removal of state controls and the restoration of free trade; they opened branches in various parts of the country and encouraged the people to hold exhibitions. The record of their representatives on the so-called government consultative council was impressive indeed, attesting to the high qualities of the pro-Istiqlal men. The reports, presented by Muḥammad al-Zaghāri, Aḥmad al-Yazīdi, Muḥammad al-ʻIrāqi, Omar al-Sabti, and Muḥammad al-Aghzāwi, were an example of mature and clear thinking. Rather than be swamped in a deluge of minor details and proposals, our representatives devoted their attention to a critique of the fundamental premises of the administration's policy in finance, economic affairs, and education.

The party representative in France, ʻAbd al-Rahīm ibn ʻUbayd, was told by M. de Peretti, our French friend in

Paris, that the President of the Republic had paid warm tribute to the work of the Moroccan representatives, and had expressed his congratulations to the Istiqlal on the performance of its men. The President of the Republic, M. Vincent Auriol, is one of France's renowned liberals who appreciate human endeavor in the fullest measure; his congratulations are a proof of his strong sense of justice and fair play.

Another of General Juin's proposed reforms was a plan for the reorganization of Moroccan municipalities on the basis of mixed councils; the King ordered the setting up of a Moroccan committee to study the plan. We learn from reliable sources that the committee had turned down the principle of mixed representation, or the granting to the French residents of the right to form municipal councils of their own in Morocco. The committee also laid down sound bases for the reorganization of Moroccan municipalities on the lines of municipal institutions in democratic countries.

The principle of administrative decentralization, which had been advocated by M. Labonne and by General Juin, and which we had criticized in several articles in the Egyptian press as a new form of feudalism, seems to be fading away; General Juin's references to it are becoming more faint and lukewarm day by day.

In short, the subsidiary reforms of the Residency-General are being considered by the Sheriffian Government and by the Moroccan people, in the light of their relevance to the aim of national liberation. That is to say, the yardstick is whether or not they are likely to further the aim of Moroccan independence and liberation from foreign control. The reforms per se are unacceptable to the Moroccans so long as they are not preceded by a recognition of the country's independence.

Failure of General Juin

In spite of General Juin's bombastic threats in support of his programs, the people maintained their solid resistance, while His Majesty the King continued to oppose all measures incompatible with the interests of the country. Naturally the General's anger mounted with his increasing failures, inducing him to resort to force. He was incensed by the people's rally behind the King and the Crown Prince, and was angered by their rallying cry of independence and freedom on every occasion. He saw in this a slight to his person and to the honor of the protecting state, although they were merely an expression of popular feelings. Eventually, the General submitted for the King's signature a decree forbidding the people to utter independence slogans in the presence of the King or in gatherings attended by the Crown Prince. The decree was presented on the occasion of the King's impending inauguration of a number of schools in Marrakech and of the Muḥammad V schools in Rabat. The King's reply was naturally a flat rejection, and a reiteration of the right of Moroccans to acclaim freedom and independence. When General Juin called on the King to ask for a reconsideration of the decision, the latter walked out of the reception hall. The Resident-General in retaliation forbade the participation of the Crown Prince in public receptions.

The wrangle occurred on November 1, 1947. A few days later, on the anniversary of the King's accession to the throne, he gave his traditional address, in which he reiterated his previous statements during the visit to Tangier. The address included the following excerpt: "We have not desisted from our plan of serving our country, of pursuing the interests of our people, of keeping faith with the democratic principles of Islam, and of exerting our utmost abilities, until our loyal subjects have attained their legitimate rights, as a free people enjoying their full rights, and constituted as an Arab Muslim nation which occupies a worthy place in the community of free nations."

General Juin regarded these utterances as an encroachment on French rights in Morocco; in fact, they were an answer to his assertions that the future of Morocco lay within the fold of the Western powers. The Resident-General sent a sharp protest to the King; the reply of His Majesty startled the General and convinced him of the futility of his terroristic methods.

But these repeated rebuffs and failures did not dissuade the General from his provocative policies and his disregard for the legitimate powers of the King. He began to appoint governors without consultation with the King; he instituted new posts--assistants to the governors--in Casablanca, Marrakech, Fez, and Rabat, to which he appointed French stooges for the explicit task of suppressing the nationalist movement and of spying on the people.

Since new posts in the Moroccan administration could only be instituted by a decree, introduced by the Ṣadr al-A'zam in his capacity as Minister of the Interior and approved by the King, and considering that the Resident-General had overstepped his limits, the Ministry of the Interior withheld recognition of the new posts, and the King refused to accept the fait accompli. The Prime Minister lodged a strong protest with the Resident-General.

When the Residency-General ignored the protest, His Majesty sent a strongly-worded message to the President of the Republic, recalling all of General Juin's violations of the protectorate treaty. The message also referred to the right of Morocco to independence and the legitimacy of the Moroccan people's strivings for its attainment, as other peoples of the world had likewise done.

The French Foreign Ministry attempted to conceal news of the growing crisis between the Palace and the Residency. Attention was diverted to speculation on possible French-Moroccan negotiations, and on news relating to the Paris mosque and the hospital adjoining it. The Istiqlal Party's office of information and publicity in Paris, however, revealed news of the crisis and of the royal message to the President. The news was first published in "Paris Presse" "Franc Tireur", and in the French news agency, and soon found its way to the rest of the French press as well as to the Belgian, Swiss, and British press. The French Foreign Ministry was obliged to acknowledge news of the royal message, attempting at the same time to minimize the seriousness of the crisis.

In an interview with the correspondent of "Paris Presse" General Juin said: "In the face of popular demonstrations, organized by Moroccan nationalists clamoring for freedom and independence, and in the face of the King's refusal to prohibit these demonstrations, the Resident-General has been compelled to forbid the King and the Princess from appearing in public gatherings, in order not to give the people a chance to express their hostile feeling towards the protectorate."

The French Foreign Ministry regarded the statement as a political blunder and a public admission of France's encroachment upon the inviolability of the Crown. The Resident-General was instructed to deny the story, and the French press published the denial with a good deal of derision and sarcasm.

While the French Government was seeking ways and means of overcoming the crisis, the Residency-General continued its hostile activities against the King. This time, its tactics were those of a defeated coward. Pamphlets were distributed purporting to be under the auspices of Ḥizb Allah (the party of God) or, the Ikhwan al-Muslimūn (Muslim Brotherhood), attacking the King, the royal family, the Crown Prince, and the Princess 'Ā'ishah. The pamphlets caused a wave of public indignation, and the situation threatened to develop into violent encounters and would have done so but for His Majesty's appeal to the people to maintain calm.

A senior official of the Moroccan administration was able to identify the handwriting of the script writer. His name was Muḥammad Farfarah, a former employee of Marshal Lyautey and of the Residency-General, and currently on the staff of the political secretariat of the Resident-General. The case was submitted to the Moroccan High Court, and the accused was summoned for interrogation by the president himself (to avoid the prosecution, which is in the hands of the French police). After initial denials, the accused confessed to his guilt. He told the court that he had copied the text of the pamphlet in Arabic; he also revealed that the original author was a French colonel by the name of Leconte, chief secretary of the political department. A car of the Residency-General had provided transport for his visits by night to the political department, where he had made copies of the script against payment of a handsome remuneration. After these confessions, he was summoned before a Sharī'ah judge in the presence of two official witnesses; the accused reiterated his previous statements and told the judge that he was giving them voluntarily and without any duress.

The French counsellor intervened as soon as the confessions of the accused were brought to his knowledge, implicating the Residency in the affair. He demanded that the case be referred to the Court of First Instance, so that it might take its natural course. The accused was interrogated anew by the Rabat Court, in the presence of two witnesses and a French government attorney. He repeated his earlier statements and affixed his signature to them, as did also all those present, including the French attorney.

The French attorney, dismayed by the confessions, defended the accused on the ground of lunacy, requesting that he be released from jail and subjected to medical examination. The president of the High Court refused this request, whereupon the French attorney broke into the prison and secured his release. When His Majesty was informed of what had happened, he sent his private physician, together with the physician of the law court, for a medical examination of the accused. The two physicians testified that the accused was in full mental health, whereupon he was returned to jail. Subsequently, the Residency-General claimed that the case should be tried before a French court. The accused was finally released, but the chief secretary of the political department, Colonel Leconte, was fired from his post for his principal role in the conspiracy.

Another Failure

Reference has been made earlier to General Juin's many attempts at reactivating the Sufi orders; mention was also made of the pamphlets, prepared by the political secretariat of the protectorate, under the fictitious label of "Islamic Unity Party". These were exploratory attempts by General Juin to secure some Moroccan collaborators, or at least to give the impression abroad that there were certain Moroccans who disapproved of the policies of the Istiqlal Party and the King.

The policy of our party had been to refuse contacts with General Juin, despite the efforts of our friend M. de Peretti to convince the executive committee otherwise.

General Juin, therefore, turned his attention to those whom he regarded, rightly or wrongly, as moderates. During the previous summer, Colonel Leconte (architect of the infamous pamphlets) contacted representatives of the moderates at a tea party, and later at the political department (which the nationalists had boycotted since the Meknes events of 1937). The talks resulted in an agreement on a modus vivendi to serve as a basis for a settlement. In a reference to these talks, the General declared in Paris that a memorandum had been submitted to him by this group, but that he had advised them to present it first to the King, through whom such proposals could be forwarded to the French Government for appropriate action.

The memorandum remains a guarded secret until the present day; but sections of it have appeared in the Cairo press and others in the press of Morocco.

The higher council of the party has decided not to take up discussion of the memorandum, or to answer the campaign of vilification which its authors have launched within the party. When fuller details are available, the party will pass judgment in the light of the country's best interests.

From what has been published in the Egyptian newspaper, "al-Balāgh", the propositions, which the report claims have received the endorsement of the Resident-General and of the King, may be summed up in the following points:

1. To restore Morocco's sovereign independence and territorial unity under a system of constitutional monarchy.

2. To launch Morocco upon a transition period which would enable her to organize freely and with utmost speed for her future condition of freedom, to be guaranteed by a treaty of alliance and friendship voluntarily contracted.

The scheme stresses the need for a calm transition period, to enable Moroccans to achieve genuine progress, politically, materially, and morally. To attain this objective, the following steps shall be taken:

1. France shall declare her official recognition of the Moroccan people's right to manage their own affairs and accord Moroccan interests priority over all others in Morocco.

2. All repressive measures and extraordinary enactments shall be abrogated.

3. There shall be a general amnesty for all Moroccans who have been victims of political persecutions.

The constitutional system during the transition period is envisaged as follows:

1. A provisional Moroccan government shall be formed, with specific responsibilities and freedom of action, deriving its authority from the confidence of the people and the support of the King; the government shall lead the country, with the guidance of a constitution, towards an independent Morocco; it shall devote primary attention to a reform of the social structure, a reorganization of the educational

system, and the encouragement of a modern cooperative movement for workers and farmers; it shall also undertake the preparation of Moroccan experts to take over the higher echelons of government.

2. The protectorate treaty, imposed on the country in March 1912, shall be abrogated and replaced by a temporary agreement for a definite period, according to the version of "al-Balāgh" (for an unspecified period, according to the correspondent of the "Observer"), after which a treaty shall be concluded between the two countries.

The plan provides that the temporary treaty shall include provisions for the coordination of Moroccan-French relation pending the working out of the final treaty.

3. A national assembly, representing Moroccan public opinion, shall undertake the drafting of a constitution for a democratic monarchy, which shall serve as the basic law of an independent Morocco; the new constitution shall provid for a separation and a delineation of powers within the state, and shall ensure freedom and equality for all Moroccans.

4. The military zone, known as the insecure areas, shal be abolished.

5. The Moroccan army and police shall be organized on the basis of an independent status.

This is what has been published of the plan submitted to General Juin by the moderates. We have gathered from various quarters that it comprises even uglier features, particularly in the preamble, which recognizes France's civilizing mission and concedes that Morocco had not yet reached the stage for unequivocal and immediate independence.

The French publicity organs gave widespread publicity to the plan in Cairo, at a time when His Majesty the King was protesting to the President of the Republic against General Juin, and when the result of the elections for the Moroccan chambers had given 98 per cent of the votes to pro-Istiqlal nominees. I wrote several articles criticizing the plan, including the following statement, which I gave to a correspondent of the Arab Maghrib Office in Cairo, for publication in its regular bulletin. The statement reads:

> The French hints of readiness to grant independence to Morocco and to the rest of North Africa are merely designed to mislead. It is hardly reasonable that France

which has just suspended the Grand Council in Tunisia on account of a mere protest over a matter pertaining to employees' salaries, which is maintaining such a shocking press censorship in Morocco, and which is continuing the wave of arrests throughout the Arab Maghrib for the most trivial reasons, should decide on anything other than the perpetuation of her persecutions.

The plan, which is reported to have emerged from talks between General Juin and certain Moroccan nationalists, has not been officially divulged till now; nor have any of those nationalists indicated approval of what has been published concerning it in the press. We have spent the entire past year in deliberations with the Residency-General, after which we emerged convinced that French plans would in no way concede the independence to which we aspire; on the contrary, they are designed to substitute for the protecorate a more heinous form of colonization. We are all too familiar with the French habit of not calling a spade a spade. That is the reason why I had made the abrupt decision to leave Paris for Cairo, whereupon the Istiqlal movement entered the phase of relentless resistance and a refusal to negotiate before independence is granted.

The protagonists of the plan allege that it had been the result of an agreement between General Juin and the King. General Juin has been following in the footsteps of his predecessor, M. Labonne--with all due allowance to their many differences. It had been the method of M. Labonne to convey the impression, in France and elsewhere, that he was in full accord with His Majesty, with a view to convincing French and world public opinion of the success of his mission. One of the foremost tasks of the Istiqlal's first delegation to Paris had been to expose the fallacy of this contention, and to reveal the extent of the gap between the Crown and the Residency, with the result that M. Labonne was recalled from his post. General Juin could not with reason claim the endorsement of the King for his policies of persecution. He had, therefore, been compelled to create a new atmosphere of cooperation with certain nationalist elements, and to claim the blessings of the King for the results of such contacts. We know for certain, however, that the conflict between the King and the General is at the peak of intensity, so much so that the King had found it necessary to address a strong protest to Paris.

As for our views on the plan itself, what has been published of it gives sufficient ground for its rejection; because it transforms the Moroccan case, during the so-called transition period, from an international dimension to a bilateral one, thereby placing us within the French sphere of influence in form as well as in fact. The existence of a form of self-government during this period is inconsequential, considering the continued circumscribing of our competence in foreign affairs, and the vesting of final authority for internal affairs in the hands of France. In addition, there would be no international guarantee of our independence, because the transition phase would have been accepted by mutual agreement between Morocco and France. This in effect means that France will be freed from her obligations under Morocco's international status and come face to face with Morocco through a bilateral agreement.

There is an old story, which however has not lost its relevance; in the course of the negotiations between Ambassador Gaillard, Minister Ibn Ghibrit, and His Majesty Mawlay 'Abd al-Ḥafīẓ over the protectorate treaty, the French Ambassador, sensing the apprehensions of the King and his rejection of a protectorate, said, "But your Majesty, the presence of the French armies in Morocco will be only for a short duration." Whereupon the King smiled and said, "God the Almighty has created the world for a short duration but it is still there." Long ago, the French novelist Balzac remarked that to the French the temporary is always eternal.

The stark fact is, that our country is still suffering under the yoke of French, Spanish, and international colonialism, and that colonial oppression has now reached a high peak of intensity. On the occasion of the royal anniversary, several hundred freedom-loving nationalists were arrested. Press censorship has become more choking, so much so, that the mouthpiece of the Istiqlal Party, "Ra'y al-Sha'b" newspaper, has been forced to suspend publication. General Juin has had the temerity to issue and implement decrees without reference to the head of state, namely, the King, in violation of the Moroccan constitutional procedure. The authorities have removed all Moroccan governors who have obeyed the instructions of their King, and have persecuted private schools for no better reason than the refusal of their pupils to greet General Juin during his visits to their towns.

In addition to all this, the Residency-General has been exerting its utmost towards reanimating the impostors of the Sufi orders; its aim here, as in contacting certain nationalists, is merely to sow the seeds of discord in the ranks of the nation, as the French had done over a long period of time in Syria.

Therefore, it is best for us to maintain the struggle with patience and fortitude, to call for complete unity within our ranks, and to refuse to entertain any move designed to undermine the will to resistance. And finally, are we not in the right in refusing to be "reasonable" and in accepting nothing less than effective and unequivocal independence?

Following the release of this statement to the press, the party branch in Paris divulged news of the royal message, which had been concealed by the French Foreign Ministry, revealing the depth of the crisis between our sovereign and General Juin. At the same time, the Committee for the Liberation of the Arab Maghrib was formed in Cairo, on the basis of "no negotiations before independence". Several leading Egyptian thinkers wrote articles urging the Moroccans to beware colonial deceptions. One of the articles was by our friend Maḥmūd Muḥammad Shākir in the Egyptian literary magazine, "al-Risālah", entitled "La Tammallu" (do not lose patience).

We do not wish to touch on persons or on parties in a complicated issue of this nature. But our duty as historians impells us not to gloss over this aspect of the struggle which the party has waged against General Juin's attempts to form a bloc, in opposition to our principle and strategy. It is, therefore, fitting to conclude this section by inserting the message which the higher council of the party addressed to all party branches on January 1, 1948. It is a historic document which serves to prove the strength of our party's loyalty to its principles and its struggle for their realization. The message reads:

We had written to you on December 15, 1947 concerning the memorandum, submitted by the moderates on that same date, and we informed you in respect to:

1. What has come to our knowledge of its contents.
2. The views of the party concerning it.
3. The attitude of the party towards it.

We had promised to acquaint you with fuller details concerning the matter. Now that excerpts from it have appeared in the press of the East and in the newspaper of the moderates themselves, and now that a widespread propaganda campaign has been launched in its behalf, we must return to the subject once again.

The position of the party in respect to the plan is the same position decided upon by the higher council, namely to refuse to engage the authors of the plan in a press duel or a campaign of vilification. But when they publish the text of their memorandum, the party will of necessity have to announce its official attitude towards it. Since the memorandum has not as yet been published, the party adheres to its previous decision and finds no reason to take an official stand. What have been published are bits here and there, and the party--as you are aware--is not prone to hasty and ill-considered judgments.

What has come to our knowledge of the memorandum is substantiated by what has been published, because it is undoubtedly the more correct, although there is an evident dichotomy between the version given in the newspaper "al-Ra'y al-'Âm" (public opinion) and that of the Egyptian newspaper, "al-Balāgh". The opinion of the party is attached herewith to each of the published section In brief, the plan suggests:

1. The creation of a calm atmosphere by means of an official declaration recognizing the right of the Moroccan people to manage their own affairs; to give first consideration to the interests of Moroccans in their country, and to respect fully the sovereignty and independence of the country, and so forth.

Our view on this point is, that the recognition of the right of the Moroccan people to manage their affairs is not of considerable value in creating the calm atmosphere; moreover, there is nothing new that the memorandum proposes to France, because:

a. Such a declaration is embodied in the Covenant of the United Nations to which France is duty-bound to adhere.

b. It has been reiterated on more than one occasion by the Resident-General, and particularly in his Qunayṭirah speech. But where is the result of those declarations? The situation remains as before, or is even worse, in spite of those declarations.

c. A declaration of the nation's right to independence, moreover, is not a recognition of the independence to which we aspire. The gap between the two is considerable.

2. They propose the initiation of a transition period, which would enable Morocco to pass from the stage of the protectorate to that of independence. This is to be done by the establishment of a provisional national government, endowed with specified responsibilities and enjoying freedom of action, so that it could perform its mission in the light of the constitution, and so forth.

Our view is that the retention of legislative powers in the hands of His Majesty the King would safeguard the rights of Morocco from being violated, the more so since he is defending those rights to the utmost of his ability. The transfer of those powers from the hands of the King would present a serious danger to the country; for the stature of the Sultan is great, and his position is inviolable, unlike a government which, no matter how patriotically imbued, could easily be replaced by the French administration at will. Such a substitute government may be weak or treasonable.

There is no difference between the provisions of this section and General Juin's reported request from the King to waive his legislative powers in favor of the Ṣadr al-A'zam. As for the replacement of the protectorate treaty by a provisional agreement of specified duration, pending the conclusion of a final treaty of alliance and friendship, before replying to it we must emphasize the failure of the protectorate treaty to bring about the development and progress of Morocco towards maturity and well-being, and we must declare once more the sufferings which it has brought upon the country. We must further state, that in spite of its shortcomings, it is based upon a recognition of the international treaties between Morocco and the foreign powers, particularly the Treaty of Algeciras, which recognizes the independence, sovereignty, and territorial unity of Morocco. The treaty, though restricting the independence of Morocco and limiting the scope of her jurisdiction, does at any rate recognize the entity and internal independence of the country. It also has the character of an international agreement. The proposed provisional treaty would transform that international position into a bilateral relation between Morocco and France, thereby placing the country within the sphere of French influence, in form as well as in fact. The establishment of self-government during the transitional phase is of no significance so long as an interdiction is maintained on our foreign policy and so long as France is accorded ultimate say in our internal affairs. In addition, there would be no international guarantee of our independence, because a transition phase will have been initiated by a mutual agreement between ourselves and France. This in fact frees France from her obligations under international agreements. Therefore, the party regards any transitional period that is not preceded by a declaration and a guarantee of independence as worse than the existing protectorate regime.

In regard to the final treaty of alliance, which in their view would end the transitional period, their memorandum states verbatim: "This treaty shall be concluded when the aforementioned conditions are met, with a view to enabling Morocco to prepare and install properly constituted authorities for the management of public affairs." This means that the final treaty, which alone will recognize the independence of Morocco, would be contingent upon fulfilling the preceding conditions. But what are these preceding conditions? The "Ra'y al-'Ām" has not divulged them, although the Egyptian newspaper, "al-Balāgh", did so in the paragraph on the duties of the national government. These included: a reform of the social structure, a reorganization of the educational system, encouragement of a modern cooperative movement for workers and farmers, and finally, the preparation of Moroccan experts to take over the major functions of government.

There is no doubt that these are the conditions referred to, but are they the only ones? Or are there other conditions which have not appeared even in "al-Balagh". It is understood from the published excerpts that these conditions would be implemented gradually. There is no doubt, therefore, that the task laid upon the national government in the transitional phase is identical with that originally laid upon the protectorate. The protectorate treaty has not been carried out and has not achieved for Morocco--over a period of thirty-six years--any of its purported aims. So what guarantees do we have that France, during this second phase, would implement any of the objectives provided for in the memorandum? The truth is that the plan involves a reckless gamble over the fate of the country, in which France only stands to gain.

3. A national assembly shall be entrusted with the drawing up of a constitution. The memorandum, or rather the newspaper, "al-Ra'y al-'Ãm", explains some of the basic questions that would be embodied in the constitution. These questions have not appeared in the version of "al-Balagh"; therefore, we are unable to ascertain whether they belong to the text of the plan or are mere additions and comments by "al-Ra'y al-'Ãm". At any rate, the position of the party with regard to the constitution is clear and unequivocal.

The constitution per se is one of the basic objectives and demands, which the Istiqlal Party had presented to His Majesty the King, in its historic document of January 11, 1944. But it is the view of the party that the constitution is a concomitant of independence and not an antecedent to it. A constitution is a manifestation of the people's authority in their control over the government. Such a popular sovereignty is incompatible with the status of an occupied country. It is perfectly evident that the transitional phase, envisaged in the program, would be within the framework and under the supervision of French occupation. On the other hand, the pillars of constitutional government are elections and liberties. As for elections, suffice it here to recall the manner in which the administration conducted the recent elections for the chambers of commerce and agriculture; the pressures, the fraud, the illegal devices, resorted to by the authorities in all parts of Morocco, are common knowledge and must not be forgotten. As for liberties, we hardly need more than to point to the administration's record of oppression and its blatant disregard for civil liberties. We might also mention General Juin's interview with a correspondent of "Paris Presse" on January 13, 1948, in which he stated: "Whereas bold meetings, such as school festivals, had been made the occasion for nationalist celebrations whenever a member of the royal family was present, I have asked the Sultan to put an end to these hostile demonstrations against France; the answer of Sidi Muḥammad ibn Yūsuf was that he could not prevent the Moroccans from giving expression to their feelings. Therefore, I have decided to remove the cause of these disturbances and to forbid the Sheriffian family from making public appearances. The King was protesting against this decision, in his message to the President of France, pointing out that it violated his inviolable position and demanding its revocation as soon as possible."

Liberation movements have preceded our own in other countries of the world. Their fundamental aim was independence; in their view, the constitution was an internal affair coming after independence. In all phases of her national struggle, Egypt's exclusive demand was for independence. Mustapha Kāmil [founder of the Nationalist Party in Egypt], was the author of the motto, "no negotiations until after evacuation". He demanded a constitution for Egypt, but only after the attainment of independence. Sa'd Zaghlūl and his Wafd colleagues concentrated on the aim of independence to the exclusion of all else. When Britain attempted to divert their attention from the cause of independence to that of a constitution and reforms, through the famous Milner Commission, the Egyptians boycotted it and compelled it to return home empty-handed. In the face of Egyptian unanimity, Britain was compelled to recognize the independence of Egypt, whereupon a government was formed to convene a national assembly and draft a constitution, over a year elapsed before a constitution was promulgated.

The demand for a constitution in the memorandum is in effect a negation of the idea of independence; for how can we ask the occupation power to draft a constitution for implementation in the era of independence? This is strange logic!

In section four, the memorandum discusses the enactment of legislation for a gradual "Moroccanisation" of the administration, and for the transfer of responsibilities from French to Moroccan hands as soon as competent Moroccans are trained to take over these tasks. But how long will Morocco have to remain in this preparatory phase preceding independence? Suffice it here to state that Egypt had to spend thirty years in this phase, though her independence had been recognized; how much longer would the duration be for a dependent Morocco?

The fifth point--proposing the removal of military zones--is sound, save that it is written in a spirit which does not put trust in independence; for the demand is made in connection with the transitional period, whereas it should more properly have been suggested among the initial steps designed to create a calm political astmosphere. The Kutlah of National Action had demanded the cancellation of the military zones thirteen years ago, in its program, "The Demands of the Moroccan People".

The sixth point pertains to the organization of the national army and police, with the assistance of French experts, whose task would also include the coordination of common defense. It is feared that the authors of the memorandum had been unaware of the dangers to their country involved in the coordination of common defense. They had also withheld mention of it, in the version published in the Egyptian newspaper, "al-Balagh". As a result of the proposed common defense, Morocco would be compelled to join in any war in which France might be involved; such a war might be with one of the Arab or Islamic states, whereas the protectorate treaty does not require Morocco to join a war in support of France.

It is strange that the memorandum should volunteer acceptance of the principle of common defense, while neglecting such matters as a reorganization of the national economy, Morocco's international status, and diplomatic representation; all these and other things seem to indicate an acceptance of Moroccan membership in the French Union.

These are the proposals as reported in the press. The proposals are either twisted awry or are unacceptable. It is feared that what has not been published may be even worse, considering the strange manner in which fragments of the memorandum had found their way to print; for it does not seem to be purely accidental that certain points which had been published in Egypt were glossed over in Morocco, and vice versa.

We conclude with general observations on the memorandum, the circumstances of its presentation, and the aura that has accompanied it:

1. The party, as you have gathered, does not support this memorandum, either in form or in substance. We have already pointed out the main flaws and dangers in the substance of the plan. As regards the form, it is our view that the timing of the plan, the person to whom it has been addressed, and the persons with whom deliberations have been conducted in relation to it, are such as to give rise to misgivings concerning the best interests of the country. The present attitude of France towards Morocco is worse than at any time in the past; for control over the press, the suppression of liberties, and the persecution of nationalists, are more intense and pervasive than they had been during the war.

2. The memorandum, with all its defects, is merely the work of the moderates and represents their views on a solution of the problem. But what is the view of the French, and what is their attitude towards it? They state in their publicity that the Resident-General Juin endorses the plan without any reservations. They also state that "the basic postulates of the memorandum do not meet in French government quarters in Paris with any serious opposition." But let us see what General Juin thinks, as reported in his interview with the correspondent of "Paris Presse". He said: "French measures against the inevitable spread of nationalism take three forms:

1. Suppression, which includes measures to forestall rebellions, control over the national press, and the detention of instigators.

2. Economic measures, designed to improve communal

life, and to expand exports of fruits, cereals, and phosphates.

3. Political measures, which include administrative and judicial reforms, with a view to affording a greater Moroccan participation in the management of their country."

This is the program, laid down by the French administration, for leading Morocco towards her goal, as General Juin states in this interview. In the same interview, the General declared: "We are determined to make Morocco capable of managing her own affairs. Our views in this regard go beyond those of the nationalists." We have seen for ourselves that his acts conform meticulously to his program and not to the views of the moderates, as expressed in their memorandum. The situation is growing more tense, pressures and repression are assuming larger proportions, not merely against the people, but even in the treatment of His Majesty and his Mekhzen government. Right now, officials are being suspended from duty without the approval of the head of the state and others are being appointed against his will. Direct rule has now reached the peak of intensity.

3. In their oral utterances and publications abroad, they claim the support of the Sultan for their plan. But when they reprinted in their newspaper, "al-Ra'y al-'Ām", the report of "al-Balagh" newspaper--which naturally emanated from them--they did not dare include reference to alleged support from the King. Instead, they deleted all reference to this matter and shifted to something else. If His Majesty had supported their plan, they would have said so at home also. This confirms our belief that the plan does not meet with the approval of the King; for it is a partisan act, and His Majesty is above parties. If there were to be negotiations enjoying his support, they would be carried on by persons in responsible positions and in an official manner.

It is amusing in this connection to note that "al-Ahram" newspaper has quoted General Juin's remarks on the moderates at his press conference in Paris. In those remarks the General said: "They have drawn up a constitutional plan for the country and presented it to me. I advised them to submit it to the Sultan because he is the head of the state and consultation with him is required. The Sultan could say to me, I want this and that, and I would convey his views to the French Government."

Finally, it is necessary to draw attention to a basic point, namely that the party's motto is "no negotiations before independence". The motto has been embodied in the constitution of the Liberation Committee, under the leadership of our hero Muḥammad 'Abd al-Karīm. This means that any negotiations with France, pertaining to military, diplomatic, economic, and cultural matters, should be conducted after and not before the attainment of independence, so that Morocco could be free to decide for herself and in a manner agreeable to her interests. But if she continued to be circumscribed in her actions, and remained under the shadow of the protectorate or some similar arrangement, how could Morocco give expression to her genuine feelings? Under duress, Morocco could give more than she would take, and would accept in humiliation what is offered. What sort of an agreement is that between the free and the slave, the master and the subject?

As for mere exploratory talks and contacts, soundings and feelers, these are activities which the party has engaged in and is still continuing to perform. The successive official delegations which have visited Paris since 1946, and the presence of a permanent party representativ in Paris, are intended to serve this purpose. But this is one thing, and what we are condemning is something else. The party has contacted, and continues to contact, influential quarters, for the purpose of exchanging views. But it does not claim that such contacts are tantamount to negotiations.

This is the message expounding the views of the higher council of the party concerning the memorandum of the moderates. It shows a good deal of restraint and a concern for gathering facts before jumping to any hasty conclusions. We in Cairo did our utmost to prevail upon the authors of the memorandum to make its official text available to the Liberation Committee, and to report on the scope of their deliberations with the Residency-General, in accordance with the basic law of the Committee. Our efforts, however, did not meet with success; for they refused to give any statement to clarify the situation.

Dr. (X) told me that during his meeting with General Juin in Paris, the General had expressed the view that the memorandum of the moderates was a sound basis for an agreement between the Residency-General and the nationalists. The General had expressed also his determination to extract authority from the hands of the King and to place it in the hands of the new ministers and deputies. The General added that he would do so even though he was well aware of the King's very strong objections to his plans.

The General told a certain Mr. (X) that he regarded the plan of the moderates as a childish affair, to which he would not give serious attention; he had listened to it merely to probe and study the situation. The General added that the refusal of the Istiqlal people to deal with him had compelled him to seek others who would. Mr. (X) replied that the Istiqlal people could not possibly contact anybody so long as an atmosphere of terror persisted. At any rate, the establishment of the Committee for Liberation of al-Maghrib, on the basis of no negotiations before independence, has restored unity in the ranks of the nationalists. I do not believe that there is anyone today who would consider the policy of gradualism, whose failure has been demonstrated by experience. We can, therefore, assert that the attempt of General Juin to create a deep conflict between the moderate and the extremist wings of the nationalist movement has also failed. All are now rallied behind the King in his efforts to save the situation and to liberate the country.

The Failure of Two Generals

The presence in Cairo of ʻAbd al-Khāliq al-Ṭarris made it possible to initiate coordinated activities in exposing the policies of the Spaniards, who while expressing their friendship with the Arabs of the East have not ceased to oppress the Arabs of the West.

It is fair to acknowledge the efforts of the Khalifiyah delegation in acquainting the Arabs of the East with the realities of the situation in their zone. Moreover, the new orientation, agreed upon between the Iṣlaḥ and the Istiqlal Parties, committed the movement in the Khalifiyah Zone to outright opposition--an indispensible step for a coordinated and smooth working of the Moroccan movement.

The delegation of the Istiqlal Party in the East--representing also the Iṣlaḥ Party--spared no efforts in working for the entire Maghrib. Naturally, our common efforts while in Egypt strengthened the activities of our brethren both at home and abroad. Thus, resistance to Spanish policy became no less pronounced than the resistance to French policy.

Our united movement dispatched a representative to the United States, and one of his principal tasks was to advocate the unity of Morocco and expose the misdeeds of Spanish colonialism. In the name of our independence movement, he submitted a memorandum to Mr. Trygve Lie on the question of the Spanish protectorate over a part of Morocco. The presentation of the memorandum coincided with Spanish declarations that they were conducting official negotiations with the Arab League concerning the Khalifiyah Zone.

The representative of the independence parties in the United States requested that the Iṣlah and the Istiqlal Parties be allowed a hearing before the United Nations Political Committee, when the item on the relations between Spain and the member states was to come up for discussion in August 1947. The representative stated in his application that right and justice required that the people be allowed to voice their views on this issue with its important bearing upon their future.

The Spanish Ambassador to Washington, Señor Manuel Aznar, anticipating the presentation of a memorandum to the United Nations concerning the Spanish Zone, similar to the one already presented concerning French Morocco, summoned al-Mahdi Benūnah and requested him to defer presentation of the memorandum until he could consult with his government. Mr. Benūnah replied that he was not competent to decide on deferment, but that he would consult with his superiors in Cairo and al-Maghrib. The following reply was cabled to al-Mahdi: "If Spain is contemplating an offer, let it be announced openly and before the world; because they would not pay any attention to any move made by Spain behind the scenes."

Mr. Benūnah presented the following demands to the Spanish Ambassador, as a condition for deferring the presentation of the memorandum:

1. That Spain declare her support for the establishment of an independent Moroccan state, comprising French Morocco, Tangier, and the Spanish Zone.

2. That a general amnesty be granted to all political exiles and prisoners.

3. That direct negotiations be initiated with the Khalifah of the Sultan towards implementation of this objective.

The Spanish Ambassador conveyed these demands to his government in Madrid. The reply came in the form of an inquiry concerning the demands of the nationalists as regards cultural and social progress; it requested also a clarification of the term "political prisoners".

Mr. Benūnah, interpreting the reply as a complete rejection of the nationalist demands, submitted the memorandum to the United Nations, depicting Spanish policies in the Khalifiyah Zone. The delegate from Pakistan pledged his support for the cause of Moroccan independence, as did also the delegates from Poland, the Philippines, and all the Arab states. The attitude of the United States, however, resulted in a postponement of the debate on Spain, and with it the opportunity for a submission of the Moroccan case and of the case of the entire Arab Maghrib before the international forum.

The success of the nationalist propaganda abroad, and the astute manner in which the case was being handled, infuriated the Spaniards and hardened their opposition to the movement. Agents were sent out to spy on nationalist circles, and the authorities imprisoned all those who had connections with Cairo and the leaders residing there.

Finally, they enacted a decree whereby the Moroccan Government was divested of its jurisdiction in matters pertaining to public security, in violation of their treaty obligations towards this government. They had apparently lost confidence in the Moroccan employees, on account of their increasing reluctance to carry out orders designed to suppress the nationalists. The new decree provides that Spanish courts only would have jurisdiction in matters relating to public security.

The Iṣlaḥ party promptly issued a statement decrying the move. The statement reads:

> This step, taken by the Spaniards, is most serious and will inevitably lead to a clash. The Spanish authorities

have virtually abolished the Moroccan Government by transferring the duties of public security to the Spanish control authorities.

Article two of the decree abolishes the Moroccan police and transfers authority to the Spanish police. Article three empowers the Spanish police to search homes without restrictions of any sort. If this unlimited power is contrary to all laws, it is also a violation of our Islamic traditions. Spanish courts have been empowered to decide all cases, with the Spanish police acting as prosecution. By virtue of article six, the Spanish police would henceforth receive direct instructions from the Residency-General. Thus, Moroccans would be subjected to the direct rule of the Residency. This constitutes a flagrant aggression upon even the protectorate treaty, which accords to Spain the power of supervision only. Article eight accords to the Spanish police a military status. Thus, Spain commits a transgression upon the Islamic judiciary and places the Moroccans under the mercy of fascist military courts. This in effect amounts to a perpetual state of marshal law in the zone. At the same time, all legislation in conflict with this decree has been abrogated.

News of this decree caused a popular furor. Large crowds assembled in the grand mosque and elected a delegation, led by Sheikh Aḥmad ibn ʿAbd al-Qādir al-Fāsi, to present a protest to the Khalifah. A general strike was observed in Tetuan, as a mark of solidarity with the delegatio His Highness the Khalifah joined the people in the protest and demanded abrogation of the decree. After negotiations between the Khalifiyah Government and the Residency-General, the decree was modified, restoring some of the jurisdiction to the Moroccans. The Khalifiyah Government is continuing its efforts with a view to restoring the rest.

But the strength and the solidarity of the opposition, both at home and abroad, sensitized the Spaniards once again to the dangers inherent in the coordination of Moroccan nationalist movements; it also made the French aware of the futility of their policy towards Franco.

Consequently, General Juin and General Varela, the French and Spanish Residents in Morocco, set to work for the coordination of their plans in Morocco, disregarding the political cleavage between Republican France and Franco Spain.

The two Generals, flanked by their top aids, met in special conference in the city of Tangier. The conferees, on February 1, 1948, agreed on a concerted plan of resistance to the nationalists of the two zones and to the Palace, and they concurred in conceding minor reforms only.

Immediately afterwards, al-Mahdi Benūnah, 'Abd al-Khāliq al-Ṭarrīs, and Muḥammad ibn 'Abbūd were on their way home from the United States and Cairo, only to be told that the Spanish Residency had forbidden their entry into the zone. The decision created a widespread wave of indignation throughout the land, and confirmed rumors of an agreement between the Spanish and the French Residents as to an all-out policy of suppression against the nationalists.

The people were quick to express solidarity with their persecuted countrymen; a two-day strike was observed in the capital, Tetuan, and large throngs marched towards the palace of the Khalifah, to protest against the decision of the Spanish authorities.

On February 8 demonstrations spread throughout the Khalifiyah Zone, shouting anti-colonial slogans. The demonstrators were led by the leaders of the Iṣlaḥ Party in the zone and by a select group of prominent citizens. The Spanish authorities were compelled to call out regular army troops to engage the nationalists who had swarmed through the main thoroughfare. The troops opened fire on the demonstrators, killing four and wounding many others. Members of the Iṣlaḥ Party's executive committee were arrested, along with many supporters of the movement. Many prominent citizens were placed under house-arrest and required to pay heavy fines. These valiant men included Sheikh Aḥmad ibn 'Abd al-Qādir al-Fāsi who, despite his advanced age, played an active part in the movement.

Other clashes occurred, in the course of which six policemen and twenty nationalists lost their lives. The Istiqlal Party expressed its condemnation of these acts of oppression; Ḥaj Aḥmad Bla-Freej sent cables of protest to the Arab League and to the Secretariat of the United Nations. The party branch in France publicized news of these events exposing the atrocities committed by the Spaniards.

In Egypt, the independence parties represented on the Liberation Committee expressed their solidarity with Morocco in her hour of crisis. The chairman of the Committee, the Amir 'Abd al-Karīm, issued the following statement:

> While all the states are seeking to improve their situations in the post-war period, events in Morocco develop only from bad to worse; it is as though a race were on between France and Spain for inflicting the maximum amount of injury upon this innocent country. No sooner do we finish counting our heavy sacrifices under the French than Spain is upon us again to inflict no less grievous injuries. Bloody events have just occurred in Tetuan, in the course of which many sons of this brave city lost their lives, for no reason other than their protest against the prevention of their loyal compatriots from returning to their birthplace. If these events prove anything, it is the bravery of the Moroccan people and the cowardice of the Spanish Fascists, because they have stabbed in the back an unarmed people. When this people had an armed force, the Spanish armies were retreating before it at the first encounter.
>
> Spain and France, notwithstanding their political differences, are in agreement when they face the countries of the Arab Maghrib. They are coordinating their plans and continuing their efforts to destroy Arabism in these countries. While appealing to our brethren in the Arab East to beware the intrigues by which Fascist Spain has been seeking to deceive them while spilling our blood, I reiterate the determination of the Maghrib peoples in Tunisia, Algeria, and Morocco, to continue the struggle until complete freedom and effective independence have been achieved, or perish to the last man in the course of it. For these countries have had to bear greater hardships than any other land, even those lands that were afflicted by the Nazi occupation.
>
> I firmly believe that we shall win in the end, and that the day of our victory draws nearer in proportion to our increased sacrifices in resistance to colonialism. Fascist Spain's persecution of us is the result of weakness and cowardice; our resistance has its basis in courage and faith.

The Office of the Arab Maghrib held a press conference, during which the statement was distributed to the press. Addresses were also made by 'Alāl al-Fāsi, al-Ḥabīb abu Raquibah, and Dr. Sulaymān ibn Sulaymān.

The Office of the Association of Islamic Societies in Cairo called a general meeting at the headquarters of the Muslim Youth Association. The speakers included Muḥammad 'Allūbah Pasha, president of the Association, Muḥammad Sālih Ḥarb Pasha, chairman of the Muslim Youth Association, Sheikh Ḥassan al-Banna, the general guide of the Muslim Brotherhood, Sheikh Ṣabri 'Abidīn, chief of the Arab Higher Committee's Palestine liaison office, and 'Alāl al-Fāsi, in the name of all the Maghrib independence parties. The gathering, which included the Amir 'Abd al-Karīm, his brother, and a throng of Arab and Muslim leaders, addressed messages of protest against Spanish acts.

The Committee for the Liberation of the Arab Maghrib held a reception for the Arab delegations on the occasion of the meeting of the Arab League's political committee. The secretary-general of the committee read the speech of its chairman, the Amir 'Abd al-Karīm, whereupon the Secretary-General of the Arab League replied with the following speech:

> I have said many times before, and I repeat now, that this Arab bird which wishes to fly will not be able to do so with one wing, while his other wing is lying low in al-Maghrib. The Arab nation will not occupy the worthy place it deserves under the sun so long as the countries of al-Maghrib remain under occupation. This blessed renascence, which has permeated all parts of the Arab world, cannot come to full fruition unless the countries of the Arab Maghrib achieve their full independence. If the peoples of the East struggle for the independence of al-Maghrib, their struggle would be for their own independence, and in the cause of fraternity, equality, and mercy. We and the Europeans along the shores of the Mediterranean have exchanged various visits; they settled in our midst and we settled in theirs; but we left to them the legacies of our civilization, while in all their visits they merely left their savage deeds. Our countries were the cradle of civilization, fraternity, and mercy; we taught the world agriculture, industry, and writing. Our countries were also the cradle of religions; we

carried all these things along with us in our visits to the northern shores of the Mediterranean.

The Easterners have been able to achieve their objectives to some extent, and the Maghāribah [peoples of the Maghrib] will succeed likewise in attaining the objectives for which they are now struggling. I struggled like yourselves for a cause whose object I considered far from attainable. I did not then have an Arab country in which I could take refuge; whereas now, you are struggling for a cause the attainment of which seems close at hand, and you have been able to take sanctuary in the East. You are in your homeland continuing your struggle, and I hav no doubt that the day will come when we shall all go to al Maghrib. Many people do not know the Maghrib well, and I say to these, that the Maghrib people have the staunchest qualities of endurance and fortitude in carrying on the hardships of struggle and in dedicating their lives to the cause of independence. They are a sturdy people whose will to struggle bends to no obstacle and whose word is their deed.

It is a happy occasion on which the veterans of struggl from Iraq, Syria, the Lebanon, Saudi Arabia, Yemen, Transjordan, and Egypt are now assembled in this hall; theirs is an example to you that God's recompense is forthcoming to those who work.

When 'Azzām Pasha concluded his speech, Riad Bey al-Ṣulḥ, the Lebanese Prime Minister, took the floor. He assured the gathering that the delegations from the Arab state were in full agreement with what 'Azzām Pasha had just siad. He added: "We have asked 'Azzām Pasha to speak for all of us; you shall see from amongst us fighters for the cause of the Maghrib, such as you have seen for the cause of the East."

When news reached us that the Spanish authorities had forbidden the imams of the mosques to deliver their usual Friday sermons, I submitted sharp protests to the various competent quarters. I also met Monseigneur Hughes, the Vatican's Apostolic Delegate in Egypt, to whom I presented a memorandum in the name of the Istiqlal Party, protesting against the policies of the Spanish authorities in Morocco and against the continuance of the Berber policy in the Fren

Zone. The Delegate promised to communicate my protest to the Vatican.

His Majesty King 'Abdullah ibn al-Ḥussein, monarch of the Hashimite Kingdom of Transjordan, had been planning to visit Spain and the Khalifiyah Zone in Morocco. Press reports concerning this projected visit had appeared two years ago, and the Spanish publicity organs had attempted to exploit it in a manner contrary to its true purport. The projected visit had two main objectives: to establish friendly relations with Spain and to serve as an anti-Moscow gesture, in retaliation against the Soviet's vetoing of the admission of Transjordan to membership in the United Nations. In addition to these two aims, His Majesty was as keenly interested in the situation of North Africa as he had been in the situation of his country and the neighboring countries of the Arab East. He had repeatedly impressed upon the representatives of France and Spain in Amman the need for a change of policy towards the Arabs of North Africa. His Majesty had thought that his visit to Spain would enable him to visit the Khalifiyah Zone, and perhaps the Sultaniyah Zone as well, where he would meet with his cousin the King of Morocco, with a view to renewing close ties between the two Hashimite Kingdoms. But the heavy burden of duties at home, in the wake of the newly-won independence, prevented a realization of the plan.

When the events of the Khalifiyah Zone occurred, causing widespread repercussions in the Arab world, and evoking protests from the Secretary-General of the Arab League and from representatives of Arab public opinion, Spain revived talk about the projected royal visit, in the hope that it might supplant the prevailing Arab indignation, and give to Moroccans the impression that there was still among the Arabs a great Arab monarch, a descendant of the Prophet, who continued to maintain friendship with Spain, regardless of what she did to Moroccans.

In a move to counter this colonial propaganda, I submitted a memorandum to the Jordanian Government, through its Minister in Cairo, expressing the hope of the Moroccans that His Majesty, whose love and sympathy for our country and King is beyond doubt, would consent to defer the projected trip until a more propitious moment.

The Minister of Jordan facilitated my mission by his

sympathetic and firm grasp of the situation. Then I travelled to Amman, accompanied by Aḥmad al-Malīh, where upon arrival I called on Dr. Fawzi al-Mulqi Pasha, Foreign Minister, at his home. I had previously met Dr. Mulqi in Cairo and had been impressed by his genial character and his staunch loyalty to the Arab cause. He assured us that His Majesty had conceded our request and had instructed him to inform the Spanish Ambassador of His Majesty's decision to postpone the visit to some future date.

The following day we were received in audience by His Majesty at the Shūnah winter palace. The meeting lasted for three hours, during which various Arab and North African questions were discussed. We were impressed by His Majesty's profundity of knowledge concerning our cause and his solicitude for its success. He related to us some of his efforts on behalf of the Maghrib cause, and assured us that he would instruct the representatives of Transjordan to the Arab League to take the initiative in defense of the Maghrib and in intensifying the efforts of the League on her behalf. We were the guests of His Majesty for dinner, and the menu included one of al-Maghrib's popular dishes (al-kiskis) to make us feel at home.

The next day we were accorded another audience at Raghadan palace in Amman, in the presence of a number of cabinet ministers and leading officials. His Majesty inquired of us concerning the Moroccan budget, the armed forces stationed in the country, and the fate of the once great Moroccan army. When we described the existing state of affairs, His Majesty was profoundly moved, as were all those present at the audience.

In conclusion, we wish to stress that in citing the failures of General Juin, it has not been our intention to disparage his person, or to belittle his standing as France's greatest general, with an exemplary record in the fight for the liberation of his people. We merely wish to demonstrate the weakness of the regime imposed upon our country; for the present Resident-General is one of France's leading personalities, and his failure is the best proof of the bankruptcy of the regime itself, regardless of the persons who might be in control. We believe that the succession of military and civilian residents will in no way alter the existing situation; because a representative of France, in a protectorate country, is compelled to act within the framework of colonial policies, which are in conflict with the national aspirations of the people. It is not within his human power to resist the will of the Maghrib people or to prevent the victory of liberal ideas in the country. The duty of France, therefore, is not to waste time in attempts foredoomed to failure. Such attempts constitute a crime not only against Morocco but against France herself. It is in her interests, no less than in ours, to recognize the situation as it is and to accept the dictates of equity by declaring our independence. Then she could send her representatives to us for a new era of French-Moroccan friendship on the basis of mutual regard and interests.

Royal Patronage of the Reform Movement

His Majesty's profound interest in the reform movement is neither secret nor new. Since he succeeded to the throne of his illustrious ancestors, he has actively aided and encouraged the cause of progress and reform. His efforts have been doubly intensified since the people requested him, in their Istiqlal charter, to take the reform movement under his distinguished patronage.

His Majesty is of the firm conviction that his people's aspirations for progress and a better life can be made possible only through learning and education for all. He has, therefore, devoted his efforts to the opening of schools and has contributed considerable sums of money--from his own private means--towards this end.

In his devoted care for the education of his children he has set an example to all parents; for the princes and princesses of the royal house have become a symbol to their people, and the esteem in which they are held has been amply demonstrated in the acclaim that greets their public appearances, on such occasions as the inauguration of a school or of a charitable foundation.

Our sovereign's interest in religious education is not less than his interest in lay education. Had it not been for His Majesty's patronage and protection of the Qarawiyīn and other religious institutions, Islamic culture in Morocco would not have survived the catastrophe wrought by the Berber Edict and by the missionary policies of the protectorate.

His Majesty has resuscitated the policy, initiated by his great reforming grandfather, Mawlay al-Ḥassan, of sending educational missions to Europe. Ten students have been sent abroad to study at his private expense.

One of His Majesty's most notable contributions has been his encouragement of the education and uplifting of the Moroccan woman, so that she could achieve her emancipation. He has designated his own daughter, Princess 'Â'ishah, to lead the Moroccan feminine movement, thereby dealing a blow to the misguided and the reactionary. He has guided the feminine movement in accordance with sound principles conformable to religious and ethical precepts. The Moroccan woman has responded to the call of her sovereign, and is now working side by side with men in the service of society for the progress and liberation of the fatherland.

His Majesty has also extended a helping hand to sports and scout movements as well as to music and to the fine arts.

His Majesty is taking an active part in the work of organized relief; charitable societies have been receiving his most devoted attention, encouragement, and active participation.

While the next chapter will be devoted to a depiction of the efforts made by the Istiqlal Party in the social and cultural fields, it should be emphasized that the moving spirit in all these popular endeavors has been His Majesty himself. The achievements of the Istiqlal Party, and of others, have been in response to his lead in initiating a new era which before long will herald an age of renascence, progres and liberation.

The Activities of the Istiqlal

In the Cultural Field

If the Istiqlal Party has fallen heir to the National Party and to the Kutlah of National Action, it has also followed in the footsteps of its predecessors in devotion to cultural and social reforms. The efforts of the party have not been restricted to political and the economic activities, which we have already described, or to the diplomatic field, to which we shall refer once more. The party has been a prime supporter of the movement towards general enlightenment. Its efforts have been many-sided, though united in their common aim and orientation. The party has a central committee on education, responsible to the executive committee. The central committee has branches in all towns and other localities. These committees supervise the educational work of the party; they open schools, draw up curricula, write books, train teachers, and send student missions. There is a special sub-committee whose task is to provide aid and loans to students. There are about one hundred schools which are run by the party, or which are offered financial or other forms of assistance; more girls and boys receive education in these schools than in the schools run by the department of education. In addition to regular schooling, the party provides extra-curricular activities in the various student centers, in youth festivals, and in collective recreational trips which are organized in the spring and summer seasons. The Istiqlal student committees are themselves doing a commendable job in propagating the noble cause and in fostering the spirit of teamwork among the student body. The special columns, assigned by the party newspapers to student contributors, afford these youths an opportunity for self-expression, and give them the feeling that they have a definite contribution to make to the cause of their country. This will prepare them for the day when they themselves will grasp the reins in the struggle both at home and abroad.

The party, following the lead of His Majesty, has sent student missions to various colleges in Algeria and France. There are about ninety students who are receiving their higher education abroad with the help of the party. The Istiqlal has founded for them a special center, comprising a dining hall and a club. A student committee guides the students in their work and publishes a regular bulletin edited by the students themselves. There is a weekly meeting during which students give talks on various problems pertaining to their country.

These are in addition to the coordinated work which is being carried on within the North African Muslim Students' Association, and in addition to the annual Arab students' conference.

It is fortunate that close contacts now exist between students from the various Arab countries who are studying in France, England, Belgium, and Switzerland. The mutual visits between students in these countries are a most effective means for clarifying the ideas of Arab nationalism, which today permeates the youths of North Africa.

The party has made a beginning towards introducing religious instruction in secondary schools. Complementary sections have been established in Fez, Rabat, and Casablanca. This is intended to provide schooling in Islamic culture, along with the regular courses obtaining in government secondary schools; the curriculum is different only in the emphasis placed upon Islamic studies. At the same time, a beginning has also been made in introducing a liberal, lay education on the secondary level, at the Jasūss school and at the Sidi Muḥammad school in Casablanca. The party is also giving free training to teachers at elementary schools. In short, it is doing all it can to fill the gap that should more properly have been filled by the Department of Education, which instead has obstructed its efforts.

Although the party has not been able, so far, to send a student mission to the East, as did its progenitor, the National Party, it has nonetheless made a modest beginning; for there are two students in Egypt now studying at the party's expense. It is to be hoped that the educational committee will fill this gap by sending a student mission, from graduates of Islamic and regular secondary schools, for advanced study at Egyptian and Syrian colleges, so that qualified Arabic scholars will be made available for Morocco.

The party has founded a literary magazine, "Risālat al-Maghrib" (the message of the Maghrib), which is regarded as the foremost Arabic literary magazine in North Africa. A select group of the country's leading literary men, who are devoted to the revival and the development of Moroccan literature, are contributing to this magazine. The party's delegation in Egypt is also making a praiseworthy contribution; a special report was presented to the higher council of the party, urging the need for greater advances in this direction. It can be safely stated that a rejuventated national culture will emerge through the efforts of the Istiqlal, which comprises the elite of university graduates in the country.

The efforts of the press committee are reflected in its various publications, which include the most advanced newspaper in the entire Arab Maghrib, "al-'Alam" (the flag), "al-Taqaddum" (progress), a weekly magazine, and "Ṣawt al-Shabāb al-Maghribi" (the voice of the Maghrib youths).

If these foundational activities have been circumscribed by the extraordinary conditions obtaining in the country, which prevent the party from attaining the cultural aims to which it aspires, efforts are continuing with a view to prevailing upon the authorities to implement a national educational program.

His Majesty the King has afforded an opportunity to a number of our brethren to express their views on the subject, when he decided upon the setting up of a royal commission to draw up an educational charter for Morocco. The Moroccan members of the commission, a group of qualified and experienced educationalists, presented a plan to the full commission, which included French members. The plan was adopted by the unanimous vote of the Moroccan members and by an overwhelming majority of the French members.

The educational charter, according to this plan, is based upon the following principles:

1. Compulsory elementary education for all Moroccans--males and females.

2. A Moroccan-oriented curriculum with Arabic as the language of instruction.

3. The provision of free schooling in all government schools.

4. A unified curriculum in elementary schools throughout Morocco.

5. Freedom of education at all levels, to be guaranteed by a special enactment for this purpose.

6. Unrestricted admission of Moroccans to all educational institutions in Morocco.

The Moroccan authors of the plan gave supporting statements for each of these principles. Concluding their report they told the commission:

> This plan will have been valueless if it has not conveyed to your esteemed committee the aspirations of the Moroccan people as regards the future of their country. Attention is now focused on us, who have been assigned

the noble task of treating the Moroccan body, and of giving it health and well-being.

The Moroccan members on this committee welcome the representatives of French culture who have come to participate with us in drafting a charter to guide the nation along the road to happiness. His Sheriffian Majesty has placed his confidence in us; let us be worthy of it.

All three French members who had come from France voted for the Moroccan plan, while only one of the three French members, selected from the staff of the Moroccan department of education, went along with it. The two others resigned from the commission, alleging that it was adopting a hostile attitude towards the French language. At any rate the plan was carried by an overwhelming majority and was submitted to the King who gave it his wholehearted endorsement. The Residency-General, however, has not approved it to the present day. His Majesty has been turning down all alternative proposals, submitted to him by the director of education. It can be stated, therefore, that His Majesty' defense of the Moroccan educational charter is the surest guarantee that it will be carried through in the near future.

We must not gloss over the achievements of the representatives of Moroccan chambers of commerce and agriculture during the recent session of the so-called government consultative council; for they have put up a defense of all the afore-mentioned Istiqlal principles, and their approach to concrete problems has been made in the light of them.

The party is endeavoring by all possible means to coordinate the cultural orientation in Morocco with that of the Arab League. The party was represented at the Arab League's cultural colloquium, held in the Lebanon during the summer of 1947, by 'Abd al-Karīm Ghallāb, who, along with Muḥammad ibn 'Abbūd, represented Morocco. Party representatives in France participated also in the Arab students' conference held in England.

In the Social Field

The party is tackling the manifold problems in the social field. One of the foremost of these problems pertains to religious and moral reforms. The Istiqlal "Society of 'Ulemas", which comprises the overwhelming majority of the faculties at the Qarawiyīn University, the Ibn Yūsuf College, the Meknes Institute, and other religious institutes, is sparing no efforts towards the modernization of Islamic instruction, with a view to transforming the entire social structure. It has directed its fire against official prostitution, a practice which the party believes should be banned. The Society has also been calling the attention of local administrators to all forms of unlicensed prostitution, in an effort to help its suppression. Narcotics and intoxicating drinks have been a principal target of attack, while at the same time the Society has been preaching a constructive approach to problems relating to the family and to society. It has also been advocating the education of women and has been resisting those who oppose it in the name of religion. This is a part of a more general attack upon the rigidities of false 'ulemas and certain Sufi adherents, who under the subterfuge of religion and nation serve their own ulterior and selfish aims. The party depends a great deal upon this Islamic group, which represents the elite of university thinkers, not only for their part in enlightening the minds of the people, but also for their help in formulating Islamic ideas to suit the spirit of the modern era in all facets of Moroccan development.

The Istiqlal 'ulemas have a special section in the weekly magazine, "al-'Alam", in which to propagate their ideas among their large and receptive public.

In the section on the Salafīyah movement, we alluded to the efforts of our learned Sheikh, Muḥammad ibn al-'Arabi al-'Alawi, towards purification of the Moroccan mind from superstitious beliefs and practices. We can now assert that all these 'ulemas are either his colleagues, his students, or his students' students. They all look to him for ultimate guidance and advice whenever they are faced by any particular problem.

The party has devoted considerable attention to improving family life; it has advocated an abandonment of polygamy, an improvement in the status of women, a plea for greater family allowances to government employees and to workers, and cheap housing. It took an active part in the royal commission's proceedings at Qunayṭirah concerning these problems.

Since family reforms are contingent upon a sound training

and education of women, the party has established a number of girls' schools and womens' training centers. There is within the party today a higher council for Istiqlal women and girls, directing the party's feminine movement. Madame Malakah al-Fāsi acts in liaison between it and the party executive and higher council. The feminine council has established several female and co-educational schools. Last year it submitted to His Majesty the King a report requesting the institution of secondary education for Moroccan girls and the establishment of a special section for girls at the Qarawiyīn for religious and literary instruction. His Majesty has responded to the request, and the first secondary school for girls was founded. He has also approved in principle the institution of a special womens' section at the Qarawiyīn, and it is to be hoped that the plan will be carried through in the near future.

Women participate today in all aspects of party activity, and particularly in relief work for the orphans and the needy at schools.

There is a special womens' section in the weekly magazine, "al-'Alam", devoted to feminine affairs; the contributions to this section constitute an interesting and novel phase in the history of Moroccan literature.

One of the most important womens' organizations is a group of counsellors devoted to the physical and the moral training of girls; one of its principal aims is to instill the spirit of teamwork among Moroccan girls.

The party, to the extent permitted by the circumstances of the country, has organized the Moroccan youths within sport and scout organizations, which are equal to the most advanced in the world.

The "Free Football League", which has recently been recognized and which comprises two hundred national teams representing ten thousand players, is one of the foremost sport organizations in North Africa. At the recent session of the so-called government consultative council, Aḥmad al-Yazīdi, president of the Rabat chamber of commerce, gave a comprehensive report on the problems of Moroccan youth organizations; he urged that they be allowed to function unhindered and be accorded every possible assistance.

It is pleasing to note that the party scouts do not restrict their activities to the conventional scout gatherings and camps; they also carry on their scout duties in relief and assistance to those in distress.

The party has its own program for combating the widespread unemployment in the country. It calls for large-scale industrialization, to which wealthy Moroccans are urged to subscribe; it also encourages the youths to go in for private enterprise rather than government jobs. It called once again for a weekday holiday on Friday, and its call has been heeded by the inhabitants of Fez, Meknes, and Taza; other towns are expected to follow suit. It will be recalled that the National Party had secured the observance of a weekday holiday in 1937; but the authorities compelled the Moroccans to abandon it following the October revolution of that year.

As a result of the efforts commenced by the National Party and continued by the Istiqlal, the government has fixed the hours of work at factories and mines and has adopted a weekday holiday. Efforts are being made to adopt similar measures in rural areas, because the plight of farmers is even worse than that of factory workers.

At the behest of the party, the chambers of commerce, industry, and agriculture have grouped together within a general association. Our friend Muḥammad al-Zaghāri, member of the party's higher council, has been elected president of the association. We have no doubt that the new body will make a valuable contribution towards the organization of the national economy and spur the industrialization of the country.

We have already described the policies of the party in regard to labor organizations. The aim has been two-fold: to achieve for Moroccans the right to establish free Moroccan labor unions; and to resist the efforts of the C.G.T. to seize control of the Moroccan workers and use them for its own purposes.

Our policy had been to prevent the affiliation of Moroccan workers with any French unions; but in view of the obstinate refusal of the Residency-General to permit Moroccans to found their own unions, we permitted Moroccan workers to join the French Confédération Générale du Travail, on condition that they be allowed to form a wing of their own within the movement and be accorded adequate representation on the council of the confederation. The conditions were conceded, whereupon unions were formed at Jarādah,

Khuraybiqah, and other working centers. Moroccan workers organized several strikes in support of their demands for bet ter conditions. Naturally, this step is regarded as a preliminary one, intended to bring pressure to bear upon the protectorate for a recognition of the Moroccan workers' right to combination. The Residency-General has promised to recognize Moroccan unions, but the promise has remained ink on paper until the present time.

Moroccan workers are very active in defense of their righ their struggle enjoys the support of the nationalist movement as well as that of the various democratic parties in France.

One of the most impressive demonstrations in the history of the Moroccan trade union movement occurred in 1947, when a general strike was observed for almost one month at the phosphate mines in Khuraybiqah; the strike was in protes against the failure of the government phosphate office to implement its promise of better working conditions.

The French authorities used all methods of suppression in an endeavor to break up labor resistance; the efforts, however, were to no avail.

Army forces cordonned off the Abī Junaybah and Abī Anwār centers, isolating the inhabitants of the two villages from the rest of Morocco. Numerous incidents followed, news of which was withheld from the Moroccan public by French censorship. It is our duty to record a number of these incidents as examples of the struggle which our worker brethren are waging to secure minimum living conditions and the right to combine in unions.

On April 29 six Moroccan workers were marched off to th central square in Abī Junaybah, and there, in the sight of all they were flogged by army forces until they bled.

On April 30 the French police commissar, with a revolver hand, and accompanied by the caid of the village and its Frenc controller, attacked the headquarters of the local union at Abī Junaybah. The leader of the union, Sayīd al-Ḫussein, was arrested, along with one hundred of his mine-worker colleagues. The arrested workers were marched off to an unknown destination. An order was issued declaring the marke place out of bounds for the inhabitants. On May 4 the water supply was cut off entirely from Abī Junaybah. Thus, by depriving the inhabitants of food and water, the authorities hoped to break the resistance of Moroccan workers.

In the village of Abī al-Anwār, the leaders of the workers

assembled in the headquarters of the union, were cordonned off by army troops and were forced to remain without food for several days; the police did not permit their families or colleagues to supply them with food unless they ordered their workers back to work. The marooned leaders, however, refused to submit to these highhanded tactics, or to give up the struggle for the liberation of their country from the grip of French financial monopolists.

Similar incidents occurred in Jarādah, in the vicinity of Ougdah, and resulted in a violent clash, in the course of which a French director and a number of his Zionist assistants were killed.

In describing the labor movement and its efforts for liberation we must emphasize that our Moroccan workers do not embrace any social creed incompatible with our Istiqlal principles. If they were forced to join a union, to which French residents in Morocco are affiliated, this is because they could not find any other way of expressing their demands. They enjoy the support of the Istiqlal Party, which comprises the majority of their leaders.

We must stress also, that we do not consider strikes anything more than a temporary device to secure basic minimum rights for the Moroccan workers; for disputes between employees and employers should be settled through arbitration and mediation boards set up by the state, whose decisions must be binding on all.

We also look upon union struggle as only a part of a general struggle for the organization of the Moroccan people and government and their mobilization to safeguard Morocco's independence and national heritage, both material and moral. We firmly believe that we have no struggle apart from our struggle for independence and a free and happy life within our fatherland, which is the fatherland of all classes and the great bond uniting all our citizens.

Efforts for Unity

The Kutlah of National Action, and later the National Party, spared no efforts towards a coordination of plans between North Africa's various parties and organizations. There was a time when the Association of North African Muslim Students in France symbolized this aspiration for unity. The Kutlah-sponsored demonstrations following our arrest in Casablanca in 1936, and the October events of

1937, gave considerable impetus to the move for unity. The representatives of the independence movements in Paris have been working in close cooperation, even though there has been no official coordination among their respective parties. One of the foremost steps, initiated by the Istiqlal Party, had been to expand and solidify the natural ties between the nationalist movements in the three countries of North Africa. Negotiations in this regard resulted in the conclusion in November 1945 of a covenant between the Istiqlal Party, the Algerian People's Party and the Tunisian Liberal Dustur Party. The preamble states:

> Whereas the people of North Africa are oriented towards the same objective, namely to combat colonialism in all its forms, to work for independence, to consolidate national sovereignty, and to strive for the unification of North Africa within the Arab League, the representatives of the political organizations, signatories of this Covenant have resolved to transform this unity of outlook from the realm of theory and emotion to concrete reality, praying God the Almighty to lead them along the right path and to grant them success in their endeavors.

The Covenant bound the signatory parties not to depart from this united political plan, except after consultations with all the other parties.

The Covenant left the door open for other North African parties to join in if they so wished.

As soon as the Second World War ended, and with it the restrictions on travel between the two parts of Morocco, the party resumed its old ties of solidarity and cooperation with the Iṣlaḥ Party in the Spanish Zone.

With the release of Wazzāni from detention, and the establishment of the Shura and the Istiqlal, efforts were made for a merger of the two parties, but these failed. As a result of high-level mediation, under the auspices of our learned Sheikh Muḥammad ibn al-'Arabi al-'Alawi, agreement was reached on a unified plan of action, though each party retained its independent existence. The plan was embodied in the following covenant:

1. Each of the two parties shall retain its present entity, so as not to disrupt the national efforts, pending agreement on the manner of unifying the common effort.

2. The manner of unifying the common effort is through a merger of the two parties; the name, organization, and functions of the new party shall be decided in due course.

3. We do not accept membership in the French Union; relations between independent Morocco and France should be based upon a new treaty.

4. There shall be no cooperation with the protectorate administration; but members of the party shall accept the calls from His Majesty for participation in technical duties, after notifying the executive committee to this effect. As for members of the executive committee, their participation must be considered by the higher council, in view of their political responsibilities in the party and their duty of adhering to the principle of independence.

5. No member of the executive committee or of the higher council shall accept a government post; the other members of the party shall consult the executive committee in this regard.

6. Talks with the responsible French authorities shall be left to the discretion of the executive committee, unless the higher council decides otherwise; such talks must not infringe upon the principle of non-cooperation with the administration of the protectorate.

7. There shall be no affiliation with the Communists in a common front, and there shall be no contacts with them except through the executive committee.

8. The Jews who do not carry a foreign nationality and who are not Zionists, shall be regarded as Moroccans, subjects of His Majesty.

9. Contacts shall be established with other Moroccan parties, in an effort to bring about unity and a coordination of efforts.

10. Methods of action: peaceful and legitimate.

11. North Africa: cooperation, solidarity, and coordination.

12. Arab League: to seek its assistance for the realization of Morocco's independence and endeavor to expedite entry into its fold.

13. The Moroccan cause abroad: to take steps for the submission of the cause before the United Nations, at the appropriate time.

If the plan of the moderates, to which reference was

made earlier, had violated provisions of this covenant, the establishment of the Committee for the Liberation of the Arab Maghrib, under the leadership of the hero, ʻAbd al-Karīm, has restored unity among all the Maghrib parties on the basis of one principle, "no negotiations until after independence."

It is our hope that the day will come when the parties in each part of North Africa will have united within one party, on the basis of the preceding recommendations; for it is in the best interests of the nation to remove all appearances of dissension which may tempt exploitation by the foreigner.

The Solidarity of the Party with Arab Liberation Movements and Others

In addition to striving for inter-North African party solidarity, we have maintained close and continuous cooperation with the Arab liberation movements and those of other peoples. In my speeches in Cairo I have urged the convening of a general conference for all subject peoples with a view to coordinating the struggle against colonialism. The party is now advocating such a conference, which, if held, would constitute a blessed step towards human emancipation. Morocco's moral support for liberation movements abroad has been demonstrated on various occasions; foremost of these has been the cause of Arab Palestine, which united the Arab peoples everywhere. The party had mobilized the Moroccan people, in protest against Zionist policies before and after the partition. Together with the rest of North Africa, we demanded a hearing before the United Nations on the matter. When the Arab forces entered Palestine to suppress the Zionist gangs, the party organized a boycott of Zionists in Morocco; subscriptions were collected and sent to the Arab League.

The efforts of the party, however, were only a part of a general national effort spontaneously made by the Moroccan people; a vigilant watch was kept on the activities of the Zionists; Moroccan volunteers braved a veritable "iron curtain" to join the ranks of Arab fighters. The number of North African volunteers amounted to five thousand, some of whom managed to get across, while the rest were turned back by the French and the Spanish control authorities.

The Ṣadr al-A'zam of the state of Morocco sent a message to 'Azzām Pasha, expressing in the name of His Majesty the King the solidarity of the Sheriffian Kingdom with the Arak kings and presidents. The French regarded the message as a violation of the protectorate treaty, because it constituted contact with foreign states without the French acting as intermediary. His Majesty the King, however, does not regard the existing boundaries between Morocco and the Arab countries as anything but artificial, and he could not as a Muslim king remain with hands folded in the face of Zionist aggression against the Holy Land.

When Egypt submitted her case before the United Nations, the secretary-general of the party, Aḥmad Bla Freej, cabled support to the Egyptian Prime Minister, Nuqrāshi Pasha. I also cabled to the Secretary-General of the United Nations, expressing Moroccan solidarity with Egypt, as did also all the other Moroccan parties.

When the Indonesians were fighting their war of liberation against the Dutch, the party took every opportunity to express solidarity with them in their noble aim.

The party organized mass celebrations on the occasion of the independence of India and Pakistan, in the course of which several party members were arrested in various parts of the land.

The party has protested against the enlistment of Moroccans for the war in Vietnam. The Amir 'Abd al-Karīm, chairman of the Arab Maghrib Liberation Committee, addressed an appeal to Moroccan soldiers urging them to join the native forces; he pointed out that it was improper for them to support colonialism while demanding liberation for their own country. Our brethren in Paris participated in joint rallies with the parties of Africa and Asia in condemnation of colonialism and in demanding justice for all.

But these are mere preliminaries to a greater solidarity for which we shall strive , so that the underprivileged throughout the world might rescue their rights from the hands of the oppressors. This makes our movement a human movement, seeking its good as well as the good of those with whom we have no ties other than our wounded human feelings.

Orienting the Country towards the Arab League

Arab unity, which had seemed to many a distant aspiration, has now become an actual fact. After generations of struggle the Arab peoples have attained their cherished goal of unity; the obstacles that had stood in the way of the idea collapsed before the surging principles of the last war. The negotiations, which had begun in 1942, culminated in the signing of the Arab People's Covenant, on March 22, 1945, by representatives of the following independent Arab Governments: Egypt, Iraq, Saudi Arabia, Syria, the Lebano Yemen, and Transjordan. The Covenant comprehends the political, social, cultural, and economic problems.

The Covenant embodied the desire of the Arab states for the strengthening and consolidation of ties on the basis of mutual respect for the independence and sovereignty of each member state, and the coordination of their efforts for the benefit of all the Arab countries. It may, therefore, be regarded as both a diplomatic and an ideological pact.

Arab public opinion, which had followed the progress of the talks with the greatest interest, received with satisfactio the results; the great step had been taken, and it was now possible to talk about an Arab bloc, capable, in conjunction with other regional formations, of contributing to the peace and tranquility of the world.

At the same time, the Allied endorsement of the Arab League during the war afforded the Arab states the opportunity to participate effectively in laying down the bases of world peace. The Arabs participated in the establishment of the United Nations and made notable contributions to the San Francisco conference.

But, though the seven Arab states have been able to strengthen their mutual ties, it is only fair to admit that Arab unity is still an unfinished task; it will remain incomplete and ineffectual if the Arab League confines its efforts to the countries bounded by Iraq in the east and Egypt in the west.

As a matter of fact, Arab unity--according to the Covenar itself--comprises all the countries between the Persian Gulf in the east and the Atlantic Ocean in the far west [Moroc co]. If the Arab Maghrib has not become a member of the Arab League, it is because of its loss of diplomatic freedom

The countries of North Africa, however, have declared all along that their fate was bound up with that of the Arab peoples, to whom they are related by the closest ties.

In this post-war period, when all small nations are seeking to reestablish their relationships on the basis of common interests, Morocco, together with Tunisia and Algeria, find in the Arab League their natural place. This view was expressed by the Istiqlal Party in the memorandum submitted on March 8, 1945 to the President of the Arab Unity Conference meeting in Cairo. The memorandum stated in part:

> If political circumstances, of which your Excellency is aware, had permitted Morocco to participate in your deliberations, an official delegation enjoying the blessings of His Majesty the King and the confidence of the Moroccan people would have represented her at your conference. Morocco has declared on all occasions her attachment to the unity of the Arab peoples, which she regards as one of the pillars of world peace; but the policy of suppression has deprived Morocco of participation in the various activities which her sister states are carrying on in the East. It has also prevented Morocco from raising her voice beyond her limited frontiers.

The League for the Defense of Morocco in Egypt made similar representations to the Arab leaders.

The participation of Morocco in the Arab League is based upon historical, linguistic, and emotional grounds. The party has published many articles with a common theme running as follows:

The history of Morocco, since the Arab conquest, is an integral part of the history of Arab civilization; no one part can be studied to the exclusion of the other. The Arabs, kindled by the Islamic faith, conquered the land of the Berbers in order to preach their faith. They successfully implanted the spirit of Arabism in this country and it has continued to flourish ever since. The new religion assisted the Arabs in spreading their influence in al-Maghrib so that it has become one of the great homelands of Arabism and Islam. The Arabs, thanks to their tolerance, encouraged and strengthened the spirit of independence among the inhabitants, thereby paving the way for the Moroccan royal families.

Although Morocco has always preserved her independenc since the rebellion of the Byzantine era, her history has re mained inextricably linked to Arab history. We need only refer to Moroccan establishments throughout the Arab coun tries. The conquest of Spain by Moroccan troops, under th command of Ṭāriq ibn Ziyād, opened the way for the supremacy of Arab civilization in Spain throughout the European medieval period. The names of distinguished Moroccan figures are too numerous to count. It is sufficient to cite such names as al-Idrīssi, the great geographer, Ibn Rushd (Averroes), the distinguished philosopher, and Ibn Baṭūtah, the famous traveller.

All movements both past and present have been connecte with the general tendencies and orientations in the Arab world.

In addition to these historical associations we find the bond of language; for the Arabic tongue--the medium of communicating the Islamic faith--prevailed in Morocco wit the spread of the new faith. The 'ulemas of Islam cultivatec in Moroccans a taste for Arabic until it became a deep-root article of faith. The universal language of reading in Moro co is Arabic, with its resourceful and fascinating vocabular It has served as the sole vehicle of communication between East and West amidst the tribulations of the past ages.

The emotional bonds between ourselves and the Arabs of the East naturally stem from the linguistic and the historica connections. The Moroccan people have always registered profoundly the impact of events--the good and the bad--occurring in the Arab countries, thus demonstrating the sense of communion which unites them with their brethren elsewhere, in adversity as well as in good fortune. Can we forget the joyous celebrations of the Moroccan people in 1936, on the occasion of Egyptian independence? Or, at the time when the government of the French Popular Front decided to grant Syrian independence, and the profound disappointment of Moroccans when the French Parliament refused ratificati of the Syrian-French treaty?

Morocco, now struggling for her freedom, expects from the Arab states effective assistance. In the annex to the Covenant of the Arab League such assistance was provided for, in the form of close cooperation between Arab states signatories of the Covenant and the other Arab states still under foreign control. It could be said, therefore, that the Arab governments in the East are convinced of the necessity for bringing Morocco and the rest of North Africa within the Arab League, and are cognizant of the role which our country could play in the Arab future, on account of her important geographic location and her potentialities in the field of economic cooperation between the Arab nations.

Various non-governmental organizations have been urging the extension of the Arab League to include the western portions of the Arab world. An appeal addressed by Jam'īyat al-Rābiṭah al-'Arabīyah (the Arab bond association) in September 1944, states, in part:

> It is regrettable that the Arab Maghrib, which is an integral part of the Arab inheritance, and which comprises nearly a half of the Arab territories, should have remained outside Arab unity, although its people have remained loyal to Arabism despite colonial pressure and the attempts of the occupation powers to sever all their relations with the Arab East. The leaders and the citizens of these countries have declared more than once their natural right to join the Arab League. The fact is, that any Arab bloc, whatever be its form, should include the Maghrib portions of Arab lands if Arab unity is to be effective and if it is to vindicate the hopes placed in it.

Several leading personages have been expounding this idea on various occasions. Dr. Ṭaha Ḥussein, one of Egypt's leading literary men, gave in the hall of the American University of Cairo, in 1944, a lecture entitled "The Cultural Relations between Egypt and the Arab States". In the course of the lecture Dr. Ḥussein declared:

> Egypt has turned towards her Eastern neighbors; but she cannot at the present time neglect the affairs of al-Maghrib, where a people live with whom we are connected by many ties. This is North Africa, which during the Middle Ages was the link between us and Spain, and which has given to us men like Ibn Khaldūn.
>
> Should Arab unity stop at Egypt's western frontiers? Such a unity would be lame, because half the Arab nation would be cut off from the other. It is the duty of those who are organizing close cooperation between the Arab

countries to remember always that there is an Arab Maghrib.

Morocco, which is a natural extension of the Arab countries, has the right to demand a place within the Arab Leagu in order to achieve her independence and to cooperate in achieving the security of all. This is particularly so in the light of the experiences of the last war, which have proved that isolated nations have no weight or consequence in the world of tomorrow. Morocco must, in order to live and prosper, join a bloc of nations. Two such blocs are open for her choosing: the French Union, whose form has not yet crystalized, and the Arab Union, which has become an actua reality.

In the promised French Union, Morocco will find herself--judging from past experience--in the utmost difficultie because there is a conflict of interests and of beliefs betwee her and France, and because she feels that she has been only an object of exploitation since France took over control The wealth of Morocco has been despoiled by a group of colonists, living as parasites at the expense of the indigenou inhabitants. The people have been subjected to the policies of assimilation, impoverishment, humiliation, and partition In short, Morocco is convinced that she would not be happy within this colonial union, but would remain as a storehouse for raw materials and as a hatching ground for soldiers to serve France.

Morocco's adherence to the Arab Union, on the other hand, would bring Morocco within this eastern family, to which she had belonged for ten centuries, and from which she had been excluded for reasons beyond her control. Morocco would be entirely free to benefit from the experiences of her more mature sisters in the rejuvenation of her systems, and then to participate in the revival of the civilization which had been built by our joint efforts and which had illuminated the entire Mediterranean basin.

Morocco, therefore, has made her choice.

Morocco's only hope is that these states would place thei confidence in a happily united Arab family animated by the desire to live in brotherly relations with the other unions and in a common attachment to freedom and peace.

This was the spirit which permeated the writings of the

Istiqlal Party as it strove to orient the Moroccan people towards the Arab League and to convince public opinion abroad that the Arab Maghrib is an integral part of the Arab world.

This advocacy was in fact nothing more than a reflection of popular sentiment in Morocco; for Arab consciousness has become strong in Moroccans, and the struggle for the Arab League has become an inseparable part of the general national struggle.

These efforts have been crowned and blessed by the attitude of His Majesty the King towards the Arab League, particularly after the historic speech in Tangier.

The Moroccan cause has gained considerable headway in Arab League circles; interest in the cause of the Arab Maghrib is growing day by day, so much so, that Arab public opinion is now exerting pressure on responsible quarters in the Arab League for increased attention to the cause of North Africa.

Facing World Opinion

The Istiqlal Party had made the necessary preparations during World War II to emerge on the international scene in the post-war period; for having despaired of the willingness of French diplomacy to abandon voluntarily its long-standing colonial policies, it was convinced that the next move should be waged abroad.

The close of World War II saw the conclusion of a series of international agreements recognizing the rights of peoples and governments to self-determination and self-government. France had been one of the powers solemnly pledged to support the Atlantic Charter, the San Francisco Charter, and other pacts. A new horizon had been opened for exposing colonialism and discrediting its oppressive policies.

There was unanimous agreement in Morocco on the need to enlighten world public opinion in preparation for submitting the Moroccan case officially before the United Nations.

We have already alluded to the efforts of the party's delegations in France, England, and America. We shall now describe some of the efforts made on the diplomatic field, and notably the memorandum submitted by the executive committee to the ambassadors of the Allied powers on

March 8, 1945, following the San Francisco conference. The memorandum was intended to recall Morocco's contribution to the Allied war efforts and to stress the right of the Sheriffian Government for a hearing before the peace conferences. Following is the text of the memorandum:

> The war of the United Nations against the forces of aggression has now entered its decisive stage, and Hitlerite Germany is at last receiving the final blow that will destroy Fascism and settle the world conflict.
>
> The Moroccan people have witnessed with great satisfaction the atmosphere that prevailed during the international conference meeting in San Francisco on April 25. Their greatest hope is that they would be accorded a place among the United Nations in acknowledgment of their contribution to the war effort and the heavy sacrifices they had borne in the common struggle.
>
> Indeed, Morocco's adherence to the democratic nation was from the beginning sincere and unequivocal. Morocc had joined the anti-Axis coalition, following a royal state ment on September 18, 1938, "that the Sultan of Morocco and his subjects were ready in the event of war breaking out to stand as one man on the side of France." This readiness became an actual fact, when on September 3, 1939 a speech by His Majesty was read in all the mosques of Morocco. The speech declared, in part: "As of this day, on which war and aggression have been unleashed, and until the day when our enemies shall have been overcome in defeat and humiliation, it is our duty to offer her [France] complete support and to assist her with all the means at our disposal, being neither calculating nor niggardly."
>
> Thus, Morocco became a belligerent against the Axis not only on account of her dependent status, but also by an explicit declaration, in which the sovereign of the country wished to express clearly his attitude towards this great conflagration for the defense of freedom.
>
> The Moroccan people have enthusiastically responded to the call of their beloved King; their response was such that the President of the French Republic, M. Lebrun, was prompted to state in a cable to His Majesty: "Morocc can, for her part, depend upon the complete support of France."

It also prompted the Resident-General to state on September 21, 1939: "France will never forget the enthusiastic support which the King and the people of Morocco have shown towards France in the defense of right and justice."

Since that time the entire country has been in a state of war. Martial law was declared; enemy property was promptly impounded; Axis nationals were interned. The country's entire resources were requisitioned to serve the needs of the Allied armies. Moroccan volunteers fought on the various battlefields, and our country was subjected to air raids. At the end of the battle of France our losses had been colossal. Moroccan prisoners are still behind barbed wires, awaiting the arrival of the liberation armies. Following the armistice of June 1940, the Moroccans conducted themselves most honorably, refusing to have anything to do with the armistice commissions or to cooperate with the enemy.

On the other hand, Allied forces were accorded a great welcome when they landed in Morocco on November 8, 1942. Here again, it was His Majesty the King who had set the course for us, by refusing categorically --with the concurrence of his ministers--to move the seat of the Mekhzen Government to the interior for a continuance of resistance, as desired by General Noguès.

The presence of Allied troops in Morocco, with their camps, arsenals, and navy units, caused the country to undergo heavy economic burdens; for Morocco, by means of self-imposed austerity, contributed substantially to the supply needs of the Allied troops in North Africa, Sicily, and Italy, as well as to the provisioning of the inhabitants of the liberated areas in France. Morocco furnished also considerable manpower for running port facilities and for the construction of airfields and road repairs. These roads, cutting across mountainous regions, could have been easy targets for local sabotage, particularly since the entire North African scene had been inundated by a deluge of Axis radio propaganda, and the impact of initial Axis victories had not worn off.

In spite of all these considerations, not one important incident, as Mr. Edward Stettinius states in his book, "Lend-Lease, Weapon for Victory", could be attributed directly to sabotage on the lines of communication in Morocco and Algeria during the fighting in Tunisia.

It is needless to emphasize the heavy financial burden arising from war expenditures, which runs into the millions, when one estimates the material sacrifices borne by Morocco in the cause of United Nations victory.

It is superfluous to recount Morocco's sacrifices in the blood of her sons, after all the official tributes to the heroism of Moroccan soldiers made by France, England, and the United States. Nor is it necessary to allude to the number of Moroccan soldiers who were in the divisio that liberated Tunisia, Italy, Corsica, Southern France, and Alsace, and who are now getting ready to cross the Rhine.

If the worth of nations is to be measured by their qualities rather than by their size, and if every nation--large or small--which had contributed to the war effort were entitled to a place in the international organization --as the United Nations Charter provides--then, it is the duty of the party of freedom to reserve for our nation a share in victory.

For all these reasons, the Istiqlal Party, which faithfully expresses the wishes of the Moroccan people, deem it just that Morocco be accorded the same rights as those of other members of the United Nations. It requests that an invitation be sent to the people's competent representa tives for direct participation in the international conferences with a view to defending their cause and establishir their rights. The party makes this demand in the name of all the sufferings which the Moroccan people have bor and in the name of the principles of right and justice whic are the noble aims of the democracies at war.

The party made other pleas for a hearing before the Unit Nations on questions in which Morocco has interests, notabl in the cases of Palestine and Libya.

We have previously alluded to the memorandum, submitt by the representative of the independence parties in the Khalifiyah Zone, on the occasion of the United Nations deba on Franco Spain. Previous to that--on September 15, 1947- the French Foreign Ministry submitted a report to the Unite Nations Trusteeship Council concerning its administration i

Morocco. The memorandum attempted to cover up the notorious record of French colonialism in our country. But the Istiqlal Party, the vigilant guardian of Morocco's interests, counteracted with a memorandum which had widespread repercussions throughout the world. The memorandum enumerated the forms of political, cultural, and judicial controls, as well as the policies of racial discrimination upon which the French protectorate regime in Morocco is based. The memorandum submitted by the secretary-general of the party to the United Nations Secretariat reads in part:

> The establishment of the United Nations has evoked great hopes in the hearts of those who are still under the yoke of the big colonial powers and are subjected to their exploitation and enslavement.
>
> Some members of the United Nations, honoring their pledges under the Charter, have been endeavoring to do away with their antiquated policies, and have shown their goodwill by granting freedom to peoples under their rule.
>
> We find with regret, however, that our country, in spite of her sacrifices for the victory of the democracies, is still subject to the most intense forms of oppression which obliterate all freedoms and are wholly incompatible with the spirit as well as the letter of the United Nations Charter.
>
> This memorandum, which our party has the honor to submit to Your Excellency, comprises a brief analysis of the contemporary situation. It concludes with a statement of the aspirations of the people who are united behind their sovereign, Sidi Muḥammad ibn Yūsuf, in his efforts to win for the Moroccan people a worthy place in the family of nations.

The memorandum summarizes the work of the protectorate over a period of thirty-five years as follows:

The division of the Kingdom into various zones of influence, and the partition of the French Zone itself into two artificial factions, with a view to playing off one against the other--this has been the Berber policy.

The establishment of a nominal government, deprived of all authority, for the benefit of a tyrannical French administration, which exercises direct control over the affairs of the country and pursues a policy of racial discrimination in all spheres of activity.

The attempt to disparage the conditions of the Moroccans which have been the result of the policy of impoverishment, of oppression, of the denial of civil rights and freedoms, an of granting to French residents in Morocco political rights, in violation of the constitution of the land and of internationa law.

The Moroccan people have never submitted to these measures because they are conscious of their past achievements and of the role which they could play once more in the history of Mediterranean civilization. The reaction to French colonialism culminated in the resolution embodied in the Istiqlal Party's covenant of January 11, 1944. The resolution, after declaring invalid the regime imposed in 1912, asserts that the only solution to the Moroccan crisis is independence of the country under a constitutional monarchy.

As for the so-called reforms announced after January 11, 1944 and the bloody disturbances that followed in their wake, these are merely designed to consolidate French economic and political control over Morocco and to deal a final blow to Morocco's separate entity. We cannot be deceived by these reforms because we are convinced that before all else an end must be put to this shameful regime and our national sovereignty restored.

It appears that France, faced with the mounting Moroccan crisis in 1944, had decided that the only solution--notwithstanding the upheavals that were shaking the world--was through the traditional colonial policy of merger between the French and the indigenous inhabitants and annexation of their territories to France. This policy has assumed a clear shape under France's last two representatives:

1. In the economic field, it manifested itself in the program, drawn up by M. Erik Labonne, following his appointment as Resident in 1946. The program is designed to control the exploitation of the country's still undeveloped resources for the benefit of French capitalists and the Frenc state, and to the detriment of Morocco's permanent interests.

2. In the political sphere, the administration of General Juin attempted to overplay the significance and scope of the

program for reorganizing the Moroccan Government. The program, in fact, introduced no changes either in the form or in the authority of the Moroccan Government. It consisted merely in the appointment of four new under-secretaries to the Ṣadr al-A'zam, whose task is restricted to liaison between the various administrations. Such changes could not be described as reforms, for most of these new posts, and others that no longer exist, had been included in the government reorganization plan of 1916, which even went so far as to include the Ministry of Finance. At any rate, the reorganization plan of 1947, like its predecessor of 1916, had been motivated by international considerations, with a view to covering up the French administration's control over all public services.

The policy of direct rule--which is at the root of the entire Moroccan dilemma--may be discerned from the various plans now being considered, with regard to conceding the demands of the French community for political representation in Moroccan public bodies, in violation of the protectorate treaty and of the international agreements upon which the Moroccan system is based.

If the Moroccan people were to accept this political orientation, they would, in effect, have decreed their own extinction and the absorption of their country into France. His Majesty has stated recently: "The time has come for democracy to all; the nations--great and small-- are aspiring to it, their aim being to secure human freedom."

The memorandum produced a visible effect in official circles. Its news was released by the United Nations Secretariat, and it was commented upon in the British and the American press. The United Press described the move as a first step towards independence from France. A spokesman for one of the big powers expressed the view that the memorandum was the first official break between the Moroccan people and France. Immediately afterwards, Poland announced that she was prepared to bring the Moroccan case before the United Nations. Cables from Lake Success quoted well-informed circles as stating that the memorandum of the Istiqlal Party was a prelude to raising the issue of Morocco before the United Nations, and that it was not unlikely that it would be placed on the agenda of the General Assembly at one of its forthcoming sessions. A number of

Latin American states expressed their willingness to support the Moroccan case.

The Istiqlal Party is continuing to send memoranda and documents to the United Nations Organization. It is also utilizing the various meetings of United Nations specialized agencies to supply relevant information pertaining to Morocco. A delegation, consisting of 'Abdullah Ibrāhim, member of the party's higher council, and Aḥmad al-'Alawi, representative of the Istiqlal press committee, was sent to the International Conference on Information, recently held in Geneva; the delegates established contacts with the various delegations to the Conference, and were assisted in their efforts by the office of the Eastern press syndicate headed by Maḥmūd abu al-Fatḥ. They were also assisted by the Egyptian, Syrian, and Pakistan delegations; the noted Egyptian writer, 'Abd al-Qādir al-Māzini, was chiefly instrumental in mobilizing support. Another party delegation was sent to the meeting of the United Nations Economic and Social Council.

Aspects of the Moroccan Case

The party is of the view that the Moroccan case is many-sided, and that the United Nations can tackle the problem from all or some of these sides, without French or Spanish colonialism being able to put up a strong or plausible defense The international standing of Morocco, for example, has always been one of complete independence. This may be evidenced by the history of the country and by the numerous pacts and treaties which had existed between the Sheriffian state and the other states in East and West, including France and Spain. This status of independence continued to be recognized even after the Algeciras Conference; for the representatives of the fifteen nations at the Conference recognized and guaranteed the sovereign independence of Morocco. There is nothing in international law, ancient or modern, that would permit a state to violate her solemn pledges; and there is also nothing in international law that would condone an aggression by one government upon the territory of another. The fact is, however, that France and Spain have occupied and partitioned the country of Morocco, in violation of all their solemn pledges and commitments at the various conferences. The occupation had been the cause of a treaty, signed under conditions of duress arising therefrom, and by a king whose mandate did not entitle him to alienate any part of the people's sovereignty. The French Declaration of the Rights of Man provides that sovereignty resides in the people and may not be alienated in any manner. Authorities on international law have always regarded any act contrary to this principle as null and void. French jurists reiterated this fact when the French parliament [sic, for National Assembly] alienated its powers to Marshal Pétain; they held that the dissolution of parliament was an act ultra vires because the deputies did not possess the authority to alienate the rights vested in them by the people. The writings of Professor Cassin, commissioner of justice and education in the French Committee of Liberation, are a categorical assertion of this fact. If experience has shown that colonialism, in all its forms, is national suicide, it is inconceivable that laws should permit nations to commit such a crime when they forbid the individual to resort to it even in the most trying situations.

The protectorate treaty, moreover, was ultra vires as long as the Treaty of Algeciras remained in force. It should have been the duty of all the states, signatories of Algeciras, to reconsider the international status they had imposed upon the country before recognizing a state of affairs at variance with their own resolution and with the obligations they had committed Morocco to observe. If the corrupt inducements, so generously distributed by France, had permitted those powers to gloss over the French and Spanish aggressions upon our country, nonetheless we, the victims of this ignoble international conspiracy, have never ceased to condemn it and demand that its perpetrators heed their consciences and endeavor to undo the crime they had inflicted upon an innocent people.

The people of Morocco have never recognized the protectorate imposed upon them; to the contrary, they have risen in an immortal rebellion which will continue ablaze until the protectorate has been erased from the Moroccan scene. The abdication of the Sultan who had signed the protectorate, in recognition of his failure to solve the problem, had satisfied the nation and preserved her honor. Thus, the draft treaty which he had initiated was rendered worthless by his abdication from the throne and his recognition that the will of the people had not endorsed his act.

As the protectorate unfolded its policies, not one aspect of our existence or sovereignty escaped aggression.

The protectorate treaty itself pledges the maintenance of the country's territorial integrity and the authority of the Crown. This pledge was the first to be violated; the country was torn into bits and shreds, and France conspired with other nations over a shabby partition of our country. Moroccan unity was reduced to a symbolic expression, emptied of all political reality. Is there any law, past or present, which permits one nation to parcel out a united country under foreign rule, whether this be national or international? And despite the fact that the component parts reject such partition and adhere to the territorial integrity of their country? This aspect alone is sufficient to impell the United Nations--if it is sincerely desirous of establishing justice and equity--to condemn French colonization and its atrocities in Morocco.

The robbery of a country's independence, which is solemnly recognized and guaranteed, is by itself a serious international crime.

The partition of the country into separate zones is a second crime no less heinous than the first.

There is also the odious question of the protectorate which lies at the root of all the evil; I refer to the system of direct rule, which lurks behind the name of "control" and "guidance". The Spanish and the French authorities have violated the protectorate compact, which had allegedly been intended merely to regulate relations with Morocco and to assist the Sheriffian state and people towards regeneration and progress. The protectorate has in fact become a system of direct and arbitrary rule, oriented towards extermination and assimilation by means of impoverishment, the perpetuation of ignorance, and ill-treatment.

The Moroccan state, which since time immemorial had been able to manage her own affairs, and still is so, is in no need of this foreign proscription and domination for her regeneration and progress.

Morocco had been a great state when France and other states were still in the primitive stages of their national formation. It is an irony of fate that she should now be subjected to the rule of those who yesterday were soliciting her friendship and learning from her experience.

The United Nations Charter, and the preceding declarations of San Francisco and the Atlantic Charter, had pledged respect for the sovereignty of each nation and its right to self-determination. This has not been an innovation in international rights and obligations; what is novel is that important states have pledged to strive for its implementation. Morocco has been struggling all along to secure its acceptance, and today she askes the pledgers--including France--to stand by their international obligations and to concede Morocco's right for liberation from colonial rule.

In demanding this right, Morocco exposes the United Nations, and the great powers that maintain it, to a severe testing of their loyalty to the cause of justice and peace. Morocco also calls upon the many member states, who had been signatories of Algeciras, to reconsider their connivance in the destruction of the country's independence, in violation of their solemn pledges.

These two aspects--the sovereignty and the territorial integrity of Morocco--are such that no law could but support them; they could not be assailed under the pretext of "reform" and "guidance", which the colonial powers might claim in support of their position; for the strivings of Moroccans for independence and unity are a priceless human possession which nothing can replace, whatever its value in terms of alleged happiness and well-being.

But there is also the bitter reality of the ill-treatment and plundering of Morocco. Do the United Nations ideals--even while conceding the principle of trusteeship--condone the trustee nation in utilizing its position to plunder the people and sequestrate their lands for the benefit of its own citizens? Are there any laws that permit a colonial power to commit crimes on the basis of racial and religious discrimination? In this regard, the representatives of the nations would be astounded if they were to read the incontrovertible figures and statistics on the record of exploitation, monopolization, persecution, humiliation, and impoverishment on the part of the French and Spanish native administrations in Morocco.

No matter how naive and unaware people might be, they could not possibly mistake the record of the French and the

Spaniards for other than what it is; or condone a mental and a moral aberration on such a colossal scale committed by United Nations statesmen.

The Moroccan case, on account of its international ramifications and its shameful reality, is more deserving of submission before the United Nations than any other case.

There are some who maintain that such a submission would be valueless; they argue that all the controlling members of the Organization have colonial interests which impell them to stand in solidarity, and they point to the attitude of these powers concerning the questions of Palestine and Indonesia. I do not concur in this view; and even if the argument is correct, it does not divest submission of the case of its substantial advantages, foremost of which would be to expose the atrocities of French and Spanish colonialism. Furthermore, any common front which the colonial powers might put up could not possibly be on the basis of principles compatible with the ideals and objectives of the United Nations. The defenders of right, from among members of the United Nations, would, therefore, be in a strong position to expose and refute the unworthy objectives of the colonial powers.

The Moroccan case, at any rate, is far less likely to come up against the same militant international adversaries who had been encountered in the Palestine case--not on account of the Jews' great influence in the international field, but because the Palestine case had not been tackled in the right manner and at the right moment by the Arabs, their friends, and the Palestinians themselves.

The Palestinian struggle had been negative; the efforts of the Arabs for Palestine had been contingent upon circumstances and international developments, and were not in accordance with a clearly worked out program of action. When the case was submitted before the United Nations, it was not at the initiative of the Arabs or their friends; rather, it was the state which had created Zionism that did so, on the grounds of her failure to work out a solution satisfactory to both parties. This meant that she had extricated herself from the case and had posed it as a conflict between two race living in the same country. France and Spain are naturally in no position to do likewise in our case.

We are convinced that the case of Morocco would find

many supporters in United Nations circles, principally from the Arab and Asian blocs, but also from other states which in the past had suffered under colonialism, such as the Philippines. It is possible to obtain support even from those states which are fearful of the spread of Communist influence and which are gradually coming to realize that no such containment of Communism could be possible so long as the people of North Africa remained in distress and enslavement.

The attitude of France and Spain during World War II is not likely to reassure the Americans and the British as to the fate of North Africa, in the event of a major war between Democracy and Communism; more particularly so since there are no guarantees that the Moroccans would not rise in rebellion, having been denied their rights in victory after two global wars, in which they sacrificed their blood and money on the side of the democracies.

The Americans will remember that Morocco had been the first state in the world to recognize their independence, even while they might forget that President Roosevelt had pledged support for the independence of Morocco to His Majesty the Sultan.

The British will feel that their policies towards the Arab League would be ineffectual, unless they supported this League in completing its formation and in realizing its long-range objectives. They would also feel that the strength of the Asian bloc, which had unanimously supported the Arab position on Palestine, could tilt the scales one way or the other.

The Slavic bloc would seize upon the opportunity to demonstrate its opposition to Western imperialism. It could not ignore the strength of the Arab Maghrib in the future, and its right to discriminate between friend and foe in its hour of need.

French diplomacy itself, representing as it does the French Republic, with its great libertarian traditions, would be ashamed to defend the work of the colonials. It would be compelled to justify its attitude by inviting Morocco to join the French Union. We can predict, therefore, that the case of Morocco would be shifted from the debate on the legitimacy or illegitimacy of the existing regime, to a fierce struggle between Morocco's aspiration for complete independence and membership in the Arab League on the one hand, and France's attempts to avert the danger by an offer of a lame independence within the French Union, on the other.

At all events, the case would depend on the strength of the Arabs' faith in themselves, and on the efforts which the members of the Arab League will make for one of the most crucial and deserving of Arab causes. The cases of Tunisia and Algeria are but a duplicate of the Moroccan case itself.

The decision of the party, therefore, to present the case to world conscience, will have beneficial effects, at least in carrying the case a step forward towards our ultimate aim of freedom, unity, and independence.

Conclusion: Summary and Orientations

We have depicted in this book the various phases of North African resistance; our aim has been to prove one fact: that the Arab Maghrib has never acquiesced in French, Spanish, or international rule; that from the moment they came to our land, the colonials met with such ferocious resistance as no other country has ever put up. We have seen how the Maghrib mentality adjusted itself to the requirements of changing times, and with them the methods of struggle for the usurped rights. We have described the spontaneous reaction of a people, astounded by the might of the conqueror --though they were by no means submissive to it--in seeking a way to salvation by methods of the modern age. We have described how the requirements of liberation had dovetailed with the needs for development to create a cultural and an educational renascence worthy of note. This renascence, however, had stumbled against the obstacles laid down by the colonials to prevent the Maghrib from attaining its objectives. The clash convinced the people of the conqueror's bad faith and confirmed them in the belief that there could be no progress or development without complete independence and liberation from the usurpers.

We have attempted, as far as possible, to indicate the various milestones within each movement, and to depict the motivations and psychological factors that had led to them. We have in no way attempted to conceal the outside factors that had contributed to the development and crystalization of these trends; thus, we have shown the connections between the Maghrib movements and the Eastern movements, the mutual impact between them, and the unification of their orientations in methods as well as in objectives.

We have endeavored to draw the main lines, running through the policies of the colonial powers in the Arab Maghrib, without delving into those aspects which have no relevance to the subject of our book. Our purpose has been to reveal the basic errors that had caused the repeated historical failures of colonialism. We have touched upon these errors as they were repeated in Tunisia and Algeria, evoking identical reactions in the three countries. The upshot had been an impasse, with no attempt on the part of the colonial authorities to amend their errors or to change their course.

We have tried to describe the circumstances under which the people of the Maghrib had appealed to principles of emancipation, which they had come across fortuitously, in the course of their search for colonial aberrations and their attempts to overcome them. It is a strange phenomenon, in individuals and in groups, that they sometimes forget the most innate and deep-rooted ethical traits within their bosoms and then return to them for refuge, as though they had discovered them anew, and for assistance in protecting themselves and their society against the assault of evil principles and their proponents.

The North African movements in the three countries had passed through identical phases, because they had developed under similar circumstances; it is fortunate that they have arrived at a unified objective; namely, the creed of independence, for which we are struggling today.

The nationalist movements in the Maghrib are perhaps foremost amongst the liberation movements in the Arab world because they alone have been able to form parties, in the real meaning of the term as used in the West. They are not based upon "sacred leadership" to which the masses adhere by means of public speeches and propaganda directed to the generality. They are guided by well-liked and popular leaders whose positions in their parties is nowise different from that of all the other members; their methods of propaganda are those of organization and education. This difference between them and the majority of parties in the Arab world--with our due respects for these parties and their leaders--might be accounted for by the gradual process of development and the constant persecution through which our movements had been obliged to pass. For they had not come into being under conditions of rebellion, where the people look to someone to organize their revolt and express their aspirations; nor did they come into existence amidst election campaigning, requiring nominations of candidates on specific and limited objectives. Our movements had their formative stages in the most critical and restrictive situations, when the Maghrib masses had not yet recovered from the shock of defeat. They consisted, moreover, or a mere handful of men, upon whom everyone looked with skepticism and reserve; not on account of a lack of popular enthusiasm for their cause, but because the might of the conqueror had been such that no one believed in the efficacy of peaceful movements, carried on by youths who could be dispersed with the greatest of ease.

This fact was most manifest in Morocco where a warrior people with long-standing military traditions could not believe in the effectiveness of peaceful and political movements. They were prepared at all times to respond to a call for armed rebellion against the foreigner, but they were lukewarm and reticent towards movements of the pen and tongue in which they had none of the faith that they have today. When we started our Moroccan movement, we were a group of men in early youth. The French themselves did not believe that we could advance our movement to the stage which has been reached today and which has evoked the admiration of such distinguished Frenchmen as Duhamel and André Gide, and such leading colonials as Labonne and Ponsot. These circumstances, which had conditioned our movement, impelled it to take shape gradually and to strike deep roots in the masses, as a nationalist movement with principles and regulations, rights, and obligations.

One of the characteristics of our movement is the all-embracing meaning attached to the term, freedom; for while demanding national liberation from foreign rule, it does not ignore the amelioration of living conditions for the masses both morally and materially, and their organization within unions, associations, and other forms of cooperative endeavor. Such efforts would not justify special mention but for the tremendous obstacles and the complete loss of freedom with which those efforts had to contend.

We have emphasized the spirit of solidarity in the relationships among the various parties of North Africa, although they belong to three states, with traditions of pride and loyalty to their respective regions. This auspicious experiment is worthy of imitation by our Arab brethren everywhere in their efforts to unify their mass organizations and parties; for the solidarity of the Arab governments is not sufficient by itself, but should be reinforced by the close association of popular organizations, so that they could spur their governments on in a sustained effort to achieve the common objective of all.

We have described the results of the inter-party solidarity in the joint efforts abroad to explain the Maghrib cause to foreign and Arab public opinions. The colonial powers had for a long time succeeded in cutting off North Africa from the rest of the Arab world and in preventing its citizens from travelling abroad. The Arab peoples at the present time, however, thanks to the efforts of the independence movements, are well informed concerning the efforts of their Maghrib brethren to catch up with the progress of the Arab caravan. The foreigners too are no longer totally in the dark as to the plight of the North African peoples. The efforts of the independence offices in Europe and America are contributing a better understanding of the true situation in North Africa.

The independence movements in the Arab Maghrib, therefore, represent genuine popular reality; they are carrying on their task thanks to the selfless devotion to their leaders and the solidarity of their supporters. They are the faithful and genuine representatives of North African feelings and aspirations. Dependence upon them for an understanding of North African realities is necessary for those who wish to face the facts straight in the face as they actually exist.

The activities of these movements in the field of resistance are characterized by prudent calculation and a regard for all possible ramifications; this is particularly the case on account of the fact that all important decisions are made according to the majority opinion of the higher councils and of party conferences.

But it is not suggested that the movements have attained perfection; it is our duty, rather, having indicated their good points, to underline the shortcomings that need to be rectified.

The foremost of these deficiencies, in our view, pertains to the field of theory, that is, the working out of a comprehensive program for the political and economic systems in the era of independence; and this because we believe that working for independence is merely a means for the realization of our great aim, the amelioration and happiness of the nation.

Although we have a general conceptual outline of what we shall do in the era of independence, we feel that it is inadequate. Our duty is to spell out our thoughts within a comprehensive program, on the lines of what we--the Moroccans--did when our movement was a purely reformative movement.

Our experts should devote themselves to specialized studies of all aspects of public life--political, administrative, cultural, financial, economic, and social, so that when the time comes we shall be ready to carry them through, without further loss of time on study and preparation.

The Spanish Republicans have utilized their exile abroad to make extensive studies on the various aspects of public affairs; it is expected that when they triumph they will do an impressive job in Spain in order to avoid the pitfalls which had led to their own collapse and to the emergence of a revolutionary situation.

Karl Marx has said that there could be no revolution without theory; this is true, because action is always a derivative of intent, which in turn is a concomitant of contemplation and comprehension. The Communists in Russia and elsewhere have succeeded--in spite of the novel and the destructive principles embodied in their program--only because they had expeditiously carried out many rural and industrial reforms in every place they occupied. We, who are anxious to prevent the spread of any destructive principle or perverted program, must utilize the opportunity of our relief from public office, and our understanding of the shortcomings of the existing regime in our country, for a study of world institutions, in the light of which we could assess our own needs and our own doctrines. By having plans ready for implementation all at once, we should gain the people's confidence in themselves, in their system, and in their government. We should not, thereby, require them, after all their exertions and sacrifices for liberation, to resume another struggle for an administrative or a social system that itself might lead to spiritual and material enslavement in a new form.

Western colonialism has impelled us to resort to many means in our efforts to contain its surging avalanche; we must not err in our orientation of the people lest the temporary and the expedient become permanently ingrained. We must learn from the lesson of Europe in this respect; and particularly from the experience of France, Belgium, and Greece, where the people, having lived through a prolonged period of resistance to the Nazi invader, remained in utmost turbulance; for in the course of their resistance to the invader they had acquired a special way of life which they were reluctant to forsake even after liberation. We are guiding the workers towards union organization and are making a vigorous fight with a view to this end. We are justified and sincere in doing so because no one is more deserving of our sympathy and support than the Moroccan worker. But our efforts on behalf of labor organization should safeguard the worker from falling into the lap of organizations which derive their moral support from abroad and their spiritual inspiration from the foreigner. We Moroccans have never known subservience to spiritual authority centered outside our country. This is our mentality and this is our history; we adhered to it in the days of our Jāhilīyah [pre-Islam], and also after we had adopted Islam as our religion. We must not, therefore, permit foreign spiritual influence to replace the foreign temporal authority. Our creeds must be of our own creation, or, if derived from others, adjusted to suit our own needs and temperaments. So, a labor union should not be regarded as anything more than one aspect of organizing the Moroccan nation. We must devote particular attention to such organization among town workers, because unionism can only be effective where workers are assembled under one roof. As for farmers, we should organize them within unions or cooperatives as they choose. Our defense of their rights should be complete, not only as regards improving their living conditions, but also with a view to restoring their lands, which had been forcibly sequestrated by the colonists. The restoration of lands to their lawful owners is a matter pertaining to our national dignity, and we can never forsake it. We must make efforts to ensure that arbitration, and not strife and strikes, is the instrument for the settlement of labor disputes, particularly since we shall be engaged in a nation-wide industrialization of our country. Our social efforts should be devoted entirely to improving the living conditions of all individuals and classes; for the individual is in reality the end of all endeavor. We must provide gainful employment, housing, education, medication, and leisure to the able-bodied, and relief to the incapacitated, in the rural as well as in the urban parts of our land.

In order to achieve these objectives, we must employ all legitimate means, as part of our struggle for liberation and development. We must mobilize the entire nation behind this task. But we must do more than that; we must instill in the hearts of the people a sense of mission, by means of lectures, writings, and conferences. Thus only can we make it a sacred creed, cherished, preserved, and sustained. We can also stimulate the creation of a national literature, which would be transmitted as an intellectual and spiritual legacy to future generations.

As a concomitant, we must utilize the instrumentality of literature both at home and in our publicity abroad which until recently had consisted merely of loud complaints and numerical figures, intelligible only to a tiny class of experts in North African affairs.

We must, therefore, create a special literature in various languages which could be called the literature of resistance, soliciting support in the name of humanism for the struggle against colonial oppression.

Further, we must do all in our power to intensify our humanist campaign for the liberation of humanity from the horrors of colonialism in all its forms. We must mobilize popular forces in dependent countries and strive to convene annual conferences of national parties from all subject territories. We must remember that the slaves were not emancipated by international covenants or by the exhortations of leaders, as the Europeans and the Americans claim. They achieved their emancipation by their own struggle and solidarity in demanding their right to life. We must recall with pride that the secret societies, formed by the African slaves in Brazil and elsewhere, had been the original propagators of the great movement for slave emancipation at a time when clergymen were telling Americans that it was not sacriligious to enslave those Africans because they were sinners condemned by their kings and chieftains and sold to the whites. The pleas of those slaves reached noble minds in white circles; they supported their cause on humanitarian grounds at some times and in self-defense at others. It was we, the North Africans, who introduced Islam to black Africa and taught its people Islam's advocacy of freedom, the equality of all people before God, and that "virtue" is the only criterion in the estimation of black and white. So why should we not today be the torchbearers of the new advocacy for human liberation from the shackles of enslavement? Why should we not call upon the weak nations to unite in opposition to one people's colonization of another.

Such advocacy, however, should not be a plea for hatred and vengeance; it should merely seek our liberation from the colonials' enslavement, and the emancipation of the colonials themselves from their degrading and evil creed.

We believe that colonialism has benefited a small class only in the countries of the imperialists, and that the vast majority of citizens have been as much victims of colonialism as the subject peoples themselves. A forthright plea for unity in resistance to colonialism would thus find supporters in all circles.

All these efforts will be to no avail unless we are able to expose before the world the real intentions of the colonials in our countries.

The colonials in our country will not stand with folded hands; their efforts to mislead their own people at home, and the world at large, will be not less than the efforts designed to exploit our resources and enslave our citizens. It is incumbent upon us, therefore, to study their methods and acquaint ourselves with their thoughts and intentions, so that we shall be the better able to resist them and expose their machinations before Maghrib and foreign public opinions.

If we have expounded our purposes and principles, it is because we wish to acquaint even the colonials themselves with their true purport. This candidness is by itself sufficient proof of the sincerity of our movement and our determination to achieve our aims. We are convinced that the just creed for which we are struggling will triumph, and that pernicious colonialism will be defeated in the face of a determined people and their faithful leaders.

The question of the Arab League and the strengthening of its edifice have become an inseparable part of our movement. This naturally imposes upon our movement certain obligations towards the League and at the same time entitles it to certain rights from the League, collectively and in respect to each of its member states.

In conclusion, therefore, we cannot pass over this focal point in the lives of the Arab peoples--the residuary of their hopes and expectations. We shall discuss its achievements as well as its failures towards the Maghrib, and the ideal of uniting the Arab world in its entirety.

We do not wish to minimize the efforts of the League during this formative phase of its existence, so abounding in tribulations and dangers; nor do we wish to overrate those achievements, because the error of exaggeration, no less than of underestimation, would merely mislead public opinion and conceal the truth which is indispensible for assessing and then avoiding existing shortcomings. Besides the leaders of the League are among the best men and heroes of the Arabs; they seek their reward in dedicated service to the cause rather than in laudations and the offerings of grateful homage.

The first two articles of the League Covenant and of the Alexandria Protocol provide that the Arab League should consist of independent Arab states. This explicitly means that Arab states which are not independent have no place in the membership of the League. However, article V of the Alexandria Protocol and of the special annex on Palestine regarded Palestine as an integral part of the Arab countries; it provided that the international status of Palestine was one of independence which would be recognized sooner or later. The League, therefore, did not see any objection to having Palestine represented by one of her own sons, provided such representative be appointed by the League itself, until Palestine should have attained her complete independence.

This, in effect, constitutes a precedent, indicating that the spirit of the Covenant aims at the achievement and consolidation of the independence of all Arab peoples. It goes even beyond that, for it permitted the representation of a non-independent country at the Arab League Council, by appointment from the Political Committee.

But the position of the Covenant concerning the other

Arab peoples has not been sufficiently forthright to merit dependability. It consists, in fact, of no more than a special annex regarding cooperation with the Arab countries not members of the League. We shall quote it in full before giving any comments. It reads:

> Whereas the member states of the League shall, at the Council and in committees, be undertaking activities whose benefit and effects will extend to the Arab World in its entirety, and considering that the Council must heed and endeavor to realize the aspirations of the Arab countries, not represented on the Council, the states, signatories of the Arab League Covenant, are particularly anxious to recommend to the Council of the League, that in considering the question of the participation of those countries in the committes provided for in the Covenant it shall carry cooperation with them to the greatest possible extent, and otherwise spare no efforts toward understanding their needs, hopes, and aspirations; it shall, moreover, strive for the amelioration of their conditions and the safeguarding of their future, with all possible political means.

Thus, the annex provides--derivatively and not basically --that the League would undertake activities of a significant bearing on the entire Arab World. The reference is merely derivative; the Arab World in its entirety--nay, the human race itself--would benefit from the efforts of the League when it makes its real and awaited contribution. But such a benefit might be derived through channels other than those of the League such as by means of imitation, animating influences, and so forth. The annex provides also--in the same incidental manner--that efforts be made towards achieving the aspirations of the Arab countries.

The annex, nonetheless, asks the Secretariat to cooperate with these countries to the fullest possible extent and to ascertain their problems and aspirations.

The preamble does not delineate or explain specifically what is meant by the Arab World. There have been many who looked to the Arab Maghrib as an area separate from the Arab World, at least from the standpoint of the political connotations of the term. Colonialism has been persistent in identifying the Arab countries with the Middle East, and in regarding North Africa as belonging either to the African region or to the French Union. The annex to the Covenant, therefore, will remain fraught with ambiguities unless the League adopts a resolution declaring the Arab Maghrib an integral part of the Arab World. It is our view that such a resolution should be in the forefront of whatever steps the League might decide to take in our case, so as to dispell this unintentional ambiguity.

In order to underline such a resolution, we believe that the second step should be the appointment of representatives from North Africa to all League councils, including the political one; the League should, for the time being, select the representatives from among prominent leaders, or persons who are considered competent to carry on the task laid upon them by the League.

The League Council might contend that the participation of those representatives would give them voting rights without the attendant obligations, financial and otherwise, which the other members have to undertake. To this we answer: a solution to this problem could be worked out, either by the willingness of the independent states to shoulder the dues which the non-independent members are unable to pay, or by withholding voting rights from those representatives on questions other than the ones pertaining to their own states.

The Arab League has taken the cause of Libya into its own hands; it gave encouragement to her nationalist movement and to the formation of Hay'ah Taḥrīr Libya (the organization for the liberation of Libya). The League demanded and was granted participation in the United Nations Commission on Libya, wherein it expressed the aspirations of this Arab people for freedom, unity, and membership in the Arab League. The League persuaded the British authorities to halt the influx of Italian immigrants, and worked for a reconciliation between the platform of the nationalists and the ambitions of Libya's spiritual leader, Sayīd Idrīs al-Sunūssi.

As regards North Africa, we cannot contend that the League has ignored or given no effective attention to its cause; it has declared its solidarity with us on all possible occasions; its leaders have spared no efforts towards encouraging our activities and giving satisfaction to our representatives, in all questions within the realm of the possible under existing circumstances. The Secretary-General of the Arab League told the Istiqlal Party's first delegation to Paris that the Maghrib question was in his hands and that the League was prepared to support us in everything we ask for.

It is fair to admit that the Maghrib movements, though at present united in their principles and demands, had not been so in the past; it is also fair to state that certain Maghrib representatives used to be satisfied with minor demands from the League, which, having been granted, became a substitute for effective action on behalf of Morocco, Algeria, and Tunisia.

But it is equally fair to state that the League has failed so far to apply to us the provisions of the Alexandria Protocol; it has not considered our problems, nor has it understood our needs. There is no organization or committee within the Secretariat of the League devoted to a study of North African affairs. It is perhaps true that the Arabs in general--including experts on foreign affairs--have but a flimsy and superficial knowledge of the Arab Maghrib cause, which they will have to come to grips with sooner or later. As long as there is a lack of specialized knowledge within the League Secretariat, we cannot state that the Arab peoples' organization is giving due attention to this part of the Arab World, let alone being prepared to assist it as it should.

The League has assisted the cause of Palestine, but its assistance was extemporary and not in accordance with a prescribed program. In spite of this, and thanks to the solidarity of its members, it has done all that Palestine could have asked for. But the League cannot claim that it performed the task without the utmost difficulties and tribulations, which arose from the impromptu nature of its performance and its unpreparedness for it. The League should not fall into the same error when dealing with the Arab Maghrib. The case should be studied carefully and exhaustively; adequate publicity should be undertaken with a view to creating a favorable public opinion in preparation for any decisive action.

The League is entitled to acquaint itself with the realities of the Moroccan movements and the degree of their popular strength. It is also its duty to seek a unification of these movements as far as possible. But it should not ignore the representative value possessed by the leaders of each of these movements. There should be no repetition of the situation which had arisen in the case of Palestine, when offices were formed with the backing of a number of member states while the Arab Higher Committee for Palestine continued to receive the support of the League Secretariat. The efforts of the Arab League should be channeled through official representatives if such is possible, or through the true representatives of the popular will in their respective countries. It is inadvisable that the present state of things should continue, wherein the League opens its doors to any and everyone, even if he is a mercenary making a living out of the Maghrib cause, and deals with the true leaders on an equal footing with those hirelings. It is the duty of the League to base its decisions upon an intimate knowledge of the internal situations in these countries; for what counts in the end is the will of the people and the wisdom of their leaders, and disorderly contacts with Maghrib representatives would be adversely registered in the direction of North African affairs.

The Arab League should conduct an objective study of the Maghrib cause and adopt if possible a secret program in agreement with the Maghrib leaders and kings. The League would work for the program according to its own methods and the Maghrib leaders according to theirs. A prior agreement on orientation would serve as a basis for cooperation in carrying out the task. Thus, the Maghrib movement would become an extension of the Arab League in aims as well as in means. The Arab peoples would be assured that the League was attending to their problems, while the League would be satisfied that it was marching forward along the path it had determined for itself, towards its objective of liberating and uniting the Arab peoples.

I have been in Egypt for one whole year, in the course of which I have expended considerable efforts and made contacts with the League and its personnel. But I am unable to claim that the Maghrib cause is given the attention it deserves in the League quarters. I am always received there with utmost respect and appreciation; but it was not for this that I had emigrated to Egypt. I had come to Egypt in order to coordinate our nationalist activity with the activities of our Arab brethren on our behalf. I must in honesty state that I have not found cognizance of this purpose, even among those most sympathetic to our cause. We are not in need of publicity in Arab circles, because publicity is designed to convince, and the Arabs in their entirety are already convinced of the need for liberation of the Maghrib. But the Arabs have only a scanty knowledge of our affairs, so they do not feel as we do the need for urgent and speedy support for our cause. It is the duty of the League to lead the way in realizing a true appreciation of this fact, and it is its responsibility to assist us in sensitizing Arab public opinion to the urgency of such a task. For the cause of Arab North Africa does not have the religious associations and significance which the Palestine case possesses; we have neither the time nor the means whereby we can mobilize Arab public opinion for pressure upon the Arab states, as was done in the case of Palestine. All this should be the burden of the Arab League and its member states. The cause of the Arab League had become an integral part of our Maghrib movement; the Maghrib cause should similarly become an integral part of Arab League objectives and strivings.

We can sum up our suggestions concerning the demands of North Africa from the Arab League in two points: firstly, in connection with the Covenant of the League; secondly, as regards its administrative apparatus.

On the first point we believe that it is necessary to modify the special annex pertaining to cooperation with the Arab countries not members of the League. We suggest the following formula:

> Whereas the basic aim of the Arab League is the establishment of Arab unity comprising the Arab peoples;
>
> Whereas an important section of the Arab countries has not as yet attained the independence that permits them to participate actively in the implementation of the resolutions of the Arab League;
>
> And whereas the principles of the League do not permit it to ignore the affairs of these non-independent Arab countries, particularly in the course of any overall consideration of the affairs of the Arab World, the Council recommends:
>
> 1. Admission of official representatives from these

nations, in cases where a national government requests participation in the Council of the League, and subject to two conditions:

a. The said national government shall pledge to work for independence from foreign control.

b. The Arab League Secretariat shall have the final decision as to the representatives whom the said government selects to represent it on the Council or committees of the League.

2. Or alternatively, the admission of people's representatives to be selected by the Arab League Secretariat with the approval of the Council, in cases where the Arab nation whose admission is proposed has no government of its own, or where such a government is unable to proclaim its political program as a result of foreign domination. It is preferable that the League select the delegates from among the leaders of parties which represent majority opinion in the country.

--and under all circumstances to give countenance to the aspirations of the non-independent Arab countries, and endeavor to orientate them towards the noble aim of the League and the achievement of the unity and the rejuvenation of the Arab nation by all possible means.

And whereas it is the aim of the League to carry out great reforms in the Arab World, and considering that a number of non-independent Arab nations would not be in a position to derive practical benefit from the resolutions of the League's specialized agencies, even though they might be represented on them, it is the duty of the Secretariat to find appropriate means whereby those resolutions may be actualized for the non-independent Arab nations. This might be achieved by encouraging and guiding the reform movements of the national parties and organizations on the one hand, and on the other, by demanding the right of the Arab states to spread culture in the Arab countries and assist in their revival--and this especially in consideration of the presence in the countries of the League of cultural and social institutions belonging to foreign states; also, by subsidizing student missions from those countries for studies in the Arab World or in Europe, and by other means which the Secretariat or its specialized committees may deem appropriate.

In addition, we believe that it is necessary for the Council of the League to make a geographic delineation of the Arab World in the following manner:

> The Arab World: Those countries whose official or popular language is Arabic. It is bounded on the north by the Mediterranean; on the west by the Atlantic Ocean; on the east by Iran, the Persian Gulf and Turkey; and on the south by the eastern equatorial regions.

As regards the Arab Maghrib, we suggest that the following resolution be adopted by the Council:

> For one hundred and fourteen years, France and Spain have by stages attacked the countries of the Arab Maghrib (Tunisia, Algeria, and Morocco), partitioned them, and then conquered them, by various diplomatic and military means, although all these countries had been free and independent, had resisted and continue to resist foreign conquest, and have now expressed their unanimous desire for liberation, independence, and membership in the Arab League.
>
> Therefore, and in view of the evil situation existing in these countries as a result of French and Spanish colonialism, and in adherence to the principles of the Atlantic Charter, the Arab League resolves:
>
> 1. To regard the Arab Maghrib as an integral part of the Arab World.
> 2. To support the states and peoples of the Arab Maghrib in their present efforts for effective independence from foreign rule.
> 3. To refuse recognition of the existing regimes in Tunisia, Algeria, and Morocco (including the Riff, Tangier, and Mauretania).
> 4. In view of the special circumstances of the Arab Maghrib and until those states have attained effective independence, the Arab League Council shall take upon itself the task of nominating representatives from Morocco, Tunisia, and Algeria.

As regards the administrative organization of the League we urge the establishment of a special section on the Arab

Maghrib within the Secretariat, under a departmental chief who is both administratively capable and well versed in North African affairs. We suggest that his terms of reference include the following assignments:

1. To study conditions in North Africa and collect all relevant documents and data for this purpose.

2. To contact the leaders of the Maghrib movements with a view to coordinating their activities with those of the Arab League and its various departments.

3. To launch widespread publicity on behalf of North Africa in the Arab World as well as in Europe and America, in cooperation with the Maghrib parties.

4. To supervise the implementation of those decisions of the Arab League which could be carried out in the countries of North Africa.

5. To look after the well-being of North African communities in the East and those that might come about in the future, and to improve their conditions, so that they might become effective members in the Arab countries in which they take up residence.

6. To study, organize, and coordinate the commercial and economic activities among the countries of North Africa

7. To advocate and promote vacationing in the countries of North Africa, so richly endowed with beautiful winter and summer resorts, instead of in Europe, where such huge sums are expended; also, to attempt to link the sport and scout movements in North Africa with their counterparts in the East; to organize exchange visits and coordinate the Arab motion picture enterprises, and so forth.

In short, the proposed department could perform all the functions that the embassies of North Africa would have had to perform if these countries had been independent.

Thus, the League could become a positive force in the lif of the Arab Maghrib, and the Arab World would thereby utilize the potentialities of one of its component parts, concerning which at present it is almost wholly uninformed. Real and effective unity cannot be achieved merely by the exchange of sentiments; it can only be achieved by participation in action and by a more profound understanding of one another.

The Arab League, furthermore, must improve upon its present organization, and should not be satisfied with the appointment of a number of second-rate officials in its various departments merely to placate some of its members, or in response to intercessions by its friends and favorites. The League Secretariat should be staffed by the best and most capable elements in the Arab World.

There has been universal criticism of the League on account of its lack of a unified economic and social program. One of the Arab kings said to me: "What the League suffers from is that each prime minister submits a program catering to the special policies of his own state; that is to say, the deliberations of the League lack a broad vision of the entire Arab World during the course of the decisional process; it is its duty, therefore, to strive for the articulation of an Arab consciousness in place of the parochial consciousness, so that a practical program could be formulated for the Arab nation in all walks of life."

Arab thinkers also blame the League for its failure to further the primary cause for which it was established, namely, the consolidation of Arab unity and the unification of the Arab states into one unitary state. That is to say, the endeavor to change the present status quo in the Arab countries, which had been brought about by Western imperialism. The shortcomings of the existing atomized status quo have become all too apparent in consequence of the recent happenings in Palestine.

It must in fairness be recognized that the Arab League has expended tremendous efforts during this short period of its existence. The machinations of imperialism against the Arab World, the pressure of Zionist propaganda, and the impetuous support accorded to Zionism by the big powers, have no doubt obstructed many of the activities which should have been performed by this crucial Arab organization. But this does not prevent us from admitting that some shameful failures have occurred in certain spheres of endeavor, notably in the social field. The League has not up to the time of writing [1948] set up the committee for social affairs, the establishment of which is provided for in its organizational procedure; it has not devoted the slightest attention to the future of Arab workers and farmers, or to the future of the Arab family. In point of fact, there is an urgent need in the Arab World for putting an end to the chaos of social life, threatened as it is with disintegration and a lapsing into the hands of destructive or reactionary movements. We have no doubt that the author of "al-Risālah al-Khālidah" (the eternal message) shares our feelings concerning this bitter reality and is endeavoring to do something about it. We do not believe that the existing conditions in some of the Arab countries, which have not as yet attained an adequate degree of modernization, are such as to prevent the League from performing its duty of formulating a charter for the Arab citizen and of recommending measures with a view to raising his material and moral standard. We therefore request the Arab League Council to expedite the formation of the social committee and the appointment of experts to draw up an Arab charter, similar to the charters drawn up for the periods of [political] awakening in Europe and America.

This problem has preoccupied my mind since my arrival in Egypt; I have discussed it with a number of leading thinkers who did not conceal their anxiety as to the appalling neglect of social problems in the Arab East; if unchecked, the situation threatens--God forbid--the ascendancy of those of ill-will who are working for the spread of foreign creeds, at the cost of the Arabs' spiritual and intellectual heritage, and to the risk of their enslavement to ideologies at variance with their own.

These deliberations resulted in the setting up of a small study group, comprising a number of distinguished men from Egypt and Morocco. The committee has drawn up a charter, with which it is fitting to conclude this book, but with the understanding that it is just a preliminary draft, intended merely to call attention to some of the questions involved.

The Arab Charter

1. The Political Structure

a. complete independence and unequivocal sovereignty

b. Arab solidarity, and non-preferential friendship with all states in the cause of world cooperation

c. government must be "consultative"

d. sovereignty resides in the people, who are its guardian

e. religious and racial minorities are entitled to a guarantee of their rights

2. The Economic Structure

a. nationalization of the basic national resources and public services

b. coordination of production and the organization of exchange and distribution

c. encouragement of cooperative endeavor

d. aid to individual investment and to private ownership, in the interest of the group

e. a graduated system of taxation

3. The Social Structure (Guarantee of Human Rights)

A. The state must provide gratuitously a basic minimum in the following spheres:

a. maternity, motherhood, child care

b. housing, food, clothing

c. health and medication

d. education

B. The state must ensure to individuals the following rights in the field of production:

a. employment

b. wages

c. rest

d. convalescence

e. insurance against old age, unemployment, and incapacitation

C. Freedoms:

a. freedom of thought and of belief

b. equality for all individuals without distinction

c. enabling women to perform their duties in society

4. Means to Resurgence

A. Morale:

a. obliteration of illiteracy, moral rearmament, the fostering of pride in the past as a means towards carrying out the Arab mission for the welfare of mankind

b. free universal elementary and secondary education; the curriculum should be based upon the national heritage and the attributes of modern civilization

c. attention to higher technical training with a view to providing a productive scientific leadership in the various fields

B. Physical well-being:

a. eradication of the causes of disease and want by providing medical care, food, and clothing free of charge to the needy

b. the construction of modern villages and residential quarters with adequate sanitary and recreational facilities

c. multiplication of hospitals and public clinics

C. Defense:

a. compulsory military service

b. the training of officers in the best military academies abroad

c. the establishment of an armament industry

d. the organization of up-to-date land, sea, and air forces

D. Economics:

a. full-fledged development of the national resources

b. the launching of large-scale industrialization

c. the construction of an adequate network of communications

d. the facilitation of the exchange of products between the Arab countries, and joint investment undertakings in the development of national resources

5. Immediate Measures

Until the governments have taken the necessary measures towards regeneration of the Arab peoples on the basis of the Covenant, the leaders of thought in the various countries shall take upon themselves the propagation of these principles and the generation of support for them through the media of free schools, the eradication of illiteracy, the subsidization of student missions, relief of the needy, the establishment of organizations for physical training, the founding of industrial and commercial companies, the convening of conferences, the publication of newspapers and articles, and the exchange of information on internal as well as on world developments. They shall also emphasize the mission of Arabism in the service of humanity and urge the Arab governments to exert themselves towards the realization of these aims.